THE FATHERS
OF THE CHURCH

A NEW TRANSLATION

VOLUME 27

THE FATHERS OF THE CHURCH

A NEW TRANSLATION

ROY JOSEPH DEFERRARI
Editorial Director Emeritus

EDITORIAL BOARD

BERNARD M. PEEBLES
The Catholic University of America
Editorial Director

PAUL J. MORIN
The Catholic University of America
Managing Editor

ROBERT P. RUSSELL, O.S.A.
Villanova University

THOMAS P. HALTON
The Catholic University of America

MARTIN R. P. MCGUIRE
The Catholic University of America

WILLIAM R. TONGUE
The Catholic University of America

HERMIGILD DRESSLER, O.F.M.
The Catholic University of America

SR. M. JOSEPHINE BRENNAN, I.H.M.
Marywood College

MSGR. JAMES A. MAGNER
The Catholic University of America

REDMOND A. BURKE, C.S.V.
The Catholic University of America

SAINT AUGUSTINE

TREATISES ON MARRIAGE AND OTHER SUBJECTS

The Good of Marriage, Adulterous Marriage, Holy Virginity, Faith and Works, The Creed, Faith and the Creed, The Care To Be Taken for the Dead, In Answer to the Jews, The Divination of Demons

Translated by

Charles T. Wilcox, M.M., Charles T. Huegelmeyer, M.M., John McQuade, S.M., Sister Marie Liguori, I.H.M., Robert P. Russell, O.S.A., John A. Lacy, and Ruth Wentworth Brown

Edited by

ROY J. DEFERRARI

THE CATHOLIC UNIVERSITY OF AMERICA PRESS
Washington, D. C.

IMPRIMATUR:
✠ FRANCIS CARDINAL SPELLMAN
Archbishop of New York

The *Nihil obstat* and *Imprimatur* are official declarations that a book or pamphlet is free of doctrinal or moral error. No implication is contained therein that those who have granted the *Nihil obstat* and *Imprimatur* agree with the contents, opinions, or statements expressed.

Copyright © 1955

THE CATHOLIC UNIVERSITY OF AMERICA PRESS

All rights reserved
Reprinted 1969 (with corrections), 1985
First short-run reprint 1999
ISBN 0-8132-0967-6

CONTENTS

THE GOOD OF MARRIAGE

Introduction 3
Text 9

ADULTEROUS MARRIAGES

Introduction 55
Text: Book I 61
      Book II 101

HOLY VIRGINITY

Introduction 135
Text 143

FAITH AND WORKS

Introduction 215
Text 221

THE CREED

Introduction 285
Text 289

FAITH AND THE CREED

Introduction 311
Text 315

THE CARE TO BE TAKEN FOR THE DEAD
Introduction 349
Text 351
IN ANSWER TO THE JEWS
Introduction 387
Text 391
THE DIVINATION OF DEMONS
Introduction 417
Text 421
INDEX 443

WRITINGS
OF
SAINT AUGUSTINE

VOLUME 15

THE GOOD OF MARRIAGE

(De bono coniugali)

Translated by
CHARLES T. WILCOX, M.M.
Maryknoll, New York

INTRODUCTION

HE PIONEER and pattern-setting treatise *De bono coniugali* has been called the most complete patristic consideration of the duties of married persons.¹ Theologians considered it most authoritative down to the time of St. Thomas Aquinas; as late as 1930, Pope Pius XI quoted from it in his encyclical, *Casti Connubii*.

St. Augustine wrote *De bono coniugali* in 401, as an answer to the false teaching of Jovinian which considered the married state equal to that of virginity. Pope Siricius and St. Ambrose had condemned this heresy before him, but it still was so rampant that many consecrated virgins were leaving their convents to marry. St. Jerome also had written his *Adversus Jovinianum* exalting virginity, but in doing so he seemed to have sacrificed the dignity and honor of married life. Therefore, St. Augustine felt that before he treated of virginity he should write on the good of marriage, both to prove false the charge of Manichaeism that was hurled against the Christian teaching and to refute Jovinian.

By calling marriage a good, St. Augustine immediately refuted the chief charge of Manichaeism. For him, the good

---
1 E. Portalié, 'Augustin,' *Dictionnaire de théologie catholique* I 2304.

of marriage was threefold: offspring (*proles*), fidelity (*fides*), sacrament (*sacramentum*). He used this terminology so often that these goods have been called pillars or columns that support his doctrine.²

To have children who would people the kingdom of God is the primary purpose of marriage. However, when Augustine spoke of the procreation of children, he was thinking also of their moral or spiritual procreation and education.

The second good of the marriage contract is that of fidelity or faithfulness. This refers to the right that the spouse has over the body of his partner. St. Augustine noted that St. Paul called this right a power. The violation of this fidelity is adultery. Fidelity in general is such a good that in matters of little importance it is worthy of praise; even in evil contracts, if it is broken the violator is looked upon as more degraded because of this added malice.

St. Augustine used the term for the third good, *sacramentum,* with what De Ghellinck calls 'an incredible diversity of meanings. . . . It is not easy to determine the exact meaning that one ought to give to each of the examples that the ten large volumes of his works contain. The penchant of Augustine for symbolism and allegorical explanation predisposed him, moreover, to the frequent use of the word "*sacramentum*" '³—for example, when speaking of the marriages of Adam and Eve, the Jews, the pagans, Joseph and Mary, and the Christians. However, Pereira believes that in *De bono coniugali* St. Augustine attributes the word only to the marriage of Christians.⁴ This is easy to explain when we realize that the pagan world repudiated the idea of the indissolubility of marriage which is attendant on this teaching. Vasquez says that the saint never called marriage a sacra-

---
2 B. Pereira, *La doctrine du mariage selon saint Augustin* 40.
3 J. de Ghellinck, *Pour l'histoire du mot 'sacramentum'* I 16.
4 Pereira, *op. cit.* 173.

ment in our sense of the term.[5] Mausbach recognizes that the term usually referred to the indissolubility of marriage,[6] as does Pourrat: 'St. Augustine calls the indissoluble bond *"sacramentum,"* because it is the figure, the symbol of the union of Jesus Christ with His Church. It is in order to secure that most holy symbolism that Christian marriage has for its essential characteristics unity and indissolubility. For St. Augustine the bond which unites the Christian husband and wife is the sacrament of Matrimony, just as the sacerdotal "character" is the sacrament of Holy Orders.'[7] Joyce writes: 'The blessing of children and the blessing of mutual fidelity belong to marriage even outside the Church. But the third benefit, the indissolubility consequent on its sacred symbolism (for *"sacramentum"* as here employed has this meaning, and is not used in its technical sense of "a sacrament") is, at least in its full perfection, peculiar to matrimony within the Catholic Church.'[8] Ladomérszky considers *sacramentum* in the sense of (1) a property or symbolic characteristic of marriage; (2) a figure, sign, or symbol; (3) an indissoluble bond; (4) a seal or sanction.[9]

To the threefold good of marriage St. Augustine added the following: the companionship between the sexes and the turning of concupiscence to the honorable task of procreation. As to the morality of the marriage act, he was most explicit. When the act is performed for the purpose of generation, he stated, it is a good act and one that is perfectly lawful. However, intercourse other than for procreation he considered sinful. This teaching dominated the patristic and early scholastic periods. Its rigorism is rooted at least to some

---
5 G. Vasquez, *Commentariorum ac disputationum in tertiam partem Sancti Thomae tomus tertius, De matrimonii sacramento,* dsp. II, c. 5.
6 J. Mausbach, *Die Ethik des heiligen Augustinus* I 323.
7 P. Pourrat, *Theology of the Sacraments* 65.
8 G. Joyce, *Christian Marriage* 149.
9 N. Ladomérszky, *Saint Augustin* 116-121.

extent in St. Augustine's defective metaphysical psychology of human nature, with its attendant misconceptions of the character of concupiscence, as well as in his imperfect theory of the nature of original sin and, above all, of its mode of transmission, which attributed to concupiscence a real instrumental causality.[10] Like all other questions on marriage, this has been exhaustively treated and carefully explored from the time of St. Thomas on, and the strict Augustinian view has been modified in part.

Another question raised in *De bono coniugali* (9, 15, 22, 24-27) is that of the polygamy of the patriarchs. The virgins and celibate men of St. Augustine's time were being challenged by the insidious questions: 'You, then, are better than Sara? You, then, are better than Abraham?' St. Augustine showed how the difference in times called for a difference in action. The patriarchs were told to rear children for the people of God, but, after Christ said: 'Let him accept it who can,' the situation had changed. The patriarchs possessed the virtue of continence even though they did not show it in practice, just as Christ was temperate although He admitted that He came eating and drinking while St. John the Baptist came in a far different way. St. Augustine pointed out that obedience is the mother virtue and the ancients by their obedience served best in the army of Christ.

---

10 E. Sheridan, *The Morality of the Pleasure Motive in the Use of Marriage* 2.

THE GOOD OF MARRIAGE 7

SELECT BIBLIOGRAPHY
for the
Treatises on Marriage and Virginity

Texts and Translations:

Sancti Aurelii Augustini Hipponensis Episcopi Opera Omnia, ed.
J. P. Migne, in *Patrologia Latina* 40 (Paris 1841).
Corpus Scriptorum Ecclesiasticorum Latinorum, ed. J. Zycha, 41
(Vienna 1900).
Oeuvres de Saint Augustin, 1ère série: 2 Problèmes moraux [Paris
1948]) 22-99 *(De bono coniugali)*, 108-233 *(De incompetentibus
nuptiis)*, both tr. G. Combès; 3 (L'ascétisme chrétien [Paris
1949]) 110-227 *(De sancta virginitate)*, tr. J. Saint-Martin.
*A Select Library of the Nicene and Post-Nicene Fathers of the
Christian Church*, First series 3 (New York 1905), tr. C. L.
Cornish.

Secondary Writings:

Adam, Karl, *Saint Augustine, the Odyssey of His Soul* (New York
1932).
Bardenhewer, Otto, *Geschichte der altkirchlichen Literatur* 4
(Freiburg im Br. 1924).
Bardy, Gustave, *Les révisions, Oeuvres de Saint Augustin*, Opuscules
12 (Paris 1950).
Batiffol, P., *Le catholicisme de saint Augustin* (Paris 1920).
Bellarmine, Robert, *De scriptoribus ecclesiasticis* (Louvain 1678).
Burkitt, F. C., *The Old Latin and the Itala* (Cambridge 1896).
Cappello, Felix, *Tractatus canonico-moralis De sacramentis* 5, *De
matrimonio* (Roma 1947).
Cavallera, F., *Saint Jérôme, sa vie et ses oeuvres* (Louvain 1922).
Cayré, F., *Manual of Patrology* 1 (Paris 1936).
Ceillier, Dom Remy, *Histoire générale des auteurs sacrés et ecclé-
siastiques* 10 (Paris 1861).
Cunningham, W., *Saint Augustine and His Place in the History of
Christian Thought* (London 1886).
Dawson, Christopher, 'St. Augustine and His Age,' in *A Monument
to St. Augustine* (London 1934).
Dermine, J., *La doctrine du mariage chrétien*, 5me éd. (Louvain
1938).
Esmein, A., *Le mariage en droit canonique* (Paris 1891).
Froget, J., 'Jovien,' *Dictionnaire de théologique catholique* 8 (Paris
1931) cols. 1577-1580.
Ghellinck, J. de, *Pour l'histoire du mot 'sacramentum'* (Louvain
1924).

Joyce, George H., *Christian Marriage: An Historical and Doctrinal Study* (New York) 1933).
Labriolle, P. de, *Littérature latine chrétienne*, rev. G. Bardy (Paris 1946).
Ladomérszky, Nicolas, *Saint Augustin docteur de mariage chrétien* (Rome 1942).
Mausbach, Joseph, *Die Ethik des heiligen Augustinus* (Berlin 1909).
Marrou, H. I., *Saint Augustin et la fin de la culture antique* (Paris 1938).
Milne, C. H., *A Reconstruction of the Old Latin Text of the Gospels Used by Saint Augustine* (Cambridge 1926).
Montgomery, W., *St. Augustine: Aspects of His Life and Thought* (London 1914).
Noldin, H., *De sexto praecepto et de usu matrimonii* (New York 1940).
Pereira, B., *La doctrine du mariage selon saint Augustin* (Paris 1930).
Perrone, E. Vincent, *Tractatus de matrimonio* (Lyons 1840).
Peters, J., *Die Ehe nach der Lehre des heiliges Augustinus*, Gesellschaft zur Pflege der Wissenschaft im katholischen Deutschland, Sekt. f. Rechts u. Socialwiss. 32 (Paderborn 1918).
Pope, Hugh, *Saint Augustine of Hippo* (Westminster, Md. 1949).
Portalié, É., 'Augustin, saint,' *DTC* 1 (Paris 1931) col. 2268ff.
Pourrat, P., *Theology of the Sacraments* (St. Louis 1910).
Reuter, A., *Sancti Aurelii Augustini doctrina de bonis matrimonii* (Rome 1942).
Serrier, G., *De quelques recherches concernant 'le mariage contrat-sacrament' et plus particulièrement de la doctrine augustinienne des biens du mariage* (Paris 1928).
Sheridan, Edward, *The Morality of the Pleasure Motive in the Use of Marriage* (Rome 1947).
Tillemont, L. de, *Mémoires pour servir à l'histoire ecclésiastique des six premiers siècles* 13 (Paris 1705).
Tixeront, J., *Histoire dogmatique* 2 (St. Louis 1914).
Vasquez, G., *Commentariorum ac disputationum in tertiam partem sancti Thomae tomus tertius* (Lugduni 1631).
Wernz-Vidal, *Ius canonicum* 5, *Ius matrimoniale*, 3rd ed. (Rome 1946).

THE GOOD OF MARRIAGE

Chapter 1

SINCE EVERY MAN is a part of the human race, and human nature is something social and possesses the capacity for friendship as a great and natural good, for this reason God wished to create all men from one, so that they might be held together in their society, not only by the similarity of race, but also by the bond of blood relationship. And so it is that the first natural tie of human society is man and wife. Even these God did not create separately and join them as if strangers, but He made the one from the other, indicating also the power of union in the side from where she was drawn and formed.[1] They are joined to each other side by side who walk together and observe together where they are walking. A consequence is the union of society in the children who are the only worthy fruit, not of the joining of male and female, but of sexual intercourse. For there could have been in both sexes, even without such intercourse, a kind of friendly and genuine union of the one ruling and the other obeying.

---

1 Cf. Gen. 2.21.

Chapter 2

(2) There is no need now for us to examine and put forth a final opinion on this question—how the progeny of the first parents might have come into being, whom God had blessed, saying, 'Be fruitful and multiply; fill the earth,'[1] if they had not sinned, since their bodies deserved the condition of death by sinning, and there could not be intercourse except of mortal bodies. Many different opinions have existed on this subject, and, if we must examine which of them agrees most with the truth of divine Scriptures, there is matter for an extended discussion:[2] Whether, for example, if our first parents had not sinned, they would have had children in some other way, without physical coition, out of the munificence of the almighty Creator, who was able to create them without parents, and who was able to form the body of Christ in a virgin's womb, and who, to speak now to the unbelievers themselves, was able to grant progeny to bees without intercourse; whether, in that passage, much was spoken in a mystical and figurative sense and the written words are to be understood differently: 'Fill the earth and subdue it,' that is, that it should come to pass by the fullness and the perfection of life and power that the increasing and multiplying, where it is said: 'Be fruitful and multiply,' might be understood to be by the advancement of the mind and by the fullness of virtue, as it is expressed in the psalm: 'Thou shalt multiply me in my soul unto virtue,'[3] and that succession of offspring was not granted to man except that later, because of sin, there was to be a departure in death; whether, at first,

---
1 Gen. 1.28.
2 Cf. *De civ. Dei* 1.14.
3 Cf. Ps. 137.3.

the body of those men had been made spiritual but animal, so that afterwards by the merit of obedience it might become spiritual to grasp immortality, not after death, which came into the world through the envy of the Devil[4] and became the punishment for sin, but through that change which the Apostle indicates where he says: 'Then we who live, who survive, shall be caught up together with them in clouds to meet the Lord in the air,'[5] so that we may understand that the bodies of the first marriage were both mortal at the first formation and yet would not have died, if they had not sinned, as God had threatened,[6] just as if He threatened a wound, because the body was vulnerable, which, however, would not have happened, unless that was done which He had forbidden.

Thus, then, even through sexual intercourse generations of such bodies could have come into existence, which would have had increase up to a certain point and yet would not have inclined to old age, or they would have inclined as far as old age and yet not to death, until the earth should be filled with that multiplication of the blessing. For, if God granted to the garments of the Israelites[7] their proper state without any damage for forty years, how much more would He have granted a very happy temperament of certain state to the bodies of those who obeyed His command, until they would be turned into something better, not by the death of man, by which the body is deserted by the soul, but by a blessed change from mortality to immortality, from an animal to a spiritual quality.

---
4 Cf. Wisd. 2.24.
5 1 Thess. 4.17.
6 Cf. Gen. 2.17.
7 Cf. Deut. 29.5.

Chapter 3

It would be tedious to inquire and to discuss which of these opinions is true, or whether another or other opinions can still be extracted from these words.

(3) This is what we now say, that according to the present condition of birth and death, which we know and in which we were created, the marriage of male and female is something good. This union divine Scripture so commands that it is not permitted a woman who has been dismissed by her husband to marry again, as long as her husband lives, nor is it permitted a man who has been dismissed by his wife to marry again, unless she who left has died. Therefore, regarding the good of marriage, which even the Lord confirmed in the Gospel,[1] not only because He forbade the dismissal of a wife except for fornication, but also because He came to the marriage when invited,[2] there is merit in inquiring why it is a good.

This does not seem to me to be a good solely because of the procreation of children, but also because of the natural companionship between the two sexes. Otherwise, we could not speak of marriage in the case of old people, especially if they had either lost their children or had begotten none at all. But, in a good marriage, although one of many years, even if the ardor of youths has cooled between man and woman, the order of charity still flourishes between husband and wife. They are better in proportion as they begin the earlier to refrain by mutual consent from sexual intercourse, not that it would afterwards happen of necessity that they would not be able to do what they wished, but that it would be a matter of praise that they had refused beforehand what they were able to do. If, then, there is observed that promise

---
1 Cf. Matt. 19.9.
2 Cf. John 2.

of respect and of services due to each other by either sex, even though both members weaken in health and become almost corpse-like, the chastity of souls rightly joined together continues the purer, the more it has been proved, and the more secure, the more it has been calmed.

Marriage has also this good, that carnal or youthful incontinence, even if it is bad, is turned to the honorable task of begetting children, so that marital intercourse makes something good out of the evil of lust. Finally, the concupiscence of the flesh, which parental affection tempers, is repressed and becomes inflamed more modestly. For a kind of dignity prevails when, as husband and wife they unite in the marriage act, they think of themselves as mother and father.

Chapter 4

(4) There is the added fact that, in the very debt which married persons owe each other, even if they demand its payment somewhat intemperately and incontinently, they owe fidelity equally to each other. And to this fidelity the Apostle has attributed so much right that he called it power, when he said: 'The wife has not authority over her body, but the husband; the husband likewise has not authority over his body, but the wife.'[1] But the violation of this fidelity is called adultery, when, either by the instigation of one's own lust or by consent to the lust of another, there is intercourse with another contrary to the marriage compact. And so the fidelity is broken which even in material and base things is a great good of the soul; and so it is certain that it ought to be preferred even to the health of the body wherein his life is contained. For, although a small amount of straw as compared to much gold is as nothing, fidelity, when it is

---
1 1 Cor. 7.4.

kept pure in a matter of straw, as in a matter of gold, is not of less importance on this account because it is kept in a matter of less value.

But, when fidelity is employed to commit sin, we wonder whether it ought to be called fidelity. However, whatever its nature may be, if even against this something is done, it has an added malice; except when this is abandoned with the view that there might be a return to the true and lawful fidelity, that is, that the sin might be amended by correcting the depravity of the will.

For example, if anyone, when he is unable to rob a man by himself, finds an accomplice for his crime and makes an agreement with him to perform the act together and share the loot, and, after the crime has been committed, he runs off with everything, the other naturally grieves and complains that fidelity had not been observed in his regard. In his very complaint he ought to consider that he should have observed his fidelity to human society by means of a good life, so that he would not rob a man unjustly, if he feels how wickedly fidelity was not kept with him in an association of sin. His partner, faithless on both counts, is certainly to be judged the more wicked. But, if he had been displeased with the wickedness which they had committed and so had refused to divide the spoils with his partner in crime on this account, that he could return them to the man from whom they were taken, not even the faithless man would call him faithless.

So, in the case of a woman who has broken her marriage fidelity but remains faithful to her adulterer, she is surely wicked, but, if she is not faithful even to her adulterer, she is worse. On the contrary, if she repents of her gross sin and returns to conjugal chastity and breaks off all adulterous unions and purposes, I cannot conceive of even the adulterer himself thinking of her as a violator of fidelity.

Chapter 5

(5) The question is also usually asked whether this case ought to be called a marriage: when a man and a woman (he not being the husband nor she the wife of another) because of incontinence have intercourse not for the purpose of procreating children but only for the sake of intercourse itself, with this pledge between them, that he will not perform this act with another woman, nor she with another man. Yet perhaps not without reason this can be called wedlock, if this has been agreed upon between them even until the death of one of them and if, although they do not have intercourse for the purpose of having children, they do not avoid it, so that they do not refuse to have children nor act in any evil way so that they will not be born. But, if both or either one of these conditions is lacking, I do not see how we can call this a marriage.

For, if a man lives with a woman for a time, until he finds another worthy either of his high station in life or his wealth, whom he can marry as his equal, in his very soul he is an adulterer, and not with the one whom he desires to find but with her with whom he now lives in such a way as not to be married to her. The same is true for the woman, who, knowing the situation and willing it, still has relations unchastely with him, with whom she has no compact as a wife. On the other hand, if she remains faithful to him and, after he has taken a wife, does not plan to marry and is prepared to refrain absolutely from such an act, surely I could not easily bring myself to call her an adulteress; yet who would say that she did not sin, when he knows that she had relations with a man though she was not his wife.

If from the union, as far as she is concerned, she wishes for nothing except children and whatever she endures beyond the cause of procreation she endures unwillingly, surely this woman is to be placed above many matrons, who, although they are not adulteresses, force their husbands, who often desire to be continent, to pay the debt of the flesh, not with any hope of progeny, but through an intemperate use of their right under the ardor of concupiscence, still, in the marriage of these women there is this good, that they are married. They are married for this purpose, that concupiscence may be brought under a lawful bond and may not waver disgracefully and loosely, having of itself a weakness of the flesh that cannot be curbed, but in marriage an association of fidelity that cannot be dissolved; of itself an increase of immoderate intercourse, in marriage a means of begetting chastely. For, although it is disgraceful to make use of a husband for purposes of lust, it is honorable to refuse to have intercourse except with a husband and not to give birth except from a husband.

Chapter 6

There also are men incontinent to such a degree that they do not spare their wives even when pregnant. Whatever immodest, shameful, and sordid acts the married commit with each other are the sins of the married persons themselves, not the fault of marriage.

(6) Furthermore, in the more immoderate demand of the carnal debt, which the Apostle enjoined on them not as a command but conceded as a favor, to have sexual intercourse even without the purpose of procreation, although evil habits impel them to such intercourse, marriage protects them from adultery and fornication. For this is not permitted because of the marriage, but because of the marriage it is pardoned. Therefore, married people owe each other not only

the fidelity of sexual intercourse for the purpose of procreating children—and this is the first association of the human race in this mortal life—but also the mutual service, in a certain measure, of sustaining each other's weakness, for the avoidance of illicit intercourse, so that, even if perpetual continence is pleasing to one of them, he may not follow this urge except with the consent of the other. In this case, 'The wife has not authority over her body, but the husband; the husband likewise has not authority over his body, but the wife.' So, let them not deny either to each other, what the man seeks from matrimony and the woman from her husband, not for the sake of having children but because of weakness and incontinence, lest in this way they fall into damnable seductions through the temptations of Satan because of the incontinence of both or of one of them.

In marriage, intercourse for the purpose of generation has no fault attached to it, but for the purpose of satisfying concupiscence, provided with a spouse, because of the marriage fidelity, it is a venial sin; adultery or fornication, however, is a mortal sin. And so, continence from all intercourse is certainly better than marital intercourse itself which takes place for the sake of begetting children.

Chapter 7

While continence is of greater merit, it is no sin to render the conjugal debt, but to exact it beyond the need for generation is a venial sin; furthermore, to commit fornication or adultery is a crime that must be punished. Conjugal charity should be on its guard lest, while it seeks for itself the means of being honored more, it creates for the spouse the means of damnation. 'Everyone who puts away his wife, save on account of immorality, causes her to commit adultery.'[1] To such a degree is that nuptial pact which has been entered upon a kind of sacrament that it is not nullified by separation, since, as long as the husband, by whom she has been abandoned, is alive, she commits adultery if she marries another, and he who abandoned her is the cause of the evil.

(7) I wonder if, as it is permitted to put away an adulterous wife, it is accordingly permitted, after she has been put away, to marry another. Holy Scripture creates a difficult problem in this matter, since the Apostle says[2] that according to the command of the Lord a wife is not to depart from her husband, but, if she departs, she ought to remain unmarried or be reconciled to her husband. She surely ought not to withdraw and remain unmarried except in the case of an adulterous husband, lest, by withdrawing from him who is not an adulterer, she causes him to commit adultery. But, perhaps she can justly be reconciled with her husband either by tolerating him, if she on her own part cannot contain herself, or after he has been corrected. But I do not see how a man can have freedom to marry another if he leaves an adulteress, since a woman does not have freedom to marry another if she leaves an adulterer.

If this is so, that bond of fellowship between married couples is so strong that, although it is tied for the purpose of procreation, it is not loosed for the purpose of procreation. For, a man might be able to dismiss a wife who is barren and marry someone by whom he might have children, yet in our times and according to Roman law it is not permissible to marry a second wife as long as he has another wife living. Surely, when an adulteress or adulterer is abandoned, more human beings could be born if either the woman were wed to another or the man married another. But, if this is not

---
1 Matt. 5.32.
2 Cf. 1 Cor. 7.10,11.

permitted, as divine Law seems to prescribe, who will not be eager to learn what the meaning of such a strong conjugal bond is? I do not think that this bond could by any means have been so strong, unless a symbol, as it were, of something greater than that which could arise from our weak mortality were applied, something that would remain unshaken for the punishment of men when they abandon and attempt to dissolve this bond, inasmuch as, when divorce intervenes, that nuptial contract is not destroyed, so that the parties of the compact are wedded persons even though separated. Moreover, they commit adultery with those with whom they have intercourse even after their repudiation, whether she with a man, or he with a woman. Yet, except 'in the city of our God, His holy mountain,'[3] such is not the case with a woman.

Chapter 8

But who does not know that the laws of the pagans are otherwise. Among them, when repudiation intervenes, both she marries whomever she wishes and he whomever he wishes, without any offense that requires human punishment. Moses, because of the Israelites' hardness of heart,[1] seems to have permitted something similar to this practice regarding a written notice of dismissal.[2] In this matter there appears to be a rebuke rather than an approval of divorce.

(8) 'Let marriage be held in honor with all, and let the marriage bed be undefiled.'[3] We do not call marriage a good in this sense, that in comparison with fornication it is a good; otherwise, there will be two evils, one of which is worse.

---

3 Ps. 47.2.

---

1 Cf. Matt. 19.8.
2 Cf. Deut. 24.1.
3 Heb. 13.4.

Or even fornication will be a good because adultery is worse—since violation of another's marriage is worse than associating with a prostitute. Or adultery will be a good because incest is worse—since intercourse with one's mother is worse than lying with another's wife—and so on, until we come to those things about which, as the Apostle says: 'It is shameful even to speak.'[4] All will be good in comparison with that which is worse. But who would doubt that this is false? Therefore, marriage and fornication are not two evils, the second of which is worse; but marriage and continence are two goods, the second of which is better. Just so, your temporal health and sickness are not two evils, the second of which is worse; but your health and immortality are two goods, the second of which is better.

Likewise, knowledge and vanity are not two evils, vanity being the worse of the two; but knowledge and charity are two goods, charity being the better of the two. For, 'knowledge will be destroyed,' says the Apostle, yet it is necessary for this life, but 'charity will never fall.'[5] So also, this mortal generation, which is the purpose of marriage, will be destroyed, but freedom from all sexual intercourse is both an angelic ideal here, and remains forever. But, as the meals of the just are better than the fastings of the sacrilegious, so the marriage of the faithful is placed above the virginity of the unbeliever. Nevertheless, neither is a meal preferable to fasting in the one case, but justice to sacrilege; nor in the second case is marriage preferred to virginity, but faith to unbelief. For, the just, when there is need, will dine for this purpose, that as good masters they may furnish for their slaves, their bodies, what is right and fitting; but the sacrilegious fast for this purpose, that they may serve devils. So, faithful women marry for this purpose, that they may join chastely with

---
4 Eph. 5.12.
5 1 Cor. 13.8.

their husbands; but the unfaithful are virgins for this purpose, that they may commit fornication against the true God.

Therefore, just as that was good which Martha did when occupied with the ministering to holy souls, yet that was better which Mary her sister did, who 'seated herself at the Lord's feet, and listened to his words';[6] so we praise the good of Susanna[7] in married chastity, yet we place above it the good of the widow Anna[8] and much more so that of the Virgin Mary.[9] That was good which they were doing who out of their substance were supplying the necessaries to Christ and His disciples, but they did better who gave away all their substance that they might follow the same Lord more readily. In both these goods, whether what the latter did or what Martha and Mary did, the better could not be done without passing over and abandoning the other.

We must understand that marriage is not to be considered an evil for this reason, that widowed chastity or virginal purity cannot be possessed unless there is abstinence from marriage. Nor was that which Martha did an evil for this reason, that, unless her sister abstained from it, she would not be doing what was better; nor is it an evil to take a just man or a prophet into one's house, because he who wishes to follow Christ unto perfection, in order that he might do what is better, ought not to own any house at all.

Chapter 9

(9) Surely we must see that God gives us some goods which are to be sought for their own sake, such as wisdom, health, friendship; others, which are necessary for something

---
6 Cf. Luke 10.39.
7 Dan. 13.
8 Cf. Luke 2.36.
9 Cf. Luke 1.28.

else, such as learning, food, drink, sleep, marriage, sexual intercourse. Certain of these are necessary for the sake of wisdom, such as learning; others for the sake of health, such as food and drink and sleep; others for the sake of friendship, such as marriage or intercourse, for from this comes the propagation of the human race in which friendly association is a great good. So, whoever does not use these goods, which are necessary for something else, for the purpose for which they are given does well. As for him for whom they are not necessary, if he does not use them, he does better. In like manner, we wish for these goods rightly when we have need, but we are better off not wishing for them than wishing for them, since we possess them in a better way when we possess them as not necessary.

For this reason it is a good to marry, since it is a good to beget children, to be the mother of a family; but it is better not to marry, since it is better for human society itself not to have need of marriage. For, such is the present state of the human race that not only some who do not check themselves are taken up with marriage, but many are wanton and given over to illicit intercourse. Since the good Creator draws good out of their evils, there is no lack of numerous progeny and an abundance of generation whence holy friendships might be sought out.

In this regard it is gathered that in the earliest times of the human race, especially to propagate the people of God, through whom the Prince and Saviour of all peoples might both be prophesied and be born, the saints were obliged to make use of this good of marriage, to be sought not for its own sake but as necessary for something else. But now, since the opportunity for spiritual relationship abounds on all sides and for all peoples for entering into a holy and pure association, even they who wish to contract marriage only to have children are to be admonished that they practice the greater good of continence.

Chapter 10

(10) But I know what they murmur. 'What if,' they say, 'all men should be willing to restrain themselves from all intercourse, how would the human race survive?' Would that all men had this wish, if only in 'charity, from a pure heart and a good conscience and faith unfeigned.'[1] Much more quickly would the City of God be filled and the end of time be hastened. What else does it appear that the Apostle is encouraging when he says, in speaking of this: 'For I would that you all were as I am myself'?[2] Or, in another place: 'But this I say, brethren, the time is short; it remains that those who have wives be as if they had none; and those who weep, as though not weeping; and those who rejoice, as though not rejoicing; and those who buy, as though not buying; and those who use this world, as though not using it, for this world as we see it is passing away. I would have you free from care.' Then he adds: 'He who is unmarried thinks about the things of the Lord, how he may please the Lord. Whereas he who is married thinks about the things of the world, how he may please his wife, and he is divided. And the unmarried woman and the virgin, who is unmarried, is concerned about the things of the Lord, that she may be holy in body and in spirit. Whereas she who is married is concerned about the things of the world, how she may please her husband.'[3]

And so it seems to me that at this time only those who do not restrain themselves ought to be married in accord with this saying of the same Apostle: 'But if they do not have self-control, let them marry, for it is better to marry than to burn.'[4]

---
1 1 Tim. 1.5.
2 1 Cor. 7.7.
3 1 Cor. 7.29-34.
4 1 Cor. 7.9.

(11) Such marriage is not a sin. If it were chosen in preference to fornication, it would be a lesser sin than fornication, but still a sin. But now what are we to say in answer to that very clear statement of the Apostle when he says: 'Let him do what he will; he does not sin if she should marry'[5] and 'But if thou takest a wife, thou hast not sinned. And if a virgin marries, she does not sin.'[6] Certainly from this it is not right to doubt that marriage is not a sin. And so it is not the marriage that the Apostle grants as a pardon—for who would doubt that it is most absurd to say that they have not sinned to whom a pardon is granted—but it is that sexual intercourse that comes about through incontinence, not for the sake of procreation and at the time with no thought of procreation, that he grants as a pardon. Marriage does not force this type of intercourse to come about, but asks that it be pardoned, provided it is not so great as to encroach on the times that ought to be set aside for prayer, and does not degenerate into that practice that is against nature, which the Apostle was not able to pass over in silence when he spoke of the extreme depravities of impure and impious men.[7]

The intercourse necessary for generation is without fault and it alone belongs to marriage. The intercourse that goes beyond this necessity no longer obeys reason but passion. Still, not to demand this intercourse but to render it to a spouse, lest he sin mortally by fornication, concerns the married person. But, if both are subject to such concupiscence, they do something that manifestly does not belong to marriage. However, if in their union they love what is proper rather than what is improper, that is, what belongs to marriage rather than that which does not, this is granted to them with

---
5 1 Cor. 7.36.
6 1 Cor. 7.28.
7 Cf. Rom. 1.26.

the Apostle as an authoriy. They do not have a marriage that encourages this crime, but one that intercedes for them, if they do not turn away from themselves the mercy of God, either by not abstaining on certain days so as to be free for prayers, and by this abstinence as by their fasts they put their prayers in a favorable light, or by changing the natural use into that use which is contrary to nature, which is all the more damnable in a spouse.

Chapter 11

(12) For, although the natural use, when it goes beyond the marriage rights, that is, beyond the need for procreation, is pardonable in a wife but damnable in a prostitute, that use which is against nature is abominable in a prostitute but more abominable in a wife. For, the decree of the Creator and the right order of the creature are of such force that, even though there is an excess in the things that have been granted to be used, this is much more tolerable than a single or rare deviation in those things which have not been granted. Therefore, the immoderation of a spouse in a matter that is permitted is to be tolerated lest lust may break forth into something that has not been granted. So it is that, however demanding one is as regards his wife, he sins much less than one who commits fornication even most rarely.

But, when the husband wishes to use the member of his wife which has not been given for this purpose, the wife is more shameful if she permits this to take place with herself rather than with another woman. The crown of marriage, then, is the chastity of procreation and faithfulness in rendering the carnal debt. This is the province of marriage, this is what the Apostle defended from all blame by saying: 'But if thou takest a wife, thou hast not sinned. And if a virgin marries, she does not sin'¹ and 'Let him do what he will; he does not sin, if she should marry.'² The somewhat immoderate departure in demanding the debt from the one or the other sex is given as a concession because of those things which he mentioned before.

(13) Therefore, what he says: 'The unmarried woman thinks about the things of the Lord, that she may be holy in body and spirit,'³ is not to be understood in such a way that we think a chaste Christian wife is not holy in body. To all the faithful, indeed, it is said: 'Do you not know that your bodies are the temple of the Holy Spirit, who is in you, whom you have from God?'⁴ Also holy, therefore, are the bodies of married people who remain faithful to themselves and to the Lord.

That an unbelieving spouse does not hinder this sanctity of either of the couple, but, rather, the sanctity of the wife profits the unbelieving husband or the sanctity of the husband profits the unbelieving wife, the same Apostle is a witness when he says: 'For the unbelieving husband is sanctified in the wife, and the unbelieving wife is sanctified in the believing husband.'⁵

Moreover, this was said in regard to the greater sanctity of the unmarried woman than of the married woman, and a more ample reward is due to this sanctity because it is better than the other good, because she thinks only of this, how she might please the Lord. For it is not that a faithful woman, observing conjugal chastity, does not think how she might please the Lord, but she does so less because she is thinking also of things of the world, how she might please her husband. This is what he wished to say about them, what

---

1 1 Cor. 7.28.
2 1 Cor. 7.36.
3 1 Cor. 7.34.
4 1 Cor. 6.19.
5 1 Cor. 7.14.

they can expect, as it were, from the demands of marriage, namely, that they must think of the things of the world, how they might please their husbands.

Chapter 12

(14) Not without reason is it doubted whether he said this of all married women or of such women of this type who are so numerous that almost all women can be considered the same. Nor does this, which he says of the unmarried: 'The unmarried woman thinks about the things of the Lord, that she may be holy in body and spirit,'[1] hold good for all unmarried women, since there are some widows who are dead in that they are living in sinful pleasures.[2] However, in regard to this certain distinction and *quasi* characteristic of unmarried and married, just as she is the most detestable who while refraining from marriage, that is, from a thing that has been granted, does not refrain from the sins whether of lust or pride or idle curiosity and gossip, so, too, rare is the married woman who in conjugal conduct thinks only how she might please God, by adorning herself 'not with braided hair or gold and pearls and expensive clothing, but by good behavior such as become women professing godliness.'[3]

The Apostle Peter also describes marriages of this type when he charges: 'In like manner also let wives be subject to their husbands; so that even if any do not believe the word, they may without word be won through the behavior of their wife, observing your reverence and chaste behavior. Let them not be such as are adorned with the curling of hair or

---
1 1 Cor. 7.34.
2 Cf. 1 Tim. 5.6.
3 1 Tim. 2.9,10.

clothed with gold or a fine robe; but let it be the inner life of your heart, in the imperishableness of a quiet and gentle spirit, which is of great price in the sight of the Lord. For after this manner certain holy women who hoped in the Lord, adorned themselves, while being subject to their husbands. So Sara obeyed Abraham, calling him lord. You have become daughters of hers when you do what is right and fear no vain disturbance. Husbands, in like manner dwell in peace and in chastity with your wives, pay honor to the weaker and subjected vessel, as if coheir of grace, and see that your prayers be not hindered.'[4]

Is it true that such spouses do not think about the things of the Lord, how they might please the Lord? They are very rare. Who denies this? And in the very rareness almost all the married people who are of this type were not joined to be this way, but, after they were united, then they became such.

Chapter 13

(15) What Christian men of our times, free from the bond of marriage, able to restrain themselves from all intercourse, when they see it is 'a time,' as it is written, 'not to embrace, but a time to abstain from embraces,'[1] would not choose to observe virginal continence or that of a widower rather than to undergo the tribulation of the flesh, without which marriage cannot exist—to pass over in silence other things which the Apostle spares us[2]—since now no duty of human society presses. But, when they have been joined under the rule of concupiscence, if they afterwards overcome it, since

---
4 1 Peter 3.1-7.

---
1 Eccle. 3.5.
2 Cf. 1 Cor. 7-28.

it is not permissible to dissolve the marriage, as it was permissible not to join together, they become such as the form of marriage professes, so that either by mutual consent they ascend to a higher grade of sanctity or, if both are not of this mind, he who is such will not be the one who demands the carnal debt but renders it, observing in all things a chaste and religious harmony.

In those times, when the mystery of our salvation was still veiled in prophetic signs, even those who were of this nature before marriage were accustomed to marry because of the obligation of procreation, not overcome by passion, but motivated by piety. If they had been given the free choice such as was given in the revelation of the New Testament when our Lord said: 'Let him accept it who can,'[3] that person does not doubt that they would have taken it upon themselves with joy who attentively and diligently reads how they used their spouses, when it was permissible for one man to have many wives, whom he had more chastely than any one of these in whose regard we see what the Apostle grants, by way of concession, now has his one wife. The patriarchs possessed their wives for the work of procreation, not 'in the passion of lust like the Gentiles who do not know God.'[4] This is so great that many today would contain themselves more easily for their whole life from all intercourse than to hold to the norm of not uniting except for offspring, if they were to be joined by marriage.

Indeed, we do have many continent brothers and associates of both sexes in the heavenly heritage, whether they have entered the marriage state or whether free from all such intercourse; in fact, they are numberless. Yet, whom have we heard in friendly talks, whether of those who are married or who have been married, saying to us that he never had

---
3 Matt. 19.12.
4 Cf. 1 Thess. 4.5.

intercourse with his wife except when hoping for conception? Therefore, what the Apostles prescribe for married people belongs to marriage; what they grant by way of a concession, or what interferes with prayer, marriage does not force but endures.

Chapter 14

(16) Still, if by chance—I do not know whether it can happen, and I rather think that it cannot—at any rate, if by chance a concubine taken for a time should seek only children from this same union, not for this reason is such a union to be preferred to the marriage of those women who take advantage of that which is pardonable. For, what belongs to marriage must be considered, not what is the action of those marrying and using marriage intemperately.

Neither does anyone, if he should use fields that have been wickedly and wrongly invaded so as to make large sums from their produce, therefore justify rapine; if another one, an avaricious man, takes over the incumbency of his father's farm or one rightly acquired, the civil statute of law whereby he became the rightful owner is not therefore to be found fault with. Neither will the wickedness of a tyrannical faction be praiseworthy if the tyrant treats his subjects with regal clemency; nor is the system of kingly power deserving of blame if a king conducts himself with tyrannical cruelty. It is one thing to wish to use an unjust power justly, and another to use a just power unjustly. So, concubines taken for a time, if they have intercourse for the sake of children, do not justify their concubinage; nor do the married wives, if they are wanton with their husbands, put a stain on the marriage state.

(17) It is clear that by a subsequent honorable agreement there can be a marriage for those who had not been rightly united.

Chapter 15

Once, however, marriage is entered upon in the City [that is, Church] of our God, where also from the first union of the two human beings marriage bears a kind of sacred bond, it can be dissolved in no way except by the death of one of the parties. The bond of marriage remains, even if offspring, for which the marriage was entered upon, should not follow because of a clear case of sterility, so that it is not lawful for married people who know they will not have any children to separate and to unite with others even for the sake of having children. If they do unite, they commit adultery with the ones with whom they join themselves, for they remain married people.

It was indeed permissible among the ancients to have another woman with the consent of the wife, from whom common children might be born by the union and seed of the husband, by the privilege and authorization of the wife. Whether this is permissible now, as well, I would not care to say. There is not the need for procreation which there was then, when it was permissible for husbands who could have children to take other women for the sake of a more copious posterity, which certainly is not lawful now. The mysterious difference of times brings so great an opportunity of doing or of not doing something justly that, now, he does better who does not marry even one wife, unless he cannot control himself; then, however, they had without fault several wives, even they who could restrain themselves much more easily, except that piety in that time demanded something else. For, as the wise and just man, who for a long time was desiring to be dissolved and to be with Christ[1] and was delighted rather by this greatest good, not the desire of living here but the duty of caring for others, took food that

---
1 Cf. Phil. 1.23.

he might remain in the flesh, which was necessary for the sake of others, so, too, for the men of those times it was not lust but duty to be joined with women by the law of marriage.

Chapter 16

(18) For, what food is to the health of man, intercourse is to the health of the race, and both are not without carnal pleasure, which, however, when modified and put to its natural use with a controlling temperance, cannot be a passion.[1] However, what unlawful food is in the sustaining of life, this is the intercourse of fornication or adultery in seeking a child; and what unlawful food is in the excessive indulgence of the stomach and palate, this is unlawful intercourse in a passion seeking no offspring; and what is immoderate appetite for some as regards lawful food, this is that pardonable intercourse in spouses. Therefore, just as it is better to die of hunger than to eat food sacrificed to idols, so it is better to die childless than to seek progeny from an unlawful union.

However, from whatever source men are born, if they do not follow the vices of their parents and if they worship God rightly, they will be honest and safe. The seed of man, from any kind of man, is a creature of God and will prove bad for those who use it wrongly; of itself, it will not at any time be an evil. Yet, just as the good children of adulterers are no defense for adultery, so the bad children of married people do not constitute an accusation against marriage. Accordingly, just as the fathers of New Testament times, taking food

---

1 Cf. *Retractationes* 2.22: 'This was said since the good and proper use of passion is not a passion. Just as it is wicked to use good things wrongly, it is good to use wicked things rightly. I argued more carefully about this matter on another occasion, especially against the new Pelagian heretics.'

because of the duty of caring for others, though they ate it with a natural delectation of the flesh—by no means, however, was their pleasure to be compared with the pleasure of those who were eating food sacrificed to idols or of those who, though they were consuming lawful foods, were doing so immoderately—so the fathers of Old Testament times had intercourse because of the duty of caring for others. That natural delight they derived was by no means given rein up to the point of unreasoning and wicked lust, nor is it to be compared to the debaucheries of lust or the intemperance of the married. Indeed, for the same fountainhead of charity, then carnally, now spiritually, were children to be propagated because of that great Mother Jerusalem; only the difference in times made the works of the fathers diverse. So, it was necessary that non-carnal Prophets copulate carnally, as it was necessary that non-carnal Apostles also eat carnally.

Chapter 17

(19) Therefore, as many women as there are now, to whom it is said: 'If they do not have self-control, let them marry,'[1] are not to be compared even to the holy women who married then. Marriage itself among all races is for the one purpose of procreating children, whatever will be their station and character afterwards; marriage was instituted for this purpose, so that children might be born properly and decently.

But the men who do not have self-control step up, as it were, into marriage by a step of honesty; those, however, who without a doubt would have practiced self-control, if the conditions of that time would have allowed this, step down, in a certain sense, into marriage by a step of piety. Therefore,

---
1 1 Cor. 7.9.

the marriage of both, inasmuch as they are marriages because they exist for the sake of procreation, are equally good; yet, married men of our times are not to be compared to married men of those days. The former have something that is granted to them as a concession because of the dignity of marriage, although it does not pertain to marriage, that is, that departure which goes beyond the need for procreating, which the other men in question did not have. But neither can these, if any by chance are now to be found who do not seek or desire in marriage anything except that for which marriage was instituted, be put on the same footing with those men. For, in these the very desire for children is carnal; in those, however, it was spiritual, because it was in accord with the mystery of the time. In our day, it is true, no one perfect in piety seeks to have children except spiritually; in their day, however, the work of piety itself was to propagate children even carnally, because the generation of that people was a harbinger of future events and pertains to the prophetic dispensation.

(20) Therefore, while it was permitted for one husband to have several wives, it was not permitted for one woman to have several husbands, not even for the sake of offspring, if, perhaps, she was able to bear while her husband was not able to beget. For, by a hidden law of nature things that rule love singularity; things that are ruled, indeed, are subjected not only each one to an individual master, but also, if natural or social conditions allow, many of them are not unfittingly subjected to one master. Neither does one servant have many masters, as many servants have one master. And so we read where no one of the holy women served two or more living husbands; we do read, however, that one man had several wives when the customs of that people permitted it and the nature of the time encouraged it, for it is not against the nature of marriage. Many women can conceive

children by one man, but one woman cannot do so by many men—this is the nature of principals—just as many souls are properly subjected to the one God. Therefore, there is only the one true God of souls; one soul through many false gods can commit fornication, but not be made fruitful.

Chapter 18

(21) Since from many souls there is to be one City of those having one soul and one heart in regard to God,[1] this perfection of our unity is to be after this peregrination, when the thoughts of all will not be hidden from one another nor in any way opposed to one other; for this reason, the sacrament of marriage in our time has been reduced and confined to one man and one woman, so that it is not lawful to ordain a minister of the Church unless he is the husband of one wife.[2] This was more keenly understood by those who believed that the person should not be ordained who as a catechumen or as a pagan had had a second wife. It is a question of the sacrament, not of sin. In baptism all sins are remitted. But he who said: 'If thou takest a wife, thou hast not sinned. And if a virgin marries, she does not sin,'[3] and 'Let him do what he will, he does not sin if she should marry,'[4] has sufficiently declared that marriage is no sin.

However, because of the sanctity of the sacrament, just as a woman, even if she has had intercourse while still a catechumen, is not able after baptism to be consecrated among the virgins of God, just so it did not seem harsh that he who has had more than one wife did not commit any

---

1 Cf. Acts 4.32.
2 Cf. 1 Tim. 3.2; Titus 1.6.
3 1 Cor. 7.28.
4 1 Cor. 7.36.

sin, but lost a certain standard, as it were, to the sacrament, necessary not for the reward of a good life, but for the seal of ecclesiastical ordination.

And on this account, just as the many wives of the ancient fathers signified our future churches of all races subject to one man-Christ, so our bishop, a man of one wife, signifies the unity of all nations subject to one man-Christ. This unity will be perfected at that time when He will reveal 'the things hidden in darkness' and make manifest 'the hidden things of the heart; and then everyone will have his praise from God.'[5] Now, however, there are open, there are hidden, dissensions, even though charity is preserved among those who are to be one and in One; these dissensions then, indeed, will be no more.

Therefore, just as the multiple marriages of that time symbolically signified the future multitude subject to God in all peoples of the earth, so the single marriages of our time symbolically signify the unity of all of us subject to God which is to be in one heavenly City. And so, just as serving two or more masters, so, too, passing from one husband while alive to the marriage of another was not lawful then, nor is it lawful now, nor will it ever be. Indeed, to apostatize from the one God and to go into the adulterous superstition of another is always wicked. Neither for the sake of a more numerous progeny did our holy father do what Cato the Roman is said to have done, that while he was still living he handed over his wife to fill the house of another with children. Indeed, in the marriage of our women the sanctity of the sacrament is of more importance than the fecundity of the womb.

(22) Therefore, even these who are joined for the sake of generation alone, for which marriage was instituted, are not to be compared with the ancients, who sought children in a

---
5 Cf. 1 Cor. 4.5.

much different way than they; since intrepid and devout Abraham, when he was ordered to sacrifice his son, whom he had received after great despair, would not have spared his sole child, but only he lowered his hand on being checked by Him at whose command he had raised it.

Chapter 19

It remains for us to see whether at least our continent men are to be compared with the married patriarchs; unless, perhaps, these continent men are to be preferred to the patriarchs, in respect to whom we have not yet found any to be compared. For there was a greater good in their marriage than the good proper to marriage, to which, without a doubt, the good of continence is to be preferred, because the ancients were not seeking children from their marriage out of an obligation such as the others are led by—a certain instinct of mortal nature requiring a replacement for a loss. Whoever denies that this is a good is ignorant of the fact that God is the creator of all good things from the heavenly even to the earthly, from the immortal even to the mortal. Yet, this instinct of generation not even the animals lack deep within, and especially the birds whose care for building a nest is obvious and to a certain extent comparable with married people as regards the procreation and nourishment of offspring.

But, the men of old, with much more holy minds, were surpassing this tendency of mortal nature whose own chastity in its kind, when the worship of God is added, is reckoned as producing fruit thirtyfold, as some have understood. They were seeking from their marriage children for the sake of Christ, to distinguish His descent according to the flesh from all others; as it pleased God to arrange it that this people before the rest should be able to prophesy Him because it was foretold from what family and from what people He was to come in the flesh.[1] Very much, then, was that a greater good that the chaste marriage of our faithful which father Abraham had known in his thigh, on which he ordered the servant to place his hand, that he might take an oath concerning the wife who was to be married by his son.[2] For, putting the hand under the thigh of a man and swearing by the God of heaven, what else did that signify except that in that flesh, which took its origin from that thigh, the God of heaven would come?

Marriage, therefore, is a good in which the married are better in proportion as they fear God more chastely and more faithfully, especially if they also nourish spiritually the children whom they desire carnally.

Chapter 20

(23) The fact that the Law orders a man to be purified even after marital intercourse does not mean that it is a sin; if it is not that intercourse which is granted as a concession, which, also, being intemperate, impedes prayers. But, just as the Law placed many things in mysteries and in the shadows of things to come, a certain material shapelessness, as it were, in the seed, which when it is formed will produce the body of a man, is placed as a sign of a life shapeless and uninstructed; so, since it is fitting that men be cleansed from this shapelessness by the form and learning of doctrine, as a sign of this, purification after the loss of seed has been ordered.

Nor is loss of seed in sleep a result of sin; yet in this case, also, purification is prescribed. Or, if anyone considers this a

---
1 Cf. Mich. 5.2.
2 Cf. Gen. 24.2.

sin, thinking that it does not happen except from some desire of this sort—which, without a doubt, is false—are, then, the cycle menstruations of women sins? However, the same Old Law ordered that the women be purified from them only because of the material shapelessness which, when conception takes place, is added, as it were, for the purpose of developing the body. And on this account, since there is a formless flow, the Law wished that by this the mind without the force of discipline, unseemly fluid and dissipated, be understood; it shows that the mind must be formed, when it orders such a flow of the body to be purified. Finally, is it a sin to die, or is not the burial of the dead also a good work of kindness? Still, purification was ordered after this, also,[1] because a dead body when life has left it is no sin, but it signifies the sin of a soul abandoned by justice.

(24) Marriage, I say, is a good and can be defended by right reason against all charges. However, with regard to the marriage of the holy patriarchs, I am asking not what marriage but what continence is comparable. Moreover, I am not comparing marriage with marriage—for a gift equal in all things has been given to the mortal nature of man—but men who make use of marriage. Since I do not find any to compare with those men of old who used marriages far differently, it must be asked what continent men can be compared to them—unless, perhaps, Abraham could not restrain himself from marriage because of the kingdom of heaven, who because of the kingdom of heaven could fearlessly immolate his single beloved son on whose account marriage was dear to him.

---
1 Cf. Num. 19.11.

Chapter 21

(25) Continence, indeed, not of the body but of the soul is virtue. Virtues of the soul, however, sometimes are manifested in work, sometimes they lie dormant in habit and character, just as the virtue of martyrdom stood out and was manifested by bearing sufferings. But how many there are in that same virtuous condition of soul for whom the temptation is lacking by which that which within is in the sight of God might also come forth into the sight of men, and at the time not begin to exist but then begin to be known!

As an example, Job had possessed patience for a long time.[1] God knew this and He bore witness to it, but it became known to men by the trial of a temptation, and what was hidden within was not born, but was manifested, by the assaults made from without. Likewise, Timothy had the virtue of refraining from wine,[2] which Paul did not take from him by admonishing that he use a little wine for the stomach's sake and his frequent infirmities—otherwise, he would have taught perniciously that for the health of the body there should be a loss of virtue in the soul—but because it was possible to do what he ordered and safeguard virtue at the same time, so the advantage of drinking was relaxed as regards the body in such a way that the habit of temperance remained in the soul.

For habit is that by which something is done when the need arises, yet, when it is not being practiced, it can be, but there is no need. They do not have this habit in respect to the continence that is from intercourse, since it is said to them: 'But if they do not have self-control, let them marry.'[3] On the other hand, they do have the habit to whom the words

---
1 Cf. Job 1.
2 Cf. 1 Tim. 5.23.
3 Cf. 1 Cor. 7.9.

are addressed: 'Let him accept it who can.'[4] Through this habit of continence perfect souls have so used worldly goods that are necessary for another purpose that by means of this habit they were not bound by these goods and were able not to use them when there was no need. Nor does anyone use them properly unless he is able also not to use them. Many, indeed, more easily abstain from them so as not to use them at all, rather than control themselves so as to use them well. Yet, no one can use them wisely except him who through continence is able not to use them. In consequence, Paul could say of this habit: 'I know how to have abundance and to suffer want.'[5] In any event, to suffer want is the lot of certain men, but to know how to suffer want belongs to great souls. So, who is not able also to have abundance? However, to know how to abound belongs only to those whom abundance does not corrupt.

(26) That it might be more clearly understood how virtue can be in habit, even if not in practice, I speak of an example regarding which there can be no doubt among Catholic Christians. That our Lord Jesus Christ in His true flesh was hungry and thirsty, ate and drank, no one doubts who is faithful in accordance with His Gospel. Therefore, was there not in Him the virtue of continence from food and drink such as was in John the Baptist? 'For John came neither eating nor drinking, and they said, "He has a devil!" The Son of Man came eating and drinking, and they said, "Behold a glutton and a wine-drinker, a friend of publicans and sinners!"'[6] Are not such things said of the members of His family, our fathers, of their use of earthly goods of another kind, such as pertain to intercourse; behold the lustful and unclean, the lovers of women and licentiousness? And just as in His case

---
4 Matt. 19.12.
5 Phil. 4.10.
6 Matt. 11.18,19.

this was not true, although it was true that He did not abstain from eating and drinking as John did, for He Himself says very openly and truly: 'John came neither eating nor drinking. The Son of Man came eating and drinking,' so neither is this true as regards the patriarchs, although the Apostle of Christ came in our time neither married nor having children, yet the pagans say: he was a magician; at that time the Prophet of Christ came marrying and begetting children, and yet the Manichaeans say: he was fond of women. 'And wisdom is justified by her children.'[7] This is what our Lord added at that point when He said these things about John and Himself. 'Wisdom,' He said, 'is justified by her children.' They see that the virtue of continence ought always to be in the disposition of the souls, to be shown, however, in practice in accord with the opportunity of the time and circumstances. So the virtue of patience of the holy martyrs appeared, indeed, in act, although equally in habit it was in the rest of the saints. Therefore, just as there was not an unequal reward for patience in Peter who suffered and in John who did not suffer, so there was not an unequal reward for continence in John who had no experience with marriage and in Abraham who begot sons. Both the celibacy of the one and the marriage of the other did service for Christ in accord with the needs of the time, but John possessed continence in practice; Abraham indeed possessed it, but only in habit.

Chapter 22

(27) Accordingly, when even the Law following the time of the patriarchs then called him accursed who did not rear children in Israel, even he who could did not show forth this continence, yet he possessed it. Afterwards, the fullness

---
7 Matt. 11.19.

of time came,¹ so that it was said: 'Let him accept it who can';² from that time up till now and henceforward to the end, he who possesses this continence puts it into practice; he who is unwilling to practice it, let him not say untruthfully that he has it. Therefore, it is with a subtlety that is empty and of no use that they who corrupt good morals by evil conversation³ say to the Christian man, continent and refusing marriage: 'You, then, are better than Abraham?' When he hears this, let him not be troubled or dare to say: 'Yes, better,' or to fall from his resolution—because the former he does not say truthfully, the latter he does not do rightly—but let him say: 'I am indeed not better than Abraham, but the chastity of the unmarried is better than the chastity of marriage. Abraham had one of them in practice, both in habit. He lived chastely in the married state, yet he could have been chaste without marriage, but then it was impossible. I, indeed, more easily do not make use of marriage, which Abraham made use of, than I could make use of marriage as Abraham used it. Therefore, I am better than those who through incontinence of mind cannot do what I am doing. I am not better than those who because of the difference of times did not do what I am doing. What I now do they would have done better, if it was to be done at that time. But what they did I would not be doing as they did, if it had to be done now.'

Or, if he feels and knows that he is of such a character that, if he would descend to the use of marriage because of some religious obligation, the virtue of continence remaining safe and secure in the habit of his mind, he would be the type of husband and the type of father that Abraham was, let him openly dare to respond to that captious questioner

---
1 Cf. Gal. 4.4.
2 Matt. 19.12.
3 Cf. 1 Cor. 15.33.

and to say: 'I am not even better than Abraham in at least this type of continence which he did not lack, though it was not apparent; but I am not such a one who has one thing but does another.' Let him say these things openly, because, even if he does wish to boast, he will not be foolish, for he speaks the truth. But, if he forbears, lest any man thinks that he is above what he sees in him or hears from him,[4] let him remove from his own person the knot of the question, and let him respond not about the man but about the thing itself, and say: 'Who can do so much, he is such a one as Abraham was.' Yet, it can happen that the virtue of continence is less in the soul of him who does not make use of marriage which Abraham made use of; still, it is greater than that in the soul of him who on this account observed the chastity of marriage because he could not observe the greater.

The same is the case of the unmarried woman who thinks about the things of the Lord, how she might be holy in body and in spirit.[5] When she hears that impudent inquirer saying: 'You are, then, better than Sara?' Let her answer: 'I am better, but better than those who lack the virtue of this continence, and I do not believe this in respect to Sara. Therefore, she possessed that virtue and did what was suited to that time. I am free from this duty so that in my body, also, there can appear what she had in her soul.'

Chapter 23

(28) Therefore, if we compare the things themselves, in no way can it be doubted that the chastity of continence is better than the chastity of marriage. Although both, indeed, are a good, when we compare the men, the one who has the

---
4 Cf. 2 Cor. 12.6.
5 Cf. 1 Cor. 7.34.

greater good than the other is the better. Moreover, he who has the greater good of the same kind has also that which is less; however, he who has only what is less certainly does not have what is greater. For, thirty is contained in sixty, but not sixty in thirty. The failure to act in accordance with one's full capacity to act depends upon the distribution of duties, not upon the lack of virtue, because he does not lack the good of mercy who does not come upon the unfortunate ones whom he could help in his mercy.

(29) We must take this into account, too, that it is not right to compare men with men in some one good. For, it can happen that one does not have something that the other has, but he has something that is to be valued more highly. Greater, indeed, is the good of obedience than the good of continence. Marriage is nowhere condemned by the authority of our Scriptures; disobedience, however, is nowhere condoned.

If, then, we have to choose between one who remains a virgin who is at the same time disobedient and a married woman who could not remain a virgin but who is nevertheless obedient—which of the two shall we say is the better? Is it the one who is less laudable than she would be if she were a virgin, or the one worthy of reproach although she is a virgin? So, if you compare a drunken virgin with a chaste spouse, who would hesitate to pass the same judgment? Marriage and virginity are, it is true, two goods, the second of them is the greater. So with sobriety and drunkenness, obedience and disobedience—the former are goods; the latter, evils. However, it is better to have everything that is good in a lesser degree than to have a great good with a great evil, since even in the goods of the body it is better to have the stature of Zaccaeus[1] together with health than the height of Goliath[2] together with a fever.

---
1 Cf. Luke 19.3.
2 Cf. 1 Kings 17.4.

(30) The right question is plainly not whether a virgin thorougly disobedient should be compared with an obedient married woman, but a less obedient to a more obedient, for there is also nuptial chastity and it is indeed a good, but a lesser one than virginal chastity. Therefore, if the woman who is inferior in the good of obedience in proportion as she is greater in the good of chastity is compared with the other, then he who sees, when he compares chastity itself and obedience, that obedience in a certain way is the mother of all virtues, judges which woman is to be placed first. On this account, then, there can be obedience without virginity, because virginity is of counsel, not of precept. I am speaking of that obedience whereby precepts are obeyed. There can be obedience to precepts without virginity, but there cannot be this obedience without chastity. For it is of the essence of chastity not to commit fornication, not to commit adultery, not to be stained with any illicit intercourse. Whoever do not observe these precepts act against the commands of God and on this account are banished from the virtue of obedience. Virginity can exist by itself without obedience, since a woman can, although accepting the counsel of virginity and guarding her virginity, neglect the precepts; just as we know many sacred virgins who are garrulous, inquisitive, addicted to drink, contentious, greedy, proud. All these vices are against the precepts and destroy them through their sin of disobedience, like Eve herself. Therefore, not only is the obedient person to be preferred to the disobedient one, but the more obedient wife is to be preferred to the less obedient virgin.

(31) In accord with this, that patriarch who was not without a wife was prepared to be without his only son and one to be slain by his own hand.[3] Indeed, I may speak of

---
3 Cf. *Retractationes* 2.22: 'What I said concerning Abraham . . . I do not entirely approve. It ought to be thought that he believed that his son, if he had been killed, must soon be returned to him by a resurrection from the dead, as it is read in the Epistle to the Hebrews' [11.19].

'his only son' not unfittingly, concerning whom he had heard from the Lord: 'Through Isaac shall your descendants be called.'[4] Therefore, how much more readily would he have obeyed if it were ordered that he was not to have a wife.

So it is that not in vain do we often wonder at some of both sexes, who, containing themselves from all intercourse, carelessly obey the commands, though they have so ardently embraced the idea of not using things that have been granted. Seeing this, who doubts that the men and women of our times, free from all intercourse but inferior in the virtue of obedience, are not rightly compared to the excellence of those holy patriarchs and mothers begetting children, even if the patriarchs had lacked the habit of mind that is manifest in the actions of the men of our day?

Therefore, let the young men singing a new canticle follow the Lamb, as it is written in the Apocalypse: 'Who have not defiled themselves with women,'[5] on no other account than that they remained virgins. Let them not think, then, that they are better than the early patriarchs, who used their marriage, if I may put it this way, nuptially. The use, indeed, of marriage is such that there is a defilement if anything is done in marriage through the union of the flesh that exceeds the need for generation, though this is pardonable. For, what does pardon expiate, if that departure does not defile entirely. It would be remarkable if the children following the Lamb would be free from this defilement unless they remained virgins.

Chapter 24

(32) The good, therefore, of marriage among all nations and all men is in the cause of generation and in the fidelity

---
4 Gen. 21.12.
5 Apoc. 14.4.

of chastity; in the case of the people of God, however, the good is also in the sanctity of the sacrament. Because of this sanctity it is wrong for a woman, leaving with a divorce, to marry another man while her husband still lives, even if she does this for the sake of having children. Although that is the sole reason why marriage takes place, even if this for which marriage takes place does not follow, the marriage bond is not loosed except by the death of a spouse. Just as if an ordination of the clergy is performed to gather the people, even if the congregation does not follow, there yet remains in those ordained the sacrament of orders. And if, because of any fault, anyone is removed from clerical office, he retains the sacrament of the Lord once it has been imposed, although it remains for judgment.

The Apostle is a witness to the fact that marriage exists for the sake of generation in this way: 'I desire,' he says, 'that the younger widows marry.'[1] And—as if it were said to him: for what reason?—he added immediately: 'to bear children, to rule their households.' But this pertains to the faithfulness of chastity: 'The wife has not authority over her body, but the husband; the husband likewise has not authority over his body, but the wife.'[2] As to the sanctity of the sacrament, this is pertinent: 'A wife is not to depart from her husband, and if she departs, that she is to remain unmarried or be reconciled to her husband,' and 'Let not a husband put away his wife.'[3] These are all goods on account of which marriage is a good: offspring, fidelity, sacrament. Yet, not to seek carnal offspring now at this time, and on this account to retain a certain perpetual freedom from all such practice and to be spiritually subject to one man, Christ, is better and indeed holier; especially if men use this freedom so acquired

---

1 1 Tim. 5.14.
2 1 Cor. 7.4.
3 1 Cor. 7.10.

in such a way as it is written, to think about the things of the Lord, how they may please God,[4] that is, that continence unceasingly consider lest obedience fall short in any way. The holy patriarchs practiced this virtue as basic and, as it is customarily called, a source and clearly a universal one; but continence they possessed in the disposition of the soul. Even if they had been ordered to abstain from all intercourse, they certainly would have done so by means of the obedience by which they were just and holy and prepared for every good work. For, how much more easily were they able not to have intercourse at the command or bidding of God who could by being obedient immolate the offspring whose propagation alone they were making possible by having intercourse.

Chapter 25

(33) Since these things are so, I have answered enough and more than enough to the heretics, whether Manichaeans or whoever else calumniate the patriarchs for their many wives, alleging that this is an argument by which they prove their incontinence, if, however, they understand that what is not done contrary to nature is not a sin, since they made use of their wives not for the sake of being wanton, but for procreation; nor against the customs, because at the time those things were being done; nor contrary to the precept, because they were not prohibited by any law. Those, indeed, who illicitly made use of women, either that divine dictum in the Scriptures convicts, or the text puts them before us as ones who are to be judged and avoided, not to be approved or imitated.

---
4 Cf. 1 Cor. 7.32.

Chapter 26

(34) However, as much as we can, we advise our people who have spouses not to dare to judge those patriarchs according to their weakness, comparing, as the Apostle says, themselves with themselves,[1] and therefore not understanding what great powers the soul that serves justice has against the passions, so that it does not acquiesce in carnal impulses of this kind and does not allow them to fall into or to proceed to intercourse beyond the need for generation, that is, beyond what the order of nature, beyond what customs, beyond what laws permit.

Men indeed have this suspicion concerning these patriarchs because they themselves either have chosen marriage because of incontinence or they make use of their wives immoderately. But let continent people, either men whose wives have died, or women whose husbands have died, or both, who with equal consent have pledged their continence to God, know that a greater reward is due them than conjugal chastity demands. But, as to the marriage of the holy patriarchs, who were joined in a prophetic way, who neither in intercourse sought anything but progeny, nor anything in the progeny itself except what would profit Christ who was to come in the flesh, let them not only not despise it in comparison with their own resolution, but also in accordance with their own resolution; let them prefer it with hesitation.

(35) Most especially do we warn the young men and the virgins dedicating their virginity to God, so that they may know that they ought to guard the life they are living in the meantime upon earth with the greatest humility, since the greater life which they have vowed is of heaven. For it is written: 'The greater thou art, the more humble thyself in

---
1 Cf. 2 Cor. 10.12.

all things.'² Therefore, it is for us to say something of their greatness; it is theirs to think of great humility. Thus, with the exception of certain of the married patriarchs and married women of the Old Testament—for these, though they are not married, are not better than they, because if they were married they would not be equal—let them not doubt that all the other married people of this time, even the ones who are continent after experiencing marriage, are surpassed by them, not as much as Susanna is surpassed by Anna, but as much as both are surpassed by Mary. I am speaking of what pertains to the holy integrity of the flesh, for who is ignorant of the other merits that Mary had?

Therefore, let them add a fitting conduct to such a high resolve, so that they may have a certain security in respect to obtaining such a splendid reward, knowing, indeed, that to themselves and to all the faithful beloved and chosen members of Christ coming from the East and the West, though shining with a light different in each case, because of their merits, this great reward is given in common, to recline with Abraham and Isaac and Jacob in the kingdom of God,³ who, not for the sake of this world but for the sake of Christ, were spouses, for the sake of Christ were parents.

---

2 Eccli. 3.20.
3 Cf. Matt. 8.11.

ADULTEROUS MARRIAGES

(De incompetentibus nuptiis)

Translated by
CHARLES T. HUEGELMEYER, M.M.
Maryknoll, New York

INTRODUCTION

WHILE CONSIDERING the state of marriage as a natural contract and a social institution regulated by the Gospel, as well as the sacramental character of matrimony in a special way, Augustine systematized the rather elementary doctrine which preceded him and developed it by establishing it on a firm foundation, largely in the course of his struggles against the Manichaean and Pelagian heretics.

The first book of the present treatise was occasioned by a letter received by Augustine from a certain Pollentius, who had some erroneous notions concerning divorce and remarriage and who had asked Augustine to answer and resolve his difficulties. After Augustine had answered Pollentius' original queries, the text of his replies were edited by some of his friends, before he could answer some later questions addressed to him also in letter form by the same Pollentius. Thus, Augustine's treatise on marriage and divorce was intended by him to appear as a unit, but the zeal of his friends forced the premature publishing of his earlier replies.

The two books, *Adulterous Marriages,* are basically exegetical in character. Augustine's conclusions are based on a carefully considered and finely drawn comparison of the passages in holy Scripture which relate to the question at hand. They are written in argumentative style and are a model of dialectic development of a main premise, which is, in this case, the statement of Mark and Luke that a Christian who divorces his spouse and remarries contracts an adulterous union, even if the divorce has as its ground adultery on the part of one of the spouses. Rarely does Augustine resort, in this work, to the finer devices of rhetoric. Rather, with a point of dogma at stake, Augustine's language is direct.

Augustine tells in the *Retractations* that this work considered a question treated many years before in his treatise, *De sermone Domini in monte,* written in 396. Augustine considers *Adulterous Marriages* in his *Retractations* immediately after the *De anima et eius origine,* which was written in the year 419, but before the work entitled *Contra adversarium legis et prophetarum,* which was written in 420. Thus the work can be dated either late in 419 or early in 420, with preference for the former period. It is included by Possidius, Augustine's earliest biographer, in his *Indiculus* under the title *De incompetentibus nuptiis.*

Augustine had given his opinion in his *Commentary on the Lord's Sermon on the Mount*[1] that women who leave their husbands because of unfaithfulness ought not to be allowed to marry again—stressing the possibility of reconciliation—and that St. Paul added a necessary condition to our Lord's command in this respect, that this prohibition is meant to extend only to the lifetime of each party. With this opinion Pollentius disagreed, maintaining that St. Paul's intention was to prohibit remarriage only to women who leave their husbands for reasons other than unfaithfulness—including clashes of temperament and difficulties of cohabitation.[2]

---
1 1.14.39; cf. translation by D. J. Kavanagh in this series, Vol. 11 (New York 1951).
2 Cf. below, 1.1; also, Gustave Combès, *Oeuvres de Saint Augustin* 2 (Paris 1948) 103-107.

Married persons who have not accused each other of conjugal infidelity have the preceptive duty to remain together, Augustine held, even if their marital obligations seem to impose an insufferable burden. In fact, nothing may relieve them of these obligations, not even the desire they may have to practice continence.[3]

In reference to the cause of fornication, the bond of marriage remains intact, no matter what the cause for separation may be—even though it be this one legitimate cause. The separated persons remain husband and wife after the separation, and the contraction of a new marriage is strictly forbidden.

In the second part of his reply to Pollentius, Augustine answered the major contention that adultery destroys the bond of marriage and allows the contraction of a new marriage. He bases his argument on Paul's text: 'The wife is bound to the husband as long as he is alive,'[4] arguing clearly that the death referred to here is the death of the body, not of the soul. Forgiveness and attempts at regeneration of the offending person are offered as better solutions than divorce.

It was Augustine's mind and intention that Christian marriage retain the stability and permanent character inherent in its institution. Undoubtedly, some Christians of his age were affected by the loose attitude of the pagans toward the marriage contract and he was adamant in his refusal to permit any but a reverential, firm, and mature attitude on the part of his own brethren toward the foundation of the Christian social structure, the sacramental bond of marriage.

The quality of unity, as it pertains to Christian marriage, excludes all other marriage bonds; such mutual fidelity

---
3 Cf. Smith and Wace, *Dictionary of Christian Biography* 4 (London 1887) 422, 'Pollentius.'
4 Cf. 1 Cor. 7.39.

excludes not only polyandry,[5] but also polygamy.[6] As to the first, as Ladomérszky says: 'A plurality of husbands destroys the principle of authority in the family by introducing many heads. It is likewise opposed in a direct fashion to the end of marriage; or, at least, propagation of children is hindered. The wife in such a case no longer will be a true wife, but simply a kept woman.'[7] Polygamy, Augustine admitted, had been allowed to the patriarchs, in order that the Israelites might increase in number, but monogamy is more in harmony with the primitive institution of marriage and more conducive to its success. Polygamy is not directly opposed to the nature of conjugal society, for it does not exclude the primary end of marriage—the generation of children; nor does it greatly impugn the authority which is demanded by the closely integrated society of marriage.[8] God, at the beginning of time, established Adam and Eve in a marriage of perfect unity. That marriage was the prototype of all subsequent ideal marriages. Then, for a reasonable motive, He relaxed His decree for a period of time. Finally, the New Covenant, in superseding the Old, restored to marriage its pristine unity.

St. Augustine regards the indissolubility of marriage as a special property, the *bonum sacramenti*.[9] Ladomérszky writes: 'Augustine indicates the necessity of restraining concupiscence within the restrictive limits of a stable marriage, so that one will not look in married life merely for the satisfaction of carnal desires, but rather to the propagation of offspring in honorable and lawful wedlock. If marriage were dissoluble, it would continue to be an occasion of immorality and never an effective remedy for concupiscence. Augustine

---

5 Cf. above, *The Good of Marriage* 18.21; also, *De nuptiis et concupiscentia* 1.10.
6 Cf. *The Good of Marriage* 17.20.
7 Nicolas Ladomérszky, *Saint Augustin* (Rome 1942) 134.
8 Cf. Wernz-Vidal, *Ius Canonicum* 5 (Rome 1946) 308-310 n. 245.
9 Cf. *The Good of Marriage* 24.32; *De gratia Christi et de peccato originali* 2.39.

does not see, however, that the nature of marriage itself demands that it be indissoluble. . . . Scripture indicates well this indissolubility, but Augustine prefers to demonstrate the stability of Christian marriage by indicating its sacramental aspect. He maintains that it is only in the Church that it has this quality. . . . In speaking of the difference between the Christian and the pagan law, a difference which consists of the fact that the former does not permit remarriages during the life of one's spouse, while the latter does, Augustine is quick to say: "Moses seems to have permitted the Israelites, through a bill of divorce, and by reason of the hardness of their hearts, something similar to this custom. However, it is clear that this permission is more of censure than an approval of divorce." '[10]

Augustine failed to appreciate fully the implications of the purely natural contract such as obtains in a marriage between two non-Christians.[11] However, certain passages indicate that Augustine attributed a certain sacramental character to marriage: 'In addition to the fidelity which spouses owe each other so as to exclude adultery, and in addition to offspring for the sake of whose generation the two sexes join together in marriage, I have also taken notice of a third good which is a necessary part of marriage—particularly a marriage between two Christians—and this good has seemed to me to be something with a sacramental character for the purpose of excluding divorce, even from a wife who cannot obey.'[12] From this text we may conclude that, according to Augustine, marriage has a sacramental character, when considered absolutely, but that Christian marriage is a sacrament in a distinct and peculiar fashion.

---
10 Ladomérszky, *op. cit.* 141-142.
11 Cf. Wernz-Vidal, *op. cit.* 809 n. 630; Felix Cappello, *Tractatus Canonico-moralis de sacramentis* 5 (5th ed., Rome 1947) 40 n. 45.
12 *Contra Julianum* 5.12.

TO POLLENTIUS ON ADULTEROUS MARRIAGES

BOOK ONE

Chapter 1

MY DEAREST BROTHER Pollentius, the first question among those which you discussed when writing to consult me is whether this statement of the Apostle, namely, 'But to those who are married, not I, but the Lord commands that a wife is not to depart from her husband, and if she departs, that she is to remain unmarried or be reconciled to her husband; and let not a husband put away his wife,'[1] is to be taken in such a way that is understood to have forbidden that woman to marry who has departed from her husband without the ground of immorality. Indeed, this is your opinion. Or, on the other hand, is that statement to be taken as a command that those women who have left their husbands for that ground which has alone been declared lawful, that is, fornication, are to remain unmarried? This was my opinion as expressed in those books which I wrote

---
1 1 Cor. 7.10,11.

many years ago on the Gospel sermon which the Saviour delivered, according to Matthew, on a mountain.

You think, then, that a woman who leaves her husband should not marry, if she departed under no constraint of immorality on the part of her husband. Nor do you revert to the fact that, if her husband has not given her the ground of immorality, she should not only remain unwed after the separation, but she should not leave him at all. For, according to that opinion of yours, the freedom to marry, and not the freedom to separate, is taken away from the woman who is commanded to remain unmarried if she separates from her husband. But, if this is the case, to wives who wish to practice the virtue of continence is given the freedom not to await any consent on the part of their husbands. And so, what has been said, 'A woman is not to depart from her husband,' seems to be a precept enjoined upon those women who might possibly choose not continence but a divorce that would render it lawful for them to espouse other husbands. By the same token, those who no longer desire to have any intercourse, and find their marriages unbearable, will be given license to leave their husbands without any grounds of immorality and, according to the Apostle, to remain unmarried. Because the nature of men and women is the same, the case of the husband is parallel to that of the wife. If husbands wish to practice continence, they will leave their wives—even without their consent—and remain unmarried. I say this because you think that they would be permitted to seek other marriages when the divorce is based on the ground of immorality. But, when this ground of immorality does not exist, it follows, according to you, that spouse must remain with spouse, or, if there is a separation, that the married person is either to remain unmarried or to return to the previous marriage. In the event, then, that there is not the ground of immorality, each and every married woman may lawfully choose one of three courses: she may lawfully decide not to depart from her spouse, or, if she has left her spouse, to remain in a state of separation, or, if she does not so remain, she may lawfully choose to return to her previous partner. However, she may not choose to seek another spouse.

Chapter 2

(2) And where is it that the same Apostle has wished husband and wife to withhold from each other without mutual consent the debt of the flesh, even for a short time to afford occasion for prayer? How will this command retain its force: 'Yet, for fear of immoralities, let each man have his own wife, and let each woman have her own husband? Let the husband render to the wife her due, and likewise the wife to the husband. The wife has not authority over her body, but the husband; the husband likewise has not authority over his body, but the wife'?[1] How will this be true except by virtue of the prohibition of a spouse's practicing continence against the will of the other partner? For, if the wife has the right to put her husband away, so long as she does not marry, she herself, and not the husband, has authority over her body. We may say the same of the husband. Then, when it is said that 'Whoever puts away his wife, save on account of immorality, causes her to commit adultery,'[2] how are we to understand it except as a prohibition against a husband's dismissal of his wife, when there is no ground of immorality? The statement was clearly made so that he would not make his wife an adulteress. We may believe, then, that the wife will be an adulteress if she remarries, even though she herself does not put her husband away, but is put away by him.

---
1 1 Cor. 7.2-4.
2 Matt. 5.32.

Chapter 3

Because of this monstrous evil, therefore, it is not lawful for a man to put away his wife except for the ground of immorality. For, in that event, he does not himself cause her to be an adulteress by the dismissal, but he puts away an adulteress. What if he should therefore say: It is true that I am putting away my wife without any ground of immorality, but I shall remain continent? Are we to say, therefore, that he has done this deed with no prospect of redress? Who is there, who recognizes the will of the Lord in those words of His, who would presume to say this? The Lord's will was not for a spouse to be put away for the sake of continence, since He expressly stated that the ground of immorality was the only valid one.

(3) Let us return, then, to the statement itself of the Apostle where he says: 'But to those who are married, not I, but the Lord commands that a wife is not to depart from her husband, and if she departs, that she is to remain unmarried.'[1] Let us interrogate him, and consult with him, as though he were present. Apostle, why have you said: 'And if she departs, she is to remain unmarried'? Is it lawful for her to depart, or not? If not, why do you command her to remain unmarried when she departs? If, on the other hand, it is lawful, there is undoubtedly some reason for its being so. But this reason, on investigation, is not found, unless it be that reason alone which the Saviour clearly determined, that is to say, the ground of immorality. Therefore, in giving the precept, the Apostle does not command the woman to remain unwed after she departs, unless she leaves her husband for that cause alone which makes it lawful for her to depart from him. For, when it is written: 'I command her not to depart, and if she departs, that she is to remain

---
1 1 Cor. 7.10,11.

unmarried,' Heaven forbid that a woman who departs and remains unmarried be thought to disregard this precept. Therefore, if we are not to understand that the Apostle is speaking of the woman for whom it is lawful to depart—she may not lawfully separate, however, except from an unfaithful husband—in what way is she commanded to remain unwed if she separates? Who is there who would say: If a woman leaves a man who is not a fornicator, she is to remain unmarried, since in no way may she lawfully separate from other than a fornicator? And so I think you now understand to what extent your opinion is opposed to the marriage bond, concerning which the Lord's will has been that no one undertake to practice the virtue of continence without mutual agreement and consent.

Chapter 4

(4) However, let us bring out the point at issue a little more clearly and examine it more closely. Observe how continence has usually been pleasing to the woman, but does not please the man. The wife leaves him and begins to lead a life of continence. She obviously intends to remain chaste, but she will make an adulterer of her husband, which the Lord does not wish. For, the husband will seek another woman when it becomes impossible for him to restrain himself. What are we to say to the woman, except to repeat what the sound doctrine of the Church maintains, that is, render the debt to your husband, lest, while you seek after a source of further glory, he find the source of his damnification. We would say the same to the husband, if he should desire to practice continence against your will. All this, because you have not authority of your body, but he does; and he has not authority of his body, but you do. Except by mutual consent, do not refuse each other his due. When we have said this and

much else pertaining to it, are you satisfied that this response of the woman is made according to your counsel? I hear the Apostle say: 'I command that a wife is not to depart from her husband, and if she departs, that she is to remain unmarried or be reconciled to her husband.' Behold, I have departed; I do not wish to be reconciled to my husband, but I am remaining unmarried. The Apostle does not say: 'If she departs, she is to remain unmarried *until* reconciled to her husband,' but he says: 'She is to remain unmarried *or* be reconciled to her husband.' He says: Do this or that. His permission was to choose between two alternatives, but he did not force a choice of either. I choose to remain unmarried, and I fulfill his precept in so doing. But, if I remarry, criticize me, accuse and upbraid me, use what severity you will.

Chapter 5

(5) What can I say to refute this, except that you do not properly understand the Apostle? He would not have commanded a woman to remain unmarried after she leaves her husband unless she has the permission to separate for that one stated cause, which he himself has failed to mention in that passage because it was so well known, the ground, that is, of immorality. God, our Master, expressly mentioned only that cause when He spoke of dismissing one's wife. He gave it to be understood that the same precept was to be observed by the husband, also, because, just as 'The wife has not authority over her body, but the husband,' so 'The husband has not authority over his body, but the wife.' Since, therefore, you cannot accuse your husband of fornication, how do you think you exonerate yourself by not marrying? You are separating from one whom you are not at all per-

ADULTEROUS MARRIAGES 67

mitted to leave. When the wife hears this from us, I do not think she will be inclined to answer that she is remaining unmarried because she has departed without any fornication on the part of her husband; for, if he committed fornication, not only would she be permitted to depart, but she would even be permitted to remarry.

Chapter 6

(6) She would by no means say this, since you yourself have been ashamed to grant this freedom to women. You said: 'If a husband dismisses an adulterous wife and marries another, disgrace will redound to the wife only. But, if the wife puts her husband away for the reason mentioned above and marries another, not the husband alone, but the wife also, will incur disgrace.' Giving a reason for this opinion, you say: 'They will maintain that she has left her husband with the intention of taking to herself another husband, although his character may be the same as that of the husband she has left. For, how extraordinarily easy it is for men to rush blindly into this disease-like vice. But, if she puts away this other husband, also, more and more will they say that she sought a plurality of husbands.' Having given your reason, you conclude with the statement: 'The woman, then, after weighing and closely considering these arguments, ought to bear with her husband or remain unmarried.' You have clearly given good advice to wives in urging them not to separate from their husbands, but, rather, to bear with them, although they are aware that the freedom has been given them to be joined to other spouses, if they put away their adulterous husbands. They are urged by you to tolerate even unfaithful husbands, so that they may not seem to be desirous of taking advantage of the opportunity which is set before

them to become involved with many men, since it is difficult for a woman to find a man to marry who is different from the one she has put away. I say this, because men are so strongly inclined toward this malady. When we say, therefore, that even the woman who has put away an unfaithful husband is not given the freedom to marry another, you still maintain that it is indeed lawful, but not expedient. We both undoubtedly agree that the woman who puts away an unfaithful husband ought not to remarry. But this fact is important, namely, that, when both spouses are Christian, we say that a wife is not allowed to marry another if she departs from a fornicator. You, on the other hand, say that, if a wife separates from her husband who is not guilty of fornication, she is forbidden by the precept to marry another. If, however, she separates from a fornicator, it is not proper for her to marry because of disgrace. Herein you grant the wife leave to depart from a husband, whether he be a fornicator or not, as long as she has no intention of remarrying.

Chapter 7

(7) Furthermore, since the blessed Apostle—nay, the Lord through the Apostle—has not permitted the wife to depart from a husband who is not guilty of fornication, it follows that he prohibits a marriage after separation on the part of the woman whom he permits to depart from a fornicator. For, concerning such a woman, it is said that, if she departs from her husband, she should not remarry. She is allowed to separate on the condition that she does not remarry. If she chooses, then, not to marry, there is no reason why she should be forbidden to separate—just as the woman, of whom it is written that if she cannot be continent she should marry, is certainly granted leave to omit the

practice, provided, of course, that she marries. So, if such a woman prefers to marry, she cannot be constrained to practice continence. And as the woman who does not restrain herself is compelled to marry, so that inability to remain continent may not redound to her spiritual death, in like manner the woman who departs from her husband is compelled to remain unmarried, so that her separation may not become subject to blame. However, not without fault does a wife separate from a husband who has not committed fornication, even though she remains unmarried. Therefore, she who departs from a fornicator is commanded to remain unmarried if she departs. Since this is the case if we understand the Apostle, in such a way that we say to women: 'Do not depart from your husbands, shameless though they be, so that, if you wish to leave them, you are to remain unmarried,' all who are attracted to a life of continence will judge that they may lawfully leave their husbands, even without their consent. Since we certainly ought not to allow that, it follows that we should point out what has already been said, that is: 'If she departs, she is to remain unmarried,'[1] and demonstrate that it was said in reference to the woman whom we have discovered to be unable lawfully to depart from her husband, unless, of course, he is unfaithful. So as not to seriously disturb Christian marriages by giving false instruction under the pretence of urging the practice of continence, let us not countermand the precept of the most merciful Lord and compel incontinent husbands to commit adultery, after they have been put away by their continent wives, or incontinent wives after they have been put away by their continent husbands.

Chapter 8

(8) Therefore, if what the Lord says elsewhere, and not, indeed, in that selfsame sermon which we were explaining, but elsewhere, namely: 'Whoever puts away his wife except for immorality, and marries another, commits adultery,'[1] is to be understood in this way, that whoever puts away a woman because of immorality and marries another does not commit adultery, it does not seem that, in reference to this cause of immorality, there is a natural equality between husband and wife. This assumption would be true, since the wife commits adultery if she departs from her husband and marries another, even on account of immorality. The husband, on the contrary, does not commit adultery if he puts his wife away and remarries for the same reason. But, if both husband and wife have the same nature, each of them commits adultery if one or the other enters into a second union, even though a union with an unfaithful spouse has been disrupted. The Apostle has indicated that there is between husband and wife a natural equality as regards this cause of immorality in that memorable passage which says: 'The wife has not authority over her body, but the husband,' and where he also adds: 'The husband likewise has not authority over his body, but the wife.'

Chapter 9

(9) 'Why, then,' you ask, 'did the Lord insert the ground of immorality? Why does He not say, in a general way: Whoever puts away his wife and marries another commits adultery, if he also is an adulterer who remarries after he puts away an unfaithful spouse?' I believe the Lord did not

---
1 Matt. 19.9.

speak thus because He wished to mention what is more important. For, who denies that in each case the adultery is greater, if another wife is taken after one who had committed no fornication has been put away, than if an unfaithful wife is put away and then another taken? This is true, not because the second mentioned is not an adulterer, also, but because the adultery is less serious when another woman is taken after an unfaithful wife is put away. The Apostle James, employing a similar expression, says: 'Therefore, he who knows how to do good and does not do it, commits a sin.'[1] Does the one, then, who does not know how to do good and so does not do it, commit sin? He certainly does, but the one who has knowledge of the good and does not do it sins more grievously. But, the sin of the one who lacks knowledge is not made null by the fact that it is less serious. Therefore, to state both cases in the same terms: Just as anyone who puts away his wife for a cause other than immorality and takes another commits adultery, so does everyone who knows how to do good and does not do it commit sin. Likewise, it cannot be correctly stated here that a man who lacks knowledge cannot sin, for there are sins even on the part of the ignorant, although they are less serious than those of men who have knowledge. It cannot be correctly affirmed either that the husband who puts away his wife because of immorality and marries another does not commit adultery. For there is adultery, also, on the part of those who marry others after the repudiation of their former wives because of immorality. Yet, this adultery is certainly less serious than that of men who put them away not because of fornication and take other wives. In fact, just as it has been said: 'He who knows how to do good, and does not do it, commits a sin,' it can likewise be asserted, according to the same principle, that he who puts away his wife without the cause of fornication and

---

1 James 4.17.

marries another commits adultery. Therefore, when, in the one case, we say that whoever marries a woman put away for other than the cause of immorality by her husband commits adultery, we most certainly state the truth; yet, we do not thereby acquit of the crime the one who marries a woman who has been put away on account of immorality, and we also have not the slightest doubt that each of them is an adulterer. We likewise declare him to be an adulterer who puts away his wife without the cause of immorality and marries another; yet we do not therein defend from the taint of this sin the man who puts away his wife because of immorality and marries another. For, while the one offense is greater than the other, we yet recognize both men to be adulterers. There is no one so unreasonable as to say that he who marries a woman whose husband has put her away because of immorality is not an adulterer, while he says that the one who marries a woman who has been cast off without the ground of immorality is an adulterer. Both of these men are guilty of adultery. So, when we say: Whoever takes a woman who has been put away by her husband for a reason other than the ground of immorality commits adultery, we are, indeed, speaking of one of them. However, we do not thereby maintain that whoever marries a woman whom her husband has put away because of immorality does not commit adultery. Also, since both of these men are adulterers, that is to say, the one who puts away his wife and marries another without the ground of immorality, and the one who puts away his wife because of immorality and marries another —since, then, both of these men are adulterers, when we read of one of them, we certainly ought not to interpret the reading in such fashion that the one is acquitted of the charge of adultery because the other is formally declared to be an adulterer.

(10) But, if Matthew the Evangelist has made the ques-

tion difficult to comprehend, because he mentioned the one case and was silent concerning the other, have not the other Evangelists treated the same matter so comprehensively that both sides of the problem can be understood? Mark wrote the following: 'Whoever puts away his wife and marries another, commits adultery against her; and if the wife puts away her husband and marries another, she commits adultery.'[2] And Luke wrote: 'Everyone who puts away his wife and marries another commits adultery; and he who marries a woman who has been put away from her husband, commits adultery.'[3] Therefore, who are we to say that there is one who commits adultery in taking another woman after he puts away his wife, and that there is another who, in doing this, does not commit adultery, when the Gospel says that everyone who performs such an act commits adultery? Furthermore, if everyone who does this, namely, marries another woman after the dismissal of his wife, commits adultery, there are undoubtedly included both the one who puts away his wife without the cause of immorality and the one who puts away his wife for this reason. For the one passage reads: 'Whoever puts away his wife,' and the other: 'everyone who puts away his wife.'

Chapter 10

(11) However, when I set forth the words of Matthew's Gospel, I did not omit—and I do not know why you believed I did—this passage of the Scripture: 'and shall marry another,' and I made this statement: 'He commits adultery.' On the contrary, I have set down those words which are contained in that lengthy discourse which the Lord delivered on the mountain, for I had undertaken to write a commentary

---
2 Mark 10.11,12.
3 Luke 16.18.

on this sermon. These words read, as I have set them down therein: 'Whoever puts away his wife, save on account of immorality, causes her to commit adultery; and he who marries a woman released by her husband commits adultery.'[1] Some passages, expressed in different words, have the same meaning when they are understood, and there is no discrepancy in their sense. For example, one text reads: 'Whoever puts away';[2] another has: 'Everyone who puts away';[3] likewise, one says: 'save on account of immorality';[4] while another says: 'without the cause of immorality.'[5] Still another reading is: 'except for immorality,' and yet another is: 'He who marries a woman released from her husband commits adultery.' Finally, there is one passage that has: 'He who marries a woman who has been put away from her husband commits adultery.' I think you realize that there is in those texts no variation from one and the same opinion. While some of the Latin and Greek codices do not have that last passage, namely, 'He who marries a woman who has been put away from her husband commits adultery,' included in that discourse which the Lord delivered on the mountain, I believe that it is omitted because the meaning of the sentence could have been thought to have been conveyed by that passage which was written just before it, that is, 'He causes her to commit adultery.' For, how does the dismissed wife become an adulteress if the one who marries her does not also become an adulterer?

---
1 Matt. 5.32.
2 Mark 10.11.
3 Luke 16.18.
4 Matt. 5.32.
5 Matt. 19.9.

Chapter 11

(12) Indeed, the words which you have set down, the result of which is that the man who puts away his wife because of immorality and marries another has not seemed to you to commit adultery, have certainly been written in an obscure fashion. Wherefore, I wonder not that the reader is at pains to understand them. However, the words do not appear in that discourse of the Lord which I was commenting upon at the time when I wrote those pages, which moved you when you read them. Elsewhere, as a matter of fact, the same Matthew has written that the Lord spoke them, to be sure, not when He delivered that lengthy sermon on the mountain, but after He had been questioned by the Pharisees as to whether it was lawful to repudiate a wife for any reason whatsoever. But what is insufficiently understood in Matthew's account can be understood from the words of the other Evangelists. Therefore, when we read in the Gospel according to Matthew: 'Whoever puts away his wife except for immorality,'[1] or, to use the better reading of the Greek: 'Without the cause of immorality and marries another commits adultery,' we should not immediately think that that man does not commit adultery who puts away his wife because of immorality and marries another. We should suspend judgment until we consult the accounts of the other Evangelists who have written this down for us. All that pertains to this question is not expressed in the Gospel of Matthew, but the portion contained therein is expressed in such a way that from it may be inferred the whole, that both Mark and Luke have preferred to state, in explanation, as it were, so that the sense might be understood in full. Therefore, not doubting that what Matthew says is true: 'Whoever puts away his wife without the cause of immorality and

---
1 Matt. 19.9.

marries another commits adultery,' as soon as we inquire if that man alone commits adultery by taking another wife who has put away his previous spouse without the cause of immorality, or whether everyone who marries another after the repudiation of the first commits adultery, so that even the one who dismisses an unfaithful spouse is included—as soon as we place these questions, shall not our answer come from Mark: Why do you ask whether this man be an adulterer, and that one not? 'Whoever puts away his wife and marries another, commits adultery.'[2] Will not Luke also say to us: Why do you doubt that the man who puts away his wife because of immorality and marries another commits adultery? 'Everyone who puts away his wife and marries another, commits adultery.'[3] Therefore, since it is not proper for us to maintain that the Evangelists, in writing on one topic, disagree in meaning and sense, although they may use different words, it follows that we are to understand Matthew as having desired to indicate the whole by the part, but, nevertheless, as having held the same opinion as the other Evangelists. As a result, neither the particular man who puts away his wife because of immorality and marries another commits adultery, nor does the particular man who puts away his wife without the cause of immorality commit adultery; on the contrary, everyone who puts away his wife and marries another is most certainly guilty of adultery.

Chapter 12

(13) For, how is the following passage in Luke's Gospel also true: 'He who marries a woman who has been put away from her husband commits adultery'? How does he

---
2 Mark 10.11.
3 Luke 16.18.

commit adultery, unless by reason of the fact that the woman
whom he has married remains the wife of that other man
who put her away, as long as he is living. For, if he is at present
united with his own wife and not the wife of another, he
surely does not commit adultery. However, he is committing
adultery, and, therefore, the woman with whom he is joined
is the wife of another. If she is in fact the wife of another,
that is to say, if she is the wife of him who put her away, she
has not ceased to be his wife, even if he put her away because
of immorality. If, on the other hand, she has ceased to be
his wife, she is now the wife of the other man she has
married, and, if this be true, the man is not to be considered
an adulterer, but a husband. Yet, since Scripture maintains
that he is not a husband, but an adulterer, the woman is
still the wife of the man who cast her off, even though it
was for immorality. We conclude, therefore, that whoever a
man takes to wife after she is put away is an adulteress,
since she engages in illicit relations with the husband of
another woman. In view of this, how can it be that he
himself is not also an adulterer who admittedly commits
adultery with the woman whom he takes to himself?

Chapter 13

(14) Let us now turn to this statement of the Apostle:
'For the rest I say, not the Lord.'[1] This certainly refers to a
marriage of unequals, wherein not both parties are Christian.
I was of the opinion that he wrote this to counsel Christians.
For, since a Christian spouse could lawfully depart from a
non-Christian, the Lord, therefore, does not forbid it to be
done, but the Apostle forbids it. For, what the Lord forbids
cannot possibly be done lawfully. The Apostle, therefore,

---
1 1 Cor. 7.12.

counsels believing spouses to forego the liberty granted them
of leaving their unbelieving partners, because they will thereby
have a great opportunity for winning souls to Christ. However, you also think that it is not permitted believers to put
away unbelievers, because the Apostle forbids it; while I say
that it is lawful, because he does not forbid it, but that it is
not expedient, because the Apostle advises against it. He
also gives us a reason why it is not expedient that it be done,
although it may be lawful. He says: 'For how dost thou
know, O wife, whether thou wilt save thy husband? Or
how dost thou know, O husband, whether thou wilt save
thy wife?'[2] Besides, where he said before: 'For the unbelieving
husband is sanctified by the wife, and the unbelieving wife
is sanctified by the husband'—which is to say by the Christian
husband—he had also said: 'Otherwise your children will be
unclean, but, as it is, they are holy.'[3] Accordingly, he seems
to have made his exhortation to win partners and children
to Christ, because of the examples that had gone before.
Therefore, the reason why it is not expedient that even
unbelieving spouses should be put away by the faithful has
been clearly stated. The Apostle forbids separation from
unbelievers, not to preserve the marriage bond with such
persons, but so that they may be assimilated in Christ.[4]

---

2 1 Cor. 7.16.
3 1 Cor. 7.14.
4 Augustine here begins his discussion of the Pauline privilege, which allows for the dissolution of a marriage between two pagans, but only after one of the parties has been converted, and the pagan refuses to cohabit at all or to do so peaceably. While the converted party is permitted to separate under the necessary conditions, Augustine urges against it on the grounds that the continuation of the union of Christian and pagans presents a marvelous opportunity for conversion of the infidel. His stand is logical, as the privilege was orginally constituted to safeguard the faith of the converted spouse, but if a Christian were to cohabit with an infidel and solicit his acceptance of the faith, the Church would profit. Making allowance for certain legal technicalities, Augustine's view is comprehensive and extensive enough to serve as a precedent for modern Church thought on this question.

Chapter 14

(15) As a matter of fact, much is to be done, not at the prescription of the Law, but from a free impulse of charity. Such actions are the more meritorious of those which duty prescribes, since it is lawful for us not to perform them, yet we do perform them for the sake of love. Wherefore, in former times, the Lord Himself paid the tribute, after He had shown that He did not owe it, so as not to give scandal to those with whose salvation He was concerned in assuming a human nature.[1] Moreover, the extent of the Apostle's approval of those words of the Saviour is attested when he says: 'For free though I am as to all, unto all I have made myself a slave, that I might gain the more.'[2] Yet, he had said just before: 'Have we not a right to eat and to drink? Have we not a right to take about with us a woman, a sister, as do the other Apostles, and the brethren of the Lord, and Cephas? Or it is only Barnabas and I who have not the right to do this? What soldier ever serves at his own expense? Who plants a vineyard and does not eat of its fruit? Who feeds the flock, and does not partake of the milk of the flock?'[3] And he says a little later: 'If others share in this right over you, why not we rather? But we have not used this right, but we bear all things, lest we offer hindrance to the Gospel of Christ.' Then, a few sentences after, he says: 'What, then, is to be my reward? That in preaching the Gospel, I deliver the Gospel without charge, so as not to abuse my right in the Gospel.'[4] Immediately he subjoins what I related a while back: 'For, free though I was to all, unto all have I made myself a slave that I might gain the more.'

---
1 Cf. Matt. 17.24ff.
2 1 Cor. 9.19.
3 1 Cor. 9.4-7.
4 1 Cor. 9.18.

Likewise, he says in another place with reference to certain matters pertaining to food: 'All things are lawful for me, but not all things are expedient. All things are lawful for me, but I will not be brought under the power of any. Food for the belly and the belly for food, but God will make void both it and them.'[5] Also, on this same subject, he says elsewhere: 'All things are lawful, but not all things are expedient. All things are lawful, but not all things edify. Let no one seek his own interests, but those of his neighbor.'[6] Therefore, to give a reason for his statement he says: 'Anything that is sold in the market, eat, asking no questions for conscience' sake.'[7] Yet, he says in another place: 'I will eat flesh no more forever, lest I scandalize my brother.'[8] Again he says: 'All things indeed are clean; but a thing is evil for a man who eats through scandal.'[9] The phrase, 'All are lawful,' is the same as 'All indeed are clean,' and the words, 'but not all things are expedient,' are equivalent to 'but a thing is evil for a man who eats through scandal.' He demonstrates how those things that are lawful, that is, forbidden by no precept of the Lord, ought preferably to be accomplished in the measure that they are advantageous, not, indeed, at the prescription of the Law, but by the counsel of charity. Such were the services rendered with uncalled-for generosity to the man whom the good Samaritan conducted to the inn to be cared for. They are not said to be prescribed by the Lord, therefore, although they are preferred at His counsel. Hence, they are understood to be more pleasing to Him to the extent that they are shown to be done without obligation.

---

5 1 Cor. 6.12,13.
6 1 Cor. 10.23,24.
7 1 Cor. 10.25.
8 1 Cor. 8.13.
9 Rom. 14.20.

Chapter 15

(16) However, it cannot be said of those actions which are included here, and which are not expedient, although lawful, that this action is good, but that one is better in the same way that it has been written that 'He who gives her in marriage does well, and he who does not give her does better.'[1] For, in this second instance, both courses are lawful, although, at times, the one may be expedient, at times, the other. Doubtlessly, those who cannot remain chaste should marry. This is expedient because it is lawful. For those, however, who have vowed to remain continent, it is neither lawful nor expedient to marry. As a matter of fact, one may lawfully separate from an unbeliever, but it is not expedient. However, if the spouse consents to cohabitate, it is both lawful and expedient to remain with him, because if it were not lawful, it could not be expedient. Therefore, an action can be lawful and not expedient, but what is unlawful cannot be expedient, because not everything that is lawful is also expedient, but everything that is unlawful is inexpedient. For, it is certain that everyone who has been redeemed by the Blood of Christ belongs to the human race; nevertheless, it is likewise true that not every human person has been redeemed by the Blood of Christ. It is just as true that everything that is not lawful is also inexpedient; but, not everything that is inexpedient is likewise unlawful. Certainly, then, there are lawful acts which are inexpedient, just as we have learned from the testimony of the Apostle.

---

1 1 Cor. 7.38.

Chapter 16

(17) But it is difficult to draw with some universal dividing line the distinction between what is unlawful and, therefore, inexpedient, and what is lawful, although inexpedient. For anyone will be quick to say that what is not expedient is sinful, and, since every sin is unlawful, that, therefore, everything that is inexpedient is unlawful. But will there be any of those actions which the Apostle has said are lawful but not expedient, if everything that is not expedient is unlawful? Wherefore, since we cannot doubt that the Apostle has spoken the truth and do not dare to say that some sins are lawful, we must maintain that some act is performed which is not expedient and yet is not a sin, providing, of course, it is lawful. Yet, since such an act is not expedient, it certainly should not be done. But if it seems foolish for a thing to be done which is not expedient, and for one who does it not to be considered a sinner, it is understood to be foolish only in a manner of speaking. Such a way of speaking has become so universal that we often say that even plodding beasts, although they are bereft of reason, ought to be beaten when they sin. Sin, however is properly predicated of no being except one that is endowed with intellect and free will. God has bestowed these on man alone of all mortal and animate creatures. It is one thing to speak in appropriate terms, quite another to interchange words, transferring them from other objects, or misusing them.

Chapter 17

(18) Therefore, let us try to distinguish, if we can, in some definite fashion between that which is lawful and not expedient, and that which is not lawful and, therefore, inex-

pedient. Those acts seem to me to be lawful and not expedient which justice, as it comes from God, permits, but which should be avoided because of some scandal to men, lest they be thereby prevented from being saved. On the other hand, those acts seem to be unlawful and, therefore, not expedient which justice herself forbids in such a way that they are not to be done, even if they are praised by those who have learned of them. But if this is so, only acts that are unlawful are forbidden by the Lord; and, as a result, acts which are lawful, but not expedient, are avoided, not because of the bond of the Law, but by the free and generous exercise of charity.

(19) Therefore, if it were not lawful to put away the unbelieving spouse, the Lord would forbid it, and the Apostle, in forbidding it, would not say 'I say, not the Lord.'[1] For, if a man is permitted to separate from his spouse because of the fornication of the flesh, how much more is to be detested the fornication of the mind on the part of the spouse, that is, the infidelity of which it has been written: 'For, behold, they that go far from Thee shall perish: Thou hast destroyed him who is disloyal to Thee!'[2]

Chapter 18

However, that separation is lawful in such a way as to be inexpedient, so that men not be offended by the separation of their spouses and repudiate the doctrine of salvation which forbids unlawful acts, and so, remaining in the same state of unbelief, be in a worse state and in danger of being lost. The Apostle, therefore, intervenes and counsels that it not be done, because, while it is lawful, it is inexpedient. The Lord

---
1 1 Cor. 7.12.
2 Ps. 72.27.

does not forbid believing husbands and wives to depart from unbelieving wives or husbands, so as to command them to do so. For, if they were commanded to put away partners of that kind, there would be no place for the advice and counsel of the Apostle against their doing it. We say this, because a good servant in no way forbids what the Lord commands to be done.

(20) The Lord formerly gave this commandment through the Prophet Esdras, and it was followed.[1] Those among the Israelites who were able at that time to have foreign wives put them away. Through them, the Israelites were being led after strange gods, while their wives were not being won over to God by their husbands. For, the powerful grace of the Saviour had not yet cast its illumination, and the greater portion of that people were still longing for the earthly goods which the Old Law promised. Wherefore, when they saw those who worshiped many false gods replete with those worldly goods which they themselves were seeking from the Lord in abundance, they were fearful, at first, of giving offense to those gods, due to the coaxing of their wives. Then, they were even induced to worship them. It was for that reason that the Lord had commanded through holy Moses that no one marry a foreign wife.[4] With reason, then, at the Lord's command, they put away the women they had married against His prohibition. But, when the Gospel came to be preached to the Gentiles, many of the pagans were discovered married to their own kind. In their case, if both spouses did not embrace the faith, but either the unbelieving husband or wife consented to live with the believing spouse, the Christian spouse should not have been either forbidden or commanded by the Lord to put away the unbeliever. I say that he should not have been forbidden, because justice

---
3 Cf. Esd. 9.7ff.
4 Cf. Deut. 7.3.

allows one to separate from a fornicator, and the fornication of an unbeliever is more serious, though it is of the spirit. Nor can the relation of the unbeliever with his spouse be said to be truly chaste, for 'All that is not from faith is sin.'[5] However, the believing spouse may preserve chaste relations with an unbeliever who does not. On the other hand, the believing spouse ought not to have been commanded to separate from the unbeliever, since both, while they were pagans, were not united contrary to the commandment of the Lord.

Chapter 19

(21) Therefore, because the Lord neither forbids nor commands the believing spouse to depart from the unbeliever, the Apostle, therefore, and not the Lord, speaks, so that he may not depart. Since he possessed the Holy Spirit, the Apostle was to be able to give both practical and reliable advice. Wherefore, when he said concerning the woman whose husband had died: 'She will be more blessed in my judgment, if she remains as she is,' he added: 'And I think I also have the Spirit of God,'[1] so that no one would think this advice worthy of condemnation, as though it came from man and not from God. Furthermore, it is to be understood that even what is not commanded by the Lord but is urged by His holy servant in a useful manner is urged under the inspiration of the same Lord. May it never happen that some Catholic will say that, when the Holy Spirit gives counsel, the Lord does not; because the Holy Spirit is Himself the Lord, and the works of the Trinity are inseparable. Yet, Paul says: 'Now concerning virgins, I have no commandment of

---
5 Rom. 14.23.

---
1 1 Cor. 7.40.

the Lord, yet I give an opinion,' in order to prevent us from considering this counsel as given apart from the Lord, inasmuch as he immediately follows with: 'As one having obtained mercy from the Lord to be trustworthy.'[2] Therefore, according to the mind of God, and also the Holy Spirit of whom he says: 'And I think that I also have the Spirit of God,' he gives trustworthy advice.

(22) However, the authority of the Lord giving a command is one thing, and the faithful counsel of His servant which has been breathed into and granted him by the Lord is another. When a commandment of God is involved, it is not lawful to act otherwise. It is lawful, however, to act against the counsel of the Apostle, so that, obviously, that which is lawful itself may be at one time expedient, but at another time inexpedient. An act is expedient when it is both permitted by that justice which is from God and also when there is no obstacle placed in the way of men's salvation. Such is the case when the Apostle advises the virgin not to marry, concerning which counsel he testifies that he has no commandment of the Lord. It is lawful to do the other, that is, to marry, and to fasten upon the goods of marriage, although they are inferior to the joys of continence. This course, which is lawful, is also advantageous, because by an honorable marriage he reinforced the weakness of the flesh, which is prone to rush into forbidden and unlawful acts, to an extent that he placed an obstacle in the way of no one's salvation. However, it would be more advantageous and more honorable for the virgin to seize upon the counsel, in virtue of which she is not constrained by any precept. On the other hand, that which is lawful is not expedient when permission is indeed granted, but the use of the power places an obstacle in the way of salvation for others. And, as we have long been saying, such is the case when the believing spouse

---
2 1 Cor. 7.25.

separates from the non-Christian. The Lord does not forbid that separation by a precept of the Law, because, in His judgment, it is not unjust. However, the Apostle forbids it by a counsel of charity, because it impedes the salvation of unbelievers, not only because the parties offended are most harmfully scandalized, but also because it is most difficult to free them from the ties of an adulterous marriage, in the event they have fallen into such marriages, while the ones who put them away are still living.

(23) Therefore, in this case, wherein that which is lawful is not expedient, one cannot say: If he puts away the unfaithful spouse, he does well; if he does not put away the unfaithful spouse, he does better, in the same way it has been said: 'He who gives his virgin in marriage does well, and he who does not give her does better.'[3] For, in the latter case, not only are both courses equally lawful—whence not everyone is compelled by a commandment of the Lord to either course—but each course is even advantageous, the one less, the other more, by reason of which fact whoever can accept it is urged by a counsel of the Apostle to that which is more expedient. However, in the following case, when the question is asked concerning putting away or not putting away the non-Christian spouse, each course is indeed as lawful as the other by reason of the justice which is of God. For this reason, the Lord forbids neither, but because of the weaknesses of men, both are not advantageous; and it is for this same reason that the Apostle forbids what is not advantageous. The Lord gives him freedom to prohibit, because He neither prohibits what the Apostle counsels nor commands what he forbids. And, if that were not so, the Apostle would not advise anything against the Lord's prohibition, nor would he forbid anything against his command. In like manner, in reference to these two questions, one of which concerns mar-

---
3 1 Cor. 7.38.

riage and non-marriage, and the other, putting away and not putting away a non-Christian spouse, some similarity and some dissimilarity exist in the words of the Apostle. On the one hand, there is a similarity between these two phrases: 'I have no commandment of the Lord, yet I give an opinion'[4] and 'I say, not the Lord.'[5] 'I have no commandment of the Lord' is similar to 'The Lord does not say,' and 'I give an opinion' is similar to 'I say.' On the other hand, there is a dissimilarity, because it may be stated in reference to the advisability of marriage or non-marriage: This would be done well, that better, since both are advantageous, the one less, the other more so. But, certainly, in reference to the advisability of putting away or not putting away a non-Christian spouse, since one course is expedient while the other is not, it should not be said: Whoever puts away the non-Christian does well, and he who does not put away the unbelieving spouse does better. Rather, one ought to say: Let not the unbelieving spouse be dismissed, because, while it is lawful to do so, it is not expedient. We can say, therefore, that it is better not to put away the unbelieving spouse, although it may even be lawful to do so, to the extent that it can be reasonably asserted that what is both lawful and expedient is better than that which is lawful but not expedient.

Chapter 20

(24) For these reasons, as I was expounding the lengthy sermon which the Lord delivered on the mount, and when I had come to the question of whether a spouse was to be put away or not, I came to say, in employing the Apostle's testimony, that there was a counsel of the Apostle and not a

---
4 1 Cor. 7.25.
5 1 Cor. 7.12.

precept of the Lord, when he says 'For the rest I say, not the Lord.' In that statement he advises those who have unbelieving spouses to consent to live with them and not to put them away. Justifiedly, then, ought this to have been advised and not commanded, because men ought not to be as forcefully forbidden to do what is lawful, however disadvantageous it may be, as they are forbidden to perform unlawful deeds. But, if the Apostle has somewhere seen fit to counsel even those actions which are commanded, he has done so out of regard for the weakness of men, without prejudice to a commandment of the Lord. Wherefore, if he has said: 'I write these things not to put you to shame, but to admonish you, as my dearest children,'[1] what connection does this have with the following: 'I say, not the Lord'? Likewise, when he says: 'Behold, I, Paul, tell you that if you be circumcised, Christ will be of no advantage to you,'[2] has he also said here, in effect: 'I say, not the Lord'? No. For those phrases are not similar, since it is not unseemly or contradictory for the Apostle to advise the very things which the Lord commands. We admonish those whom we cherish to abide by the precepts and commandments of the Lord. But, when the Apostle says: 'I say, not the Lord,' he shows sufficiently that the Lord does not forbid what he himself forbade. The Lord, however, would have forbidden it if it were unlawful. Therefore, in keeping with what we have long been saying and expounding, the act was lawful by reason of the justice of God, but, even though lawful, it was not to be done because of free good will.

---
1 1 Cor. 4.14.
2 Gal. 5.2.

Chapter 21

(25) But you are pleased to think that what the Lord does not forbid but the Apostle does is unlawful to as great an extent as what the Lord does forbid. When you wished to show what these words of the Apostle mean, that is, 'I say, not the Lord'—which the Apostle addressed to the Christians who were married to unbelievers—you said: 'because the Lord has commanded that marriages between persons of different faiths be not contracted,' and you used the very testimony of the Lord, who says: 'Thou shalt not take a wife for thy son from the daughters of other nations, lest she lead him after her gods and his soul perish.'[1] You also added the words of the Apostle, wherein he said: 'A woman is bound as long as her husband is alive, but if her husband dies, she is free. Let her marry whom she pleases, only let it be in the Lord.'[2] But, in giving your exposition, you added: 'that is, a Christian.' Then you went on to say: 'The following, therefore, is a precept of the Lord in the Old as well as in the New Testament, namely, that only those marriages are to remain joined that are between members of one religion and one faith.' Therefore, if that is a precept in the Old as well as in the New Testament, and if the Lord commands and the Apostle teaches it, so that only marriages between persons of one religion and faith remain joined, why does the Apostle, contrary to the precept of the Lord, contrary to his own teaching, and contrary to a precept of the Old and New Testaments, command that marriages between persons of different faiths remain joined? For, you say: 'Paul, the Preacher and Apostle of the Gentiles, not only admonishes, but even commands, those living in marriage not to put away the other spouse who does not

---
1 Deut. 7.3,4.
2 1 Cor. 7.39.

believe, if he or she consents to cohabit, in the event that either husband or wife should be converted.' In these your own words you show clearly enough that this latter case is one thing; the former, another. The first quotation concerns those marriages which are contracted for the first time, so that a woman will not marry a man not of her religion or a man marry a woman of another faith. For, as you say: 'God orders, the Apostle teaches, both Testaments prescribe.' Who would deny that this case is different, since here the concern is not with projected marriages, but with couples already joined? In this case, surely, both parties are of one and the same unbelief when they were joined, but, when the Gospel had come, a husband believed without the wife, and she without him. If, then, this case differs from the other—which fact is clear without any trace of doubt—why does not the Lord also command the believer to remain in wedlock with the unbeliever, just as the Apostle does? Unless, perhaps, there is lacking in that place what he so confidently states: 'Do you wish to have proof of the Christ who speaks to me?'[3] And, surely, Christ is the Lord. Do you understand what I am saying, or shall I pause to give a somewhat more careful explanation?

(26) Please give me your attention, so that I may put the heart of the matter more fully before you, for your consideration. Consider, then, two married people of one belief. They were so when they were joined. There is no question concerning these which may refer to that commandment of the Lord, the teaching of the Apostle, and the precept of the Old and New Testament, by which the believer is forbidden to join marriage with an unbeliever. They are already man and wife, and until now both have been unbelievers. Until the present, they have been such as they were, both before and when they were married. The preacher of the Gospel comes;

---
3 1 Cor. 13.3.

the husband or the wife has accepted the faith, but in such a way that the unbelieving party consents to live together with the believer. Does the Lord command the believer not to put away the unbeliever, or not? If you say He does command him, the Apostle cries out in protest: 'I say, not the Lord.' If you say He does not command him, I ask for your reason. You do not intend to give in answer the reason which you included in your letter, namely: 'Because the Lord forbids believers to be joined to unbelievers.' That reason in no way applies here; we are speaking of persons already married, not about those who are to be married. If, therefore, you have discovered no reason why the Lord does not forbid what the Apostle forbids—for you are now coming to realize, I believe, that the reason is not the one you had thought—consider whether the reason be the one, perhaps, which I thought best to advance at that time and then to defend, so that we may understand the Lord to be uttering what His absolutely inviolable justice dictates, that is to say, what He commands or forbids in such a way that to do otherwise is absolutely unlawful. But, what he leaves to the authority of the free individual in such wise, that a person either do it or omit it lawfully, in this case He gives an opportunity for the advice of His servants, so that they may urge more strongly what they will see to be expedient.

(27) In this matter, then, first and foremost, let it be accepted that unlawful acts are not to be performed. When some action is lawful in such a way that to act otherwise is not unlawful, what is expedient or that which is more expedient ought to be done. What the Lord says as Master, therefore—that is, not in the nature of counsel on the part of one advising, but in the nature of a command on the part of one who is master—cannot lawfully be left undone, and is therefore inexpedient. So, the Lord commands: 'The woman is not to depart from the man, but if she departs,'

for the one reason, at any rate, which makes the departure lawful, 'to remain unmarried or to be reconciled to her husband.'[4] 'For the married woman is bound by the Law, while her husband is alive; and, while her husband is alive, she will be called an adulteress, if she lives with another man,'[5] because 'the married woman is bound as long as her husband lives.'[6] Wherefore, 'If the wife puts away her husband and marries another, she commits adultery,'[7] and 'He who marries a woman who has been put away by her husband commits adultery.'[8] Therefore, we have this same precept of the Lord: 'Let not a husband put away his wife,'[9] because 'Everyone who puts away his wife, save on account of immorality, causes her to commit adultery.'[10] But if he put her away for this reason, even so: let him remain unmarried. For, 'Everyone who puts away his wife and marries another, commits adultery.'

Chapter 22

This dicipline, established by the Lord, is to be preserved without any reservation. Justice, which is of the Lord, imposes it whether men approve or disapprove. Therefore, it ought not be said that it is not to be preserved because of scandal to men, or so that men may not be withheld from the salvation which is in Christ. For, what Christian would presume to say: So as not to offend men and to gain men for Christ, I will cause my wife to commit adultery, so that I myself may become an adulterer.

(28) For it can happen that, after each Christian has

---
4 1 Cor. 7.10,11.
5 Rom. 7.2,3.
6 1 Cor. 7.39.
7 Mark 10.12.
8 Luke 16.18.
9 1 Cor. 7.11.
10 Matt. 5.32.

put away his unfaithful wife, he be tempted in such a way that some woman who has not yet become a Christian, but is desirous of entering wedlock with him, may promise that she will become a Christian. She does not promise this falsely, but she promises that, if she marries him, she will become a complete Christian. And so the Tempter will be able to suggest to this man who now refuses to marry: The Lord said 'Whoever puts away his wife, save on account of immorality, and marries another, commits adultery.'[1] But you who have put your wife away because of immorality will not commit adultery if you marry another. As the Tempter suggests this, let him, from the depths of his knowledge, answer that he indeed commits a more serious adultery who marries another after putting away his wife without the cause of immorality. But, even he who marries another wife after putting away an adulterous spouse is not then free from adultery because he leaves an adulteress. In like manner, he who marries a woman who is put away without the cause of immorality commits adultery, but not on that account is that man free from adultery who marries a woman whom he finds to be put away without the cause of immorality. And, therefore, what Matthew has put down somewhat obscurely, because the whole has been signified by the part, has been explained by those who expressed the whole in a general way, just as we read in Mark: 'Whoever puts away his wife and marries another commits adultery,'[2] and in Luke: 'Everyone who puts away his wife and marries another commits adultery.'[3] For, they have not said that some who marry others after putting away their wives commit adultery, and some do not; but they have said: 'Whoever puts away,' that is, absolutely everyone, without exception, who puts away his wife and marries another commits adultery.

---
1 Matt. 5.32.
2 Mark 10.11.
3 Luke 16.18.

Chapter 23

(29) However, if that Christian makes this reply to the Tempter in the knowledge that permission has indeed been granted him to put away an adulteress, but that he may not remarry, what if the Temptor should say: Commit the sin so that you may gain for Christ the soul of this woman, living as it is in the death of unbelief. She is prepared to become a Christian, if she marries you? What else is the Christian to say in answer, except that, should he act thus, he will not be able to avoid the judgment which the Apostle mentioned, when he says: 'As some accused us of teaching, do evil that a good may come of it? The condemnation of such is just.'[1] How, then, will this woman be able to be saved in becoming a Christian, since she will commit adultery along with the man who marries her?

Chapter 24

(30) However, not only must adultery not be committed, which not a certain one, but everyone, commits who puts away his wife and marries another, even though he does this for the purpose of making her a Christian, but also everyone who is not bound to a wife and has made a vow of continency ought not to sin under the pretext that he believes he should marry the woman who seeks to be his wife, because she has promised to be a Christian. What was lawful to each one before his vow will not be permitted to him when he has vowed he will never do it, that is, if he vowed what ought to have been vowed, such as the vow of perpetual virginity or continency, either on the part of those who have been married but are released from the bond of marriage, or on

---
1 Rom. 3.8.

the part of those who make a vow from mutual consent, and, remaining faithful and chaste spouses, release each other from the debt of the flesh. Such a vow is not proper, if either husband or wife makes it without the other. Therefore, when men make these vows, or any others which are vowed most properly, they should on no condition break them, because these vows were made unconditionally, and because it is to be understood that the Lord commanded this very thing where it is read: 'Vow ye, and pay to the Lord, your God.'[1] Wherefore, the Apostle says in reference to certain women who vow to practice continence and afterwards wish to marry, because it was lawful for them to do so before the vow: 'They are to be condemned, because they have broken their first troth.'[2]

Chapter 25

(31) Therefore, there is nothing which is at the same time expedient and unlawful, and nothing which the Lord forbids is lawful. But, in these matters, in reference to what has been left to personal discretion, without any restraining precept of the Lord, let us heed the Apostle, advising and counseling in the Holy Spirit that either the better be fastened upon or that which is not expedient be avoided. Let him be heard as he says: 'I have no commandment of the Lord, yet I give an opinion,'[1] and 'I say, not the Lord.'[2] If a man would follow the better course, let him listen to this: 'Let not him who has been freed from his wife seek another; but if he does take a wife, he does not sin.'[3] Here there is

---

1 Ps. 75.12.
2 1 Tim. 5.12.

---

1 1 Cor. 7.25.
2 1 Cor. 7.12.
3 1 Cor. 7.27.

advice against a virgin's marrying: 'Therefore, both he who gives his virgin in marriage does well, and he who does not give her does better.'[4] Let the woman be happier by remaining as she is, as long as it is within her power after the death of her husband 'To marry whom she pleases, only let it be in the Lord.'[5] These last words can be understood in two ways: either that she remains a Christian, or that she marries a Christian. For, during the era of the revealed New Testament, I do not recall that either in the Gospel or in any letters of the Apostles was it stated without ambiguity whether the Lord forbade Christians to be joined to unbelievers. However, most blessed Cyprian does not hesitate in this matter and does not reckon marriage with an unbeliever among the less serious sins. He also says that it is a prostitution of the members of Christ to the Gentiles.[6] But, because the question of those already married is different, let the Apostle again be heard as he says: 'If any brother has an unbelieving wife and she consents to live with him, let him not put her away. And if any woman has an unbelieving husband and he consents to live with her, let her not put away her husband.'[7] And let him be heeded in such wise that, although it may be done lawfully, because the Lord makes no mention of it, still, because it is not expedient, it is not to be done. The Apostle, as we have pointed out already, most clearly teaches that not all that is lawful is also expedient.[8] Because of any kind of fornication—whether it be of the flesh or the spirit, wherein also is understood—it is not lawful for a wife to marry after a husband has been put away, nor is it lawful for the husband to remarry after his wife has been put away, because the Lord has left no place for exception, in saying:

---
4 1 Cor. 7.38.
5 1 Cor. 7.39.
6 Cf. Cyprian, *De lapsis* (Hartel) p. 249.
7 1 Cor. 7.12,13.
8 Cf. 1 Cor. 10.23.

'If the wife puts away her husband and marries another, she commits adultery,' and 'Everyone who puts away his wife and marries another commits adultery.'

(32) After this rather paltry treatment and discussion of mine, I am not ignorant of the fact that the question of marriage still remains very obscure and involved. Nor dare I say that either in this work or in any other up to the present have I explained all its intricacies, or that I am to explain them now, if urged to do so. In reference to the point, however, on which you have a mind to consult me in another letter, I would also take care to explain it separately to you, if it seemed different to me than to you. Since, however, both our opinions are the same, there is, on that account, no need to discuss the matter further.

Chapter 26

(33) Therefore, if catechumens are at the end of this life, whether they be stricken by disease or some misfortune, and if they cannot request baptism for themselves or answer questions, although they still are alive, let baptism be administered to them, because the disposition of their will toward Christianity has long been known. Let them be baptized after the manner of infants, whose will, to be sure, is not yet in evidence. Nevertheless, we ought not to condemn for this reason those who act more timidly than seems proper to us, lest we be judged for having desired to judge with too little foresight, rather than with caution, concerning a treasure entrusted to a fellow servant.[1] In such matters, adequate attention must be paid to this statement of the Apostle: 'Each one of us will render an account of himself to God.'[2]

---
1 Cf. *Confessions* 4.4.8.
2 Rom. 14.12.

Let us not, then, go on to judge each other further. As a matter of fact, there are men who think that, in these matters and in others, what we read that the Lord said must be observed, namely: 'Do not give to dogs what is holy, neither throw your pearls before swine.'[3] Therefore, in deference to these words of the Saviour, they dare not baptize those who are unable to answer for themselves, lest, perhaps, the decision of theirs will be contrary. This cannot be said of children, in whom there is not as yet the use of reason. However, it is not alone incredible for a catechumen not to wish to be baptized at the end of this life, but, even if his will is uncertain, it is much more satisfactory to give it against his will than to deny it to him when he desires it. When it is not clear whether he desires it or not, it is easier to conclude that, if he could speak, he would more likely say that he wished to receive those sacraments without which he had already believed that it was not proper for him to die.

Chapter 27

(34) However, if the Lord, when He says: 'Do not give to dogs what is holy,' wished it to be understood—as they think it to be—a thing to be guarded against, He would not have given over to His betrayer what he, unworthy as he was, received together with the Worthy to his own destruction, without any fault of the One giving. Wherefore, when the Lord said this, we must believe that He wished to signify that unclean hearts do not bear the light of spirtual understanding. And if a teacher implants something to be carried away by them, which they receive perversely, because they do not grasp them, they either lacerate them with words of censure or crush them with reprobation. For, if the blessed

---
3 Matt. 7.6.

Apostle says that he has given milk and not solid food to those who, while they have just been reborn in Christ, are yet but spiritual children—'For you were not yet ready for it, nor are you now ready for it'[1]—if, accordingly, the Lord Himself said to the chosen Apostles: 'Many things have I yet to say to you, but you cannot bear them now,'[2] how much less can the sordid intellect of the wicked bear what is said of the incorporeal light?

Chapter 28

(35) But, more fittingly to conclude this exposition with relation to its beginning, I think that not only those other catechumens, but also the ones who are joined to living spouses and persist in adulterous unions—although we do not admit them to baptism when they are sound in body, yet, if they have fallen critically ill and are not able to answer for themselves, I say that I think they are to be baptized, so that even this sin, along with the rest, may be cleansed by the laver of regeneration. For, who knows whether they had perhaps decided to persevere in the unlawful pleasure of an adulterous union until baptism? But if, recovered from that grave illness, they continue to live, they will do what they had resolved, or, as they have been taught, they will obey, or, if they refuse, they will be dealt with as one should deal with such baptized persons. For, the motive of reconciliation is the same as that of baptism, if, perchance, the threat of life's end preoccupies the penitent. Mother Church ought not to wish them to depart from this life without the gage of her peace.

1 1 Cor. 3.2.
2 John 16.12.

BOOK TWO

Chapter 1

IN ANSWER TO THE LETTER you wrote me, my holy brother Pollentius, I had already written in reply a rather large volume about persons who marry others while their spouses are still living. When this came to your Charity and you were pleased, you added a few points to your original queries, desiring me to answer them, also. Although I proposed to do this by way of an addition to my previous book, so that there would be a single book that would contain this response also, the work I had previously completed was published without any warning, at the demand of my brethren who were ignorant that something was still to be added. Thus it happened that, perforce, I answered your further questions in another, separate book. However, your additional questions were placed, not at the end of your letter, but were interspersed in the body, wherever it seemed best.

Chapter 2

(2) The following words of the Apostle bear on one of your questions which I think I ought to answer at the outset: 'For to the rest, I say, not the Lord, that the woman is not to depart from her husband, and if she departs, that she is to remain unmarried or be reconciled to her husband.'[1] You do not think that the expression 'if she departs' has been used so as to be understood that she departs from an unfaithful husband—for this reason alone is a departure lawful—you conjecture, rather, that a departure from a Christian husband is understood; and, therefore, the wife has been commanded to remain unmarried so that she can be reconciled to him if he is unwilling to remain continent. This will prevent her, while unreconciled, from compelling her husband to commit fornication, that is, to marry another, while she is still alive. Furthermore, you think that, if she departs from an unfaithful husband, she is not commanded to remain unwed, and it is your opinion that, if she wishes to practice continence, she does, in fact, remain unwed, but not so as to be considered as violating a precept if she does marry. This rule you think applies also to the husband, so that he may not put away his wife, except because of immorality. Yet, if he does put her away, he is to enter no other union so that he can be reconciled to his chaste wife—unless, perhaps, she chooses to practice continence—lest, avoiding a reconciliation with a chaste wife, he force her to commit adultery. This she will do if she does not remain continent and marries another during his life. You think also that, if he separates from an adulterous wife, he is not bound by any precept commanding him to remain continent, nor is he at all guilty of adultery if he remarries while his

---
1 1 Cor. 7.12,10,11.

first wife is still living. This you say because of what the same Apostle says, namely, 'A woman is bound as long as her husband is alive, but if her husband dies, she is free. Let her marry whom she pleases,'[2] is to be understood, in your opinion, in such a way that, if a man or woman commits adultery, he or she is considered to be dead. Therefore, it is permitted both of them to remarry after the adultery, just as though after death.

Chapter 3

(3) After considering your interpretation, I ask you whether everyone is to be considered an adulterer who marries a woman who is not bound to a husband. I think that your answer would be no. For 'A woman, while her husband is alive, will be called an adulteress, if she be with another man,'[1] because 'she is bound as long as her husband is alive.'[2] But, if this bond with her living husband were dissolved, she would marry another with no accusation of adultery. Accordingly, if she is bound as long as her husband lives, she is in no wise said to be freed from this bond except after the death of her husband. Furthermore, if the death of either severs the bond between husband and wife, and if fornication also is equivalent to death, as you say, a woman will undoubtedly be loosed also from this bond when she has committed fornication. Nor will one be able to say that she is bound to her husband, when her husband has been freed from her. Hence, as soon as she afterwards ceases to be bound to her husband by reason of her fornication, no one who marries her will be guilty of adultery.

---
2 1 Cor. 7.39.

---
1 Rom. 7.3.
2 1 Cor. 7.39.

Chapter 4

See how absurd it is for him not to be considered an adulterer, therefore, since he has married an adulteress. Yes, and what is more unnatural: the woman herself will not be an adulteress, because she will be to her second husband, not the wife of someone else, but his own wife. For, since the bond of her previous marriage has been dissolved through adultery, no matter whom she now marries, as long as he has no wife, her second marriage will not be regarded as a union of two adulterers, but one, rather, between husband and wife. How will these words be true: 'A woman is bound as long as her husband is alive'? See! Her husband is alive. He has neither died a physical death, nor committed fornication, which you wish to be regarded as death, yet his wife is not now bound to him. Do not you realize how contrary this is to the Apostle's words: 'A woman is bound as long as her husband is alive'? Or are you, perhaps, going to say: As a matter of fact, he is alive, but he is no longer her husband, because he ceased being her husband at the time when she dissolved the marriage bond by her adultery? How, then, these words, 'While her husband is alive, she will be called an adulteress, if she be with another man,' since he is not now her husband after the marriage bond has already been dissolved through the adultery of the woman? For, during what husband's life, if not her own husband's, will she be called an adulteress, if she be found with another man? But, if he has now ceased to be her husband, she will not be called an adulteress, even if her husband is alive, and she be with another man. However, not having a husband, she will obtain one through her second marriage. Do you not perceive how contrary to the Apostle is the opinion of the one who thinks this way? As a matter of fact, you yourself do not think this, but it follows from your opinion.

Therefore, if you wish to avoid the consequences, change the premises. Do not say that an adulterous spouse, whether husband or wife, should be considered dead.

(4) For these reasons, the accepted teaching is: 'The woman is bound as long as her husband is alive,' that is to say, as long as he has not yet departed from the body. 'For the married woman is bound by the Law, as long as her husband is alive,' that is to say, with body intact. 'If he dies,' that is, if he departs from the body, 'she is released from the Law which binds her to her husband. Therefore, while her husband is alive, she will be called an adulteress, if she be with another man; but if her husband dies, she is set free from the law [of her husband] so that she is not an adulteress, if she has been with another man.'[1] The words of the Apostle, so often repeated, so often impressed, are true, living, rational, and unequivocal. The woman begins to be the wife of no later husband, unless she has ceased to be the wife of her former one. But, she will cease to be the wife of the former one, if he should die, and not if he should commit fornication. As a consequence, a spouse is lawfully put away because of fornication, but the bond of chastity remains. For this reason, whoever marries a woman who has been put away, even for the reason of fornication, incurs the guilt of adultery.

Chapter 5

Just as a person guilty of some crime is excommunicated, yet the sacrament of regeneration remains in itself, and the person does not lack that sacrament even if he should never be reconciled to God, so does the bond of the marital contract persist in itself when the wife is dismissed because of fornication, and she will not be free from the bond even if she

---
1 Rom. 7.2,3.

should never be reconciled to her husband. However, she will be free if her husband dies. Indeed, the guilty person who has been excommunicated will never, simply for that reason, be without the sacrament of regeneration, even though he has not been reconciled, because God never dies. So it follows that we should not say—if we wish to be wise with the wisdom of the Apostle—that the adulterous husband is to be reckoned as dead, and that, therefore, it is lawful for his wife to marry another. For, while adultery may be death, it is not the death of the body; what is worse, it is the death of the soul. Yet, the Apostle was not speaking of this second type of death when he said: 'but if the husband dies, let her marry whom she pleases'; he was speaking of that death alone which consists in departure from the body. For, if the marital bond is dissolved by the adultery of either spouse, this perversity follows, that must be avoided, as I pointed out above, that the wife also would be freed from this bond by reason of her unchastity. If she is released, she will be freed from the law of her husband; therefore, she will not—as it is most foolishly maintained—be an adulteress if she is with another man, because she has been freed from her former husband by her adultery. But, if this conclusion is so far removed from the truth that no human—I do not say Christian—intelligence will admit it, then, assuredly, 'A woman is bound, as long as her husband is alive,' that is, to speak more plainly, as long as he is physically alive. The husband, being subject to the same law, is likewise bound as long as his wife is physically alive. Wherefore, if he wishes to dismiss an adulteress, he is not to marry another, lest he himself commit what he reproaches in her. And so with the wife. If she puts away her adulterous husband, she is not to join herself to another husband. She is bound as long as her husband lives. She is not freed from the law of her husband, unless he be dead, so that she will not be guilty of adultery if she has been with another man.

Chapter 6

(5) It appears harsh to you that, after adultery, spouse should be reconciled to spouse. If faith is present, it will not be harsh. Why do we still reckon as adulterers those who we believe have either been cleansed by baptism or have been healed by penance? Under the Old Law of God, no sacrifices wiped away these crimes, which, without a doubt, are cleansed by the Blood of the New Covenant. Therefore, in former times, it was forbidden in every way to take unto oneself a woman sullied by another man, although David, as a figure of the New Testament, took back, without any hesitation, the daughter of Saul, whom the father of the same woman had given to another after her separation from David.[1] But now, afterwards, Christ says to the adulteress: 'Neither will I condemn thee. Go thy way, and from now on sin no more.'[2] Who fails to understand that it is the duty of the husband to forgive what he knows the Lord of both has forgiven, and that he should not now call her an adulteress whose sin he believes to have been eradicated by the mercy of God as a result of her penance?

Chapter 7

(6) However, the pagan mind obviously shrinks from this comparison, so that some men of slight faith, or, rather, some hostile to true faith, fearing, as I believe, that liberty to sin with impunity is granted their wives, remove from their Scriptural texts the account of our Lord's pardon of the adulteress, as though He who said: 'From now on, sin no more,' granted permission to sin, or as though the woman

---
1 Cf. 2 Kings 3.4.
2 John 8.11.

should not have been cured by the Divine Physician by the remission of that sin, so as not to offend others who are equally unclean. The ones whom that act of the Lord displeases are themselves shameless, nor is it chastity that makes them stern. They belong, rather, to those men of whom the Lord says: 'Let him who is without sin among you be the first to cast a stone at her.'[1] But the men, terrified by their consciences, departed, and they ceased to try Christ and to vilify the adulteress. These men, on the contrary, sick as they are, censure the physician, and, themselves adulterers, rage at the adulteress. If one were to say to them, not what they heard: 'Let him who is without sin'—for who is without sin?—but: Let him who is without that particular sin 'be the first to cast a stone at her,' then, perhaps, those who were incensed at the fact that they had not killed the adulteress will consider how great is the mercy of God which spares them so that they may live as adulterers.

Chapter 8

(7) When we speak thus to these men, they not only are not willing to detract at all from their severity, but also become enraged at the truth. They say in answer: We are men; will the dignity of our sex sustain this affront, so that we become like women in paying the penalty for our sins if we have relations with women other than our own wives? As if for this very reason, that they are men, they ought not all the more to bridle their sinful desires, as becomes men; as though, for the very reason that they are men, they ought not all the more to offer themselves to their wives as exemplars of this virtue; as though, for the same reason, they ought not to be less overcome by lustful desire; and, as though, for the

---
1 John 8.7.

same reason that they are men, they ought not to be less servile to their wanton flesh. Yet they become indignant if they should hear that men, guilty of adultery, pay the same penalty as adulterous women, although they should be punished as much more severely as it befits them to surpass the virtue of their wives and to govern them by their example. I am definitely speaking to Christians who heed faithfully the words: 'A husband is head of the wife,'[1] whereby they realize they are to be the leaders; their wives, on the other hand, followers. Therefore, the husband must avoid entering upon a path of conduct which he may fear his wife will follow in imitation. However, there are some who are not pleased at the fact that, in the matter of chastity, there is a single norm for both husband and wife. In this matter, particularly, they would rather be subject to the standard of the world than the law of Christ, because civil law does not seem to restrict men with the same bonds of chastity as it does women. They should read the decree, passed by the Emperor Antoninus, who certainly was not a Christian. In the decree, he did not allow the husband whose conduct did not furnish an example of chastity to accuse his wife of the crime of adultery. As a result, both were condemned if the investigation proved that both were equally unchaste. The following are the words of the emperor, mentioned above, as they appear in the Gregorian Code: 'Surely, my letter will in no way prejudice the case. For, if the blame for the dissolution of your marriage lies with you, and if it is entirely your fault that Eupasia, your wife, avails herself of the privilege of the Julian Law to remarry, she will not be condemned by my rescript as an adulteress, unless she has already been proven one. However, the judges must consider whether you, by your chaste life, have been her inspiration to also cultivate virtuous habits. It seems to me the height of

---

1 Eph. 5.23.

injustice for a husband to demand of his wife a chastity which he himself does not practice. This fact may serve to condemn the husband, also, but it will not serve to conciliate both parties, or remove the cause of the deed, of the establishment of the mutual guilt.'[2] If these things are to be observed for the decorum of the earthly city, how much more chaste are the men who are sought by the heavenly fatherland and the company of the angels. Since this is the case, is this proud and unwarranted boasting on the part of men a lesser, or rather, a greater and more debased, form of unchastity? Therefore, let not men be shocked because Christ forgave the adulteress; let them, rather, realize their own danger, and let them, struggling as they are with the same disease, flee with pious supplication to that same Saviour. Let them acknowledge that they also require what they read was accomplished in that woman; let them receive the remedy of their own adulteries; let them now cease to commit adultery; let them praise the forbearance of God shown to them; let them perform works of penance, receive pardon, and, finally, let them alter their opinion of the punishment of women and their own impunity.

Chapter 9

(8) After these matters have been considered and discussed, if the reflection is made with humility and faith that for all men there is a common lot, a common evil, a common danger, a common weakness, and a common salvation, the reconciliation of the spouses will be neither dishonorable nor difficult, even after perpetuated and cleansed adulteries, since the remission of sins is undoubtedly effected by means of the keys of the kingdom of heaven, not so that after the divorce

---
2 *Ulpiani de adult.* 13.3.

of her husband a woman may be called an adulteress, but so that, after her participation with Christ, she may not be called an adulteress. Rest assured that not everyone will follow this counsel. No one compels it, because, perchance, some law of this world forbids it, according to the manner of the earthly city, wherein the removal of sin is not reckoned through the sacred Blood. Therefore, let continence be undertaken because no law prohibits it. Further adultery should not be entered upon. But, of what concern is it to us, if an adulteress, not yet at least cleansed by the mercy of God, be not reconciled to her husband, as long as no other so-called marriages which are proven to be adulterous are attempted by unreconciled adulterers? 'For a woman is bound, as long as her husband is alive.'[1] As a consequence, therefore, the husband is also bound, as long as his wife is alive. This bond renders any further union impossible without the implication of adultery. Hence, four adulterers are produced of necessity from the two marriages, whenever the wife remarries and the husband marries an adulteress. However, a more infamous adultery is imputed to the one who remarries after the dismissal of his wife for other than the cause of fornication. Matthew spoke of this type of adultery. Such a one is not the only one who commits adultery, but, as we read in Mark: 'Whoever puts away his wife and marries another, commits adultery against her; and if the wife puts away her husband, and marries another, she commits adultery,'[2] and, as we read in Luke: 'Everyone who puts away his wife and marries another commits adultery; and he who marries a woman who has been put away from her husband commits adultery.'[3] Their testimony was sufficiently discussed in my previous book.

---
1 1 Cor. 7.39.
2 Mark 10.11,12.
3 Luke 16.18.

Chapter 10

(9) However, you answer me: A few can live continently. Therefore, those who have put away their unfaithful spouses, because they cannot be reconciled to them, realize that they endanger themselves only in so far as they proclaim the law of Christ to be fit for beasts and not for men. My brother, as far as the incontinent are concerned, they can have many complaints, among which, you say, they proclaim that the law of Christ is fit for beasts and not for men. However, we ought not to pervert or alter the Gospel of Christ on their account. Certainly, only the complaint of those men who put away their wives by reason of the intervening cause of adultery would move you, if otherwise they would not be permitted to marry, because only a few can practice continence. These should be urged to do so by the prospect of glory, not compelled by the Law. Therefore, if there is no second marriage after the dismissal of the first wife, the incontinence of men, you think, will have a reasonable complaint. But, take notice of how many cases will arise, when we must permit adultery to be committed, if we ackowledge the complaints of these men. What are we to do if the wife is gripped by some chronic, incurable disease which prevents her having relations with her husband? Again, suppose they are separated by captivity or some other calamity, so that the husband knows his wife is still alive, whose favors are denied him. Do you think that the mutterings of the incontinent are to be allowed and that adultery is to be countenanced? What about this case, when the Lord, upon being questioned, answered that it ought not to be done, but, in view of the hardness of their hearts, Moses had permitted a bill of divorce to be granted and to dismiss a wife for any reason whatsoever?[1] Does not Christ's law displease the in-

---
1 Cf. Matt. 19.8.

continent, who wish to cast off, through a process of divorce, wives who are quarrelsome, insulting, domineering, finicky, and ill-disposed toward rendering the marriage debt, and wish to marry others?[2] Is Christ's law to be altered at their discretion, for this reason, because their incontinence has been in dread of that law?

(10) However, if a wife should leave her husband, or the husband his wife, not because of immorality, but for the sake of continence, and if the one should be incontinent to whom the separation is granted because of this, I ask whether either the husband or wife will not be an adulterer if he or she marries another. If either of them will not be, the Lord is contradicted, for His words are as follows: 'Whoever puts away his wife, let him give her a written note of dismissal! But I say to you that everyone who puts away his wife, save on account of immorality, causes her to commit adultery; and he who marries a woman who has been put away commits adultery.'[3] But look! She has been put away; she has not put away her husband, but, because it is possible for only a few to practice continence, she has given in to her carnal desires and married. Nevertheless, an adulterer has married an adulteress. Both are party to the act and both are condemned, that is, the woman who has married while her husband was still living, and the man who married a woman whose husband was still living. And are we to say here that the law of Christ is inhuman by which a woman is convicted of so great a crime whose husband has put her away without any previous infidelity on her part and has, by putting her away, forced her to marry, in so far as it is possible for only a few to remain continent? Why do we not say here that whoever prematurely severs the marriage bond by an unjust dismissal is to be considered as one dead?

---
2 Cf. 1 Tim. 5.13.
3 Matt. 5.31,32.

Why are you going to say that the husband who, although an adulterer, has not put away his wife has severed the marriage bond, and that the one who has put away even a chaste wife has not broken it? However, I maintain that this bond remains intact in either case, because the 'woman is bound as long as her husband is alive.' She is bound whether he be continent or an adulterer, and, therefore, she commits adultery who remarries after her dismissal. He also commits adultery who marries a woman who has been put away, whether she has been put away by an adulterous or a continent husband, because 'A woman is bound as long as her husband is alive.' But, now, to mention something about the complaints of incontinent men. For what seems more just than the complaint of this woman who says: I have been put away; I have not put away my husband, and, because it is possible for only a few to remain continent, I have not remained so. I have married to avoid committing fornication, and am I to be called an adulteress because I have married? Shall we think that, because of the seemingly warranted complaint of this woman, the divine Law is to be altered so that we may not judge that woman to be an adulteress? Heaven forbid! But you will answer: She should not have been put away, because there was no antecedent cause of fornication. You would be correct, for the Lord indicated the sin of her husband when He said: 'Whoever puts away his wife, save on account of immorality, causes her to commit adultery.' But has not that woman sinned by her later marriage for the very reason that her husband sinned by previously putting her away? What does it avail her, therefore, incontinent woman that she is, to complain about the law of Christ, except to be punished as a grumbler.

Chapter 11

(11) And now let us also consider the points that you added and inserted in another section of your letter. You looked for an answer from me on those points. When you are concerned and feel sorry for the man who is constrained to lie with an adulteress, if not by his incontinence, certainly by the necessity for procreating children, if it is not permitted him to so dismiss his wife that he may remarry during her life—in this case, you would be justly concerned if it would not be adultery to remarry while one's wife is alive, regardless of how unfaithful she may be. But, if this be adultery, as the points discussed have indicated, why is the motive of procreating children advanced as a plea? For, not on that account is license to sin to be permitted. Or, indeed, is death without heirs to be avoided, just as life hereafter is to be chosen? This will not be granted to adulterers, for after their first death they will be condemned to an everlasting second death. For that motive of begetting children compels women who are not adulterous, and even those who are most chaste, to be put away, and other women to be taken, if, perchance, they be sterile. I do not think that this pleases you.

(12) Wherefore, if adulteries are not to be excused for the sake of incontinence, how much less are they to be excused for the sake of procreating children?

Chapter 12

It is that weakness, namely, incontinence, that the Apostle wished to remedy by the divinity of marriage. He did not say: If he does not have sons, let him marry, but: 'If he does not have self-control, let him marry.'[1] Indeed, the con-

---
1 1 Cor. 7.9.

cessions to incontinence in marriage are compensated for by the procreation of children. Incontinence surely is a vice, although marriage is not. So, through this good, that evil is rendered pardonable. Since, therefore, the institution of marriage exists for the sake of generation, for this reason did our forebears enter into the union of wedlock and lawfully take to themselves their wives, only because of the duty to beget children. There then was a certain necessity for having children which does not exist now, because 'the time to embrace,'[2] as it is written, was in those days, but now is 'the time to refrain from embracing.' Alluding to the present age, the Apostle says: 'But this I say, brethren, the time is short; it remains that those who have wives be as if they had none.'[3] Whence, with perfect conviction, the following can be said: 'Let him accept it who can,'[4] but 'let her marry who cannot control herself.' In former times, therefore, even continence was made subordinate to marriage for the sake of propagating children. Now, the marriage bond is a remedy for the vice of incontinence, so that children are begotten by those who do not practice continence, not with a disgraceful display of unbridled lust, but through the sanctioned act of lawfully wedded spouses. Then why did the Apostle not say: If he does not have sons let him marry? Evidently, because in this time of refraining from embrace it is not necessary to beget children. And why has he said: 'If he cannot control himself, let him marry'? Surely, to prevent incontinence from constraining him to adultery. If, then, he practices continence, neither let him marry nor beget children. However, if he does not control himself, let him enter into lawful wedlock, so that he may not beget children in disgrace or avoid having offspring by a more degraded form of inter-

2 Esdras 3.5.
3 1 Cor. 7.29.
4 Matt. 19.12.

course. There are some lawfully wedded couples who resort to this last, for intercourse, even with one's lawfully wedded spouse, can take place in an unlawful and shameful manner, whenever the conception of offspring is avoided. Onan, the son of Juda, did this very thing, and the Lord slew him on that account.[5] Therefore, the procreation of children is itself the primary, natural, legitimate purpose of marriage. Whence it follows that those who marry because of their inability to remain continent ought not to so temper their vice that they preclude the good of marriage, which is the procreation of children. The Apostle was certainly speaking of the incontinent where he said: 'I desire, therefore, that younger widows marry, bear children, rule their households, and give the adversary no occasion for abusing us. For already some have turned aside after Satan.'[6] So, when he said: 'I desire that the younger widows marry,' he surely gave the advice to bolster their collapsing self-control. Then, lest thought be given only to this weakness of carnal desire, which would only be strengthened by the marital act, while the good of marriage would be either despised or overlooked, he immediately added: 'to bear children, rule their households.' In fact, those who choose to remain continent certainly choose something better than the good of marriage, which is the procreation of children. Whence, if the choice is continence, so that something better than the good of marriage is embraced, how much more closely is it to be guarded so that adultery may be avoided! For, when the Apostle said: 'But if they do not have self-control, let them marry, for it is better to marry than to burn,'[7] he did not say that it is better to commit adultery than to burn.

---

5 Cf. Gen. 38.8-10.
6 1 Tim. 5.14,15.
7 1 Cor. 7.9.

Chapter 13

(13) Therefore, there is nothing to which we may exhort those who fear reconciliation with their adulterous spouses, who have been healed by their repentance, except to safeguard their continence, because 'A woman is bound as long as her husband lives,' whether he be adulterous or chaste. She is guilty of adultery if she remarries. The husband also is bound as long as his wife lives, whether she be adulterous or chaste, and he, too, commits adultery if he marries another. This bond is never dissolved at any time, even if a spouse is separated by divorce from a chaste partner. Much less is the bond dissolved if she commits adultery before the separation. From this we may know that she is freed only by the death of her husband, whose death is reckoned, not from his lapse into adultery, but from his departure from the body. As a result, if the wife leaves her adulterous husband and does not wish to be reconciled to him, let her remain unmarried. And if a husband dismisses an adulterous wife and is unwilling to take her back, even after her repentance, he must preserve his continence, if not with the desire of choosing the greater good, certainly from the necessity of avoiding a deadly evil. I would urge this even if the wife were afflicted with a chronic, incurable disease, and even if she were physically separated in a place where her husband could not go to her. Finally, I would urge the practice of continence even if the wife, in her desire to live continently—although against the general rule, since it is without his consent—would nevertheless dismiss him though both he and she were chaste. I do not think that any Christian will maintain that he is not an adulterer who has had relations with another woman, in the event that his wife has long been sick or absent or is desirous of living continently. Therefore, he is also an adulterer if, after the dismissal of an adulterous

wife, he is found with another woman, because not this or that man, but 'everyone who puts away his wife and marries another commits adultery.'[1] For this reason, if one free from the marriage bond strives less to live a saintly life, he is to fear the punishment of the adulterers, and let his lust be bridled at least by fear, if continence is not chosen because of love. For, where there is fear it is toilsome to strive, and where there was toil there will be love. We must not confide in our own strength, but prayer must be added to our endeavors so that He who deters us from evil may fill us with good.

Chapter 14

(14) Let us also answer your argument wherein you think that husbands are constrained to punish adulterous women unmercifully, when they wish them to die, if it is not permitted them to remarry while their wives are alive. In your desire to exaggerate this cruelty, you said: 'It does not seem to me, my most beloved father, that this can be the mind of God, when kindness and love are excluded.' You say that as though husbands ought to spare their adulterous wives on the ground that it is lawful for them to marry other women, so that, if it is not lawful, they would not spare them, in order that it would become lawful. On the contrary, they ought to show mercy to their sinful wives so as also to obtain merciful treatment themselves for their sins. Much more is this to be done by those who, after the dismissal of their adulterous wives, desire to live continently. They ought, in truth, to be as much more merciful as they wish to be holy, so that in the preservation of chastity in themselves they may gain divine aid, while they themselves do not avenge in human fashion the violation of chastity on the part of their

---
1 Luke 16.18.

wives. These words of the Lord are particularly to be recalled: 'Let him who is without sin be the first to cast a stone at her.'[1] He did not say: who is without that particular sin. Since we are discussing chaste men, the man 'who is without sin'—if they say that they are without sin, they are deluding themselves and 'there is no truth in them.'[2] If they are not deluding themselves and there is truth in them, they will not be savagely harsh. In the knowledge that they are not without sin, they forgive, in order that they may be granted forgiveness. Likewise, kindness and love will not be withheld from them. These are excluded the more if their unbridled lust, and not pious solicitude, secures pardon for the sins of their spouses, that is to say, if they pardon them because it is permitted them to marry others, and not rather because they also crave the Lord's pardon for themselves.

Chapter 15

(15) It is proper, then, and much more honorable and worthy of men professing Christianity not to seek the blood of their adulterous spouses. We quote to them what has been written: 'Forgive the injustice of thy neighbor, and then shall thy sins be forgiven thee, when thou prayest. Man to man reserveth anger: And doth he seek remedy of God? He hath no mercy on a man like himself: And doth he entreat for his own sins? Since he is but flesh, he nourisheth anger.... Who shall obtain pardon for his sins?'[1] And the following is from the Gospel: 'Forgive and you shall be forgiven,'[2] so that we can say: 'Forgive us our debts, as we

---

1 John 8.7.
2 Cf. John 1.8.

---

1 Eccle. 28.2,5.
2 Luke 6.37.

also forgive our debtors.'³ This is from the Apostle: 'To no man render evil for evil.'⁴ We might also quote other passages in holy Scripture of a like nature, by which the human spirit, when roused to vengeance, may be mollified, in so far as it is Christian. How much better it is, I maintain, to express those sentiments than to say: Merely dismiss your adulterous wives and do not seek their blood. For, whatever discomfort you experience as a result of their derelictions others whom you wed will console you. Not without reason would you wish to remove them from the ranks of the living if their lives were to prevent your marrying others. But now, since it is permitted you, even during their lives, to look forward to other marriages, why do you wish so strongly to kill them? If we say this, do you not see how far removed our counsel is from the spirit of Christianity? We also say wrongly that something is lawful for them which is not, namely, that it is lawful to join themselves to others while their wives are still alive; and, if they spare them for that reason, they do not spare them because of piety but because of the complete freedom to remarry. Finally, I ask you whether it is lawful for a Christian husband to kill an adulterous wife according to the old law of God, or according to Roman Law. If it is lawful, it is better for him to refrain from either course, that is, both from lawful chastisement, in case she sins, and from unlawful wedlock, during her life. But, if he has decided to choose either of the two, it is more proper for him to have the adulteress punished because it is lawful than to do what is not lawful, that is, to commit adultery while she is alive. If, however, to speak more truthfully, it is not lawful for a Christian to kill an adulterous spouse, but only to put her away, who would be so foolish as to say to him: Do what is lawful, so that what is not

---
3 Matt. 6.12.
4 Rom. 12.17.

permitted may become lawful for you? Since each action is unlawful according to the law of Christ, both to kill an adulteress and to remarry while she lives, one must refrain from both. One unlawful act must not be done in lieu of another. The one who intends to do what is unlawful must commit adultery now and not murder, so that he will remarry during the life of his spouse and not shed human blood. If each is a heinous crime, he ought not to commit either in preference to the other, but should avoid both.

Chapter 16

(16) At this point, I realize what can be said by the incontinent, namely, that it is evident that the man who puts away his adulterous wife and permits her to live is, while his former wife is living, an adulterer all the while and does not repent fruitfully as long as he does not withdraw from sin. Also, if he is a catechumen, he is not admitted to baptism, because he does not turn aside from its impediment. And if he is persistent in the same evil, he cannot be reconciled as a penitent. If, however, accusing her of adultery, he kills her, this sin, since it is over and done with and does not perdure in him, is absolved in baptism, if the crime has been committed by a catechumen; if by a baptized person, it is healed by penance and reconciliation. Are we to say, therefore, that that adultery is not adultery which is committed without doubt, if another wife is taken while the adulterous spouse is still living? With the exception of this species of adultery, you surely do not doubt that it is adultery for anyone to take the wife of a living husband who has been put away by her husband through a bill of divorce with no infidelity on her part. What then? When he sees that he is neither admitted to baptism, if he is a catechumen, and that he is

not usefully performing penance, if he has done this after being baptized, in not correcting or abandoning what he has done, if he wishes and is able to kill the man whose wife he has taken, so that this sin may be cleansed by baptism or forgiven by penance, that, on the one hand, adultery may not remain, after the wife has been freed from the law of her husband once he has died, and, on the other hand, that satisfaction through penance may be had for the deed committed, and that it may be blotted out by baptism—if any of these things is done, is the law of Christ therefore to be accused, as though it compelled the crime of murder, when it states that it is adultery to marry a woman repudiated without the crime of fornication?

(17) Here, if we pay too little attention to what we are discussing, there can be much more serious conclusions than you yourself have drawn. For, while you wish there to be no adultery if there is remarriage after the dismissal of adulteresses, you have reached the following conclusion: 'Because, if we maintain that this is adultery, husbands will be constrained to kill adulterous wives, whose lives prevent their marrying others.' And, to magnify the issue, you said: 'My beloved father, it does not seem to me that the mind of God is expressed where kindness and piety are excluded.' Then, if anyone, unwilling to believe it to be adultery for a woman to be taken to wife after she has been repudiated by her husband without being guilty of adultery, should discover this also to be contrary to your opinion, because for that reason men are persuaded to commit murder and to seek out by any possible trickery and calumny, or accuse of some actual crime and kill the husbands of the women they marry after such a repudiation, so that the marriages which had been adulterous during their life are possible after their death—if anyone, I say, were to find this flaw in your reasoning, is he not going to say to you, to exaggerate his

case: It does not seem to me, most beloved father, that the mind of God can be here, where not only kindness and devotion are excluded, but where also great malice and impiety are fostered? Therefore, for husbands to kill their adulterous wives is much less serious and easier to countenance than for adulterers to kill husbands. Does it please you that we cease to defend the Lord's opinion because of this most fruitless envy, or, what is more, for us to cast aspersions on it by saying that adultery should not be determined, even if a woman who has been repudiated for other than the cause of fornication is joined to another man, so that she may not be constrained to kill her husband who put her away, while she desires to convert adultery into marriage by the death of her former husband? I know that this does not please you to say that the law of Christ is harsh and inhumane because of this fruitless envy, when it is found to be true and reasonable. Thus, you should not feel that it is not to be considered adultery when a second wife is taken during the life of an adulterous wife, because a husband can be forced to kill the adulteress for this reason, while he desires to be permitted to marry another after her death, if he is not permitted to do so during her life. Why? Because, if those who scoff at the Christian faith should also say that men are compelled to kill, by wicked and insidious means, their troublesome wives whom they cannot tolerate, whether because they are afflicted with a chronic illness and are not able to perform the marriage act, or because they are poor or sterile or deformed, in hope of taking other wives who would be healthy, wealthy, fruitful, and exceedingly beautiful, because it is not permitted them to divorce, save on account of fornication, those whom they are unwilling to tolerate, nor to marry others, so that, unhampered by perpetual adultery, they can be baptized and healed by penance, are we to say, then, that there is no adultery when they take other women, after their wives have been divorced for other than the cause of fornication, so that those foul deeds of murder may not be perpetrated?

Chapter 17

(18) But now, since it is your opinion that there is no adultery if a man puts away his wife because of fornication and takes another, do not you think that care must be taken that husbands do not learn to force their wives, whom they cannot bear for numberless other reasons, to commit adultery, to enable them lawfully, according to your mind, to remarry after the bond of marriage has been removed from them through fornication, and also, after they have constrained their wives to adultery, to enable them to be cleansed by baptism or be healed by penance, because both grace and spiritual remedy will be denied them as long as they live with adulteresses, if they remarry after they divorce their former spouses for other than the cause of fornication—unless, perchance, someone may say that no man can cause his wife to commit adultery if she is chaste. Yet, the Lord says: 'Everyone who puts away his wife, save on account of immorality, causes her to commit adultery.'[1] Certainly, while she remains chaste when with her husband, yet, after she has been put away, she is constrained by her lack of self-control to have relations with another man while her former husband is still alive. And this is to commit adultery. If she does not do this, her husband compels her to it, as best he can. God will lay this sin to his account, even though she remains chaste. But, who does not know how few wives there are who live so chastely with their husbands that, even though put away by them, they do not look for others?

1 Matt. 5.32.

Indeed, incomparably greater is the number of women who, while they cling chastely to their husbands, do not defer marriage if they have been put away by them. Therefore, when men lend credence to this saying of the Lord: 'Everyone who puts away his wife, save on account of immorality, causes her to commit adultery,' if they believe you who say that it is lawful for a husband to remarry if his wife is unfaithful, everyone shall wish to separate for any other difficulty you may mention from the wife to whom he is joined prior to his forcing her to commit adultery by putting her away without any fornication, so that he may then take a second wife, although she becomes an adulteress by the marriage, and so that, freed from his former sin by which he caused her to commit adultery, either by baptism or penance, he may seem to have the second wife, whom he has taken after the adultery of the former, as though the marriage bond had been dissolved thereby. As a matter of fact, if he contrives to do this, and makes his wife an adulteress, he himself will likewise be an adulterer by taking a second wife, even after the adultery of his former spouse. It will avail him nothing that he has believed you and not rather Him who said: 'Everyone who puts away his wife and marries another, commits adultery.'[2]

Chapter 18

(19) After considering and discussing these points, it remains for those who receive them faithfully to quote to us what was said to the Lord in the Gospel: 'If the case of a man with his wife is so, it is not expedient to marry.'[1] And

---
2 Luke 16.18.
---
1 Matt. 19.10.

what are we to answer to them, if not what He Himself answers? 'Not all accept this teaching; but those to whom it has been given. For there are eunuchs who were born so from their mother's womb; and there are eunuchs who were made so by men; and there are eunuchs who have made themselves so for the kingdom of heaven's sake. Let him accept it who can.'[2] Therefore, let him who can accept it accept what not all men do accept. However, they to whom the hidden, but not unjust, mercy of God offers it can accept it. And that just mercy is shown all those 'who have made themselves eunuchs for the kingdom of heaven's sake.' There are some of either sex who have no knowledge of marital relations; there are others who have had such experience, but have turned away. Some of these, indeed, have secured their knowledge of marriage unlawfully; others, lawfully. Accordingly, among those who have had their experience in lawful wedlock there are some who have had only such lawful knowledge of marriage, and others who have had both lawful and unlawful marital relations. There are certainly among them some who have had relations only with their own wives, but there are those who also know other women as well as any form of immorality you may mention. But those who make themselves eunuchs for the kingdom of heaven either lose their spouses through death, after marital experience, or through their consent, when they make known their intention to live continently with them, or through the necessity of separation, lest they commit adultery in joining themselves to others while their spouses live. These make themselves eunuchs for the kingdom of heaven's sake, not so that they can be greater in glory there, but because they are not able to be there otherwise. For, those who practice the virtue of continence, not because of that necessity, but in their quest of the greater good, would

---

2 Matt. 19.11,12.

be able to attain heaven even by the practice of chastity in their marriage. They would reach heaven, although their reward would be less. Those who practice continence because they fear to join themselves to other women while their former wives are still living should exercise greater care for their salvation than those have exercised who have chosen continence in view of a greater reward. Surely they will then attain heaven, if they are not adulterers. If, on the contrary, they do not restrain themselves, they will be adulterers, because, during the lives of their former spouses, they will cleave, not to other spouses, but to adulterers. And if they are not in heaven, where will they be, except in the place where they will not be saved?

Chapter 19

(20) I exhort them, therefore, to do what men should do, if they have wives who are afflicted with a protracted disease, or wives who are apart from them in an inaccessible place or practicing continence with unlawful zeal. When they have wives who are besmirched with the foul stain of adultery, and although they be separated from their companions, I urge them for that very reason to treat their spouses as they are bound to do in the former instances; and I urge them not to seek other marriages, because they will not be marriages, but adulterous unions. For, since the husband and wife are equal as regards the marriage bond, just as 'The wife, while her husband is alive, will be called an adulteress, if she be with another man,'[1] so will the husband also be called an adulterer if, while his wife is living, he is with another woman. For, although the adultery is more serious on the part of the one who puts his wife

1 Rom. 7.3.

away for other than the cause of fornication and marries another, 'Everyone who puts away his wife and marries another commits adultery.'[2] The burden of self-restraint must not terrify them. It will be lighter if it is Christ's and it will be Christ's if that faith is present which obtains from the Lawgiver the grace to do what He has ordained. Let them not be crushed by the fact that their self-restraint seems to be forced and not to come from the will, because even those who have freely chosen it have made it a matter of necessity, since they cannot deviate from its practice without condemnation, and those who have been forced into its practice make it a matter of free choice, providing they do not rely upon themselves but upon Him from whom is every good. The former have embarked upon its practice for the sake of greater glory, in order to come upon something of greater worth; the others have fled to it with a mind to their final salvation, lest they perish. Both must persist and walk unto the end in the path they have entered. Let them burn with zeal and importune God with their prayers, because their salvation is to be considered by the former group, so that they fear to fall away from what their will has fastened upon, and because the latter are not to lose the hope of final glory, if they choose to persevere in that which necessity has thrust upon them. For it can happen that, with God frightening, exhorting, changing, and flooding them with grace, the disposition of men may change for the better, and also that they desire so strongly to live with the greatest impure and lustful desire that, even if an opportunity for new marriage is presented, after they have been separated from their spouses by death, the course, lawfully opened to them, is closed by a vow, and what began of necessity becomes perfect through charity. Undoubtedly, these persons will be repaid in the same manner as those who have either

---

2 Luke 16.18.

made this vow along with their spouses by mutual consent, or have chosen continence for the sake of a greater good, although they were bound to no wife. If, however, they restrain themselves in such a manner that they are of a mind to remarry, if those women should die whose lives are an impediment to marriage, marital chastity assuredly would be imputed to them, even though they themselves depart from the body in such a state of continence, for the sake of which they are not doing anything which they would do, if it were lawful. To live continently with this intention is, in fact, too little to receive the reward of that self-restraint which is freely chosen, but it suffices as a safeguard against adultery.

Chapter 20

(21) You will remember that I am making these observations about both sexes, but particulary on account of men who think themselves superior to women, lest they deem themselves their equals in the matter of chastity. They should have taken the lead in chastity, so that their wives would follow them as their heads. But, since the law forbids adultery, if weakness of the flesh should be admitted as an excuse for incontinence, an occasion for losing their souls is offered to many under the guise of a false impunity. Women also have flesh, to whom their husbands are unwilling to make some such allowance, as though it were granted them because they are men. Never believe that something is owed the stronger sex as an honor which is detrimental to chastity, since meet honor is owed to virtue and not to vice. On the contrary, when they demand such great chastity on the part of their wives, who assuredly have flesh, so that, when they go on long journeys away from their wives, they wish them

to pass their glowing youth, untarnished by any adulterous relations—in fact, a great many women pass their days most virtuously, particulary the women of Syria, whose husbands, absorbed in business affairs, leave them as young men and hardly return to their old wives in their advanced age—by the very fact that they pretend that they are unable to practice continence they prove more clearly that it is not impossible. For, if the weakness of men could not accomplish this, much less could the weaker feminine sex.

(22) Wherefore, when we frighten those men who think virile excellence to be nothing other than license to sin to prevent their being lost for eternity by reason of their persistence in adulterous marriages, we habitually hold up to them the restraint of clerics, who, usually against their will, are constrained to bear this same burden, and, once accepted, carry it through to its proper end with the help of the Lord. Therefore, we say to them: Look here! If you were forced to undergo this by the violence of the people, would you not chastely carry out your duty, once you had taken it upon yourself, after you had turned to the Lord to secure the strength you had never before considered? But they say that honor affords them the greatest consolation. We answer that fear should also govern them much more. For, if many of God's ministers have taken this upon themselves, although it has been imposed suddenly and unexpectedly, with the hope that they will shine with greater brightness in the inheritance of Christ, how much more ought you to live continently, avoiding adultery, not in the fear that you may shine with less splendor in the kingdom of God, but fearing lest you burn in the fiery abyss. This and similar statements we make, as the opportunity presents itself, to those who, at the departure of their wives in any manner at all, or after their dismissal because of adultery, wish to remarry, and, when

they are forbiden, place before us as an excuse the weakness of the flesh. Now, this book also must be closed and God be sought that He either not permit them to be tempted by the separation of their wives, or else permit it in such a way that fear for their imperiled salvation may become for them the occasion of a fuller and more praiseworthy chastity.

HOLY VIRGINITY

(De sancta virginitate)

Translated by
JOHN McQUADE, S.M.
Marist College
Washington, D. C.

INTRODUCTION

AUGUSTINE'S TREATISES, *The Good of Marriage* and *Holy Virginity*, constitute his answer to the heresy of Jovinian.[1] This monk, whose early life was characterized by austerity, gained notoriety during the pontificate of Pope Siricius (384-398). He left his monastery in 385 and went to Rome, where he became a scandal to the Church both by his conduct and his teaching. His writings are entirely lost. Their contents are known only through the answers of his opponents. From these we learn that he centered his attack principally on the practice of virginity, denying its superiority over marriage, and accusing the Catholics of Manichaeism in their preference for celibacy.[2]

The doctrine met with considerable success. Many monks and consecrated women were persuaded by Jovinian's specious reasoning to desert their monasteries and marry.[3] The situation became grave enough to call for papal action. In 389, Pope Siricius, in the presence of the Roman clergy, solemnly

---
1 Cf. Augustine, *De haeresibus* 82; Jerome, *Adv. Jovinianum libri duo*, *passim;* J. Froget, 'Jovinien,' *DTC* 8, cols. 1577-80.
2 *De nuptiis et concupiscentiis* 2.23.
3 *Retract.* 2.22.

condemned the doctrine of Jovinian, declaring him, together with eight of his followers, excommunicated for the crimes of heresy and blasphemy.[4]

The renegade monk answered with a series of tracts called *Commentarii* or *Commentarioli,* which Jerome describes in his own caustic manner: 'Indeed, the barbarity of the writings is such, and the language, extremely corrupt, is befuddled with such defects, that I was able to understand neither what he says nor with what arguments he would prove what he says.'[5]

Finding the opposition in Rome too great, the condemned men moved to Milan in the hope of continuing their operations in a locality where they were unknown. This hope was thwarted by the vigilance of Siricius, who immediately dispatched a copy of the condemnation to Ambrose. The latter convoked a provincial synod. The condemnation was read and a letter warmly supporting the papal action was penned by Ambrose and signed by the assembled bishops.[6]

Meanwhile, Jerome had received copies of the *Commentarii* from friends in Rome, with a request to write a refutation. He responded in 392 with his two works *Against Jovinian* (*Adversus Jovinianum libri duo*) in which he unleashes the full fury of his pen against the sophisms of the unhappy heretic.

This combination of papal authority and capable defenders of Christian truth quickly broke the power of the heresy as an organized and open threat to the Church.

St. Augustine says: 'This heresy was quickly crushed and extinguished, nor could it succeed in deceiving any priests.'[7] Nevertheless, its effects were still felt when Augustine wrote

---

4 Cf. letter of Siricius to Ambrose, in Mansi, *Sacrorum Conciliorum nova et amplissima collectio* 3, col. 663; *PL* 13.1168.
5 *Adv. Jovinianum* 1.1.
6 Cf. reply of Ambrose to Siricius, *Ep.* 42 (*PL* 16.1123).
7 *De haer.* 82.

Holy Virginity, about 401. In the *Retractations* he gives us an accurate summary of the circumstances of its composition. Deprived of the power to teach publicly, the heretics still clung tenaciously to their views and continued to foster them surreptitiously: 'But these contentions of his, which no one dared to defend openly, had survived in the prattlings and innuendoes of certain men.'[8]

The accusation was made that the champions of virginity could defend its superiority only by joining company with the Manichaeans in condemning marriage. Some of Jerome's expressions regarding married people were open to such a false interpretation, and his subsequent explanations failed to dispel the bad impression.[9]

It was to meet such continuous sly insinuations of the heretics that Augustine took up his pen: 'But even the stealthily creeping poisons had to be fought, especially since it was boastfully maintained that Jovinian could not be answered by praising, but only by maligning marriage.'[10]

He entered the controversy with *The Good of Marriage,* demonstrating in detail its goodness and beauty before establishing its inferiority to the state of perpetual continence. The wisdom of this cautious procedure is demonstrated by the fact that, in spite of his effort to avoid the possibility of misinterpretation, he was forced subsequently to defend himself against the charge of Manichaeism.[11]

'After I wrote *The Good of Marriage,* it was expected that I would write on holy virginity; nor did I delay. And, in so far as I was able, in a single book, I portrayed that gift of God, both how great it is, and with what great humility it is to be guarded.'[12]

---

8 *Retract.* 2.22.
9 Cf. Jerome, *Ep.* 48,49.
10 *Retract.* 2.22,23; *De s. virg.* 1.
11 Cf. *Contra secundam Juliani responsionem imperfectum opus* 1.123.
12 *Retract.* 2.23.

The details furnished by Augustine are helpful in determining the precise date of the treatise, *Holy Virginity*. In the *Retractations*, *The Good of Marriage* follows *The Work of Monks*, published in 400. Since Augustine assures us that he lost no time in turning to the praise of virginity, and since the next work in the *Retractations*, *The Literal Interpretation of Genesis*, was begun in 401, *Holy Virginity* was probably completed in 401.[13]

The subject of virginity had been dear to the hearts of Christian writers from the very beginning. Chrysostom, Ambrose, and Jerome had already made valuable contributions to the stream of Christian thought on this theme.[14] That stream is even more richly endowed as it passes through Augustine's hands.

His theological insight finds depths of meaning in the virginal consecration which his predecessors had failed to fathom. His investigation, moreover, is made with characteristic breadth of vision. Virginity is viewed, not in isolation, but in relation to fundamental Christian teachings. We are enriched with Augustinian thought on a variety of doctrines.

Jovinian's attack on Mary's virginity was a logical step in the development of his doctrines. It does not seem to have entered into his original teachings, and is not mentioned either in the letter of Pope Siricius or by Jerome in *Against Jovinian*.[15] It is, however, listed by Ambrose in the letter of the Synod of Milan to the Pope, and by Augustine in *On Heresies*.[16]

Since the champions of virginity always pointed to Mary as the most perfect model of virgins, Jovinian was led, in

---
13 Cf. *ibid.* 2.21-24.
14 Chrysostom, *De virginitate*; Ambrose, *De virginibus*; *De virginitate*; *De institutione virginis*; *Exhortatio virginitatis*; Jerome, *Adv. Jovinianum*.
15 Cf. *Adv. Jov.* 1, where he lists the errors of Jovinian.
16 Cf. above, notes 6,7.

defense of his position, to claim that her virginity was lost at the birth of Christ.

To this denial we owe one of the richest passages in *Holy Virginity*. Chapter 4 could, indeed, form the nucleus for a treatise on Augustinian Mariology. It includes the following teaching of Christian tradition: (1) Mary remains perpetually a virgin, in the conception of Christ, in His birth, and throughout her life. (2) Mary had made a vow of virginity. This teaching, found implicitly in Jerome and Ambrose, is stated explicitly by Augustine. (3) Mary is spiritually the Mother of Christ's Mystical Body, the Church.[17] She fulfills this function by her union with Him through charity and obedience in carrying out the will of His heavenly Father. (4) Mary preserved her virginal integrity, yet gave physical birth to Christ; the Church, though virginal, is spiritually the mother of Christ in His members through baptism; the consecrated virgin, likewise, while preserving her integrity, has a spiritual motherhood by co-operation with Christ through charity in bringing souls to eternal life.

The second part of the treatise, the practical exhortation on the conduct of virgins, rests on the thought taken from the Apocalypse,[18] that the virgins follow the Lamb wherever He goes. From this Augustine draws the twofold lesson of the unique glory of virginity and of the necessity of deep humility for the preservation of true Christian virginity, meritorious for heaven.[19]

In its style, *Holy Virginity* bears the imprint both of the rhetoric of the contemporary schools and of the Christian Scriptures.

There is hardly a device of the schools that is not used. The very first sentence exemplifies the flair for circum-

---

17 Cf. *De s. virg.* 2-7.
18 Cf. Apoc. 14.2-4
19 Cf. *De s. virg.* 27-56.

locution so foreign to modern style. At times word is piled upon word and phrase upon phrase for the cumulative effect. Member is balanced against member for the purpose of stressing similarity or contrast of ideas, with due attention to the effect of the cadence on the ear. Emphasis is produced by repetition of words or phrases. Metaphor abounds. Exclamation and rhetorical question are mingled in profusion.

The Scriptural influence on Augustine's style is inescapable. The text is richly sprinkled with direct citations and obvious allusions, and the very language of the man himself is evidently colored by his intimate association with the inspired books. His vocabulary includes a rich treasure of Scriptural terms. His phraseology is frequently molded after the pattern of the sacred text. His thoughts, especially in many sections which approach the oratorical style, seem to flow naturally into a form of expression akin to that of the Prophecies and Psalms.

The modern reader, accustomed to a less ornate and less artificial style, is apt to find Augustine's rhetoric foreign to his taste. It can be appreciated only through a sympathetic understanding of the literary heritage which forms its background and of the tastes of the times in which it was used by him. In any other form he would not have been representative of the age which produced him.

On the whole, even for the modern reader *Holy Virginity* possesses both power and beauty of style. Aside from a few complicated sentences, an excessive indulgence in alliteration, and a preoccuption with parallelism and rhyme, Augustine displays throughout an artistic reserve in his use of figures. The form, in most instances, is worthy of the lofty thought it is meant to convey.

Since style is personal, it would be impossible for the strong personality of Augustine to be lost in his rhetoric. It does shine through in all its deep sincerity, charm, and persuasiveness. His keen logic is mingled with his profound theological penetration. Under the inspiration of his pure mystical insight and burning love for eternal Truth, many passages attain a delicacy and beauty of expression that defy translation or paraphrase.

Augustine's concept is full and rich in its implications. Without overlooking the element of suppression of self entailed in the surrender of natural rights and inclinations, he goes straight to the heart of the mystery of divine grace which raises the soul to angelic heights. He places the essence of virginal consecration in the positive element, the throwing of one's whole being into intimate, loving union with God, so that He becomes the center of thought and action.

In this union the soul finds its deepest satisfaction and noblest self-expression. It achieves a fruitfulness immeasurably superior to that of carnal generation. Like Mary, like the Church, it becomes in a special way, in a spiritual way, the mother of Christ in His members.

The modern mind often tends to miss the deep significance of consecrated virginity by placing excessive emphasis on the surrender of natural human affections. Augustine leads us into the broad realms of traditional Christian thought. With him we contemplate the virgin, not as one who has coldly rejected love, but as one who lives in the embrace of the love of Christ.

HOLY VIRGINITY

Chapter 1

E RECENTLY PUBLISHED a book, *The Good of Marriage*,[1] in which we also admonished and warned the virgins of Christ that they must not, because of the superiority of the more perfect gift which they have received from on high, despise, by comparison with themselves, the fathers and mothers[2] of the people of God; and that, because by divine law continence is preferred to matrimony and holy virginity to wedlock, they must not belittle the worth of those men whom the Apostle praises as the olive tree, that the ingrafted wild olive may not boast;[3] who,

---

1 *De bono coniugali*.
2 The patriarchs and holy women of the Old Testament, through whom the Jewish race was propagated.
3 Cf. Rom. 11.16-22. St. Paul pictures the Church as an olive tree with its roots anchored deeply in Judaism, thus preserving an organic unity between the Old and the New Dispensations. The full-developed tree is the Church herself. The root and stem are the patriarchs. The many branches are the various members of the Church, some of whom (those of Jewish descent) belong to her by natural growth, while others (the Gentile Christians) have been grafted from wild stock. These latter should preserve a humble respect for the natural branches, and especially for the root and stem; for it is only by being grafted into the stem that the wild branches share in the life of the tree. Cf. *Sermones* 77.10; 201.2; 203.3; 218.7; also, Fernand Prat, S. J., *The Theology of Saint Paul*, trans. John L. Stoddard (New York 1927) 2 275-276. St. Augustine here makes particular application of the analogy in defense of the sacred character of the conjugal life as practiced by the patriarchs.

by the very begetting of children, served the Christ who was to come.

In them, indeed, were prepared and brought to term those future events which we now behold marvelously and efficaciously fulfilled, of which their conjugal life was, in fact, prophetic.[4] Wherefore, not after the manner of human vows and pleasures, but by the most profound design of God, in some of them fecundity deserved to be honored,[5] in others sterility even merited to become rendered fruitful.[6]

At the present time, however, those to whom it is said: 'If they do not have self control, let them marry,'[7] are not to be exhorted, but consoled; but those to whom it is said: 'Let him accept it who can,'[8] are to be exhorted lest they be frightened, and to be frightened lest they be proud. Therefore, virginity must not only be praised that it may be loved, but also admonished that it may not be puffed up.

---

4 Cf. *Contra Faustum* 22.24: 'Not only the speech of these men, but their life also was prophetic. . . . So, as regards those [Hebrews] who were then made wise of heart in the wisdom of God, . . . a prophecy of the coming of Christ and of the Church ought to be discovered both in what they said and in what they did.' It was especially in their conjugal life that they typified the marvelous mysteries that would be revealed in Christ and in His Church. Cf., above, *De bono coniugali* 16; 19-23. The patriarchs typified Christ. Their marriage typified His union with the Church. Cf. *Contra Faustum* 22.38. Their numerous offspring, constituting the chosen people, typified the multitudes who would be born to the faith through the mystical union of Christ with His Spouse, the Church. Cf. *Contra Faustum* 22.57 *et passim*; *Sermo* 213.7. Even in the practice of polygamy among the patriarchs St. Augustine finds something prophetic; cf. above, *De bono coniugali* 18.
5 Cf. Gen. 12.2.; 26.4; 35.11.
6 Cf. Gen. 18.10; 25.21; 30.22.24.
7 1 Cor. 7.9.
8 Matt. 19.12.

Chapter 2

(2) That is what we have undertaken in this treatise. May Christ, the Son of a virgin and Spouse of virgins, born bodily from a virginal womb, wed spiritually by a virginal espousal, help us.

Since, therefore, the whole Church is espoused as a virgin to one man, Christ, as the Apostle says,[1] how great honor her members deserve who preserve in their very flesh this which the whole Church, imitating the Mother of her Spouse and Lord, preserves in the faith. The Church, too, is both mother and virgin.[2] For, about whose integrity are we solicitous if she is not a virgin? Or of whose progeny do we speak if she is not a mother?

Mary bore the Head of this body in the flesh; the Church bears the members of that Head in the spirit. In neither does virginity impede fecundity; in neither does fecundity destroy virginity.

Therefore, since the whole Church is holy, both in body and in spirit, yet is not exclusively a virgin in body, but only in spirit, how much more holy is she in those members where she is a virgin both in body and in spirit.

Chapter 3

(3) It is written in the Gospel that when the Mother and brethren of Christ, that is, His relatives according to the flesh, were announced to Him, and were waiting outside because they could not get near Him for the crowd, He answered: ' "Who is my mother, or who are my brethren?"

---
1 2 Cor. 11.2; also, Eph. 5.27-32; Apoc. 21.9; 22.17; Matt. 9.15; 25.1-13. St. Augustine explains more fully in his commentary on the marriage feast at Cana (*In Joannis Evangelium* 8.4).
2 St. Augustine places the virginity of the Church in her integrity of faith, hope, and charity; cf. *De bono viduitatis* 10.

Stretching forth His hand over His disciples, He said: "These are my brethren; and whoever does the will of my Father, he is my brother and mother and sister." [1] What else was He teaching us except to prefer our spiritual kinship to carnal affinity, and that men are not blessed by being connected with just and holy people through blood relationship, but by being united to them through obedience to their teaching and imitation of their life?

Thus, Mary was more blessed in accepting the faith of Christ than in conceiving the flesh of Christ.[2] For, to someone who said: 'Blessed is the womb that bore Thee,' He replied: 'Rather, blessed are they who hear the word of God and keep it.'[3]

Finally, for His brethren, that is, His relatives according to the flesh, who did not believe in Him, of what advantage was that relationship? So, even her maternal relationship would have done Mary no good unless she had borne Christ more happily in her heart than in her flesh.

Chapter 4

(4) Indeed, her virginity was itself more beautiful and more pleasing, because Christ, in His conception, did not Himself take away that which He was preserving from violation by man; but, before He was conceived He chose one already consecrated to God of whom He would be born.[1]

---

1 Matt. 12.48-50; also, *In Joan.* 10.3.
2 Cf. *In Joan.* 10.3; *Contra Faustum* 29.4; *De peccatorum meritis et remissione* 2.24; *Sermones* 69.3; 196.1; 233.3.
3 Luke 11.27,28.

1 Here St. Augustine summarizes the belief in the perpetual virginity of Mary. With St. Ambrose he champions the Catholic doctrine that she was a virgin, not only in the conception of Christ, but also in His birth, and that she remained virginal throughout her life in fulfillment of the vow made to God previous to her marriage. Cf. *Enchiridion* 34; *De bono vid.* 10; *Contra Faustum* 29.4; *Sermones* 69.3; 110.3; 184.1; 191.1; 196.1; 213.7; 215.3; 233.3; *et passim.*

The words which Mary addressed to the angel who announced her Child to her indicate this. 'How shall this happen, she asked, 'since I do not know man?'[2] And this she would certainly not have said unless she had previously vowed herself to God as a virgin. But, because the customs of the Jews as yet forbade this,[3] she was espoused to a just man; not to one who would ravage by violence, but to one who would protect against violent men that which she had already vowed.

Although, even if she had only said: 'How shall this happen?' and had not added 'since I do not know man,' she would never have asked at all how a woman was to bear the son promised to her if she had married with the intention of cohabiting.

Again, she could have been commanded to remain a virgin in whom the Son of God would, by a fitting miracle, take upon Himself the nature of a slave,[4] but, in order to be a model for holy virgins, lest it be thought that only she ought to be a virgin who had merited to conceive a child even without carnal intercourse, she consecrated her virginity to God while she was still ignorant of what she would conceive, so that the imitation of the heavenly life in her earthly and mortal body might come about by vow, not by precept, by a love of her own choice, not by the compulsion of obedience.

Thus, Christ, in being born of a virgin who, before she knew who was to be born of her, had resolved to remain a virgin, chose rather to approve holy virginity than to impose it. So, even in that woman in whom He took upon Himself the nature of a slave, He desired virginity to be free.

---
2 Luke 1.34.
3 Perpetual virginity was not unknown among the Jews. The sect of the Essenes demanded absolute continence of its members. However, since the great glory of the race lay in the propagation of the people of God and in providing the carnal generation of the Messias, marriage and parenthood were more highly esteemed than virginity. Cf *De sancta virginitate* 1, 9; *De bono coniugali* 19; *De bono vid.* 7
4 Cf. Phil. 2.7.

Chapter 5

(5) There is no reason, therefore, why the virgins of God should be troubled because they cannot likewise, while preserving their virginity, be mothers in the flesh. For, virginity could appropriately bear Him alone who in His birth could not have an equal.

Nevertheless, the Child of the one holy Virgin is the glory of all holy virgins, and they, together with Mary, are the mothers of Christ if they do the will of the Father. On this account Mary herself is more praiseworthily and more happily the Mother of Christ, according to His saying mentioned above: 'Whoever does the will of my Father in heaven, he is my brother and sister and mother.'[1]

All these relationships to Himself He manifests spiritually in the people whom He has redeemed. He regards holy men and women as His brothers and sisters because they are co-heirs[2] with Him in the inheritance of heaven. The whole Church is His mother, because she most truly brings forth His members, that is, His faithful, through the grace of God. Every holy soul who carries out the will of His Father is likewise His mother by a most fruitful charity toward those for whom it is in labor until He be formed in them.[3] Mary, therefore, in fulfilling the will of God, is merely the Mother of Christ in the body, but both Sister and Mother in the spirit.

---

1 Matt. 12.50.
2 Cf. Rom. 8.17.
3 Cf. Gal. 4.19.

HOLY VIRGINITY 149

Chapter 6

(6) That one woman, therefore, is both Mother and Virgin, not only in spirit, but also in body. She is mother, indeed, in the spirit, not of our Head, who is our Saviour Himself, of whom she was rather born spiritually, since all who believe in Him (among whom she, too, is included) are rightly called children of the bridegroom,[1] but she is evidently the mother[2] of us who are His members, because she has co-operated by charity that the faithful, who are members of that Head, might be born in the Church. Indeed, she is Mother of the Head Himself in the body.

It behooved our Head to be born of a virgin according to the flesh, for the sake of a wonderful miracle by which He might signify that His members would be born according to the spirit, of a virgin, the Church.[3]

Mary alone, therefore, is mother and virgin both in spirit and in body, both Mother of Christ and Virgin of Christ. The Church, on the other hand, in the saints who are to possess the kingdom of God, is indeed wholly the mother of Christ, wholly the virgin of Christ in spirit; in the body, however, not as a whole, but in some she is a virgin of Christ, in others a mother, although not Christ's mother.

Both married women of the faith and virgins consecrated to God, by holy lives and by charity 'from a pure heart and a good conscience and faith unfeigned,'[4] are spiritually the mothers of Christ because they do the will of His Father. But those who, in married life, give physical birth bring forth not Christ, but Adam;[5] and they therefore hasten that

---
1 Cf. Matt. 9.15.
2 For a detailed treatment of Mary's universal Motherhood cf. M. J. Scheeben, *Mariology* (1947) 2.245-246 *et passim*.
3 Cf. also, *Sermones* 189.4; 192.2; 213.7.
4 1 Tim. 1.5.
5 I.e., having the stain of original sin. Cf. 1 Cor. 15.22. Cf. *De peccatorum meritis et remissione, passim*; *Ep.* 166 (*ad Hier.*), *passim*.

their offspring may be initiated into the sacraments,[6] and may become members of Christ, for they know what they have borne.

Chapter 7

(7) I have said this lest, perhaps, conjugal fecundity might dare to quarrel with virginal integrity, and adduce Mary herself, and say to the virgins of God: 'She possessed in her body two things deserving of honor: virginity and fecundity, since she remained inviolate and yet conceived. As we could not each possess this boon in its entirety, we have divided it, so that you are virgins, we are mothers. Let the preservation of your virginity console your lack of progeny, and let our loss of virginal integrity be compensated for by the reward of children.'

This claim of the faithful who are married ought to be brought in some way or other against consecrated virgins if those whom they brought forth in the body were Christians, so that Mary's fecundity of the flesh, apart from her virginity, would be superior only in this, that she brought forth the Head itself of these members, whereas they would bring forth the members of that Head. But now, even though they argue in this fashion who are united and cohabit with their husbands for the sole purpose of having children, and who have no other concern for their children than that they

---
6 Infant baptism was the common custom in the Church at this time; St. Augustine defends the practice as of apostolic origin in *Ep.* 166.7.21, 8.23; cf. *De peccatorum meritis et remissione* 3.5.10; 13.22. His use of the plural, 'sacraments,' can be understood as referring merely to baptism as the gateway to the others, or as indicating his familiarity with the custom of admitting infants to confirmation and Holy Eucharist immediately after baptism. Cf. *Sermo* 174.6.7; *Ep.* 98.4; *Contra Julianum opus imperfectum* 2.30; also, Innocent I, *Ep.* 25 (*ad Decentium*) 6, DB 98; G. Bareille, 'Bapteme d'aprés les pères grecs et latins,' *DTC* 3 col. 215; H. Leclercq, 'Communion des enfants,' *DACL* 3 cols. 2440-2442.

may gain them for Christ, and who see to this as soon as they are able, those born of their flesh are not Christians, but become such afterwards through the motherhood of the Church, inasmuch as she is spiritually the mother of Christ's members, as she is also spiritually His virgin.

In this holy birth the mothers also co-operate who have brought forth non-Christians in the body, that these may become what they know they could not bring forth in the body. Yet they co-operate through this in which they are also both virgins and mothers of Christ, namely, in faith 'which works through charity.'[1]

Chapter 8

(8) No fecundity of the flesh, therefore, can be compared with holy virginity, even of the flesh. Even this itself is not honored because it is virginity, but because it is consecrated to God; although it is preserved in the flesh, it is nevertheless preserved by religion and devotion of soul. Therefore, even bodily virginity, which a loving chastity vows and preserves, is spiritual. For, just as no one uses the body impurely except through wickedness already conceived in the spirit, so no one preserves purity of body except through chastity already rooted in the spirit.

Moreover, if conjugal chastity, although it is preserved in the flesh, is nevertheless attributed not to the flesh, but to the soul, under whose command and direction the flesh itself is used in no other except its own proper union, how much the more, and how much the more honorably, is that continence to be numbered among the goods of the soul by which integrity of body is vowed, consecrated, and preserved for the Creator Himself of the soul and of the body.

---
1 Gal. 5.6.

Chapter 9

(9) So, the physical fecundity, even of those who at the present time desire nothing in marriage except children whom they may hand over to Christ, must not be thought capable of making up for the loss of virginity. In former times, it is true, carnal generation in a certain numerous and prophetic nation was itself necessary for the coming of Christ in the flesh.[1] Now, however, since the members of Christ can be gathered from every race of men and from all nations into the people of God and the city of the kingdom of heaven, 'let her accept it who can'[2] accept holy virginity, and let only her who does not have self-control marry.[3]

What if some rich woman devote a large sum of money to the good work of ransoming slaves from various nations and making Christians—will she not provide more fruitfully and more abundantly for the begetting of Christ's members than by the very greatest fruitfulness of the womb? Yet, she will not presume on that account to compare her money with the gift of consecrated virginity. But, if fecundity of the flesh shall compensate fully for the loss of virginity because it makes Christians of those who are born, this will be a more profitable exchange, to surrender virginity for a large sum of money with which many more children might be purchased to be made Christians than would be born of one womb, no matter how fertile.

1 Cf. above, *De bono coniugali* 9.
2 Cf. Matt. 19.12.
3 Cf. 1 Cor. 7.9.

Chapter 10

If it is the height of foolishness to say this, let the married faithful have their blessing, which we discussed in so far as seemed necessary in another book;[1] and let them honor more highly in consecrated virgins (as they have been most rightly accustomed to do) their greater blessing, which we are discussing in this treatise.

(10) Married people ought not to claim a share in the merits of the continent even from the fact that virgins have their birth from them; this is not the blessing of marriage, but of nature, which is so constituted by God that the daughter born of any human union of both sexes, whether lawful and good or base and illicit, must be a virgin. But no woman is born a consecrated virgin. So it is that a virgin is born even of fornication, but a consecrated virgin not even of wedlock.

Chapter 11

(11) So, we do not praise in virgins the fact that they are virgins, but that they are virgins dedicated to God by holy chastity. A married woman seems more blessed to me (and I am not rash in saying it) than a virgin who intends to marry, because the former already possesses what the latter still desires, especially if she is not even betrothed to anyone. The former strives to please one man to whom she has been given; the latter, many, not knowing to whom she will be given. In this alone she protects her purity of thought against the multitude, that she seeks not an adulterer, but a husband from the multitude.

That virgin, therefore, is rightly preferred to the married woman, who neither places herself before the multitude to

---

1 *De bono coniugali.*

be loved, while she is seeking the love of one out of the multitude, nor unites herself to one already found, concerned with 'the things of the world' how she may please her husband,[1] but who so loves Him who is 'beautiful above the sons of men'[2] that, since she cannot, like Mary, conceive Him in the flesh, she preserves even her body intact for Him who has been conceived in her heart.

Chapter 12

No corporal fecundity has brought forth this race of virgins; they are not the offspring of flesh and blood. If their mother is sought, she is the Church. No one brings forth consecrated virgins except a consecrated virgin, she who has been betrothed to be presented undefiled to one Spouse, Christ.[1] Of her, not wholly virginal in body, but wholly virginal in spirit, are born holy virgins, both in body and in spirit.

(12) Let spouses have their blessing, not because they beget children, but because they beget them honorably and lawfully and chastely and for society, and bring up their offspring rightly, wholesomely, and with perseverance; because they keep conjugal fidelity with each other; because they do not desecrate the sacrament[2] of matrimony.

---

1 1 Cor. 7.34.
2 Ps. 44.3.

---

1 Cf. 2 Cor. 11.2.
2 St. Augustine sometimes uses the term 'sacrament' in a wide sense for any sacred symbol. Here, however, he employs the term in the strict sense, as it later came to be used exclusively for the seven sacraments.

Chapter 13

These, however, are all duties of a human office, but virginal integrity and freedom from all carnal relation through holy chastity is an angelic lot, and a foretaste in the corruptible flesh of perpetual incorruption. Let all carnal fecundity and all conjugal chastity bow to this. The former is not within one's own power, the latter is not found in eternity; free choice does not control carnal fecundity, heaven does not contain conjugal chastity.[1] Certainly they shall possess something greater than others in that common immortality, who in the flesh already possess something not of the flesh.

(13) They are amazingly foolish, therefore, who think that the perfection of this continence is necessary, not because of the kingdom of heaven, but because of the present life, that is, because married people are distraught by so many urgent worldly cares, while virgins and celibates are freed from such affliction; as though it were better not to marry for this reason alone, that the cares of this life may be lightened, not because continence is of value for the future life.

Lest they seem to have conceived this foolish opinion from their own foolishness of heart, they allege proof from the Apostle, where he says: 'Now concerning virgins I have no commandment of the Lord, yet I give a counsel,[2] as one having obtained mercy from God to be trustworthy. I think, then, that this is good on account of the present distress—that it is good for a man to remain as he is.'[3]

'Notice,' they say, 'where the Apostle teaches that this is good because of the present distress, not because of future

---
1 Cf. Matt. 22.30.
2 The Confraternity edition of the New Testament renders *consilium* by 'opinion.'
3 1 Cor. 7.25,26.

eternity.' As though the Apostle would take account of the present distress except to provide and counsel for the future, when his whole teaching is directed only to eternal life!

Chapter 14

(14) The present distress should be avoided, therefore, but for this reason, that it hinders some of our future rewards. By this distress conjugal life is forced to be concerned about the things of the world: the husband how he may please his wife, and the wife how she may please her husband. Not that these things exclude from the kingdom of God, as do sins, which are therefore forbidden by precept, and not by counsel, because to disobey a commandment of the Lord is deserving of damnation, but what would be more fully possessed within the kingdom of God if more thought were given to the manner of pleasing God shall certainly be less when this itself is given less thought due to the cares of marriage.[1]

Therefore, 'Concerning virgins,' he says, 'I have no commandment of the Lord.' Whoever disobeys a commandment is a criminal, and subject to punishment. Hence, because it is no sin to take a wife and to marry (for if it were a sin it would be forbidden by precept), therefore there is no commandment of the Lord concerning virgins. Since eternal life is to be reached by avoiding sins or by having them forgiven, and in it a special glory is to be given, not to all who shall live forever, but to certain ones, and since to obtain this it is not enough to be freed from sins, but something must be vowed to the Deliverer Himself which it would not be wrong to have left unvowed, but to have vowed and to have rendered is worthy of praise, he adds:

---
1 Cf. above, *De bono coniugali* 11.13.

' "I give a counsel, as one having obtained mercy to be trustworthy;" for I must not jealously withhold the trustworthy counsel, who am trustworthy, not by my own merits, but by the mercy of God. "Therefore, I think that this is good on account of the present distress." '²

'The thing,' he says, 'about which I do not have a commandment of the Lord but give a counsel, is this: "Concerning virgins, . . . I think that this is good on account of the present distress." For I know the character of the present time, to which married people are subject. Necessity compels them to think less of the things of God than is necessary to secure that glory which will not be the lot of all, even though they dwell in eternal life and salvation. "For star differs from star in glory. So also with the resurrection of the dead."³ Therefore, "it is good for a man to remain as he is." '⁴

Chapter 15

(15) Then the same Apostle goes on to say: 'Art thou bound to a wife? Do not seek to be freed. Art thou freed from a wife? Do not seek a wife.'¹

The first of these two things which he lays down is in the nature of precept, against which it is not lawful to act. For it is not lawful to put away one's wife except because of fornication, as our Lord Himself says in the Gospel.² But, what he adds: 'Art thou freed from a wife? Do not seek a wife,' is the statement of a counsel, not of a precept; therefore, it is lawful to do it, but it is better not to do it.

---

2 1 Cor. 7.25,26.
3 1 Cor. 15.41,42.
4 1 Cor. 7.26.

1 1 Cor. 7.27.
2 Cf. Matt. 19.9.

Moreover, he immediately adds: 'But if thou takest a wife, thou hast not sinned. And if a virgin marries, she has not sinned.'[3]

But when, in the first place, he said this: 'Art thou bound to a wife? Do not seek to be freed,' did he add: 'and if thou dost free thyself, thou hast not sinned'? He had already said above: 'But to those who are married, not I, but the Lord commands that a wife is not to depart from her husband, and if she departs, that she is to remain unmarried or be reconciled to her husband.'[4] (For it can happen that she departs, not through her own fault, but through that of her husband.)

Then he says: 'And let not a husband put away his wife,'[5] which he laid down no less by the command of the Lord. Nor did he there add: 'And if he does put her away, he does not sin.' For this is a precept, and disobedience to it is a sin; not a counsel by refusing to follow which you will choose a lesser good, but will not do anything wrong.

Therefore, after he had said: 'Art thou freed from a wife? Do not seek a wife,'[6] because he was not commanding that an evil thing should not be done, but counseling that something better be done, he immediately added: 'And if thou takest a wife, thou hast not sinned. And if a virgin marries, she has not sinned.'

Chapter 16

(16) However, he added: 'Yet such will have tribulation of the flesh. But I spare you that,'[1] in this manner exhorting

---
[3] 1 Cor. 7.28.
[4] 1 Cor. 7.10,11.
[5] 1 Cor. 7.11.
[6] 1 Cor. 7.27,28.

---
[1] 1 Cor. 7.28.

to perpetual virginity and continence, even to the extent of discouraging a little from marriage, moderately, indeed, not as from something evil and illicit, but as from something burdensome and difficult.

It is one thing to engage in carnal vice; another, to have tribulation of the flesh. To do the former is a sin; to bear the latter is a hardship; and men, for the most part, do not shirk hardship, even for the sake of the most honorable positions.

But it would be very foolish, for the sake of enjoying marriage even at the present time, when the coming of Christ is not served through carnal generation by the very begetting of children, to take upon oneself the burden of this tribulation of the flesh which the Apostle predicts for those who marry—unless those who cannot remain continent feared that under the temptation of Satan they would fall into sins leading to damnation.

When he remarks, however, that he is sparing those who he says will have tribulation of the flesh, nothing seems more certain to me than that he was unwilling to reveal and explain in words that same tribulation of the flesh which he had predicted for those who choose marriage, in the suspicions of marital jealousy, in the bearing and raising of children, in the fears and anguish of bereavement. For, what man is there who, when he has bound himself by the bonds of wedlock, is not torn and harassed by these emotions? Yet, we must not exaggerate them, lest we might fail to spare those who the Apostle thought ought to be spared.

Chapter 17

(17) Merely from what I have briefly set forth, the reader ought to have been put on his guard against those

who, from what was written: 'Such will have tribulation of the flesh. But I spare you that,' falsely charge against marriage that this pronouncement implicitly condemns it, as though he were unwilling to pronounce the condemnation itself when he said: 'But I spare you that'; so that, as a matter of fact, while he spares them, he did not spare his own soul, if he lied in saying: 'And if thou takest a wife, thou hast not sinned. And if a virgin marries, she has not sinned.'

Those who believe this, or would have it believed, concerning the sacred Scripture, as though they are paving the way for themselves for freedom to lie or for the defense of their erroneous opinion, hold a view altogether opposed to what sound teaching demands.

For, if something clear shall be adduced from the divine books by which their errors are refuted, they keep this at hand like a shield—with which, as if defending themselves against the truth, they expose themselves to be wounded by the Devil—in order to claim that the author of the book spoke this falsehood, now that he might spare the weak, and again that he might frighten the contemptuous, just as the occasion demands when their erroneous teaching is being defended.

And thus, while they prefer to uphold rather than to correct their opinions, they attempt to break the authority of the Holy Scriptures, by which, single-handed, all proud and obdurate necks are broken.

Chapter 18

(18) Wherefore, I admonish the men and women who have embraced perpetual continence and sacred virginity to prefer their blessing to marriage in such a way that they may not consider marriage an evil, and may acknowledge

that it was not said falsely, but in all truth, by the Apostle: 'He who gives his virgin in marriage does well, and he who does not give her does better.¹ . . . And if thou takest a wife, thou hast not sinned. And if a virgin marries, she has not sinned'; and a little further on: 'But she will be more blessed, in my judgment, if she remains as she is.' And, lest it should be regarded as a human judgment, he adds: 'And I think that I also have the spirit of God.'²

This is the teaching of the Lord, the teaching of the Apostle, the true teaching, the sound teaching: so to choose the greater gifts as not to condemn the lesser. The truth of God in the Scripture of God is better than virginity in the mind or in the flesh of any man.

Let what is chaste be so loved that what is true be not denied. For, what evil are they not capable of thinking, even concerning their own flesh, who believe that the tongue of the Apostle, in the very place where it was commending virginity of the body, was itself defiled by the corruption of falsehood?

In the first place, therefore, and above all, let those who choose the blessing of virginity believe with the utmost steadfastness that the holy Scriptures contain no falsehood, and that, therefore, this saying is also true: 'And if thou takest a wife thou hast not sinned. And if a virgin marries, she has not sinned.' And let them not think that so great a blessing of integrity is diminished if marriage shall not be evil. Nay, more, let her rather be confident that a palm of greater glory has been prepared for her who did not fear to be condemned if she married, but who aspired to be more honorably crowned for not marrying.

Wherefore, let not those who have chosen to remain unmarried flee marriage as a pitfall of sin, but let them

---
1 1 Cor. 7.38.
2 1 Cor. 7.28,40.

surmount it as a hill of inferior blessing, that they may come to rest on the mountain of the greater blessing of continence.

Indeed, that hill is dwelt upon under this law, that one may not leave it at will. For 'a woman is bound as long as her husband is alive.' Truly by it, as by a step, the chastity of widowhood is reached. But for the sake of virginal chastity, it is either to be avoided by rejecting suitors, or to be surmounted by forestalling suitors.

Chapter 19

(19) However, lest anyone think that the rewards of the two works, that is, of the good and of the better, shall be equal, we had to refute those who so interpreted the words of the Apostle: 'I think, then, that this is good on account of the present distress,' as to claim that virginity is useful, not because of the kingdom of heaven, but because of the present life, as though they who had chosen the higher good were going to possess nothing more than the rest in that eternal life.

In the argument, when we came to this saying of that same Apostle: 'Yet such will have tribulation of the flesh. But I spare you that,' we turned against the other opponents who did not make nuptials equal to perpetual chastity but who condemned them altogether.

For, while either one is an error, either to make nuptials equal to holy virginity or to condemn them, these two errors, in their overeagerness to avoid each other, attack from opposite extremes, since they have refused to cling to the middle position of truth, in which, both from certain reason and from the authority of the holy Scriptures, we find that marriage is not sinful, yet we do not make it equal to the blessing, either of virginal, or even of widowed continence.

Chapter 20

Some, indeed, in embracing virginity, have regarded marriage as a loathsome adultery; others, on the contrary, in defending marriage, have desired the perfection of perpetual continence to merit nothing more than conjugal chastity; as though either the blessing of Susanna[1] were an humiliation of Mary, or Mary's greater blessing ought to be a condemnation of Susanna.

(20) God forbid, therefore, that the Apostle spoke thus to those married or about to be married: 'But I spare you that,'[2] as though he were loath to pronounce the punishment which would be due to married people in the world to come! God forbid that Paul consigned her to hell who had been freed from the temporal tribunal by Daniel! God forbid that her marriage bed be a source of punishment for her before the tribunal of Christ, who, by preserving her fidelity to it, chose either to run the risk of being put to death or even to die under the false accusation of adultery.

What was the use of that exclamation: 'It is better for me to fall into your hands than to sin in the sight of God,'[3] if God was not going to deliver her for preserving her nuptial chastity, but was going to condemn her for having married?

And now, as often as conjugal chastity is defended by the truth of the holy Scripture against those who abuse and denounce marriage, Susanna is defended by the Holy Spirit against her false accusers, and is again exonerated of the false charge—and this in a much more serious matter. Then the accusation was made against one spouse, now it is made against all spouses; then it concerned a secret and sham

---
1 Cf. Dan. 13; Susanna is a symbol of marital fidelity.
2 1 Cor. 7.28.
3 Dan. 13.23.

adultery, now it concerns true and public marriage; then one woman was accused on the word of the wicked elders, now all husbands and wives are accused on the word that the Apostle was unwilling to utter.

'He withheld your condemnation,' they say, 'when he said: "But I spare you that."' Who did this? He, in truth, who had previously said: 'But if thou takest a wife, thou hast not sinned. And if a virgin marries, she has not sinned.'

Why, then, do you detect an accusation against husbands and wives in that which, through moderation, he refrains from saying, and do not recognize a defense of spouses in that which he says plainly? Or does he condemn by his silence those whom he has exonerated by speech?

Is not Susanna more leniently accused, not of marriage, but of adultery itself, than the teaching of the Apostle is accused of a lie? What would we do in such a plight, if it were not as evidently certain that chaste nuptials ought not to be condemned as it is evidently certain that the holy Scripture cannot lie?

Chapter 21

(21) At this point, someone will ask: 'What has this to do with sacred virginity or perpetual continence, whose praise was undertaken in this treatise?' To this I answer: First, as I explained above, the glory of that greater blessing is greater from this, that to obtain it the blessing of marriage is foregone, not that the sin of marriage is avoided. Otherwise, it would suffice for perpetual continence not to be especially praised, but merely not to be disparaged, if it were embraced on this account, that to marry were sinful.

Moreover, since men ought to be urged to such an excellent gift, not by human opinion, but by the authority of the divine Scripture, this divine Scripture must not be handled in an indifferent or cursory manner, or it may appear to someone to have lied on some point.

They rather discourage than encourage virgins who compel them to persevere in their state by condemning marriage. How will they rely on the truth of what is written: 'And he who does not give her does better,' if they shall consider false that which, as shown above, is just as surely written: 'And he who gives his virgin in marriage does well'?[1]

But, if they have believed the Scripture without hesitation when it speaks of the blessing of marriage, they shall press on with ardent and confident eagerness, sustained by the same truthful authority of the divine Word, to their own more perfect blessing.

But we have said enough for the purpose undertaken. And, in so far as we were able, we have also shown that neither is this saying of the Apostle: 'I think, then, that this is good on account of the present distress,'[2] to be so understood as though consecrated virgins were better off than married women of the faith in this world, but that in the kingdom of heaven and in the world to come they will be equal; nor is that in which he says to spouses: 'Yet such will have tribulation of the flesh. But I spare you that,' to be so understood as though he preferred to conceal rather than to pronounce the sinfulness and the condemnation of marriage.

Two mutually contradictory errors have, indeed, each espoused one of these two statements by failing to understand them. For, those who claim that married people are equal to the unmarried interpret the one concerning the present distress in their favor; while those who take it upon themselves to condemn married people interpret the other, where it is said: 'But I spare you that,' in their favor.

---
1 1 Cor. 7.38.
2 1 Cor. 7.26.

We, however, according to the trustworthiness and sound teaching of the holy Scriptures, do not claim that marriage is sinful, yet we place its blessing not only beneath virginal continence, but even beneath that of widowhood.

We also claim that the present distress of married people is an obstacle to their attainment, not, indeed, of eternal life, but certainly of that eminent glory and honor which is reserved for perpetual chastity. We claim likewise that at the present time marriage is not expedient except for those who do not have self-control,[3] and that the Apostle, as the prophet of truth, was unwilling to conceal the tribulation of the flesh springing from carnal emotions, from which the marriage of those who lack self-control can never be free, but that, as the consoler of human weakness, he was unwilling to explain it more fully.

Chapter 22

(22) We hope now to demonstrate even more clearly from the most obvious pronouncements of the divine Scriptures which, within the limits of our memory, we are able to recall, that perpetual continence is to be embraced, not for the sake of the present earthly life, but for the sake of the future life which is promised in the kingdom of heaven.

Who does not, in fact, detect this in the words of the same Apostle, spoken a little later: 'He who is unmarried is concerned about the things of the Lord, how he may please the Lord. Whereas he who is married is concerned about the things of the world, how he may please his wife. And the unmarried woman, or the virgin, is set apart. She who is unmarried thinks about the things of the Lord, that she may be holy in body and in spirit. Whereas she who is

3 Cf. 1 Cor. 7.9.

married thinks about the things of the world, how she may please her husband'?¹

He certainly does not say: 'She is concerned with the things that make for security in this world, that she may pass her time free from more pressing cares.' He does not say that the virgin or the unmarried woman is set apart, that is, separated and distinguished from the married woman, for this purpose, that the unmarried woman may be secure in this by avoiding the temporal cares which the wife does not escape; but 'she thinks,' he says, 'about the things of the Lord, how she may please the Lord,' and 'she thinks about the things of the Lord, that she may be holy in body and in spirit.'

Unless, perchance, anyone is even so stupidly contentious that he will attempt to maintain that we desire to please the Lord, not because of the kingdom of heaven, but because of the present world; or that we desire to be holy in body and in spirit for the sake of this life, not for the sake of eternal life.

What is the one who believes this but the most pitiable of all men? For so the Apostle says: 'If with this life only in view we have had hope in Christ, we are of all men the most pitied.'² Is he, indeed, foolish who shares his bread with the hungry, if he does it merely for the sake of this life, and shall he be wise who restrains his body to the extent of continence, by which he refrains even from marriage, if it shall bring him no reward in the kingdom of heaven?

Chapter 23

(23) Finally, let us listen to the Lord Himself, pronouncing the most conclusive argument on this point. When

---
1 Cf. 1 Cor. 7.32-34.
2 1 Cor. 15.19.

He proclaimed in a divine and terrifying manner that spouses must not separate except because of fornication, the disciples said to Him: 'If the case of a man with his wife is so, it is not expedient to marry!' And He replied: 'Not all accept this teaching. . . . For there are eunuchs who were born so from their mother's womb; and there are eunuchs who were made so by men; and there are eunuchs who have made themselves so for the kingdom of heaven's sake. Let him accept it who can.'¹

What truer, what clearer word could have been spoken? Christ, the Truth, the Wisdom, and the Power of God, proclaims that they who, by a holy resolve, have refrained from taking a wife make themselves eunuchs for the kingdom of heaven's sake. On the other hand, human foolishness, with impious temerity, contends that those who do this merely escape the present distress of conjugal cares but receive nothing more than others in the kingdom of heaven!

Chapter 24

(24) But who are the eunuchs about whom God speaks through Isaias the Prophet,¹ to whom He says He will give a place of renown in His house and within His walls, a place much better than that of sons and daughters, if not those who make themselves eunuchs for the sake of the kingdom of heaven?

For those whose generative faculty itself is so weakened

---

1 Matt. 19.10-12.

1 Isa. 56.4,5. Isaias represents a more tolerant view than that of Deut. 23.1, which excluded eunuchs from the Jewish religion. The prophecy is concerned primarily with the statement that eunuchs will enjoy equality with others in the Messianic Kingdom. The Fathers generally see in the text a reference to the superior position of virgins over that of parents of children.

that they are unable to procreate (such as are the eunuchs of the wealthy and of kings), when they become Christians and observe the laws of God, but are of such a mind that they would have married if they had been able, it is quite enough that they be placed on the same level as the other married faithful in the house of God, who bring up in the fear of God the progeny legitimately and chastely begotten, teaching their children to place their hope in God. However, they are not to receive a higher place than that of sons and daughters. For they do not remain unmarried through virtue of soul, but through necessity of the flesh.

Let him contend, then, who will that the Prophet foretold this concerning those eunuchs who have been mutilated in body. This error also lends support to the cause which we have defended. God did not prefer these eunuchs to those who have no place in His house, but undoubtedly to those who store up the merit of conjugal life by generating children. For, when He said: 'I shall give them a much better place,' He made it clear that a place shall be given also to the married, but a much lower one.

Let us concede, therefore, that eunuchs according to the flesh, who were not numbered among the people of Israel, are foretold to dwell in the house of God, since we see that, while they do not become Jews, they do become Christians. And let us concede that the Prophet did not speak of those who, refraining from marriage from a resolution of continence, make themselves eunuchs for the kingdom of heaven's sake. Is anyone so fanatically opposed to the truth as to believe that those made eunuchs according to the flesh possess a higher place than married people in the house of God, and to contend that the continent by holy vow, who mortify their body to the point of spurning marriage, who make themselves eunuchs, not in body, but at the very root of concupiscence, who enjoy a foretaste of the heavenly and angelic life in their earthly mortality, are on an equal level with the merits of spouses? And will a Christian contradict Christ, who praises those who have made themselves eunuchs, not for the sake of the present world, but for the sake of the kingdom of heaven, by asserting that this is valuable for the present, not for the future life?

What else remains for them, except to assert that the kingdom of heaven itself refers to this temporal life in which we dwell at present? Why does not blind presumption proceed even to this absurdity? What is more absurd than this assertion? For, although the Church which exists at this time is also called the kingdom of heaven, she is called so precisely for this reason, because she is connected with the future and eternal life.² Therefore, although she has 'the promise of the present life as well as of that which is to come,'³ nevertheless, in all her good works, she looks not at the things 'that are seen, but at the things that are not seen. For the things that are seen are temporal, but the things that are not seen are eternal.'⁴

Chapter 25

(25) Indeed, the Holy Spirit did not fail to utter the clear and invincible word that would prevail against these shameless and fanatic assailants, and would, with irresistable force, drive their brutish ranting from His sheepfold. For, when He had said concerning eunuchs: 'I will give to them

---
2 Matt. 19.12.
3 1 Tim. 4.8.
4 2 Cor. 4.18.

in my house, and within my walls, a place of renown much better than sons and daughters,[1] lest anyone excessively carnal might think that something temporal should be hoped for from these words, He immediately added: 'I will give them an everlasting name which shall never perish,' as though He were saying: 'Why do you equivocate, O unholy blindness? Why do you equivocate? Why do you spread the clouds of your deception over the clear sky of truth? Why do you seek in so great a light of the Scriptures a source from which to spread darkness? Why do you promise nothing but temporal gain to holy celibates?

' "I shall give them an everlasting name." Why do you strive to limit those who abstain from all carnal relations to an earthly reward? And that also through the very thing by which they do abstain from them, that is, by being concerned about the things of the Lord, how they may please the Lord?

' "I will give them an everlasting name." Why do you argue that the kingdom of heaven, for the sake of which holy eunuchs make themselves eunuchs, is to be understood only in this life?

' "I will give them an everlasting name." And if, perchance, you attempt to interpret "everlasting" itself in this place as a long period of time, I add, I amplify, I insist: "which shall never perish." '

What more do you ask? What more do you have to say? This everlasting name for the eunuchs of God (whatever it is), which certainly signifies some special and eminent glory, will not be possessed in common with the multitude, even though they dwell in the same kingdom and in the same house. Perhaps it is even called a name from this, that it distinguishes those to whom it is given from others.

---
1 Cf. Isa. 56.5.

Chapter 26

(26) 'What, then,' they ask, 'does that denarius[1] signify, which at the completion of the work in the vineyard is paid equally to all, whether to those who have worked from the first hour, or to those who have worked for one hour?' What, indeed, unless it signifies something which all shall have in common, such as eternal life itself, the very kingdom of heaven, where all shall dwell whom God has predestined, called, justified, and glorified?[2]

'For this corruptible body must put on incorruption, and this mortal body must put on immortality.'[3] This is that denarius, the reward of all. Nevertheless, 'star differs from star in glory. So also with the resurrection of the dead.'[4] These are the different rewards of the saints. For, if heaven be signified by that denarius, is not to be in heaven common to all the stars? Yet, 'there is one glory of the sun, and another glory of the moon, and another of the stars.'[5] If the denarius were to represent health of body, is not health common to all the members when we are in good health? And if it persist even till death, it is not just as equally present in all? Nevertheless, 'God has set the members, each of them, in the body as He willed,'[6] so that it is not all eye, nor all ear, nor all nose; everything else has its own individuality, although it has health in common with all the members.

Thus, because eternal life itself shall belong to all the saints, the same sum of a denarius is given to all, but, because in that eternal life the splendor of merits will present a

---
1 Cf. Matt. 20.9,10.
2 Rom. 8.30.
3 1 Cor. 15.53.
4 1 Cor. 15.41,42.
5 1 Cor. 15.41.
6 1 Cor. 18.18.

varied luster, 'there are many mansions'[7] with the Father. Therefore, in the equality of the denarius, one will not live longer than another, but, in the many mansions, one will be honored with greater glory than another.

Chapter 27

(27) Press on, then, saints of God, youths and maidens, men and women, celibates and virgins, press on unflaggingly toward the goal! Praise the Lord more sweetly, to whom your thoughts are more fully devoted; hope in Him more eagerly, whom you serve more eagerly; love Him more ardently, whom you please more carefully. With loins girt, and lamps lit, await the Lord when He returns from the wedding.[1]

You shall offer, at the nuptials of the Lamb, a new canticle, which you shall accompany on your harps; by no means such as the whole earth sings, to which it is said: 'Sing ye to the Lord a new canticle, sing to the Lord, all the earth,'[2] but such as no one shall be able to sing except yourselves. Thus you saw in the Apocalypse[3] the one who was loved above others by the Lamb, who was accustomed to lean upon His breast, and to drink in and pour forth the supercelestial wonders of the word of God.

He saw you, twelve times twelve thousand blessed harpers, of undefiled virginity of body, of inviolate truthfulness of heart; because you follow the Lamb wherever He goes, he wrote about you.

---

7 John 14.2.

---

1 Cf. Luke 12.35,36.
2 Ps. 95.1.
3 Apoc. 14.2-4.

Where do we think this Lamb goes, where no one either dares or is able to follow, except yourselves? Where do we think He goes; to what heights and what meadows? I think where the delights of rich pasture are—not the empty delights of the world, which are deceitful follies; nor such delights as belong to the others, not virgins, in the kingdom of God itself—distinct from the portion of delights of all others, the delight of the virgins of Christ, from Christ, in Christ, with Christ, after Christ, through Christ, because of Christ.

The special delights of the virgins of Christ are not the same as those of non-virgins, although these be Christ's. There are other delights for the others, but such delights for no others. Enter into these. Follow the Lamb, because the flesh of the Lamb is also virginal. For He preserved in Himself in His manhood what He did not take away from His Mother in His conception and birth.

You deservedly follow Him wherever He goes because of your virginity of heart and of body. For, what is it to follow Him except to imitate Him? 'For Christ has suffered' for us, 'leaving' us 'an example,' as the Apostle Peter says, 'that' we 'may follow in His steps.'[4] Each one follows Him in that in which he imitates Him.

Not inasmuch as He is the only Son of God, through whom all things were made, but inasmuch as He is the Son of Man, because it was fitting, He exemplified in Himself the things to be imitated. Many things in Him are proposed to all for imitation, but virginity of the flesh is not proposed to all, for there is nothing they can do to become virgins whom it has befallen not to be virgins.

---
4 1 Peter 2.21.

Chapter 28

(28) Let the rest of the faithful, therefore, who have lost virginity of body, follow the Lamb, not wherever He goes, but wherever they are able. And they are able to follow Him everywhere, except when He walks in the splendor of virginity.

'Blessed are the poor in spirit.'[1] Imitate Him who, 'being rich, became poor for your sakes.'[2]

'Blessed are the meek.'[3] Imitate Him who said: 'Learn from me, for I am meek and humble of heart.'[4]

'Blessed are they who mourn.'[5] Imitate Him who wept over Jerusalem.[6]

'Blessed are they who hunger and thirst for justice.'[7] Imitate Him who said: 'My food is to do the will of Him who sent me.'[8]

'Blessed are the merciful.'[9] Imitate Him who succored the man wounded by robbers and lying in the road, half dead and in despair.[10]

'Blessed are the merciful.' Imitate Him who did no sin, neither was deceit found in His mouth.'[11]

'Blessed are the peacemakers.'[12] Imitate Him who pleaded for His persecutors: 'Father, forgive them, for they do not know what they are doing.'[13]

---

1 Matt. 5.3.
2 2 Cor. 8.9.
3 Matt. 5.4.
4 Matt. 11.29.
5 Matt. 5.5.
6 Luke 19.41.
7 Matt. 5.6.
8 John 4.34.
9 Matt. 5.7.
10 Luke 10.30-35.
11 1 Peter 2.22; cf. Isa. 53.9.
12 Matt. 5.9.
13 Luke 23.34.

'Blessed are they who suffer persecution for justice' sake.'[14] Imitate Him 'who suffered for you, leaving you an example, that you may follow in His steps.'[15]

Those who imitate these things follow the Lamb in them. But certainly, even married people can walk in these footsteps, although not placing their foot perfectly in the same imprint, nevertheless walking in the same paths.

Chapter 29

(29) But behold, the Lamb walks in the path of virginity. How shall they follow Him who have lost this path, which they do not accept in any way? Therefore, you, you His virgins, follow Him. Follow Him even there, since because of this one thing you do follow Him wherever He goes. We can exhort spouses to any other gift of sanctity in which they may follow Him except to this, which they have irreparably lost.

Follow Him, therefore, by steadfastly preserving what you have eagerly vowed. Take care while you can that you may not lose the blessing of virginity, which you can do nothing to regain.

The other multitude of the faithful, which was unable to follow the Lamb to this blessing, shall see you; it shall see you and shall not envy you; by rejoicing with you, it shall possess in you what it does not possess in thyself. It will not be able to sing that new canticle which will be yours alone; however, it will be able to hear, and to delight in your blessing so marvelous.

But you who shall both sing and listen (since you shall also hear what you sing rising from yourselves) shall rejoice more

---
14 Matt. 5.10.
15 1 Peter 2.21.

fully, and reign more joyfully. There will be no regret, however, concerning your great delight on the part of those who do not possess it. Indeed, the Lamb, whom you follow wherever He goes, will not desert those who are unable to follow Him where you are able. We are speaking of the omnipotent Lamb. He will both go before you and will not desert them, since God will be 'all in all.'[1] And those who shall possess less shall not turn away from you. For, where there is no envy, variety is harmonious.

Take courage, therefore: have confidence; be strengthened; persevere, you who vow, and who fulfill 'to the Lord your vows'[2] of perpetual continence, not for the sake of the present world, but for the sake of the kingdom of heaven.

Chapter 30

(30) You, also, who have not yet vowed this, accept it, you who can.[1] Run with perseverance, 'that you may obtain.'[2] 'Bring up your sacrifices,' each one of you, 'and come into the courts of the Lord,'[3] not through compulsion, since you are masters of your will. For, not in the same way as it is said: 'Thou shalt not commit adultery; thou shalt not kill,'[4] can it be said: 'Thou shalt not marry.' Those things are demanded; these are freely offered. If the latter are observed, they merit praise; unless the former are observed, they merit condemnation. In the former, the Lord lays an obligation on you; in the latter, whatever extra you have

---

1 1 Cor. 15.28.
2 Ps. 75.12.

1 Matt. 19.12.
2 Cf. 1 Cor. 9.24.
3 Ps 95.8.
4 Exod. 20.13,14.

expended in fulfilling them, He, on His return, will repay you.[5]

Consider the place of honor within His walls (whatever it is) much better than that of sons and daughters; consider there the eternal name.[6] Who will explain what kind of a name it will be? Nevertheless, whatever it will be, it will be eternal. In believing in, and hoping for, and loving this, you have been able, not to avoid a forbidden marriage, but to ascend above a lawful marriage.

Chapter 31

(31) Hence, in proportion as the gift, the embracing of which we have urged as forcefully as we were able, is more excellent and divine, so much the more does its sublimity urge us to say something with great care, not only about the exceeding glory of chastity, but also about its most excellent safeguard, humility.

Therefore, since the proponents of perpetual chastity, comparing themselves with spouses, according to the Scriptures, have found them to be inferior both in work and in merit, both in vow and in reward, there immediately comes to mind what was written: 'The greater thou art, the more humble thyself in all things, and thou shalt find grace before God.'[1] A standard of humility is given to each one from the very measure of his greatness, to which pride is a menace, since it lays more cunning snares for those of superior station.

Envy follows pride as her daughter and handmaid. Indeed, pride immediately begets her, and is never without this

---

5 Cf. Luke 10.35.
6 Isa. 56.5.

---

1 Eccli. 3.20.

offspring and companion. By these two vices, that is, pride and envy, the Devil is the Devil. Therefore, the whole Christian way of life wages war above all against pride, the mother of envy; for it inculcates humility, by which it acquires and preserves charity, concerning which, when it was said: 'Charity does not envy,'[2] as though we sought a reason whence it comes about that it does not envy, it was immediately added: 'It is not puffed up, as if to say: 'It is not envious for this reason, because it is not proud.'

Wherefore, Christ, the Teacher of humility, first emptied himself, taking the nature of a slave and being made like unto men. And appearing in the form of man, He humbled himself, becoming obedient to death, even to death on a cross.'[3]

But who can readily explain, and collect all the testimony to prove this point, how carefully His teaching itself instills humility, and how strongly it insists in commanding it? Let whoever desires to write expressly on humility attempt or accomplish this. But this treatise has a different scope. It is concerned with virginity, a thing so great that it must be especially warned against pride.

Chapter 32

(32) Therefore, I mention a few testimonies, which the Lord vouchsafes to call to my mind, from the teaching of Christ on humility, which will perhaps suffice for what I have undertaken.

The first lengthy discourse which He delivered to His disciples began thus: 'Blessed are the poor in spirit, for theirs

---
2 1 Cor. 13.4.
3 Phil. 2.7,8.

is the kingdom of heaven.'¹ And these we understand without any question to be the humble.

This is why He especially praised the faith of the centurion, and said that He had not found so great faith in Israel, because he believed so humbly that he said: 'I am not worthy that thou shouldst come under my roof.'² Wherefore, the only reason why Matthew says that He came to Jesus, while Luke very clearly indicates that he himself did not come, but sent his friends,³ is that, by a most trusting humility, he himself did come more than those whom he sent.

Therefore, this is also prophetic: 'The Lord is high, and looketh on the low; and the high he knoweth afar off,'⁴ undoubtedly as those who do not draw near.

Hence, He also said to the Canaanite woman: 'O woman, great is thy faith. Let it be done to thee as thou wilt.'⁵ He had already called her a dog, and had answered her that the bread of the children was not to be cast to her. She had humbly accepted the remark, saying: 'Yes, Lord; for even the dogs eat of the crumbs that fall from their masters' table.' Thus, what she did not receive through importunate pleading, she merited by a humble confession.

In the same way, the two men are portrayed praying in the temple, 'the one a pharisee, and the other a publican,' because of those who regard themselves as just, and despise others, and the confession of sins is preferred to the enumeration of merits.⁶

Now, the pharisee undoubtedly thanked God for those things in which he was very self-complacent. 'I thank thee,' he said, 'that I am not like the rest of men, robbers, dishonest,

---

1 Matt. 5.3.
2 Matt. 8.5-10.
3 Cf. Luke 7.6,7.
4 Ps. 137.6.
5 Matt. 15.28,27.
6 Luke 18.10,9,14.

adulterers, or even like this publican. I fast twice a week: I pay tithes of all that I possess. But the publican, standing afar off, would not so much as lift up his eyes to heaven, but kept striking his breast, saying: "O God, be merciful to me, the sinner!"' The divine judgment follows: 'Amen, I tell you, the publican went out of the temple justified rather than the pharisee.' Then the reason is shown why this is just: 'For he who exalts himself shall be humbled, and he who humbles himself shall be exalted.'[7]

It can happen, therefore, that someone avoid real sins, and be conscious of real virtues in himself, and give thanks for them to the Father of lights, from whom every good gift and every perfect gift comes,[8] yet be damned because of the vice of pride if in his superiority he despise the other sinners, especially those who confess their sins in prayer, or even only in thought, since this is evident to God. Such sinners, indeed, deserve not an arrogant upbraiding, but mercy untouched by despair.

Why was it that, when the Apostles were disputing among themselves which one of them would be greater, He placed a little child before their eyes, saying: 'Unless you become like this child, you will not enter into the kingdom of heaven'?[9] Did He not praise humility most highly, and place the merit of greatness in it?

Or when He answered the sons of Zebadee[10] in such a way, when they desired to occupy the seats of honor at His side, that they considered the drinking of the chalice of His passion, in which He 'humbled Himself even to death, even to death on a cross,'[11] rather than asked through proud ambition to be preferred to others, what lesson did He teach,

---

7 Luke 18.11-14.
8 James 1.17.
9 Cf. Matt. 18.3.
10 Matt. 20.21-23.
11 Phil. 2.8.

except that He would be the dispenser of honor to those who would follow Him beforehand as the Teacher of humility?

Moreover, when, as He was about to go forth to His passion, He washed the feet of His disciples[12] and gave them the clearest instruction to do for their fellow disciples what the Master and the Lord had done for them, how highly this recommended humility! He even chose that time to recommend this when they were watching Him with great eagerness, as He was very close to His death. They would surely hold fast in their memory the last lesson which the Master whom they were to imitate had shown them. Yet He performed at that time this action, which He could certainly have done several days before while He was going about in their company. And if it had been done then, He would, indeed, have taught the same thing, but they would by no means have received it in the same way.

Chapter 33

(33) Therefore, while humility ought to be observed by all Christians, since they are named Christians from Christ, whose Gospel no one studies carefully without finding in Him the Teacher of humility, yet it especially becomes those who by some great blessing excel over others to be followers and adherents of this virtue, so that they earnestly observe what I proposed in the first place: 'The greater thou art, the more humble thyself in all things, and thou shalt find grace before God.'[1]

Wherefore, because perpetual continence and, above all, virginity is a great blessing in the saints of God, it must be

---

12 John 13.1-15.

1 Eccli. 3.20.

guarded with the utmost vigilance, lest it be corrupted by pride.

(34) The Apostle mentions evil unmarried women who are gossipers and busybodies, and says that this vice springs from idleness. 'And further,' he says, 'being idle, they learn to go about from house to house, and are not only idle, but gossipers as well as busybodies, mentioning things they ought not.'[2]

He had previously said of these: 'But refuse younger widows, for when they have wantonly turned away from Christ, they wish to marry, and are to be condemned because they have broken their first troth,'[3] that is, they did not persevere in what they had first vowed.

Chapter 34

However, he does not say: 'They marry,' but: 'They wish to marry,' for it is not the love of their noble vow which prevents many of them from marrying, but fear of outright indecency; and this itself springs from pride by which the displeasure of men is more dreaded than that of God.

Those, therefore, who wish to marry, and do not marry because they cannot do it with impunity; those who would do better to marry than to be burnt[1] (that is, than to be consumed by concupiscence itself while concealing the fire of concupiscence); those who regret their profession, and are ashamed to confess their regret—unless they reform and control their heart, and once more shackle their lust with the fear of God, they will be counted with the dead; no matter whether they give themselves over to pleasure (whence the

---

2 1 Tim. 5.13.
3 1 Tim. 5.11,12.

---

1 Cf. 1 Cor. 7.9.

Apostle says: 'She who gives herself up to pleasures is dead while she is still alive'[2]), or whether they give themselves up to hardships and fasts, useless without conversion of heart, and serving rather for display than for correction.

I do not urge a great solicitude for humility on such persons, in whom their very pride is confounded and tortured by remorse of conscience. Nor do I impose this great solicitude for holy humility on drunkards or misers or those languishing from any other form of loathsome disease, since they keep up the profession of corporal continence and give the lie to their name by their sinful manner of life—unless, perhaps, they shall even dare to flaunt themselves in these crimes and are not content to have their punishment postponed.

Neither am I concerned with those in whom there is a certain inclination to attract admiration, either by a more elegant dress than the necessity of their kind of profession demands,[3] or by an unusual headdress, whether by protruding knots of hair, or by veils so thin that the little braids set underneath show through.[4] Admonitions are not yet to be given to these on humility, but on chastity itself, or on the perfection of modesty.

Give me someone professing perpetual continence, and free from these and all similar vices and blemishes of conduct. For her I fear pride; for her I dread the swelling of self-conceit from so great a blessing. The more there is in her

---

[2] 1 Tim. 5.6.
[3] By Augustine's time, consecrated virgins had adopted a distinctive dress; cf. *Contra Julianum* 5.6.24. There was no absolute uniformity, although he mentions a veil and cincture, but the garb was expected to be modest and unadorned. Cf. *Ep.* 211.10,12; 242.9.
[4] Christian women, even consecrated virgins, were apparently not immune to the allurement of the elaborate and worldly coiffures of the Roman ladies. Cf. *Ep.* 211.10; Tertullian, *De cultu feminarum* 2.6; Cyprian, *De habitu virginis* 16; *De lapsis* 6.30; Jerome, *Ep.* 107.5; also H. Leclercq, 'Chevelure,' *DACL* 3 col. 1307ff.

from which she finds self-complacence, the more I fear lest by pleasing herself she will displease Him who 'resists the proud, but gives grace to the humble.'[5]

Chapter 35

(35) Certainly, the principal teaching and example of virginal integrity is to be observed in Christ Himself. Therefore, what more shall I prescribe for the continent concerning humility than He did, who said to all: 'Learn from me, for I am meek and humble of heart'?[1] When He had proclaimed His greatness above, and, desiring to show this very thing: how great a being became how little for our sakes, He said: 'I praise thee, Lord of heaven and earth, that thou didst hide these things from the wise and prudent and didst reveal them to little ones. Yes, Father, for such was thy good pleasure. All things have been delivered to me by my Father; and no one knows the Son except the Father; nor does anyone know the Father except the Son and him to whom the Son chooses to reveal Him. Come to me, all you who labor and are burdened, and I will give you rest. Take my yoke upon you, and learn of me, for I am meek and humble of heart.'[2]

He to whom the Father has delivered all things, and whom no one knows except the Father, and who alone knows the Father, together with him to whom He chooses to reveal Him, does not say: 'Learn from Me to make the world, or to raise the dead,' but 'for I am meek and humble of heart.'

O salutary doctrine! O Master and Lord of mortal men to whom death was passed and shipped in the cup of pride!

---

5 James 4.6; cf. Prov. 29.23.

1 Matt. 11.29.
2 Matt. 11.25-29.

He would not teach what He Himself was not; He would not command what He Himself did not practice. I see you, good Jesus, with the eyes of faith which Thou hast opened for me, as though in the assembly of the human race, crying out and saying: 'Come to me, and learn from me.' What, I beg of Thee, through whom all things were made, Son of God, and who wast Thyself made among all things, Son of Man, what do we come to learn from Thee? 'For I am meek,' He says, 'and humble of heart.'

Is 'all the treasures of wisdom and knowledge hidden in Thee'[3] reduced to this, that we learn from Thee as something great that Thou art meek and humble of heart? Is it so great a thing to be humble that, unless it were learned from Thee who art so great, it could not be learned at all? So it is, indeed! For in no other way is rest found for the soul, except by curing the infectious tumor by which it was great in its own eyes when it was diseased in Thine eyes.

Chapter 36

(36) Let those who seek Thy mercy and truth hear Thee, and let them come to Thee, and let them learn from Thee to be meek and humble, by living for Thee; for Thee, and not for themselves. Let him who labors and is burdened hear this, who is weighed down under such a load that he dare not lift his eyes to heaven, the sinner, who strikes his breast and draws near from afar.[1] Let the centurion hear, who is unworthy that Thou shouldest enter under his roof.[2] Let Zachaeus, the chief of the publicans, hear, who restores four-

---
3 Col. 2.3.

---
1 Cf. Luke 18.13.
2 Cf. Matt. 8.8.

fold the gain of his detestable sins.³ Let the woman, the town's sinner, hear, who is so much the more contrite at Thy feet as she had been further away from Thy footsteps.⁴ Let the harlots and publicans hear, who enter the kingdom of heaven before the scribes and pharisees.⁵ Let every sort of diseased person hear, with whom Thou didst dine and wast charged with a crime, as if, indeed, by the healthy who had no need of the physician, since Thou didst not come to call the just, but sinners to repentance.⁶

All these, when they turn to Thee, easily become meek and humble, mindful of their own most wicked life and of Thy most tender mercy, for 'where the offense has abounded, grace has abounded yet more.'⁷

(37) But turn Thy gaze upon the companies of virgins, of holy youths and maidens. This generation has been brought up in Thy Church. There it was nurtured for Thee at its mother's breasts. With its first speech it invoked Thy name. It drank in Thy name, instilled into it like the milk of its childhood. No one out of this company is able to say: 'I formerly was a blasphemer, a persecutor, and a bitter adversary; but I obtained mercy because I acted ignorantly, in unbelief.'⁸ They have, indeed, even embraced and vowed what Thou hast not commanded, but hast only recommended to be embraced by those who will, when Thou didst say: 'Let him accept it who can.' And not because Thou hast threatened, but because Thou hast exhorted, they 'have made themselves eunuchs for the kingdom of heaven's sake.'⁹

---
3 Cf. Luke 19.2-8.
4 Luke 7.37,38.
5 Cf. Matt. 21.31.
6 Matt. 9.11-13.
7 Rom. 5.20.
8 1 Tim. 1.13.
9 Matt. 19.12.

Chapter 37

Cry out to these, and let them hear Thee, that Thou art meek and humble of heart. Let these, in proportion as they are great, so humble themselves in all things that they may find grace with Thee. They are just, but do they, like Thee, make the sinner just?[1] They are chaste, but their mothers nurtured them in sins in their womb.[2] They are holy, but Thou art even the Holy of Holies. They are virgins, but they were not also born of virgins. They are inviolate both in spirit and in flesh, but they are not 'the Word made flesh.'[3]

Yet, let them learn, not from those whose sins Thou forgivest, but from Thee Thyself, the Lamb of God who takest away the sins of the world,[4] 'for thou art meek and humble of heart.'[5]

(38) I do not send you, O holy and chaste soul, who have not yielded to carnal instinct even to the extent of lawful marriage, who have not indulged your mortal flesh even for the propagation of a descendant, who have constrained your weak earthly members to a heavenly way of life, I do not send you to the publicans and sinners that you may learn humility—although they enter the kingdom of heaven before the proud. I do not send you to these, for these, who have been freed from the abyss of uncleanness, are not worthy that unspotted virginity be sent to imitate them.

I send you to the King of heaven, to Him through whom men were created, and who was created in the midst of men for the sake of men; to Him who is 'beautiful above the sons of men,'[6] and despised by the sons of men for the sake of

---

1 Cf. Prov. 17.15.
2 Cf. Ps. 50.7.
3 John 1.14.
4 John 1.29.
5 Matt. 11.29.
6 Ps. 44.3.

the sons of men; to Him who, although ruling over the immortal angels, did not disdain to serve mortal men.

Not iniquity, certainly, but charity made Him humble, charity which is not puffed up, is not ambitious, is not self-seeking';[7] for Christ did not please Himself, but, as it is written concerning Him: 'The reproaches of those who reproach thee have fallen upon me.'[8]

Hasten! Come to Him, and learn, for He is meek and humble of heart. You shall not go to him who, through the weight of his sinfulness, did not dare to raise his eyes to heaven, but to Him who, through the weight of charity, came down from heaven. You shall not go to her who washed the feet of her Lord with tears, seeking the forgiveness of grievous sins, but you shall go to Him who, although He granted pardon of all sins, washed the feet of His servants.

I know the dignity of your virginity. I do not propose for your imitation the publican humbly confessing his sins, but, in your behalf, I fear the pharisee proudly boasting of his merits. I do not say: 'Be like her of whom it was said: "Many sins are forgiven her because she has loved much," '[9] but I fear lest, since you think that little is forgiven you, you will love little.

Chapter 38

(39) I greatly fear for you, I say, lest, while you glory that you will follow the Lamb wherever He goes, you will not be able to follow Him through the narrow ways, because of swollen pride.

It is your blessing, O virginal soul, that, just as you are a virgin, thus preserving perfectly in your heart what you

---
7 1 Cor. 13.4,5.
8 Rom. 15.3; cf. Ps. 68.10.
9 Luke 7.47.

are by rebirth, while preserving in your flesh what you are by birth, you conceive of the fear of the Lord and bring forth the spirit of salvation.[1]

Truly, 'there is no fear in love; but perfect love,' as it is written, 'casts out fear';[2] the fear of men, however, not of God; the fear of temporal evils, not of the final divine judgment.

'Be not high minded, but fear.'[3] Love the goodness of God; fear His severity. They both forbid you to be proud. For, in loving, you fear lest you seriously offend your loved one and your lover. And what would be a greater offense than that you displease by pride Him who for you displeased the proud? And where ought that 'holy fear which endures for ever and ever'[4] be greater than in you who are not concerned with the things of the world, how you may please a husband, but with the things of the Lord, how you may please the Lord?[5]

That other fear is not found in love, but this chaste fear never departs from love. If you do not love, fear lest you perish; if you do love, fear lest you displease. Love casts out that one fear; it runs, bearing this other fear within itself.

The Apostle Paul also says: 'Now we have not received a spirit of bondage so as to be again in fear, but we have received a spirit of adoption as sons, by virtue of which we cry: Abba! Father!'[6] I believe he is speaking of the fear which was inspired in the Old Testament, lest the temporal be lost which God had promised to those who were not yet His sons under grace, but still servants under the Law. It is also the fear of eternal fire, and to serve God in order to

---
1 Cf. Isa. 26.18.
2 1 John 4.18.
3 Rom. 11.20.
4 Ps. 18.10.
5 Cf. 1 Cor. 7.32.
6 Rom. 8.15.

avoid this is not yet by any means the work of perfect charity. The desire of reward is one thing; the fear of punishment is another.

The words, 'Whither shall I go from thy spirit? Or whither shall I flee from thy face,'[7] are one thing, but these words are a different matter: 'One thing I have asked of the Lord, this will I seek after, that I may dwell in the house of the Lord all the days of my life, that I may see the delight of the Lord, and may visit[8] his temple,'[9] and 'Turn not away thy face from me,'[10] and, on the other hand, 'My soul longeth and fainteth for the courts of the Lord.'[11]

He will speak the former words who did not dare to raise his eyes to heaven,[12] and she who washed the feet with tears to obtain the pardon of grave sins;[13] but speak the latter, you who are concerned about the things of the Lord, that you may be holy both in body and in spirit.[14]

A tormenting fear accompanies the former words, and perfect love casts it out; a holy fear of the Lord accompanies the latter words, and it remains for ever and ever. And both classes must be told: 'Be not high minded, but fear,'[15] so that man will exalt himself neither by the defense of his sins, nor by the presumption of righteousness.

The same Paul who said: 'Now you have not received a spirit of bondage so as to be again in fear,'[16] says, since fear is the companion of charity: 'I was with you in fear

---

7 Ps. 138.1.
8 The Vulgate *visitem* ('visit') has been used here in preference to *protegar*, ('I may be protected'), which is found in St. Augustine's text.
9 Ps. 26.4.
10 Ps. 26.9.
11 Ps. 83.3.
12 Cf. Luke 18.13.
13 Cf. Luke 7.37,38.
14 1 Cor. 7.34.
15 Rom. 11.20.
16 Rom. 8.15.

and in much trembling.'¹⁷ And he employs that pronouncement which I have cited:¹⁸ that the ingrafted wild olive is not to lord it over the broken olive branches, when he says: 'Be not high minded, but fear.'¹⁹

Admonishing all the members of Christ in general, he says: 'Work out your salvation with fear and trembling. For it is God who of His good pleasure works in you both the will and the performance,'²⁰ lest what was written: 'Serve ye the Lord with fear, and rejoice unto him with trembling,'²¹ might seem to be confined to the Old Testament.

Chapter 39

(40) And what members of the holy body which is the Church ought to have greater care that the Holy Spirit rest upon her than those who profess virginal holiness? But how does He rest where He does not find His dwelling place? What else is His dwelling place but a humble heart which He fills, not one from which He recoils; a heart which He lifts up, not one which He crushes? It is most clearly said: 'But upon whom shall my Spirit rest? Upon him who is humble and peaceful, and who trembleth at my words.'¹

You already live justly; you already live piously; you live modestly, holily, in virginal chastity. Nevertheless, do you still dwell here and are not made humble by hearing: 'Is not the life of man upon earth a trial?'² Does not this restrain you from presumptuous pride: 'Woe to the world

---

17 1 Cor. 2.3.
18 Cf. above, Ch. 1.
19 Rom. 11.20.
20 Phil. 2.12,13.
21 Ps. 2.11.

---

1 Cf. Isa. 66.2.
2 Job 7.1; the Vulgate differs slightly.

because of scandals'?³ Do you not tremble lest you be numbered among the many whose 'charity' grows 'cold because iniquity abounds'?⁴ Do you not strike your breast when you hear: 'Therefore let him who thinks he stands take heed lest he fall'?⁵ In the midst of these divine warnings and human perils, do we still labor thus to persuade holy virgins to humility?

Chapter 40

(41) Or, indeed, is it to be thought that God permits that many men and women who will fall away be included in the ranks of your profession for anything else than that by their fall your fear may be increased and by it pride may be crushed?

God so hates pride that against it alone the Almighty humbled Himself so much. Unless, perhaps, you will on this account so fear less and be more puffed up that you will love Him less who loved you so much that He gave Himself up for you,¹ because He forgave you less; that is, since you have from childhood lived religiously, modestly, in holy chastity and inviolate virginity. As though you ought not in truth love Him all the more ardently who forgave all things whatsoever to the profligates who turned to Him, but who did not allow you to fall into them! Or was the pharisee who loved little on this account, that he judged that little was forgiven him,² blinded by this error because of anything else than because, 'ignorant of the justice of God' and seeking

3 Matt. 18.7.
4 Matt. 24.12.
5 1 Cor. 10.12.

1 Gal. 2.20.
2 Luke 7.36-47.

'to establish his own,' he was 'not submitted to the justice of God'?³

But you, also, a chosen people, and preferred even among the elect, choirs of virgins who follow the Lamb, 'by grace you have been saved through faith; and that not from yourselves, for it is the gift of God; not as the outcome of works, lest anyone may boast. For his workmanship we are, created in Christ Jesus in good works, which God has made ready beforehand that we may walk in them.'⁴

Will you, then, the more richly you are adorned with His gifts, love Him so much less? May He avert so detestable a folly! Therefore, since the Truth has said truly that he to whom less is forgiven loves less, do you, that you may love Him more ardently, out of love for whom you live free from the bonds of matrimony, account as entirely pardoned to you whatever evil you have, through His power, not committed.

Your 'eyes are ever towards the Lord, for he shall pluck' your 'feet out of the snare,'⁵ and, 'unless the Lord keep the city, he watcheth in vain that keepeth it.'⁶ And, speaking of continence itself, the Apostle says: 'For I would that all men were as myself; but each one has his own gift from God, one in this way, and another in that.'⁷ Who, then, bestows these things? Who 'distributes to everyone according as he wills'?⁸ God, certainly, with whom there is no iniquity.⁹ And for this reason, with what justice He makes some in this way and others in that, it is either impossible or exceedingly difficult for men to understand, but to doubt that He does it in justice is wicked. Therefore, 'what hast thou that thou

---
3 Rom. 10.3.
4 Eph. 2.8-10.
5 Ps. 24.15.
6 Ps. 126.1.
7 1 Cor. 7.7.
8 1 Cor. 12.11.
9 Cf. Rom. 9.14.

hast not received?'¹⁰ And by what perversity do you love less Him from whom you have received more?

Chapter 41

(42) Wherefore, let the first thought of the virgin of God be to be filled with humility, lest she think that it comes to her from herself that she is such, and not think rather that this best gift comes from above, from the Father of lights, with whom there is no change nor shadow of alteration.'¹ Thus, she will not think that little is forgiven her, and so love little, and, 'ignorant of the justice of God, and seeking to establish'² her own, be unsubmissive to the justice of God.

In this vice was Simon ensnared, and the woman to whom many sins were forgiven because she loved much, surpassed him.³ But she will more safely and more truly consider that all the sins which God has preserved her from committing ought to be reckoned as though they are forgiven.

The words of pious supplications in the holy Scriptures are witnesses. Through them it is shown that the very things which are commanded by God are not carried out except by the gift and the help of Him who commands. They are insincerely requested if we were able to do them without the help of His grace.

What is so generally or so forcefully commanded as obedience, by which the commandments of God are observed? Yet we find that it is the object of petition. 'Thou hast commanded thy commandments to be kept most diligently.' Then

---

10 1 Cor. 4.7.

1 James 1.17.
2 Cf. Rom. 10.3.
3 Cf. Luke 7.36-47.

follows: 'O! that my ways may be directed to keep thy justifications. Then shall I not be confounded, when I shall look into all thy commandments.'[4] He begged that this thing be fulfilled by him, which he stated God had commanded.

This is done, clearly, that sin may not be committed. But if sin has been committed, it is commanded that it be expiated, lest he who committed it perish by pride in the defense and justification of his sin, while he is unwilling that what he has committed perish by his repentance. Even this is requested from God, that it may be understood that it is not accomplished except by His help from whom it is begged.

'Set a watch, O Lord,' he says, 'before my mouth, and a restraining door round about my lips. Incline not my heart to evil words, to make excuses in sins, with men that work iniquity.'[5] If, therefore, even the obedience by which we observe the commandments, and repentance, by which we do not excuse but accuse our sins, is requested and prayed for, it is evident that, when it is carried out, it is had by His gift, it is accomplished by His help.

It is even more clearly said because of obedience: 'By the Lord are the steps of a man directed, and he shall like well his way.'[6] And concerning penance the Apostle says: 'In case God should give them repentance.'[7]

(43) Further, concerning continence itself, was it not most clearly said: 'And as I knew that no one can be continent, except God give it, and this itself as a point of wisdom, to know whose gift it was'?[8]

---

4 Ps. 118.4-6.
5 Ps. 140.3,4.
6 Ps. 36.23.
7 2 Tim. 2.25.
8 Wisd. 8.21.

Chapter 42

Perhaps continence is a gift of God, but man acquires for himself the wisdom by which he acknowledges that gift to be not his own, but God's. In truth, 'God maketh the blind wise,'[1] and 'The testimony of the Lord is faithful; he gives wisdom to little ones,'[2] ad 'if anyone is wanting in wisdom, let him ask it of God, who gives abundantly to all men and does not reproach; and it will be given to him.'[3]

It behooves virgins to be wise, lest their lamps be extinguished.[4] How will they be wise except by 'not setting their mind on high things, but condescending to the lowly'?[5] Wisdom itself has said to man: 'Behold the fear of the Lord is wisdom.'[6]

If, therefore, you have nothing that you have not received, 'Be not high minded, but fear.'[7] And do not love little, as though little is pardoned you by Him; rather, love Him much, by whom much has been given to you. For, if he loves to whom pardon was granted from paying his debt, how much more ought she to love to whom it was granted that she might have possessions!

For, whoever remains chaste from the beginning is ruled by Him, and whoever is made chaste from impurity is corrected by Him, and whoever is unchaste to the very end is abandoned by Him. He can accomplish this, indeed, by a mysterious judgment; He cannot accomplish it by an unjust judgment. And perhaps it is mysterious, that fear may be increased and pride diminished.

---

1 Ps. 145.8.
2 Ps. 18.8.
3 James 1.5.
4 Cf. Matt. 25.4.
5 Rom. 12.16.
6 Job 28.28.
7 Rom. 11.20.

Chapter 43

(44) Next, knowing now that he is what he is by the grace of God, let man not fall into another snare of pride, so that, by exalting himself because of the grace of God itself, he despises others. By this vice that other man, the pharisee,[1] gave thanks to God for the good things which he had, yet exalted himself above the publican who confessed his sins.

What, then, shall a virgin do? What shall she keep in mind that she may not exalt herself over those men or women who lack so great a gift as this? She must feign humility, but must actually practice it, because the pretense of humility is greater pride. Thus, the Scripture, wishing to show that humility must be genuine, when it had said: 'The greater thou art, the more humble thyself in all things,' immediately added: 'and thou shalt find grace before God,'[2] before whom it is altogether impossible to feign self-abasement.

Chapter 44

(45) What shall we say, then? Is there something which the virgin of God will consider truthfully from which she will not presume to prefer herself to the faithful woman, not only the widow, but even the spouse? I am not speaking of a faithless virgin. For, who does not know that an obedient wife is to be preferred to a disobedient virgin? But when both are obedient to the commandments of God, will she be so afraid to prefer holy virginity even to chaste nuptials, and continence to marriage, and for the hundredfold fruit

---
1 Luke 18.10-14.
2 Eccli. 3.20.

to precede the thirtyfold?[1] No. Let her not hesitate in the least to place this state above the other. Nevertheless, let not this or that obedient and God-fearing virgin presume to set herself above this or that obedient and God-fearing wife. Otherwise, she will not be humble, and 'God resists the proud.'[2]

What, then, will she consider?—The hidden gifts of God, of course; and only the proof of trial reveals these to each one, even within herself. For, not to mention other things, how does the virgin know, although she be 'concerned with the things of the Lord, how she may please the Lord,'[3] whether, perhaps, because of some weakness of soul unknown to her, she is not yet ready for martyrdom, whereas that woman to whom she seeks to prefer herself is already able to drink the cup of the Lord's humiliation, which He presented to be consumed first to the disciples who desired honors?[4] How does she know, I ask, whether, perhaps, while she is not yet Thecla,[5] the other is already Crispina?[6]

Chapter 45

(46) Certainly, unless it be tried, there is no proof of this gift.

---

1 Cf. Matt. 13.23.
2 James 4.6; Prov. 29.23
3 1 Cor. 7.32.
4 Cf. Matt. 20.22.
5 A virgin martyr, greatly venerated in the early Church, heroine of the apocryphal Acts of Paul and Thecla. She is said to have been born of noble parents at Iconium, to have been a disciple of St. Paul, to have spurned marriage for the sake of perpetual virginity, and to have been subjected to a series of tortures during the reign of Nero, from which she escaped miraculously. The account in the Roman Breviary states that she lived to be ninety and was buried at Seleucia.
6 A noble woman of Thagara, martyred at Thebeste on December 5, 304, under Anulinus, proconsul of Africa, during the persecutions of Diocletian. Augustine comments on her courage in *Enarr. in ps.* 120.13 and 137.3. As Thecla was the model of virgin martyrs, Crispina was the pride of Christian matrons.

And this gift is so great that some take it to be the hundredfold fruit. Ecclesiastical authority offers most excellent testimony, by which it is known to the faithful in what place the martyrs and in what place the departed nuns are commemorated at the Sacrifice of the Altar.[1]

Let those who understand these things better than we do investigate what the distinction of fruitfulness signifies, whether the virginal life is found in the hundredfold fruit, widowhood in the sixtyfold, and conjugal life in the thirtyfold;[2] or whether the hundredfold fruitfulness is rather attributed to martyrdom, the sixtyfold to continence, and the thirtyfold to marriage;[3] or whether virginity, together with martyrdom, constitutes the hundredfold fruit, virginity alone is discovered in the sixtyfold, but spouses, who bear the thirtyfold, advance to the sixtyfold if they become martyrs; or whether (and this seems more probable to me), since the gifts of divine grace are manifold, and one is greater and better than another (whence the Apostle says: 'Strive for the greater gifts'[4]) it must be understood that they are too numerous to be divided into three categories.

In the first place, we must neither reckon the continence of widowhood without any fruit, nor reduce it to the rank of conjugal chastity, nor make it equal to the glory of virgins; nor must we think that the crown of martyrdom, whether it is placed in the disposition of soul, even though the test of suffering be lacking, or in the experience of suffering

---

[1] The practice of commemorating the names of the living and dead—civil officials and clerics, martyrs and confessors, the faithful departed—was well established long before Augustine's time. Names were sometimes inscribed on ornate tables of wood, metal, or ivory, called diptychs; where the list was long, a book was used. Cf. *Conf.* 9.13.37; *Sermo* 273.7.; Cyprian, *Epistolae* 1.9; also, F. Cabrol, 'Dyptiques,' *DACL* 4 cols. 1045-1094.
[2] Matt. 13.8,23. Cf. Jerome, *Comment. in ev. Matt.* 2.13.23; *Contra Jovin.* 1.3.
[3] Cf. *Quaest. in ev. sec. Matt.* 1.9; Cyprian, *De habitu virg.* 21.
[4] 1 Cor. 12.31.

itself, is added to each of these three grades of chastity without any increase of fruitfulness.

Moreover, where do we place this, that many men and women preserve virginal continence, in such a manner, however, that they do not carry out what the Lord says: 'If thou wilt be perfect, go, sell all that thou hast, and give to the poor, and thou shalt have treasure in heaven; and come, follow me';[5] nor do they venture to join the company of those among whom no one calls anything his own, but who have all things in common?[6] Do we judge that no fruitfulness is added to the virgins of God when they do this, or that virgins of God are without fruit even though they do not do it?

Chapter 46

So, there are many gifts, some more glorious and more exalted than others; to each is given that which is proper to him. Sometimes one is fruitful through fewer but more perfect gifts, another through inferior but more numerous ones. And what man will dare to decide in what way they are equal to one another, or different from one another, in receiving eternal honors; while it is clear both that these different gifts are many and that the better ones are advantageous, not for the present time, but for eternity?

But I think that the Lord wished to designate three categories of fruitfulness, and that He left the rest to those who understand. Another Evangelist[1] mentions only the hundredfold. Is he therefore to be judged either to have disapproved of, or to have been ignorant of, the other two, and not to have left them to be understood?

---

5 Matt. 19.21.
6 Cf. Acts 2.44; 4.32.

---

1 Cf. Luke 8.8.

(47) But, as I began to say, whether the hundredfold fruit be virginity consecrated to God, or whether the distinction of fruitfulness is to be understood in some other way (either one which we have mentioned, or one which we have not mentioned), in any case, no one, in my opinion, could have dared to prefer virginity to martyrdom, and no one could have doubted that this gift is hidden if the test of suffering is lacking.

Chapter 47

Thus, the virgin has something which she will consider, which will help her to preserve humility, that she may not violate that charity which surpasses all gifts, without which, whatever other things she has—whether few or many, whether great or small—are nothing at all.

She has, I say, something which she will consider, so that she will not be puffed up, will not envy; namely, that the blessing of virginity professes to be much greater and better than the conjugal blessing, so that it does not know whether this or that married woman is already able to suffer for Christ, while itself is not yet able, and whether it is being spared in this, that its weakness is not tested by suffering. 'God is faithful,' says the Apostle,[1] 'and will not permit you to be tempted beyond your strength, but with the temptation, will also give you a way out that you may be able to bear it.'

Perhaps, therefore, some or other adherents of the state of conjugal life, praiseworthy in its own class, are already able to fight, even by disembowelment and the shedding of their blood, against the enemy who urges them to iniquity, while some or other of those men and women who have been continent from childhood, 'and who make themselves eunuchs

---
1 1 Cor. 10.13.

for the kingdom of heaven's sake,'² are, nevertheless, still unable to undergo such things, either for justice, or even for chastity itself.

It is one thing, for the sake of truth and the holy vow, not to give in to him when he entices and cajoles; it is something else not to yield to him when he tortures and buffets. These things lie hidden in the faculties and powers of the soul; they are called forth by temptation; they are revealed by test.

Therefore, that no one may be puffed up over that which he sees he is able to do, let him humbly consider that he is unaware that he may not be able to do something more noble, but that others, who neither possess nor profess that for which he glorifies himself, can do this which he cannot do. Thus, he will be preserved, not by false, but by true humility, 'anticipating one another with honor,'³ and 'each one regarding the other as his superior.'⁴

Chapter 48

(48) Now, what shall I say concerning caution itself and vigilance against falling into sin? 'Who will boast that he has a chaste heart? Or who will boast that he is pure from sin?'¹ Holy virginity is, indeed, intact from its mother's womb. But 'no one,' it is said, 'is clean in thy sight, not even the child whose life is one day upon the earth.'²

In the inviolate faith there is also preserved a kind of

---

2 Matt. 19.12.
3 Rom. 12.10.
4 Phil. 2.3.

---

1 Prov. 20.9; the Vulgate reading is slightly different.
2 Job 25.4; the wording of the Vulgate is quite different.

virginal chastity, by which the Church is joined as a chaste virgin to one Spouse.³ But that one Spouse taught not only the faithful virgins in body and soul, but each and every Christian, to pray, from the spiritual even to the carnal, from the Apostles even to the lowliest penitents, as though 'from end to end of the heavens,'⁴ and He admonishes them to say in the prayer itself: 'Forgive us our debts as we also forgive our debtors,'⁵ wherein, through that which we ask, He teaches us to be mindful of what we are.

It is not for those debts of our whole past life, which we trust were forgiven us in baptism through His peace, that He commands us to pray and to say: 'Forgive us our debts as we also forgive our debtors.' Otherwise, the catechumens ought rather to say this prayer up to the time of baptism. But, since those who have been baptized—prelates and people, pastors and flocks—say it, it is sufficiently demonstrated that in this life, the whole of which is a trial, no one ought to glorify himself as though free from all sins.

Chapter 49

(49) Wherefore, the irreproachable virgins of God also follow the Lamb wherever He goes, both by perfect purification from sins and by the preservation of virginity, which, once lost, does not return. Since this very same Apocalypse, wherein like were revealed to like,¹ also praises them for this, that no lie is found in their mouth, let them remember to be truthful in this, too, that they are without sin.

---
3 Cf. 2 Cor. 11.2.
4 Matt. 24.31.
5 Matt. 6.12.

---
1 Apoc. 14.4,5. The glorious virgins were revealed to the Virgin Disciple.

In fact, the same John who witnessed that said this: 'If we say that we have no sin, we deceive ourselves, and the truth is not in us. But if we acknowledge our sins, he is faithful and just to forgive us our sins and to cleanse us from all iniquity. But if we say that we have not sinned, we make him a liar, and his word will not be in us.'[2] This is said, surely, not to some or to others, but to all Christians, among whom virgins must also recognize themselves. Thus they will be free from untruth, such as they appeared in the Apocalypse, and in this way, as long as their perfection is not yet attained in the heights of heaven, their confession renders them irreproachable to humility.

(50) Again, lest by reason of this pronouncement anyone sin through fatal rashness and allow himself to be seduced, as though sins are to be quickly washed away by a prompt confession, he immediately added: 'My dear little children, these things I have written to you in order that you may not sin. But if anyone sins, we have an advocate with the Father, Jesus Christ, the just; and he is the propitiator of our sins.'[3] Let no one, therefore, fall away as though he will quickly return from sin, nor bind himself by a kind of pact with iniquity, of this nature, that it pleases him to confess it rather than to avoid it.

Chapter 50

Since, even in those who are careful and who watch lest they sin, sins do arise in some way because of human frailty— however small, however few, yet sins—these very same sins become great and grievous if pride shall add growth and weight to them. But, if they are enveloped by holy humility,

---
2 1 John 1.8-10.
3 1 John 2.1,2.

they are cleansed with perfect felicity by the Priest whom we have in heaven.[1]

(51) I do not argue with those who affirm that man can live in this life without any sin; I do not argue; I do not contradict them. Perhaps we measure the great by our own misery, and, comparing ourselves with ourselves,[2] we do not understand. One thing I know: These great ones, such as we are not, such as we have not yet encountered, the greater they are, let them humble themselves so much the more in all things, that they may find grace before God.[3] For, no matter how great they may be, 'no servant is greater than his Lord, nor is the disciple greater than his master.'[4] And He is by all means the Master who says: 'All things have been delivered to me by my Father'; He is likewise the Master who says: 'Come to me all you who labor . . . and learn from me.' Yet, what do we learn? 'For I am meek,' He says, 'and humble of heart.'[5]

Chapter 51

(52) At this point someone will say: 'But this is not to write on virginity, but on humility.' As if, indeed, we had undertaken the praise of any kind of virginity whatsoever, and not of that which is according to God. The greater I see this blessing to be, the more do I fear pride in it, lest it perish in the hereafter.[1]

---

1 Cf. Heb. 4.4-16.
2 2 Cor. 10.12.
3 Eccli. 3.20.
4 John 13.16; the Vulgate reading differs slightly.
5 Matt. 11.27-29.

---

1 *In futurum.* Some Mss. read *furem* ('the thief'). The meaning is the same; St. Augustine fears that through pride the virgin will be robbed of her merits for heaven.

No one, therefore, protects the virginal blessing except God Himself, who bestowed it, and 'God is love.'[2] Therefore, the protector of virginity is love, but the dwelling place of this protector is humility. He indeed dwells there who said that His Spirit rests upon him who is humble and peaceful and who trembles at His words.[3]

Wherefore, what have I done that is out of order, if, desiring the blessing which I have praised to be more safely guarded, I have also taken care to prepare a place for its protector? I say confidently (and I have no fear that those whom I earnestly admonish to fear with me will be angry with me): Humble spouses follow the Lamb, although not wherever He goes, certainly as far as they are able, more easily than proud virgins. How does she follow Him whom she does not wish to approach? And how does she approach Him to whom she does not come to learn that He is 'meek and humble of heart'?[4]

The Lamb, therefore, leads those who follow Him wherever He goes, those among whom He has already found a place where He may lay His head. For, a certain proud and deceitful fellow also said this to Him: 'Master, I will follow thee wherever thou goest.' And He answered him: 'The foxes have dens, and the birds of the air nests; but the Son of Man has nowhere to lay his head.'[5] He condemned cunning deceitfulness by the title of foxes, and puffed-up pride by the title of birds of the air, in this man, in whom He did not find the loving humility whereon He might lay His head. For this reason, he who had promised that he would follow the Lord, not up to a certain point, but wherever He would go, never followed Him at all.

---

2 1 John 4.8.
3 Cf. Isa. 66.2.
4 Matt. 11.29.
5 Matt. 8.19,20.

Chapter 52

(53) Wherefore, do this, O virgins of God, do this! Follow the Lamb wherever He goes. But first, come to Him whom you will follow, and learn that He is 'meek and humble of heart.'[1] Come humbly to the humble One, if you love, and do not depart from Him, lest you fall away. For, whoever fears to depart from Him pleads, and says: 'Let not the foot of pride come to me!'[2] Advance on the road to sublimity by the footstep of humility. He Himself exalts those who follow Him humbly, who was not ashamed to descend to the fallen.

Entrust His gifts to Him to be preserved; keep your strength for Him.[3] Whatever evil thing you do not commit through His protection consider as remitted by Him, lest, by judging that little has been forgiven you, you may love little, and may, by a ruinous pride, despise the publicans striking their breasts.

Beware of those powers of yours which have been tested, lest, because you are able to bear something, you be puffed up; but pray regarding those powers which have not been tested, lest you be tempted beyond what you are able to bear. Esteem as superior to you in what is hidden some of those whom you excel in what is evident. When you kindly believe the blessings of others, perhaps unknown to you, your own blessings, which are known to you, are not lessened by the comparison, but are strengthened by love. And those which are perhaps yet wanting are so much the more readily bestowed as they are so much more humbly desired.

Let those who persevere in your company be an example to you, but let those who fall by the wayside increase your

---
1 Matt. 11.29.
2 Ps. 35.12.
3 Ps. 58.10.

fear. Love that perseverance, so that you will imitate it; weep for this defection, lest you be puffed up. Do not desire to proclaim your own righteousness; submit yourself to God who vindicates you. Pardon the sins of others; pray for your own. Avoid future falls by vigilance; repair those of the past by confession.

Chapter 53

(54) Behold, you are already such that you conform in the rest of your conduct to the virginity you have professed and preserved. Behold, you already not only abstain from murder, sacrifices to devils and abominations, theft, robbery, cheating, lying, drunken reveling, all extravagance and avarice, deceit, envy, irreverence, cruelty, but even those things which either are or are considered less grave are not found and do not arise in your midst: neither immodest mein, nor wandering eyes, nor unbridled tongue, nor coquettish smile, nor indecent jest, nor unbecoming dress, nor haughty or undignified carriage.

Even now you do 'not render evil for evil, nor abuse for abuse.'[1] Finally, even now you fulfill that measure of love, that you lay down your life for your brethren.[2]

Behold, you are already such, because you truly ought to be such. These things, combined with virginity, display an angelic life before men, and a heavenly manner of deportment before the world. The greater you are, whoever are so great, 'the more humble yourselves in all things, that you may find grace before God,'[3] lest He resist you as proud,[4] lest He humble you who exalt yourselves,[5] lest He not lead you who

---
1 1 Peter 3.9.
2 1 John 3.16; cf. John 15.13.
3 Eccli. 3.20.
4 James 4.6; 1 Peter 5.5.
5 Luke 18.14.

are puffed up through the narrow places—although there is no reason for anxiety that, where charity is on fire, humility will be wanting.

Chapter 54

(55) If, therefore, you have despised the nuptials of the sons of men, out of which you would beget sons of men, love Him with all your heart who is 'beautiful above the sons of men.'[1] You have the opportunity; your heart is free from bonds of marriage. Contemplate the beauty of your Lover; consider Him, equal to His Father, subject also to His Mother; ruling even over the heavens, and serving upon earth, making all things to exist, and being made to exist in the midst of all things.[2]

That very thing which the proud deride in Him, see how beautiful it is. By your interior illumination contemplate the wounds of the Crucified, the scars of the risen One, the blood of the dying One, the ransom of the believer, the price paid by the Redeemer.

Chapter 55

Consider how much these things are worth. Weigh them in the scale of charity, and whatever love you were holding in reserve to be devoted to your marriage repay it to Him.

(56) Surely, since He desires your interior beauty, wherein He gave you power to become children of God,[1] He does not seek bodily beauty from you, but beauty of conduct,

---

1 Ps. 44.3.
2 Cf. above, Ch. 37.

1 John 1.12.

by which you even subdue the flesh. He is not the kind to whom someone may lie about you and cause Him to fly into a jealous rage. See how securely you love Him whom you do not fear to displease through suspicions. A husband and wife love each other because they see each other, and they fear in each other what they do not see. They do not rejoice with certainty from that which is evident, since they suspect in secret what, for the most part, does not exist.

You, in Him whom you do not behold with your eyes, but contemplate by faith, do not find anything true of which you will disapprove; nor do you fear that perhaps you will offend Him by something falsely alleged.

If, therefore, you owed great love to husbands, how much ought you to love Him for whose sake you have chosen not to have husbands! Let Him be placed in complete possession of your heart, who for you was placed upon the cross; let Him possess entirely within your soul whatever you did not wish to be usurped by marriage. It is not lawful for you to love sparingly Him for whose sake you did not love even what was lawful. I have no fear of pride in you who so love Him who is meek and humble of heart.

Chapter 56

(57) And so, within the limits of our ability, we have said enough, both concerning that sanctity by which you are properly called 'holy nuns,' and concerning humility by which is preserved whatever greatness is attributed to you.

Let the three children,[1] to whom He whom they loved with a most fervent heart granted coolness in the fire, more worthily admonish you from this little work of ours. They

---
1 Dan. 3.20-90.

do it much more briefly, indeed, by the measure of words, but much more grandly by the weight of authority, in the hymn through which God is praised by them.

For, combining humility with sanctity in those who praise God, they taught most clearly that each one take so much greater care not to be deceived by pride, in proportion as something more holy is professed.

Wherefore, do you also praise Him who vouchsafes to you in the midst of the fire of this world that, although you do not enter into the union of marriage, you nevertheless do not burn,[2] and, praying also for us: 'O ye holy and humble of heart, bless the Lord; sing a hymn and exalt him above all for ever.'[3]

---
2 Cf. 1 Cor. 7.9.
3 Dan. 3.87.

FAITH AND WORKS

(De fide et operibus)

Translated by
SISTER MARIE LIGUORI, I.H.M., Ph.D.
Marygrove College
Detroit, Michigan

INTRODUCTION

'I RECEIVED LETTERS,' St. Augustine wrote in the *Retractations*, 'from certain brethren—of the laity to be sure, but nevertheless, well advanced in religious studies—who so divorce Christian faith from good works that they are convinced that one is able to attain eternal salvation, not without faith, of course, but without good works. I wanted to answer these brethren and, accordingly, wrote a book entitled *Faith and Works*. In that book I have not only set forth how Christians should live who through the grace of Christ have been regenerated in baptism, but also what manner of persons are to be admitted to the font of rebirth.'[1]

This work—short but significant enough for him to mention it three times in the course of his writings[2]—is engaged with three problems that reveal the mentality of a not uncommon class of catechumens, catechists, and converts in early Christian times. These were as true products of the environment, culture, and tradition of their day as are the secularized Christians of our own. The problem of dealing gently but firmly with well-intentioned, yet essentially pagan,

1 *Retractationes* 2.64.
2 Cf. *Enchiridion* 18.67; *De quaestionibus Dulcitii* 1.2; *Ep.* 205.4.18.

minds and attitudes taxed to the utmost the persuasive power, learning, and patient endurance of the Fathers of the Church. They faced the difficulty as frankly as St. Paul had done a few centuries earlier; they struggled and grappled with it and in their fervent agony brought forth some of their most vigorous and apostolic writings.

The first part of St. Augustine's discussion (1-6.8) is a dogmatic answer to the gravely erroneous contention that there is no necessary connection between faith and the personal good works of the Christian, and that, therefore, everyone is to be admitted indiscriminately to baptism, even avowed and deliberate sinners who intend to remain in their state of iniquity. In the second place, he refutes (6.9-13.20) the argument that candidates for baptism must only be taught the tenets of belief before baptism, and Christian morals not until after baptism. The third error he confounds is, according to his own opinion (14.21-26.48), the most serious because of its insidious and far-reaching consequences: namely, that the baptized will be eventually saved by fire even though they refuse to reform their lives.

A brief summary of the normal procedure of the catechumenate will afford better understanding and deeper appreciation of the Bishop of Hippo's position and of the serious necessity for and timeliness of *Faith and Works*.

At the time of a pagan's application for admission to the Catholic Church, he was questioned as to his motive for applying. A carefully adapted instruction—long or short, depending on the previous knowledge of the individual—followed the declaration of his sincerity of purpose. After the instruction, the applicant expressed his belief in what had been explained and promised to live in accordance with the precepts he had just received. His profession of faith was acknowledged by a signing with the cross, imposition of hands, and exorcism through the administration of salt. Thereafter, the candidate was looked upon as belonging to the Church as a catechumen. At this time he received no further instruction, but he had the right and the duty to attend the Mass of the Catechumens, and either to read holy Scripture by himself or have it read to him. Usually, he remained a catechumen for two or three years.

When a catechumen was ready for baptism, he applied for the reception of the sacrament at the beginning of Lent and was listed in the official register of the Church as a competent. With this registration began a period of continuous instruction through lectures by the bishop. There also was the usual scrutiny, exorcism (which consisted in the signing with the cross), imposition of hands, and insufflation. A special and solemn ceremony was the imparting of the Creed of Baptism (*traditio symboli*) which was carefully guarded by the discipline of the secret and could not be shared with a non-Christian. The competent memorized the Creed and the Lord's Prayer. On Easter Sunday morning, he was baptized and made his baptismal profession by reciting the Creed (*redditio symboli*). After that, he received his first Communion. During Easter Week, sermon-instruction on baptism and Communion continued. On Low Sunday, having laid aside his white garments, he recited the Lord's Prayer with the Church. Then only did he enjoy full membership in the Church community.[3]

In view of this normal procedure, it is easy to see how disturbed St. Augustine was over the growing tendency that had crept into the catechumenate of cutting down the period of preparation for baptism and limiting instruction to one lesson on doctrine alone. Those who promoted this practice maintained that it mattered not at all whether the candidate

---

3 Cf. S. Mitterer, O.S.B., *Einleitung, Büchlein vom ersten katechestischen Unterricht, Bibliothek der Kirchenväter* VIII 49 (Munich 1925) 229-230.

had any intention of conforming his normal life to Christian teaching.

The traditional date[4] for the composition of *De fide et operibus,* 413, has been accounted for by some scholars from a remark Augustine makes in its Chapter 14. While commenting on the literal interpretation of certain somewhat obscure statements of St. Paul, Augustine mentions in passing that he has published a detailed answer to the question of literal interpretation of Scripture in a book bearing the title, *The Letter and the Spirit.* Since the Maurist text carries the temporal modifier *modo*—which the Zycha text in the Vienna *Corpus* rejects—those[5] who base their reading on the Migne edition logically conclude that the work mentioned has just been completed and that *Faith and Works* follows closely upon *The Letter and the Spirit* issued late in 412.

In *Enchiridion* 18.67, written about 412, St. Augustine refers to *De fide et operibus* in an almost similar manner to his reference to the *De spiritu et littera,* and for the length of an entire chapter repeats much of the thought, expression, and Scriptural passages of Chapters 15-16. Again, in *De quaestionibus Dulcitii* 1.2, written about 421 or 425, he says: 'I am answering him from my book entitled *Faith and Works* where I spoke as follows on this matter,' and reproduces exactly section 14.23. Sometime during the year 419, in his letter to Consentius,[6] St. Augustine says that he has written a not inconsiderable book dealing with the current question of whether the baptized who die impenitent will eventually attain pardon. This treatise was written, then, sometime between 412 and 421 or 425. Since, however, in

---
4 Cf. E. Portalié, 'Saint Augustin,' *DTC* I 2 (Paris 1909) 2303; M. Schanz, *Geschichte der römischen Litteratur* IV 2 (Munich 1920) 420, 422; H. Pope, O.P., *Saint Augustine of Hippo* (Westminster, Md. 1946) 376.
5 Cf. Mitterer, *Einleitung, Vom Glauben und von den Werken, BKV* VIII 49 (Munich 1925) 313-314.
6 *Ep.* 205.4.18.

Retractations 2.64, St. Augustine reports his purpose for having written on *Faith and Works* immediately after his review of *The Letter and the Spirit*, it would be reasonable to accept 413 as the more probable date of publication.

The present translation of *De fide et operibus* follows the text of J. Zycha in *Corpus scriptorum ecclesiasticorum Latinorum* 41 (Vienna) 35-97.

---

7 Mitterer, *Des heiligen Kirchenvaters Aurelius Augustinus ausgewählte praktische Schriften homiletischen und katechetischen Inhalts aus dem Lateinischen übersetzt, BKV* VIII 49 (Munich 1925) 313-385; 229-230.

FAITH AND WORKS

Chapter 1

THERE ARE CERTAIN PERSONS who are of the opinion that everybody without exception must be admitted to the font of rebirth which is in Christ Jesus our Lord, even those who, notorious for their crimes and flagrant vices, are unwilling to change their evil and shameful ways, and declare frankly—and publicly—that they intend to continue in their state of sin. Suppose a man to be strongly attached to a harlot; he would not need to be instructed to give her up before he comes for baptism, but even while staying with her and confessing, or even professing, that he is going to continue living with her, he should be admitted and baptized and not prevented from becoming a member of Christ, even though he persists in being one with a harlot.[1] Let him subsequently be taught how evil this is; after he has been baptized, let him be instructed on changing his habits for the better. They consider it perverse and preposterous first to show a man how he ought to live as a Christian and then to baptize him. But they maintain that

---
1 Cf. 1 Cor. 6.15.

the sacrament of baptism ought to come first, so that instruction on the conduct of life may follow. And if he should wish to accept and abide by this instruction, it would be to his advantage; if, however, he should prefer not to, as long as he retains the Christian faith, without which he would perish forever, he will be saved, as it were by fire. This would hold regardless of his stubborn attachment to any sin of impurity, as if it were perfectly possible to build upon the foundation, which is Christ, not gold, silver, precious stone, but wood, hay, stubble,[2] that is, not just and chaste, but unjust and impure habits.

(2) Now, it would seem that these who argue in this fashion are impelled to do so because, if baptism is refused such persons, it would have to be denied also to men who have put away their wives[3] and remarried, or to women who, having put away their husbands, have married again, since the Lord Christ has shown beyond any doubt that such marriage is not marriage at all, but adultery. Since, therefore, they could not deny that that is adultery which Truth in no uncertain terms confirms as adultery, and since they were willing to recommend for the reception of baptism those whom they saw so ensnared by a snare of this kind that, if they were not admitted to baptism, they would prefer to live and even die without any sacrament than to free themselves by deliberately breaking the bond of adultery, they have been moved by a sort of human pity to support, therefore, the cause of those involved in adulterous marriage, even to the extreme of maintaining that everyone must be admitted to baptism—the vicious and profligate, even those most insensible to prohibitions, impervious to instruction, and unmoved by penances. They judge that, if this indulgence be not granted,

2 Cf. 1 Cor. 3.11-15.
3 Cf. Matt. 19.9; Mark 10.11,12; Luke 16.18; 1 Cor. 7.10,11.

these souls would be lost for all eternity; if, however, it were, even though they persevered in these evils, they would be saved by fire.

Chapter 2

(3) In answer to these persons I say first and foremost: No one should so misconstrue these testimonies of sacred Scripture, which recognize in the Church either a present mingling of both the good and the wicked or foretell a future mingling, as to conclude that the solicitude and severity of discipline must be relaxed altogether, and even omitted. Such a one is misled by his own preconceptions and is not taught by those very words of sacred Scripture. The fact that Moses, the servant of God, endured with so much patience that mingling of bad with good among the chosen people did not stop him from punishing many offenders with the sword. And Phinees the priest thrust his avenging dagger through the adulterers found in each other's company.[1] Nowadays, since the visible sword has become inactive in the discipline of the Church, retribution has to be visited on the culprits by reduction in rank and excommunication. And though the blessed Apostle groaned deeply with utmost patience among false brethren,[2] and although some of them were stirred up by the diabolical goad of envy, he even permitted them to preach Christ;[3] on this account he does not think the man ought to be spared who had 'his father's wife,' and advised the assembled Church to deliver the incestuous man 'to Satan for the destruction of the flesh, that his spirit may be saved in the day of our Lord Jesus.'[4] On this account he would even

---
1 Cf. Num. 25.5-8; Exod. 32.27.
2 Cf. 2 Cor. 11.26.
3 Cf. Phil. 1.15-18.
4 Cf. 1 Cor. 5.1-5.

deliver others up 'to Satan that they may learn not to blaspheme.'[5] Otherwise, he says in vain: 'I wrote to you in the letter not to associate with the immoral—not meaning, of course, the immoral of this world, or the covetous, or the greedy, or idolators; otherwise you would have to leave the world. But now I write to you not to associate with one who is called a brother, if he is immoral, or greedy, or an idolator, or evil-tongued, or a drunkard, or a robber; with such a one not even to take food. What have I to do with judging those outside? Is it not those inside whom you judge? For those outside God will judge. Expel the wicked man from your midst.'[6] It is true that some take the phrase 'from your midst' to mean that each one is to expel the wicked man from out of himself, in order that he may be good, but, no matter how it is interpreted, whether that the wicked in the Church are checked by the severity of excommunication or whether each one by self-blame and self-discipline drives wickedness out of himself, there can be no misunderstanding of the teaching of the Apostle in the passage of Scripture just quoted: to refrain from association with brethren who are accused of any of the vices mentioned above, that is, with those who are notoriously scandalous.

Chapter 3

With what intention and with what charity this merciful severity is to be administered is evidenced not only by his statement, 'that his spirit may be saved in the day of our Lord Jesus Christ,'[1] but appears elsewhere even more clearly

---
5 1 Tim. 1.20.
6 Cf. 1 Cor. 5.9-13.

---
1 1 Cor. 5.5.

where he says: 'if anyone does not obey our word by this letter, note that man and do not associate with him, that he may be put to shame. Yet do not regard him as an enemy, but admonish him as a brother.'[2]

(4) Even the Lord Himself, an unsurpassed model of patience, who suffered a devil[3] among His twelve Apostles up to the moment of His Passion, and who said: 'Let both grow until the harvest; lest in gathering the weeds you root up the wheat along with them,'[4] and announced that the net[5] represented the Church as a net that would hold good and bad fish all the way up to the shore, that is, up to the end of the world, whenever He spoke about a mixture of good and wicked, directly or by analogy, it was not to counsel that the discipline of the Church was to be laid aside. Indeed, He urged strongly that it should be enforced when He said: 'Give heed; if thy brother sin against thee, go and show him his fault, between thee and him alone. If he listen to thee, thou hast won thy brother. But if he do not listen to thee, take with thee one or two more so that on the word of two or three witnesses every word may be confirmed. And if he refuse to hear them, appeal to the Church, but if he refuse to hear even the Church, let him be to thee as the heathen and the publican.'[6] Then He laid down the fearful gravity of this severity when He said, also in this place: 'whatever you loose on earth shall be loosed also in heaven; and whatever you bind on earth shall be bound also in heaven.'[7] He also forbids giving holy things to dogs.[8] The Apostle, moreover, does not contradict the Master because he says: 'When they sin, rebuke them in the presence of

---

2 2 Thess. 3.14,15.
3 Cf. John 6.71.
4 Matt. 13.30,29.
5 Cf. Matt. 13.47-49.
6 Matt. 18.15-17.
7 Cf. Matt. 18.18.
8 Cf. Matt. 7.6.

all, that the rest also may have fear,'[9] although the Lord says: 'show him his fault between thee and him.'[10] Both remedies must be used according to the malady of those whom we undertake to treat, certainly not to their destruction, but for their correction and cure. One must be restored to health in one way; another in a different way. This, then, is the reason for ignoring and tolerating the wicked in the Church; again, this the reason for punishing and reproaching them; but not the reason for admitting to or removing from the community of the Church.

Chapter 4

(5) Men fall into error when they do not observe a happy mean. When they begin to incline too much to one side, they cease to consider other testimony of divine authority which could recall them from their aberration and establish them in the mean position of truth and restraint which is the proper measure of both sides. Not on this question only do men lose their balance, but in many others, too. Some, for instance, on examining the testimony of sacred Scripture which teaches us that one God is to be worshiped, think that the same One who is the Son is the Father and also the Holy Spirit. Others again, when laboring, as it were, under an opposite disorder, in applying their mind to those passages in which the Trinity is revealed, are not able to understand how there can be one God, since the Father is not the Son, nor is the Son the Father, nor the Holy Spirit either Son or Father, and even think that a difference of substance must be posited. Others, in considering the praise of virginity in sacred Scripture, condemn marriage. Still others, following

---
9 1 Tim. 5.20.
10 Matt. 18.15.

the testimony in which chaste espousals are lauded, make virginity the equal of wedlock. When some read: 'It is good, brethren, not to eat meat and not to drink wine'[1] and some similar passages, they have interpreted the words to mean that the created things of God, even those that they wish for food, are unclean. Others who read: 'For every creature of God is good, and nothing is to be rejected that is accepted with thanksgiving,'[2] actually succumb to greediness and wine-bibbing and are unable to rid themselves of one vice without falling into more and greater ones.

(6) Similarly, in this question we have been discussing, some people, intent on severe disciplinary precepts which admonish us to rebuke the restless not to give what is holy to dogs,[3] to consider a despiser of the Church as a heathen,[4] to cut off from the unified structure of the body the member which causes scandal,[5] so disturb the peace of the Church that they try to separate the wheat from the cockle[6] before the proper time and, blinded by this error, are themselves separated instead from the unity of Christ. Of the same nature is our cause against the schism of Donatus. Here our contention is not with those who knew that Caecilian had been charged falsely and calumniously yet nevertheless, to their fatal shame, did not abandon their pernicious opposition; but with the others, to whom we say: Even if there were in the Church the wicked people because of whom you have left it, you ought to have remained in it, patiently bearing with those whom you could not either reform or expel from the flock. Certain others, on the contrary, being in danger, when they find that a mixture of good and evil in the Church

---
1 Rom. 14.21.
2 1 Tim. 4.4.
3 Cf. Matt. 7.6; Mark 7.27.
4 Cf. Matt. 18.17.
5 Cf. Matt. 18.8,9; 5.30; Mark 9.42.
6 Cf. Matt. 13.29,30.

is pointed out or prophesied and learn the precepts of patience (which precepts render us so strong that, even if cockle is seen to exist in the Church, neither our faith nor our charity is entangled, so that when we perceive that cockle does exist in the Church we ourselves do not withdraw from it), these, I repeat, believe that the disciplinary action of the Church should be done away with. They quote the passages of Scripture mentioned above to excuse an utterly perverse indifference. They would be concerned only with stating what should be avoided and what should be done and not be bothered with the conduct of the individual.

Chapter 5

(7) We sincerely believe that it is a part of sound doctrine to govern our lives by both testimonies. We, therefore, tolerate dogs in the Church for the sake of the peace of the Church; on the other hand, as soon as the peace of the Church is ensured, we do not give what is holy to dogs.[1] When we discover in the Church wicked members who have gained entrance through the carelessness of superiors or some understandable necessity or by concealed intrusion, and who are not corrected or restrained by ecclesiastical discipline, then we must not permit an impious and wicked presumption to find its way into our hearts and think that we must be separated from them in order to escape defilement from their sins. Nor may we attempt to attract disciples, presumably clean and holy, from the bond of unity under the false supposition that we are thereby segregating them from the society of the wicked. Rather, we should recall those similes and divine oracles from Scripture, or explict examples which distinctly prophesy that in the Church the wicked will be

1 Cf. Matt. 7.6.

mingled with the good until the end of the world and the last judgment and will not harm the good in the union with and participation in sacraments which are not at all in harmony with their conduct. Since, indeed, those who govern the Church possess, for the peace of the Church, the salutary power of disciplining the reprobate or hardened sinners, I say once more, we must not sleep in slothful neglect. We must be aroused by the goad of those other precepts that justify the severity of coercion. We must do this so that by following in the steps of the Lord as our Leader and Guide, we neither become torpid in the name of patience nor violent under the pretext of zeal.

Chapter 6

(8) Let us see what course to follow if we are going to uphold that moderation which is in accordance with sound doctrine, on the question of whether or not men ought to be admitted to the reception of baptism without diligent guard against giving what is holy to dogs. Apparently, the most open and stubbornly persistent perpetrators of adultery are not to be withheld from a sacrament so great and holy; whereas there is no question of admitting candidates who, during the days of preparation for this grace, having submitted their names and having been duly cleansed by abstinence, fasts, and exorcisms, declare that they will cohabit with their lawful and true wives, but, as to the matter of conjugal pleasure permissible at other times, they do not intend to practise continence during these few solemn days of preparation. How, then, is the adulterer who refuses correction to be admitted to the sacred rite, when the married man who refuses to observe ecclesiastical prescriptions is not admitted?

(9) Let him be baptized first, they say; then let him be instructed in what contributes to the good life and to good habits. This is exactly what is done whenever it happens that the end of life is at hand and the final day suddenly presses upon a man. Such instruction is then given in very few words, in which, nevertheless, are contained all the essentials of faith and for the reception of the sacrament. If afterwards the newly baptized departs from this life, he goes forth freed from the guilt of all past sins. If, however, a well person asks for baptism and there is time to instruct him, when would it be more propitious for him to hear how it behooves him to become a faithful Christian and to live accordingly than the very time when, his mind attentive and aroused by religion itself, he asks for the sacrament of life-giving faith? Do we repress the testimony of our own experience so far as to forget how intent and anxious we were over what the catechists taught us when we were petitioning for the sacrament, and for precisely this reason were called *competentes?* Do we also refrain from observing others who year by year hasten to the cleansing waters of regeneration, and note how they comport themselves during the days they are being catechized, exorcised, scrutinized: their careful vigilance when assembling, their fervent zeal and eagerness, their solicitous suspense? If that is not the proper time to tell them what manner of life befits that wonderful sacrament for which they are yearning, when will be? Or, indeed, is that the proper time when they have been baptized and continue in their many and serious sins even after baptism, not new men but old culprits? If that is the time, then with what remarkable perversity you may say to them, prior to the reception of the sacrament: Put on the new man; and afterwards, when the new man has been put on, say: Strip off the old. The Apostle maintains a sound order in saying: 'strip off the old man and

put on the new,'¹ and the Lord Himself exclaims: 'no one puts a patch of raw cloth on an old garment, nor do people pour new wine into old wine-skins.'² What, moreover, is all that time for, during which they hold the name and place of catechumens, except to hear what the faith and pattern of Christian life should be, so that first they may prove themselves and then eat of the Bread of the Lord and drink of the Chalice, since 'he who eats and drinks unworthily, eats and drinks judgment to himself'?³ This training actually goes on during all that time which the Church has beneficially appointed for the candidates⁴ for admission to the catechumenate. Their study, too, becomes far more earnest and intensive during the period in which they are called *competentes,* that is, when they have already given in their names for the reception of baptism.

Chapter 7

(10) What about the case, they say, of a virgin who unknowingly marries a married man? As long as she does not know that he is the husband of another, there is no question of adultery. If, however, she becomes aware of the fact, from the moment that she realizes that she is enjoying conjugal intercourse with the husband of another she commits adultery. So in the right to estates one is rightfully said to be the owner in good faith as long as he does not know that he is in possession of the property belonging to another. When, however, he understands that he is and does not withdraw from the possession of that property, he is said to be in bad

---
1 Cf. Col. 3.9,10.
2 Matt. 9.16,17.
3 Cf. 1 Cor. 11.28,29.
4 *ad nomen Christi accedentes.*

faith and is properly called unjust. God forbid, therefore, that we should lament when wrongs are set right as if actual marriages were being dissolved. That would not be grief worthy of man, but a foolish delusion, especially so 'in the city of our God, in his holy mountain,'[1] that is, in the Church where not only the bond, but also the sacrament of marriage, is so cherished that it is not lawful for one man to give his wife to another, as in time of the Roman Republic Cato is said to have done, not only blamelessly, but laudably.[2] But why prolong the argument along this line, since even they whom I am answering do not dare to assert that there is no sin in the instance I have just cited, nor deny that it is adultery. They would then be openly convicted of opposing the Lord Himself and His holy Gospel. It seems right to them that such sinners must be admitted to the reception of the sacrament of baptism and to the Lord's table even if they have unquestionably and publicly refused correction. Indeed, they believe that it is absolutely unnecessary that the adulterers be admonished for their sins; only afterwards are they to be taught that, if they choose to observe the commandments and correct their faults, they will be among the wheat; if, however, they despise the commandments, they still will be tolerated among the cockle. The promotors of this view make it sufficiently clear, nevertheless, that they do not defend these sins or treat them as inconsiderable or inculpable; for what Christian of good hope would view adultery as no sin or a small one?

(11) Furthermore, they think that they derive from sacred Scripture regulations whereby these vices in others are either to be corrected or to be endured. They declare that the Apostles followed his method and adduce certain proofs from their letters in which they are found to have

---
1 Ps. 47.2.
2 Plutarch, *Cato min.* 25.

introduced the doctrine on faith prior to having rules for the conduct of life. In addition, they would force this testimony to prove that only the rule of faith had to be taught to those who were to be baptized; after they had already been baptized, they were to be given rules for amending their lives. Just as if they understood that to the candidates for baptism some letters had been written containing discussions on faith, and that, to the baptized, others with precepts for guarding against evil habits and forming good ones. But, since everybody knows that the Apostles wrote letters to those already baptized as Christians, why were both types of sermons, one pertaining to faith the other to a good life, woven into one letter? Does it by any chance seem right that we should not give both doctrine and counsel to those to be baptized, yet give both to those who have been baptized? If this is said foolishly, they must at least admit that the Apostles included in their letters instructions that were complete both in doctrine and counsel, and generally introduced faith first and then appended a pattern for correct behavior, because, unless faith comes first in man himself, the good life cannot follow. For instance, whatever good act a man performs, unless it leads him to piety, that is, to God, ought not to be called meritorious. But if some were so foolish and so inexperienced as to believe that the letters of the Apostles had been written to the catechumens, they themselves assuredly would admit that precepts for conduct in accordance with faith had to be brought in at the same time with the rules of faith. Yet perhaps, by this argument they compel us to conclude that the first part of the Apostolic letters, where they speak on faith, was intended to be read to the catechumens; the latter part prescribing the Christian way of life, to the faithful. Now, if it is most stupid to say this—and there is no justification for this opinion in the letters of the Apostles—why, then, should we think that those to be baptized must be exhorted on faith, alone, and the baptized on conduct, simply because the Apostles have recommended faith in the first part of their letters and afterwards have admonished the faithful, as evidence of their belief, to lead good lives? Although, frequently enough, faith comes first and admonitions follow, very often, nevertheless, in any sermon, both are given to catechumens, both to the faithful, both to the candidates for baptism, both to the baptized. Whether for their instruction or warning against heedlessness, whether to inspire or to confirm their faith by sound doctrine, both have to be very earnestly preached. To the letter of Peter and the letter of John, from which they have cited their testimony, they also add the letters of Paul and the other Apostles. The process of reasoning we must employ against their observations and interpretation of Scripture in regard to teaching faith first and morals later, I have, if I am not mistaken, explained with sufficient clarity.

Chapter 8

(12) But, they argue, in the Acts of the Apostles, on the occasion of the conversion of the 3,000 who, having heard the word, were baptized in one day, Peter preached to them faith alone by which they believed in Christ. When they had asked: 'What shall we do?' Peter answered: 'Repent and be baptized every one of you in the name of Jesus Christ for the forgiveness of your sins; and you will receive the gift of the Holy Spirit.'[1] Why do they not notice that he said: 'Repent'? That means the stripping off of the old life so that those who are being baptized may put on the new. Of what avail is repentance for dead works, if one persists in

---
1 Acts 2.37,38.

FAITH AND WORKS 235

adultery and all the other sins with which the love of this world is entangled?

(13) To this they answer: Peter wanted them to repent only for their lack of faith in not believing in Christ. Strange presumption (I do not want to say anything more serious) if when the expression 'repent' is heard, it merely indicates an act of infidelity, when the evangelical teaching on the necessity of changing the old way of life for the new has been continuously handed down. What, too, is the purport of what the Apostle puts in this tenor: 'He who was wont to steal, let him steal no longer,'[2] and similar expressions which indicate how to put off the old man and put on the new? In the very words of Peter quoted above they have the source from which they could have been admonished, if they had cared to study them diligently. When he had said: 'Repent and be baptized every one of you in the name of Jesus Christ for the forgiveness of your sins; and you will receive the gift of the Holy Spirit. For to you is the promise and to your children and to all who are far off, even to all whom the Lord our God calls,' the writer of the book immediately added the words: 'And with very many other words he bore witness, and exhorted them, saying: Save yourselves from this perverse generation. Now they who received his word accepted it eagerly and believed and were baptized, and there were added that day about three thousand souls.'[3] Who does not here understand that, with the 'very many other words' which were omitted by the writer for the sake of brevity, Peter with strong appeal had urged them to tear themselves away from this perverse generation, since this very thought is itself concisely contained in the many words with which he was urging it upon them? It was, in fact, placed last in the most important position with the words:

2 Eph. 4.28.
3 Acts 2.38-41.

'Save yourselves from this perverse generation'; and with many more words besides, Peter pressed his exhortations upon them. In these words there was condemnation of dead works which the lovers of this world perform wretchedly, but commendation of the good life which those who save themselves from this perverse generation hold and strive after. Now, if it seems right, let them attempt to affirm that he who just believes in Christ is saving himself from this perverse generation, although he continues to sin deliberately, even to the public acknowledgment of adultery. If, however, it is wrong, let those to be baptized hear not only what they ought to believe, but also how they may save themselves from this perverse generation. Certainly at this time it is necessary for them to hear how, as believers in Christ, they are bound to live.

Chapter 9

(14) The eunuch, they insist, whom Philip baptized, said nothing more than: 'I believe Jesus Christ to be the Son of God,'[1] and immediately after this profession of faith he was baptized. Does it really seem right that upon simply making this response men should straightway be baptized? Is nothing to be said by the catechist, nothing to be professed by the believer about the Holy Spirit, about holy Church, nothing about the forgiveness of sins, the resurrection of the dead, nothing, finally, about the Lord Jesus Christ Himself except that He is the Son of God—nothing about His Incarnation in the womb of a virgin, His passion, His death on the cross, His burial, His resurrection on the third day, His ascension and sitting at the right hand of the Father? When the eunuch answered: 'I believe Jesus Christ to be the Son of God,' if this was enough for him to say in order to go right

---
1 Acts 8.38.

down into the waters of baptism, why do we not follow his example? Why not imitate it and do away with all the rest of the preparation that we consider so necessary even when the time for baptism is short and urgent? Why not so place our questions that the one to be baptized gives all the right answers even if he has no chance to commit them to memory? If, however, Scripture is silent and dismisses the rest of what Philip talked over with the eunuch as understood and taken for granted, the words 'Philip baptized him'[2] imply that everything was fulfilled which, for the sake of brevity, may be passed over in Scripture, but which, nevertheless, we know from the unbroken chain of tradition must have been carried out. Likewise, where it says that Philip had preached the Lord Jesus to the eunuch,[3] there must be no doubt that the ensuing catechism embraced all the necessary instruction on the duties and proper mode of living for one who believes in the Lord Jesus. To preach Christ consists in declaring not only what must be believed about Him, but also what precepts must be observed by one hoping for membership in the unity of the Body of Christ. Indeed, to preach Christ is to state everything that must be believed about Christ, not only whose Son He is, whence begotten according to His divinity, whence according to His flesh, what He suffered and why He suffered, what is the virtue of His resurrection, what gift of the Spirit He promised and gave to the faithful; but also what kind of members He, the Head, seeks, ordains, loves, frees from bonds of sin, and leads to eternal life and glory. When these facts are related, sometimes more briefly and with restriction, other times more comprehensively and in greater detail, Christ is being preached. At the same time, what pertains to the habits and morals of the faithful as well as what pertains to faith is not left unsaid.

---
2 Acts 8.39.
3 Acts 8.36.

238   SAINT AUGUSTINE

Chapter 10

(15) This point of view is again easily perceived in how they quote from the Apostle Paul, as if 'For I determined not to know anything among you, except Jesus Christ and Him crucified'[1] could possibly mean that nothing else had been taught the Corinthians except what induced belief in Christ in order that they might first be baptized and later be presented a pattern for living. This, they hold, was all the Apostle required of them; yet he said 'although they had ten thousand tutors in Christ yet they had not many fathers' because he himself had begotten them 'in Christ Jesus through the gospel.'[2] If, then, he who begot them through the Gospel, although he thanked God because he baptized none of them but Crispus and Gaius' and 'the household of Stephanas,'[3] taught them nothing more than Christ crucified, what if someone should say that they had not heard that Christ had risen from the dead, when were they begotten through the Gospel? How could he say to them: 'I delivered to you first of all, what I also received, that Christ died for our sins according to the Scriptures, and that he was buried, that he rose again the third day, according to the Scriptures,'[4] if he had taught them nothing but the crucifixion? If, however, they do not understand it in this way but claim that all this is part of the teaching of Christ crucified, may they know that there is a great deal to learn in Christ crucified and, above all, that 'our old self has been crucified with him, in order that the body of sin may be destroyed, that we may no longer be slaves to sin.'[5] Why, then, does he also say this about himself: 'But as for me, God forbid that

---
1 1 Cor. 2.2.
2 Cf. 1 Cor. 4.15.
3 Cf. 1 Cor. 1.14,16.
4 1 Cor. 15.3,4.
5 Rom. 6.6.

I should glory save in the cross of our Lord Jesus Christ, through whom the world is crucified to me, and I to the world.'⁶ Let them attend carefully and see how Christ crucified is to be taught and learned. Let them know how it is a part of His cross that we, too, are crucified to the world in His Body, by which is understood the entire repression of all our evil concupiscences. For this reason it is utterly impossible that open adultery be permitted those who are formed by the cross of Christ. In teaching the mystery of the cross, that is, the passion of Christ, the Apostle Peter likewise exhorts that they who are saved by the passion of Christ must cease from sin: 'Since Christ therefore has suffered in the flesh, do you also arm yourselves with the same intent; because he who has died in the flesh has ceased from sins; that during the rest of his time in the flesh he may live no longer according to the lusts of man, but according to the will of the Lord God.'⁷ In other places again he shows that he logically belongs to Christ crucified—that is, through the suffering of the flesh—who, having crucified the desires of the flesh in his own body, lives well by the Gospel.

(16) What is to be said of their contention that even the two commandments upon which the Lord says the whole Law and Prophets depend⁸ support their theory? Their argument goes this way: Since the first commandment states 'Thou shalt love the Lord thy God with thy whole heart, and with thy whole soul, and with thy whole mind, and the second is like it, thou shalt love thy neighbor as thyself,'⁹ the first, with its command to love God, they might believe applies to those ready for baptism; the second, because of its apparent reference to human intercourse, refers to the already baptized.

---
6 Gal. 6.14.
7 Cf. 1 Peter 4.1,2.
8 Cf. Matt. 22.40.
9 Matt. 22.37,39.

Apparently they forget the text: 'For how can he who does not love his brother, whom he sees, love God whom he does not see?'[10] and that other declaration in the same epistle of John: 'If anyone loves the world, the love of the Father is not in him.'[11] To what do the enormities of evil habits tend if not to the love of this world? For that very reason, the first commandment, which they think applies to the candidates for baptism, can in no way be carried out without good habits. I do not want to delay over too many considerations, however. Briefly, these two commandments, on careful reflection, are found to be so intrinsically united that there can be no love of God in man without love for his neighbor, nor love of neighbor without love of God. What we have said now about these two commandments is sufficient for our present purpose.

Chapter 11

(17) The people of Israel, it is further objected, were first led across the Red Sea, an event signifying baptism. Afterwards, they received the Law which gave them rules for living. If this is so, why do we even teach the Creed to those to be baptized and demand it be repeated from memory? Nothing of that kind was required of those whom God delivered from the Egyptians through the Red Sea. If, however, they understand correctly the significance of the preceding mysteries[1]—the blood of the lamb smeared on the door posts and the unleavened bread of sincerity and truth—why do they not also see that the escape from the Egyptians signifies the separation from sin which they who are going to

---
10 1 John 4.20.
11 1 John 2.15.

---
1 Cf. Exod. 12.7-17.

be baptized profess to make? To this effect are the words of Peter: 'Repent and be baptized every one of you in the name of the Lord Jesus Christ,'[2] as if he were saying: Depart from Egypt and cross over the Red Sea. Then, too, in the Letter to the Hebrews, repentance from dead works is included in the elementary instruction of those who are going to be baptized. The Apostle says: 'Therefore, leaving the elementary teaching concerning Christ, let us pass on to things more perfect, not laying again a foundation of repentance from dead works and of faith towards God, of the doctrine of baptism and the laying on of hands, of the resurrection of the dead and of eternal judgment.'[3] That all these teachings belong to the initial instruction of the neophytes is sufficiently and clearly attested by Scripture. What, moreover, is 'repentance from dead works' unless it be from works which must be slain that we might live? If adulteries and fornications are not such, what are to be named among dead works? Thus, the intention to abandon such dead works is not sufficient unless all past sins which, so to speak, pursue them are destroyed by the cleansing of regeneration. In the same way it would not have sufficed the Israelites to withdraw from Egypt unless the multitude of the pursuing enemy had perished in the waves of the sea that opened for the passage and liberation of the people of God. How, then, will anyone who professes that he does not want to change from his state of adultery cross over the Red Sea while he is still determined to abide in Egypt? Further, they pay no attention to the first injunction of the Law which was given the Jews after their passage of the Red Sea: 'Thou shalt not have strange gods before me. Thou shalt not make thyself a graven thing, nor likeness of anything that is in the heaven above, or in the earth beneath, nor of those things that are in the

---
2 Acts 2.38.
3 Heb. 6.1,2.

waters under the earth. Thou shalt not adore them, nor serve them,'[4] with all the other statements pertinent to this commandment. Let them insist, if they like, in contradiction to their own assertion, that worship of the one true God and the prohibition against idolatry is not to be preached to the unbaptized, but to the already baptized. Do not, however, let them any longer say to those who are going to receive baptism that they need be instructed only on belief in God, and after the reception of the sacrament they will be taught the manner of living required by the second precept on the love of neighbor, for both are contained in the Law which the people received after the Red Sea, that is, after baptism. The commandments were not so distributed that before crossing the Red Sea the Jews were warned against idolatry, and not until after their escape taught to honor father and mother, not to commit adulery, not to kill, and the remaining prescriptions for a rational and godly way of living.[5]

Chapter 12

(18) If anyone were to so petition for the sacred cleansing as to declare that he was not going to absent himself from idolatrous sacrifices, unless perhaps later if it should please him to do so, and even if he repeatedly requested baptism and pleaded ardently to be made a temple of the living God, continuing at the same time not only to worship idols, but even to execute some sacrilegious office of the priesthood, I ask them whether they agree that such a person ought even be made a catechumen? Undoubtedly, they will declare that this ought not to be done. From their very hearts they could not say otherwise. Accordingly, they would support their

4 Exod. 20.3-5.
5 Cf. Exod. 20.12-17.

reasoning with the testimony of Scripture which they think
should be so interpreted as to afford reason for daring to
oppose him and not agreeing that he should be admitted
despite his protest and insistence: 'I have learned of Christ,
and I adore Him; I believe that Christ Jesus is the Son of
God; you may not put me off any longer nor may you at
this time require any more of me. You claim the Apostle did
not ask those whom he begot through the Gospel to know
anything more than Christ crucified and that, after the
eunuch expressed his belief that Jesus Christ was the Son of
God, Philip did not put off baptizing him. Why do you then
forbid me to worship idols and refuse to admit me to the
sacrament of Christ until I repudiate this worship? In my
childhood the practice of worshiping idols was deeply impressed upon me; I shall give up the habit when I can—when
it is convenient to do so; but, even should I not renounce
idolatry, I should not be forced to die without Christ's
sarcrament, lest God exact my soul at your hands.' Now, I
ask, in their judgment, what answer must be given him?
Would they want to admit him to the sacrament? God forbid!
Under no circumstance could I believe that they would go
that far. But what answer will they give one who urges
these questions and who declares, further, that nothing should
be said to him before baptism about the necessity of disavow-
ing idolatry; the chosen people heard nothing of such re-
nouncement before they crossed the Red Sea; the prohibition
was contained in the Law that was given them only after
they had been delivered from Egypt. Surely, they would say
to that man: 'You are going to be a temple of God when
you shall have received baptism.' Besides, the Apostle asserts:
'And what agreement has the temple of God with idols?'[1]
Why do they not see that this is just the same as saying:
when you are baptized you will belong to Christ; the members

---

1 2 Cor. 6.16.

of Christ cannot be the members of a harlot,[2] can they? The Apostle says they cannot. In another place he says: 'Do not err; neither fornicators, nor idolators'—and other abominations which he lists—'will possess the kingdom of God.'[3] Why, then, do we refuse baptism to idolators and contend that fornicators must be admitted to it, since the Apostle specifically mentions fornicators and other evil-doers, saying: 'And such were some of you, but you have been washed, you have been sanctified, you have been justified in the name of our Lord Jesus Christ, and in the Spirit of our God'?[4] What is my reason for permitting baptism to an invincible fornicator and yet refusing an idolator, since the way lies open to denying both and since the same words are said to both: 'And such were some of you, but you have been washed'? They are pushed to their position because they suppose that salvation is secure, although through fire, for those who believe in Christ and receive His sacrament, that is, have been baptized, even if they are completely indifferent about reforming their lives and therefore live wickedly. With the help of God, I shall presently show what is, according to the Scriptures, the right opinion on this matter.

Chapter 13

(19) For the moment, I am still concerned with the contention that the baptized are to be admonished to acquire habits that befit the Christian way of living, but, for those to be baptized, only faith need be instilled. But if this were so, consider the following passages of Scripture in addition to the many I have mentioned: John the Baptist would not have said to those coming to his baptism: 'Brood of vipers!

---
2 Cf. 1 Cor. 6.15.
3 1 Cor. 6.9,10.
4 1 Cor. 6.11.

who has shown you how to flee from the wrath to come? Bring forth therefore fruit befitting repentance'[1] and the rest of his urgent appeals, obviously not for faith, but for good works. Why to the soldiers asking 'what are we to do?' did he not answer: 'For the time being, believe and be baptized; after that you will hear what you must do'? Before giving his answer, he warned them that as the precursor he would make the way into their hearts clean for the Lord who was about to come: 'Plunder no one, neither accuse anyone falsely, and be content with your pay.'[2] In like manner, to the publicans who inquired what they should do, he said: 'Exact no more than what has been appointed you.'[3] With a brief mention of these exhortations, the Evangelist, for it was not fitting to insert the entire catechism, indicates clearly enough that it is the duty of the catechist to indoctrinate and to encourage good morals and right habits in the one to be baptized. On the other hand, if they had replied to John: 'We absolutely shall not bring forth fruit worthy of repentance; we intend to calumniate, to plunder, to exact more than has been appointed us,' and if even in spite of this declaration he had consented to baptize them, it still could not be said, no matter whence the objection, that before baptism is not the time to inculcate the essentials of a good life.

(20) I might mention other testimony, but let my adversaries recall the answer given by our Lord Himself when the rich young man asked Him what works he should do to gain eternal life: 'if thou,' He said, 'wilt enter into life, keep the commandments.' And the young man asked: 'Which?' Then the Lord repeated the commandments of the Law: 'Thou shalt not kill, Thou shalt not commit adultery,' and the rest of them. When the rich young man replied that he

---
1 Matt. 3.7,8.
2 Luke 3.14.
3 Luke 3.12,13.

had kept all of these from his youth, the Lord added the counsel of perfection: that he was to sell all his possessions and give to the poor, in order that he might have a treasure in heaven, then follow the Lord Himself.[4] Let them note carefully that He did not say that he had only to believe and be baptized—the sole requirement for eternal salvation according to their reasoning—but that He gave him precepts for the conduct of his life, precepts which certainly cannot be guarded and kept without faith. Just because the Lord seems to have been silent here about teaching faith, we shall most certainly not prescribe and maintain that only precepts for living well must be preached to men desiring eternal life. The two phases of instruction are mutually interrelated and connected, as I have said before, because there can be no love for God in the man who does not love his neighbor, nor love of neighbor without the love of God. Although in Scripture one set of instructions sometimes is found without the other, either faith alone or good works alone instead of the complete doctrine, it is to be understood that one cannot be without the other, because whoever believes in God ought to do what God commands and whoever does what God commands because He commands it necessarily believes in God.

Chapter 14

(21) Therefore, let us now see what must be torn away from the hearts of the God-fearing to prevent the loss of salvation through a treacherously false security, if, under the illusion that faith alone is sufficient for salvation, they neglect to live a good life and fail by good works to persevere in the way that leads to God. Even in the days of the Apostles

---
4 Matt. 19.16-21.

certain somewhat obscure statements of the Apostle Paul were misunderstood, and some thought he was saying this: 'Let us do evil that good may come from it'[1] because he said: 'Now the Law intervened that the offense might abound. But where the offense has abounded, grace has abounded yet more.'[2] These words are true only because the receivers of the Law were men presumptuous of their own strength, with too much pride to beg God in right faith to help them overcome their evil concupiscence. They were burdened, therefore, with many and serious sins and even with the Law itself by reason of their perversion of it. Compelled by deep guilt, they took refuge in faith to obtain for them the mercy of indulgence and 'help from the Lord, who made heaven and earth.'[3] With charity poured forth in their hearts by the Holy Spirit,[4] they effected through love the conquest of the concupiscence of this world as predicted in the psalm: 'Their infirmities were multiplied: afterwards they made haste.'[5] When the Apostle says, then, that in his opinion man is justified through faith without the works of the Law,[6] he does not intend by this decision to express contempt for the commandments and the works of justice by the profession of faith, but to inform anyone that he can be justified by faith even if he has not previously fulfilled the works of the Law; for they follow when one has been justified, and do not come before for one to be justified. There is no need, however, for further discussion of this problem in the present work, especially since I have published a detailed answer to the question in a book bearing the title, *The Letter and the Spirit*. Since this problem is by no means new and had already arisen at the time of the Apostles, other apostolic letters of

---

1 Cf. Rom. 3.8.
2 Rom. 5.20.
3 Ps. 120.2.
4 Cf. Rom. 5.5.
5 Ps. 15.4.
6 Cf. Rom. 4.

Peter, John, James, and Jude are deliberately aimed against the argument I have been refuting and firmly uphold the doctrine that faith does not avail without good works. Paul himself also does not approve any kind of faith whatever as long as it achieves belief in God, but only that salutary and definitely evangelical faith from which good works proceed through love, for he says very plainly: 'but faith which works through charity.'[7] That is why he claimed that the faith which seems to some sufficient for salvation is useless, so that he says: 'and if I have all faith so as to remove mountains, yet do not have charity, I am nothing.'[8] It follows that where charity is operative in the Christian, there is no doubt that he is living the right kind of life: 'Love therefore is the fulfillment of the Law.'[9]

(22) From this it is clear that Peter, in his second letter, had a special motive when he urged his readers to holiness in living and character and declared that this world would pass and that new heavens and a new earth were expected[10] which would be given to the just to inhabit. He wished that they might take care how to live, and might become worthy of that dwelling. He knew that certain unjust persons had taken occasion from some obscure passages of the Apostle Paul to have no care for a right mode of life, as if secure in salvation through faith alone. He mentioned that Paul's letters contained certain places hard to understand and that men twisted them, as also other Scriptures, to their own ruin. When Paul refers to eternal salvation which will be given only to them who have lived good lives, he is in perfect agreement with the other Apostles. Here is what Peter says: 'Seeing therefore that all these things are to be

---

7 Gal. 5.6.
8 1 Cor. 13.2.
9 Rom. 13.10.
10 2 Peter 3.13.

dissolved, what manner of men ought you to be in holy and pious behavior, you who await and hasten towards the coming of the day of God, by which the heavens, being on fire, will be dissolved and the elements will melt away by reason of the heat of that fire! But we look for new heavens and a new earth, according to his promises, wherein dwells justice. Therefore, beloved, while you look for these things, endeavor to be found by him without spot and blameless, in peace. And regard the long-suffering of our Lord as salvation. Just as our most dear brother Paul also, according to the wisdom given him, has written to you, as indeed he did in all his epistles, speaking in them of these things. In these epistles there are certain things difficult to understand, which the unlearned and the unstable distort, just as they do the rest of the Scriptures also, to their own destruction. You therefore, beloved, since you know this beforehand, be on your guard lest, carried away by the error of the foolish, you fall away from your own steadfastness. But grow in grace and knowledge of our Lord and Saviour, Jesus Christ. To him be the glory, both now and to the day of eternity.'[11]

(23) James was so severely annoyed with those who held that faith without works avails to salvation that he compared them to evil spirits, saying: 'Thou believest that there is one God. Thou doest well. The devils also believe, and tremble.'[12] What could be said more tersely, with greater truth and more vehemence? We also read in the Gospel that, when the evil spirits confessed Christ to be the Son of God, He rebuked them.[13] He praised Peter for making this same acknowledgment.[14] 'What will it profit, my brethren,' James says, 'if a man says he has faith, but does not have works?

---
11 2 Peter 3.11-18.
12 James 2.19.
13 Cf. Mark 1.24,25,27; Luke 4.41.
14 Cf. Matt. 16.16,17.

Can the faith save him?' and again, 'faith without works is useless.'[15] How long are they going to cling to deception and promise themselves eternal life from dead faith!

Chapter 15

(24) From all the foregoing discussion it is necessary to take careful note of the right interpretation of that passage of the Apostle Paul which is clearly difficult to understand, where he says: 'For other foundation no one can lay, but that which has been laid, which is Christ Jesus. But if anyone builds upon this foundation, gold, silver, precious stones, wood, hay, straw—the works of each will be made manifest, for the day of the Lord will declare it, since the day is to be revealed in fire. The fire will assay the quality of everyone's work: if his work abides, which he has built thereon, he will receive reward; if his work burns he will lose reward, but himself will be saved, yet so through fire.'[1] By some this passage is taken to mean that they who add good works to faith in Christ seem to build gold, silver, precious stones upon the foundation of Christ; they who with the same faith work evil, build wood, hay, straw. As a result, they arrive at the conclusion that through the efficacy of certain punishments of fire they can be purified unto salvation by merit of their foundation, which is Christ.

(25) If this be true, we grant that they, with a charity that is laudable, attempt to admit all to baptism indiscriminately, not only adulterers and adulteresses who adhere stubbornly to false nuptials against the will of the Lord, but also public harlots, who persist in a most disgraceful pro-

---

15 James 2.14,20.

1 1 Cor. 3.11-15.

fession, and whom not the most negligent of churches has been accustomed to receive unless they first freed themselves from that prostitution. How, according to their reasoning, harlots are excluded, I do not at all see. Who would not prefer, once the foundation has been laid—granted it is permissible to gather wood, hay, and straw—that they be purified by a considerably longer burning rather than they be lost for all eternity? But the following statements will be false: 'and if I have all faith so as to remove mountains, yet do not have charity, I am nothing';[2] and 'What will it profit, my brethren, if a man says he has faith, but does not have works? Can the faith save him?'[3] False, too, will be the words: 'Do not err; neither fornicators, nor idolators, nor adulterers, nor the effeminate, nor sodomites, nor thieves, nor the covetous, nor drunkards, nor the evil-tongued, nor the greedy will possess the kingdom of God.'[4] False again: 'Now the works of the flesh are manifest, which are immorality, uncleanness, licentiousness, riotous living, idolatry, witchcrafts, enmities, contentions, jealousies, anger, quarrels, factions, envies, drunkenness, carousings, and suchlike. And concerning these I warn you, as I have warned you, that they who do such things will not attain the kingdom of God.'[5] These warnings and entreaties will be false, for, if they only believe and are baptized, although they persist in such evils, they will be saved by fire; and so the baptized in Christ, even those who do such things, will possess the kingdom of God. Also to no purpose does Scripture say: 'And such were some of you, but you have been washed,'[6] since they also have been washed who hold on to these even after baptism. In vain, also, will Peter seem to have said:

---
2 1 Cor. 13.2.
3 James 2.14.
4 1 Cor. 6.9,10.
5 Cf. Gal. 5.19-21.
6 1 Cor. 6.11.

'Its counterpart, baptism, now saves you also (not the putting off the filth of the flesh, but the inquiry of a good conscience . . .)'[7] if certain ones with very bad consciences, full of all vices and sins and unchanged by repentance, are nevertheless saved by baptism. Because of the foundation laid in the same baptism, they will be saved, even if by fire.

Then, too, I do not see why the Lord said: 'if thou wilt enter into eternal life, keep the commandments'[8]—mentioning the commandments pertaining to good behavior—if without observing these commandments one is able to enter life by faith alone, which 'unless it has works, is dead.'[9] How, under the circumstances, will there be any truth in what He will say to those whom He places on His left hand: 'Depart from me into everlasting fire which was prepared for the devil and his angels'?[10] He will not unbraid them because they did not believe in Him, but because they had not done good works. Actually, it was lest anyone promise himself eternal life from a faith which without works is dead that our Lord said that He would separate[11] all the nations formerly gathered together under the protection of the same shepherds, that He might make known those who will say to Him: 'Lord, when did we see thee' suffering this or that 'and did not minister to thee?'[12] These are the ones who had believed in Him but had not bothered to do good works, as if they expected to attain everlasting life from dead faith alone. Or perhaps, indeed, they who have not performed works of mercy will go into everlasting fire, but they who have robbed another of his possessions or who have been unmerciful to themselves by corrupting the temple of God within them

---

7 1 Peter 3.21.
8 Matt. 19.17.
9 James 2.17.
10 Matt. 25.41.
11 Matt. 25.32.
12 Matt. 25.44.

will be spared—as if the works of mercy might profit anything without charity! The Apostle says: 'If I distribute all my goods to the poor, yet do not have charity, it profits me nothing.'[13] Does one love his neighbor as himself who does not love himself: 'He that loveth iniquity hateth his own soul.'[14] Nor will that opinion hold here by which many are seduced, which claims that the fire is said to be everlasting, not the punishment itself. To be sure, they suppose that they to whom they promise salvation by fire because their faith is useless will pass through fire that will last forever. As they judge, the flames themselves are everlasting; their burning, that is, the work of the fire on sinners, is not for eternity. But the Lord, as if He anticipated this misunderstanding, pronounces His own sentence upon it: 'These will go into everlasting punishment, but the just into everlasting life.'[15] The burning will be just as everlasting as the fire, and Truth has warned that they whom He has declared to be wanting in good works—not faith—will go into that burning fire.

(26) If all these admonitions and innumerable others which can be found throughout the Scriptures stated in very plain terms are false, then that interpretation of the wood, hay, and straw can be true which maintains that they will be saved through fire who, although they have neglected good works, hold fast solely to faith in Christ. If, however, these words of Scripture are both true and clear, another interpretation assuredly must be sought for them, and these expressions of the Apostle Paul must be counted among the passages in his writings which Peter says are difficult to understand[16] and which men must not distort to their own destruction. This they do when, contrary to the evident

---
13 1 Cor. 13.3.
14 Ps. 10.6.
15 Matt. 25.46.
16 Cf. 2 Peter 3.16.

testimony of Scripture, they assure salvation to the most wicked who cling tenaciously to their wickedness and are neither changed nor improved by repentance.

Chapter 16

(27) Perhaps at this point I shall be asked what I think about the opinion of the Apostle Paul and how I think it should be interpreted. I confess that I would rather listen to the more understanding and learned who could so explain and demonstrate this problem that all those proofs I have assembled above would remain true and unshaken. The same holds for whatever others I have not mentioned by which Scripture very clearly reveals that faith avails nothing unless it is that faith described by the Apostle as the 'faith which works through charity.'[1] Moreover, without works there is no possible salvation, neither apart from nor through fire, because, if faith saves by fire, it is faith itself that saves. Positive and clear is the meaning of the words: 'What will it profit if a man says he has faith, but does not have works? Can the faith save him?'[2] Nevertheless I shall explain, in as few words as possible, how I feel about this perplexing problem in the writings of the Apostle Paul, provided that my sentiments in regard to this matter be clearly recalled, namely, that I said I preferred to hear my superiors elucidate these difficulties. In the first place, Christ is the foundation of the house of the wise builder. This needs no exposition, for it is clearly said: 'For other foundation no one can lay, but that which has been laid, which is Christ Jesus.'[3] If, moreover, Christ is the foundation, that foundation is indisputably the faith of Christ; 'through faith' indeed Christ dwells 'in

---
1 Gal. 5.6.
2 James 2.14.
3 Cf. 1 Cor. 3.10,11.

our hearts'[4] as the same Apostle affirms. If, then, it is the faith of Christ, it is no other than that defined by the Apostle as the faith 'which works through charity.'[5] Manifestly, we cannot accept as a foundation the faith of the devils by which they believe and tremble and confess Jesus the Son of God.[6] Why? Theirs is a faith impelled by fear, not the faith which works through charity. The faith of Christ, the faith of Christian grace, that is, this faith which works through love, when laid as the foundation, allows no one to perish. If I attempt to elaborate in greater detail what it means to build gold, silver, precious stones, or wood, hay, straw upon this foundation, I am afraid that my very explanation will become more difficult to understand. Nevertheless, with the help of God, briefly, and as well as I can, I shall make an effort clearly to set forth my convictions.

Consider with me the young man who asked the good Master what he should do to gain eternal life and was told that, if he wanted life everlasting, he must keep the commandments. He asked which commandments, and the answer was: 'Thou shalt not kill; Thou shalt not commit adultery; Thou shalt not steal; Thou shalt not bear false witness; Honor thy father and mother; and, Thou shalt love thy neighbor as thyself.'[7] If he observed these commandments in the faith of Christ, he indubitably would have the faith which operates through love. He could not love his neighbor as himself if he had not received love from God without which he would not love himself. Then, if he went further and carried out the counsels that our Lord added: 'if thou wilt be perfect, go, sell what thou hast, and give to the poor, and thou shalt have treasure in heaven; and come, follow me,'[8] he would be building upon the foundation of Christ

---
4 Cf. Eph. 3.17.
5 Gal. 5.6.
6 Cf. James 2.19.
7 Matt. 19.16-19.
8 Matt. 19.21.

gold, silver, precious stones. He would be 'concerned about the things of the Lord, how he may please God,'[9] and such considerations are, in my judgment, gold, silver, precious stones. If, on the other hand, he had an essentially human affection for his wealth, although he generously gave alms from it and did not plan to increase it by any fraud or robbery, or fall into any guilt or shame through fear of diminishing or losing it, or otherwise draw away from the stability of that foundation, but if on account of a too human affection, as I have said, he could not part with such goods without pain, he would be building wood, hay, straw upon that foundation. This would be especially true if he were married besides, and on account of his wife were 'concerned with the things of this world, how he might please his wife.'[10] Since possessions loved with a carnal affection are not lost without pain, they who base their holdings on faith in the foundation 'which works through charity'[11] and under no circumstance or desire prefer their possessions to faith, when they suffer deeply in the loss of them, they attain salvation through a sort of fire of grief. Now, one is more secure from so great grief and pain of loss the less one loves these temporal things or possesses them as if not possessing them. But, he who commits murder, adultery, fornication, idolatry and the like in order to hold fast to his wealth, or acquire it, will not be saved by fire by merit of the foundation. Having lost the foundation, he will be tormented in everlasting fire.

(28) Those who argue in favor of the potency of faith alone for salvation use also the following text from the Apostle: 'But if the unbeliever departs, let him depart. For brother or sister is not under bondage in such cases.'[12] This is to say that by reason of his faith in Christ a man may leave

---
9 1 Cor. 7.32.
10 1 Cor. 7.33.
11 Gal. 5.6.
12 1 Cor. 7.15.

the wife to whom he is legitimately bound, without any fault on his part, if she does not want to remain with him, her Christian husband, because he is a Christian. They take no cognizance of the fact that she is quite justly dismissed in the event that she were to say to her husband: 'I am not your wife unless you amass wealth for me by fraud or unless, even though you are a Christian, you continue to ply your trade in prostitution by which you used to support our household,' or if she knew any other shameful or disgraceful act of her husband by which, once seduced, she had grown accustomed to satisfy her lust, to live a life of ease, or appear more elegant. If that husband to whom his wife says these things had sincerely repented of his dead works when he approached the sacrament of baptism, and if he has faith in the foundation 'which works through charity,'[13] the love of divine grace is sure to have mastery over him and not love for the body of his wife, and the member which scandalizes him he firmly amputates. Whatever grief of heart he endures by this separation because of a sensual attachment to his spouse is the pain of loss which he will suffer. This is the fire through which by the burning hay he will be saved. If, on the contrary, he has his wife as if he had none,[14] that is, not for the sake of concupiscence, but out of mercy, paying rather than exacting the conjugal debt, unless perhaps he might save her, assuredly he will not grieve in a purely human manner when a union of that kind is broken. As such a one is solely preoccupied with the things 'which are of the Lord, how he may please God,'[15] to the extent that he builds a superstructure of gold, silver, precious stones upon his solicitude for the things of God, he will suffer no real loss. His structure, not built of hay, will escape the ravages of any fire.

---

13 Gal. 5.6.
14 Cf. 1 Cor. 7.29-35.
15 1 Cor. 7.32.

(29) Whether men endure these sufferings only in this life or whether similar judgments come after death, the interpretation that I have offered of Paul's thought is not, in my opinion, inconsistent with the principles of truth. But, as I was saying, even if there is a better selection of proof which does not occur to me, the fact remains that we do not have to say to the unjust, the rebellious, criminals, and the defiled, parricides, matricides, murderers, immoral people, sodomites, kidnappers, liars, perjurers, 'and whatever else is contrary to the sound doctrine, according to the gospel of the glory of the blessed God':[16] 'as long as you only believe in Christ and receive His sacrament of baptism, you will be saved even if you do not reform from that most evil life of yours.'

(30) Nor does the case of the woman of Canaan force us to conclude otherwise because the Lord granted her petition although He had previously said: 'It is not fair to take the children's bread and cast it to the dogs,'[17] because that Searcher of the heart saw the change in her when He praised her. And so He does not say: 'O dog, great is thy faith!' but: 'O woman, great is thy faith!'[18] He changed the word because He saw that her affection had changed and knew that His correction had borne fruit. I wonder if He would have praised in her a faith without works, that is, not a faith such as could now operate through charity, but a dead faith which James did not hesitate in the least to call the faith of devils,[19] not the faith of Christians. Finally, if they refuse to realize that the Canaanite woman had changed her corrupt ways when Christ rebuffed her with contempt and correction, whenever they come upon one who only believes in Christ and makes no attempt to conceal a really

---

16 Cf. 1 Tim. 1.10,11.
17 Matt. 15.26.
18 Matt. 15.28.
19 Cf. James 2.19.

FAITH AND WORKS 259

depraved life, but freely boasts of it, and is unwilling to change it, let them heal their sons if they can, just as the daughter of the Canaanite woman was healed. They must not, however, make him a member of Christ, since he does not cease to be united to a harlot. They are not illogical, of course, in recognizing the sin against the Holy Spirit and the unpardonable guilt of an eternal offense against God in one who up to the end of his life does not want to believe in Christ. If they only rightly understand what it means to believe in Christ! To believe in Christ is not to have the faith of devils, accurately termed a dead faith; it is to have a faith 'which works through charity.'[20]

Chapter 17

(31) Bearing in mind all that has been said, when we refuse baptism to such as I have described, it is not that we are attempting to uproot the cockle before it is time, but we are unwilling to sow cockle, as the Devil does, among the good.[1] We are not, moreover, preventing those who want to go to Christ from going to Him. We are convicting of guilt those who by their own profession do not want to go to Christ. We are not making belief in Christ prohibitive. We are pointing out that they do not believe in Christ who either defend as not adultery what He says is adultery, or who believe that adulterers may be members of His Body, although He says through the Apostle that they do not possess the kingdom of God and are opposed 'to the doctrine, according to the gospel of the glory of the blessed God.'[2]

---

20 Gal. 5.6.

---

1 Cf. Matt. 13.24-30.
2 1 Tim. 1.10,11.

These opponents of Christ are not to be reputed among those who come to the marriage feast,[3] but among those who do not want to come. When they dare, without the least disguise, to contradict the teaching of Christ and resist the holy Gospel, it is not that they are rejected when they seek admission; they reject themselves by making light of coming. Moreover, they who renounce the world, at least in words if not in deeds, come indeed to the feast and are sown among the wheat and are gathered into the barn and are joined with the sheep and are caught in the net[4] and are mingled with the banqueters. Whether their misconduct is open or secret, once within the Church, if there is no possibility of reforming them, there will be reason for toleration. And there should be no presumption of ejecting them. God forbid that we should so interpret the statement of the Gospel that those were brought into the marriage feast 'whom they found, both good and bad,'[5] that they are believed to have won over those who declared that they would persist in evil. If that were so, the servants of the householder sowed the cockle themselves, and that accusation will be false which states: 'and the enemy who sowed them is the devil.'[6] Still, the words, 'his servants . . . gathered . . . both good and bad,'[7] cannot be false whether the bad were hidden and hence unknown, or whether they were discovered after they had already been invited in, or whether 'both good and bad' is merely a stock phrase conveying the usual praise or censure of those who are still among the unbelievers. What about the Lord's directions to His disciples the first time He sent them to preach the Gospel that: 'whatever town or village' they entered they should inquire 'who in it is

---

3 Cf. Matt. 22.2-14; Luke 14.16-24.
4 Cf. Matt. 13.47.
5 Cf. Matt. 22.10.
6 Matt. 13.39.
7 Cf. Matt. 22.10.

FAITH AND WORKS 261

worthy,'[8] that they might stay with him until they were ready to leave? Who, in truth, is the worthy one if not he who is so acclaimed by his fellow townsmen; and who unworthy if not he who is condemned by them? Converts to faith in Christ are of both kinds and so it happens that both good and bad are brought in because the evil ones, too, do not refuse to repent of their dead works. But, if they refuse to repent, they are not driven away when they desire to enter, but of their own accord they withdraw from entering by an open contradiction.

(32) Therefore, even that servant will be safe and not damned among the slothful because he was unwilling to pay out his master's talent,[9] since they were indeed unwilling to accept what the Lord was paying out to them. This parable was also preached on account of those who are unwilling to undertake the duty of a dispenser in the Church, offering for an excuse the slothful pretext that they do not want to render an account of the sins of others. They are the ones who hear but do not heed, that is, who receive but make no return. When, in truth, a faithful and loving dispenser of God, zealously prepared in paying out and eagerly alert for the Lord's gain, says to an adulterer: 'do not be an adulterer if you want to be baptized; believe in Christ who says that this that you are doing is adultery, if you want to be baptized; do not be a member of a harlot[10] if you want to become a member of Christ.' If the adulterer in his turn replies: 'I will not obey: I will not do it,' it is because he does not want to receive the Lord's true money, but prefers to bring his own adulterous money into the treasury of the Lord. If, however, he should promise to amend his ways and then does not keep his promise and after baptism is by no

---
8 Cf. Matt. 10.11.
9 Cf. Matt. 25.15-30.
10 Cf. 1 Cor. 6.15.

means able to be reformed, measures would be found to make such persons, who are so unprofitable to themselves, harmless to others. This is to say that, if within the good net of the Lord there should be a bad fish, he nevertheless would not catch his Lord's fish with bad nets. By analogy, if within the Church he should lead a bad life, he still would not on that account teach an evil doctrine. When persons of that kind who defend such conduct of their own, and who at the same time are frankly and wilfully determined to persevere in their evil ways, are admitted to baptism, there apparently would be nothing else except to preach that fornicators and adulterers who persist in their wickedness even to the end of their lives will possess the kingdom of God and, by merit of a faith which without works is dead,[11] will attain eternal life and salvation. These are the bad nets[12] which fishermen ought especially guard against, if in that parable fishers are to be understood as bishops or superiors of a lower order in the Church, because of the words: 'Come, and I will make you fishers of men.'[13] With good nets can be caught fish good and bad: with bad nets, however, good fish cannot be caught, since from good teaching one can be good—he who hears and heeds—and another can be bad—he who hears and does not heed, but from bad doctrine he who thinks that the teaching is true although he does not submit to it is bad and he who submits is worse.

---

11 Cf. James 2.17,20.
12 Cf. Matt. 13.47,48.
13 Matt. 4.19.

Chapter 18

(33) It is truly remarkable that brethren who are wise in other respects, when they ought to discard that pernicious opinion whether old or new, instead raise the objection that this is a new dogma indeed which teaches that the exceedingly wicked who declare openly that they will persist in their licentious practices are not to be admitted to baptism. I scarcely understand such aberrations, since harlots and actors and all others professionals in public indecency are not permitted to approach the Christian sacrament without having first loosened, or broken themselves away altogether from, their filthy bondage. All these, according to my adversaries' way of thinking, surely would be admitted to baptism if holy Church did not retain her ancient and healthy practice, based on a truth so evident that they cannot miss it, 'that they who do such things will not attain the kingdom of God,'[1] and not allow them to approach baptism before they repented of their dead works. If it should happen that they receive the sacrament through deception, they still cannot be saved unless their behavior indicates that they have amended their ways. Drunkards, on the other hand, the covetous, the evil-tongued,[2] if they cannot be convicted or charged with open commission of any other damnable vice, are rigorously disciplined according to the precepts and manuals of instruction, and all such persons seem to approach baptism with a change of heart for the better. But, if by chance they notice that in some places, through carelessness, it has become customary to admit adulterers—that is, men who use the wives of others as if their own, or women, the husband of others—whom divine Law, not human law, condemns, they ought to try to correct these evil practices

---
1 Gal. 5.21.
2 Cf. 1 Cor. 6.10.

by right custom, that is, that even these be not admitted. They ought not pervert right custom by these corrupt practices. They should not think that it is unnecessary to instruct the *competentes* in the reformation of their manner of living, and, consequently, should think that all perpetrators even of public obscenities and outrages, that is, harlots, seducers, gladiators, and whoever else there are of this kind, ought to be admitted even if resolute in the pursuit of their evil activities. All those vices, to be sure, which the Apostle enumerates, concluding: 'they who do such things will not attain the kingdom of God,'[3] they should readily acknowledge, and should fittingly rebuke, on exposure, those who do such things excessively. They should refuse them baptism if they resist correction and publicly declare themselves inflexible.

Chapter 19

(34) They who believe that other things are easily compensated for by the giving of alms do not doubt, however, that there are three deadly sins that must be punished by excommunication until the offenders are cured by humble repentance: impurity, idolatry, murder. It is not now our task to inquire into the nature of this opinion or to determine whether it is to be corrected or approved. We want to avoid the risk of extending too long the work we have undertaken to answer questions not at all necessary for the resolution of our problem. Let it suffice to say that if some vices exclude one from the sacrament of baptism, among them is adultery. If, however, only three kinds of sin prevent the reception of baptism, among the three is adultery, the source of our whole discussion.

(35) Since the morals of bad Christians, who were even

---
[3] Gal. 5.21.

far more wicked before they became Christians, do not seem to have included the evil of men marrying others' wives and women wedding others' husbands; perhaps on that account the negligence crept in among certain churches of not inquiring into or uprooting such evil practices during the instructions of the candidates for baptism. In this way it came about that those evils began to be defended, which up to the present time are rare enough among the baptized—if we do not cause them to increase rapidly through our own lack of vigilance. In certain instances, of course, their appearance is due simply to neglect; in others, it is a matter of inexperience; while in still others, probably ignorance, as the Lord is understood to have signified under the term 'sleep,' when He says: 'but while men were asleep, his enemy came and sowed weeds.'[1] From this we must not conclude that such vices have appeared for the first time in the lives of bad Christians, inasmuch as blessed Cyprian in his letter on the fallen-away Christians, while bemoaning and rebuking them, mentioned[2] many evil practices which he asserts deservedly called down the indignation of God, so that He permitted His Church to be scourged by an intolerable persecution. He does not, however, mention the vices I have spoken of, although he is not silent in regard to a particular evil which he affirms belongs to those same bad practices. He maintains that the union with unbelievers in the bond of matrimony is nothing short of prostituting the members of Christ with heathens, a condition no longer considered sinful in our times. Because in the New Testament there is nothing explicitly prescribed about it, it is either believed to be lawful or it is passed over as a doubtful matter. So, too, it is questionable whether Herod[3] had married the wife of a dead or living brother, and

---

1 Matt. 13.25.
2 Cyprian, *De lapsis* 6.470.
3 Cf. Matt. 14.3,4.

for that reason it is not quite clear what John was declaring unlawful for him. Similarly, in the case of a concubine, if she has publicly promised that she will cohabit with no other, even if she should be dismissed by the one to whom she has been subject, there is just doubt whether she should be admitted to the reception of baptism. Furthermore, it does not seem right that whoever puts away his wife caught in adultery and marries another ought to be reduced to the equality of those who put away their wives for another reason than adultery, and remarry.[4] In the divine expressions themselves it is not clear whether one would be considered an adulterer if, having lawfully put away an adulteress, he should marry again; so that in this case, according to my judgment, one might be pardonably mistaken. On this account, those guilty of a misconduct of impurity which has been exposed must in every way be barred from baptism except where they have been straightened out by voluntary amendment and repentance. On the other hand, wherever there is a doubt, everything possible must be done to prevent questionable unions. What is the need of racking one's brains about an ambiguous distinction? If, however, such unions have been made, I question whether the contracting parties ought to be admitted to baptism.

Chapter 20

(36) So far as it belongs to the healthy teaching of truth to prevent granting a dangerous security and an unwholesome warrant to any death-bringing sin, there is this order of spiritual remedy: the candidates for baptism believe in God, Father, and Son, and Holy Spirit as formulated in the Creed; and especially they repent of dead works. They may

---
4 Cf. Matt. 5.32.

then be confident that in baptism they will receive complete remission of all past sin. The purpose of the remedy is not to make sinning lawful, but to remove the harm wrought by sin; not to give permission to sin, but to effect the remission of sin. The spiritual connotation becomes evident in: 'Behold, thou art cured. Sin no more'[1]—words which our Lord spoke as He healed the body of a man, since He knew that his body had been struck by an affliction, the just result of sin. I wonder, indeed, how they think the Lord's sentence, 'Behold, thou art cured,' can be passed on a man who enters baptism as an adulterer, and, after having been baptized, goes away still an adulterer. If adultery is health, what grave and deadly disease can there be?

Chapter 21

(37) But among the three thousand, they insist, whom the Apostles baptized in one day, and the many thousands of believers upon whom the Apostle 'from Jerusalem round about as far as Illyricum completed the gospel,'[1] there certainly were some married to the wives of other men and women to the husbands of other women. The Apostles ought to have established the rule then which would thereafter be observed in the churches, whether such were not to be admitted to baptism unless they had rectified these adulteries. As if the rule did not hold on that occasion just because they do not find anyone mentioned who had been admitted although he was an adulterer! Truly was it possible that the crimes—infinite in number—of individual men be enumerated, since the general rule more than covers all where Peter,

---
1 John 5.14.

---
1 Cf. Rom. 15.19.

bearing witness with many words, says to the baptismal candidates: 'Save yourselves from this perverse generation.'[2] Who would ever doubt that the perversity of this generation refers to adultery and those who choose to remain in this state of iniquity? It could just as well be asserted that public harlots, whom, certainly, no church admits to baptism before they have been released from such disgraceful bonds, could be found among the thousand believers of that time throughout the many nations and that the Apostles ought to have set them up as examples of those to be received or rejected. Nevertheless, from certain minor examples, we can conjecture greater. If the publicans coming to the baptism of John were forbidden to exact anything more than what had been appointed them,[3] I wonder if adultery could be permitted those coming to the baptism of Christ.

(38) They also recount how the Israelites had committed many serious offenses and had shed so much blood of the prophets, and yet not for these deeds entirely had merited destruction, but particularly for the infidelity by which they wilfully disbelieved in Christ. They pay no attention to the fact that this was not their only sin, that they did not believe in Christ, but that they killed Christ. Their one sin belongs to the crime of incredulity, the other to the crime of cruelty; one is contrary to the right faith, the other to right living. But he is free from both outrages who has the faith of Christ, not a dead faith without works[4] found even among devils, but the faith of grace 'which works through charity.'[5]

(39) This is the faith of which it is said: 'the kingdom of God is within you.'[6] This is the faith the violent have been

---
2 Acts 2.40.
3 Cf. Luke 3.12,13.
4 Cf. James 2.18,19.
5 Gal. 5.6.
6 Luke 17.21.

seizing by credence; they, by fulfillment of the Law,[7] are obtaining the spirit of love without which the Law, through the observance of the letter only, made them guilty of transgression. The saying, therefore: 'the kingdom of heaven is enduring violent assault, and the violent are seizing it by force,'[8] must not be thought to mean that the wicked, merely by believing and at the same time leading the worst kind of lives, enter the kingdom of heaven. It means, rather, that that guilt of transgression which was caused by the Law alone, that is, by the letter of the Law without the spirit commanding, is absolved by believing. By the violence of faith the Holy Spirit is obtained, through whom with 'charity poured forth in our hearts'[9] the Law is fulfilled, not in the fear of punishment, but in the love of justice.

Chapter 22

(40) By no means should the unwary make the mistake of thinking that they know God if they confess God with a dead faith, that is, without works after the manner of devils, and firmly trust that they will come to life everlasting because the Lord says: 'Now this is everlasting life, that they may know thee, the only true God, and him whom thou hast sent, Jesus Christ.'[1] They must also remember that Scripture says: 'And by this we learn of him, if we keep his commandments. He who says "I know him," and does not keep his commandments, is a liar and the truth is not in him.'[2] Lest anyone should think that His commandments pertain to faith alone—

---
7 Cf. Rom. 13.10.
8 Cf. Matt. 11.12.
9 Cf. Rom. 5.5.

---
1 John 17.3.
2 1 John 2.3,4.

although no one has dared to say this, especially since He said 'commandments,' of which, lest their number distract attention, He said: 'On these two commandments depend the whole Law and the Prophets'[3]—it may be said quite rightly that the commandments of God pertain to faith alone, if not a dead but a living faith which works through charity is understood. John explains later on exactly what he meant, when he says: 'And this is his commandment, that we should believe in the name of his Son Jesus Christ, and love one another.'[4]

(41) This, then, is beneficial, to believe in God with the right kind of faith, to worship God, to know God, that He may help us to live the right kind of lives, and, if we sin, that we may merit His pardon, not continuing with persistence and rash security in deeds that are hateful to Him, but withdrawing from them and saying to Him: 'I said: O Lord, be thou merciful to me: heal my soul, for I have sinned against thee,'[5] a prayer which, for those who do not believe in Him, has no auditor. In vain, too, do they utter these words who are estranged from the grace of the Mediator because they have strayed far from Him. Therefore, we have those words from the Book of Wisdom which I certainly do not understand how a rash confidence interprets: 'For if we sin, we are thine,' since we have a good and great Lord who both wills and has the power to heal the sins of penitents, One who by no means would fail to destroy the persistently malicious. Finally, when Solomon had said 'we are thine,' he added: 'knowing thy power, a power indeed from which the sinner is neither able to hide nor withdraw. He went on to add: 'But we shall sin not, knowing that we are counted with thee.'[6] Who, worthily reflecting on our habitation with God,

3 Matt. 22.40.
4 1 John 3.23.
5 Ps. 40.5.
6 Cf. Wisd. 15.2.

FAITH AND WORKS 271

to which all who are called according to plan are appointed by predestination,[7] does not strive to live in a manner befitting that dwelling place? John, too, says: 'these things I have written to you in order that you may not sin. But if anyone sins, we have an advocate with the Father, Jesus Christ the just; and he is a propitiation for our sins.'[8] He does not say this to give us protection in sinning. Rather, that if we have sinned we may, by forsaking sin utterly, have every hope of forgiveness because of that Advocate of whom infidels are deprived.

Chapter 23

(42) From these words we must be careful not to promise a too lenient condition to those willing to believe in God but with a faith that permits them retain their corrupt ways. Much more so must we be cautious of the words of the Apostles: 'Whoever have sinned without the Law, will perish without the Law; and whoever have sinned under the Law, will be judged by the Law,'[1] as if there were any difference between perishing and being judged, since the same idea is signified by another word. Scripture often employs the term 'judgment' for eternal damnation, just as the Lord does in the Gospel: 'for the hour will come in which all who are in the tombs shall hear the voice of the Son of God. And they who have done good shall come forth unto resurrection of life; but they who have done evil unto resurrection of judgment.'[2] Our Lord does not say those who have believed in the resurrection of life and, on the other hand, those who have not believed in the resurrection of

---
7 Cf. Rom. 8.28-30.
8 1 John 2.1,2.

1 Rom. 2.12.
2 Cf. John 5.28,29.

judgment; He says: 'those who have done good'; 'those who have done evil.' Truly, the good life is inseparable from faith, 'which works through charity.'³ This, indeed, is the good life itself, and hence we see that when the Lord had said the resurrection of judgment He meant the resurrection to eternal damnation. In regard to the final resurrection of all—among whom, of course, will be total unbelievers, who obviously will not be left in their tombs—He made two divisions, declaring that some would rise again unto resurrection of life; others, unto resurrection of judgment.

(43) If they presume to say that the reference above must not be assumed to concern those who are complete unbelievers, but those who will be saved by fire because they have believed even if they have lived wicked lives—for a passing punishment is signified by the term 'judgment'—they do so brazenly. The Lord plainly divided that last resurrection of all, among whom without question will be the incredulous, into two groups: 'life' and 'judgment.' Now, by 'judgment' He intended to infer eternal judgment, although He did not add the word 'eternal' to judgment; just as He did not qualify 'life' and say 'unto the resurrection of eternal life,' when certainly He did not mean any other but eternal. Let them see what answer they will give when He says: 'but he who does not believe is already judged.'⁴ Here, no doubt, either they understand that judgment has been used for eternal punishment or they will venture to say that even unbelievers will be saved by fire, since He says: 'he who does not believe is already judged,' that is to say, his destiny is already determined. That promise of theirs of judgment to believers, even those living bad lives, will not be such a great benefit after all, since even unbelievers will not necessarily be lost, but will be judged. If they do not dare to say this, then they dare

---
3 Gal. 5.6.
4 John 3.18.

not promise anything more clement to those about whom the Scriptures say: 'they will be judged by the Law,'[5] since it is agreed that judgment is the usual expression for eternal damnation. What about the fact, moreover, that we find the lot of those who sin knowingly, not only not very mild, but, even, far worse? They are those especially who have received the Law, for the words of Scripture are: 'where there is no law, neither is there transgression';[6] and again: 'I had not known lust unless the Law had said: Thou shalt not lust. But sin, having found an occasion, worked in me by means of the commandment all manner of lust.'[7] There are many other places where the Apostle expresses the same thought. From this more serious guilt the grace of the Holy Spirit sets one free through Jesus Christ our Lord. Grace, 'because the charity of God is poured forth in our hearts,'[8] gives justice satisfaction by which the inordinance of lust is overcome. It is evident, therefore, that nothing milder, but something even more serious, must be understood about those of whom the Apostle says: 'whoever have sinned under the Law, will be judged by the Law,' than about those who, sinning without the Law, will perish without the Law. Nor in this passage does the word 'judged' imply a passing punishment, but that punishment by which even unbelievers will be judged.

(44) Their whole aim is, of course, to promise salvation by fire to those who, while believing, continue to lead very bad lives. To this end they say to them: 'whoever have sinned without the Law, will perish without the Law; and whoever have sinned under the Law, will be judged by the Law,' as if they meant 'they will not perish, but will be saved by fire.' They are not able to comprehend the Apostle's distinction of sinners without the Law and sinners under the

---
5 Rom. 2.12.
6 Rom. 4.15.
7 Rom. 7.7,8.
8 Rom. 5.5.

Law, when he was speaking about pagans and Jews in order to emphasize the necessity of the liberating grace of Christ not only for the pagans, but for both pagans and Jews, as the entire Letter to the Romans very clearly testifies. Surely, then, even to the Jews sinning under the Law, who, the Apostle said, 'will be judged under the Law,' they may not promise, in virtue of the liberating grace of Christ, salvation, if you please, by fire, since Scripture said: they 'will be judged under the Law.' But, if they do not make such a promise, lest they contradict themselves—they who claim that the most serious sin of disbelief was an obstacle to the Jews— why do they apply to the problem of faith in Christ in unbelievers and believers what was written regarding those who sinned without the Law and those who sinned under the Law, since this was written about Jews and pagans in order to invite both to the grace of Christ?

Chapter 24

Scripture does not say: 'whoever have sinned without faith will perish without faith; and whoever have sinned in faith will be judged by faith, but 'without the Law' is said and 'under the Law,' to make it very evident that the reference was to the judgment being passed on pagans and Jews, and not on good and bad Christians.

(45) In the citation above, if they want to accept Law for faith, which is a great deal less unreasonable and absurd, even here they can apply the most clear judgment of the Apostle Peter in speaking of those who had taken occasion for sensuality and found a cloak for malice[1] in the words of Scripture: 'we' who belong to the New Testament 'are' not the children 'of a slave-girl' but 'of the free woman—in

---

1 Cf. 1 Peter 2.16.

virtue of the freedom wherewith Christ has made us free'[2]—
and had thought that to live in freedom meant that, secure,
as it were, by such great redemption, they could consider
lawful for themselves whatever released them from obligation,
ignoring the words: 'you have been called to liberty, brethren;
only do not use liberty as an occasion for sensuality.'[3] Peter
himself says: 'Live as freemen, yet not using your freedom
as a cloak for malice,'[4] and in his second letter: 'These
men are dry springs and mists driven by storms; the blackness
of darkness is reserved for them. For by high-sounding, empty
words they entice with sensual allurements of carnal passion
those who are just escaping from such as live in error. They
promise them freedom whereas they themselves are the slaves
of corruption; for by whatever a man is overcome, of this
also he is a slave. For if after escaping the defilements of the
world through the knowledge of our Lord and Saviour Jesus
Christ, they are again entangled therein and overcome, their
latter state has become worse for them than their former.
For it were better for them not to have known the way of
justice, than having known it, to turn back from the holy
commandment delivered to them. For what that true proverb
says has happened to them: A dog returns to his vomit, and:
A sow even after washing wallows in the mire.'[5] Why,
contrary to this manifest truth, is a better condition promised
to them for having known the way of justice, that is, the
Lord Christ, and yet living inordinately, than if they had not
known it at all, since the text says without reserve: 'it were
better for them not to have known the way of justice, than
having known it, to turn back from the holy commandment
delivered to them'?

---
2 Cf. Gal. 4.31; 5.1.
3 Gal. 5.13.
4 1 Peter 2.16.
5 Cf. 2 Peter 2.17-22.

Chapter 25

(46) In this passage the 'holy commandment' is not to be interpreted as the precept whereby we should believe in God, although everything is contained in that very precept if we understand the faith of believers to be that faith 'which works through charity.'[1] What the 'holy commandment' means is clearly expressed, namely, the precept whereby, withdrawing from the defilements of this world, we lead a life of purity. It states: 'For if after escaping the defilements of the world through the knowledge of our Lord and Saviour Jesus Christ, they are again entangled therein and overcome, their latter state has become worse for them than the former.'[2] It does not say 'escaping the ignorance of God' or 'escaping the unbelief of the world' or anything like that, but 'the defilements of the world,' in which, certainly, is included every foulness of sin. In speaking of those mentioned previously, he said: 'while banqueting with you, they have eyes full of adultery and turned unceasingly towards sin.'[3] On this account, he even calls them dry springs;[4] springs, to be sure, because they have received knowledge of the Lord Christ; dry, however, because they do not live in accordance with that knowledge. The Apostle Jude, also, when speaking of such person, says: 'These, who after becoming stained join in your feasts, feeding themselves without fear, are clouds without water,'[5] and so on. Where Peter says: 'while banqueting with you they have eyes full of adultery,' Jude says: 'after becoming stained they join in your feasts,' for they have mingled with the good at sacramental banquets

---
1 Gal. 5.6.
2 2 Peter 2.20.
3 2 Peter 2.13.14.
4 Cf. 2 Peter 2.17.
5 Cf. Jude 1.12.

and the feasts of the people. Where Peter says 'dry springs,' Jude says 'clouds without water,' and James says 'a dead faith.'[6]

(47) It is obvious, therefore, that a passing judgment of fire may not be promised to such as live disgracefully and sinfully, because they know the way of justice, although it were better for them not to know, as the unquestionably true Scripture testifies. About these very people, in fact, the Lord says: 'and the last state of that man will be worse than was the first.'[7] Because they have not received the Holy Spirit as the indweller of their purged soul, they cause a more insidious unclean spirit to return within them. Unless, perhaps, those under consideration are to be considered better because they have not returned to the uncleanness of adultery, but they have not withdrawn from it, or those who do not defile themselves after they have been cleansed, but they have refused to be cleansed! In order to receive baptism with a clear conscience, they do not disdain to vomit out the foulness of their former manner of living, but, like a dog, they lap it up again. In the holiness of their purification by baptism, with unfeeling heart, they stubbornly strive to retain their undigested filth. They do not conceal it with promises and deception, but belch it forth with the impudence of a public acknowledgment. Going out from Sodom, they do not, like Lot's wife,[8] turn and gaze back upon the things of the past, but they refuse to depart from Sodom; nay, rather, clinging to Sodom, they attempt to enter Christ. Paul the Apostle says: 'I formerly was a blasphemer, a persecutor, and a bitter adversary; but I obtained the mercy of God because I acted ignorantly, in unbelief';[9] to the wilfully wicked they

---
6 James 2.20.
7 Cf. Matt. 12.45.
8 Cf. Gen. 19.26.
9 1 Tim. 1.13.

would say: then rather will you obtain mercy, if, knowing evil, you will have lied by faith alone. It would be an almost endless task to wish to assemble all the testimony from Scripture which would evince conclusively that the condition of those who knowingly lead extremely wicked and unjust lives is not only less clement but actually much graver than those who lead such lives in ignorance; hence, this proof must suffice.

Chapter 26

(48) With the help of our Lord God, let us diligently beware henceforth of giving men a false confidence by telling them that if only they will have been baptized in Christ, no matter how they will live in His faith, they will arrive at eternal salvation. Let us not so make Christians as the Jews made proselytes, to whom the Lord says: 'Woe to you, Scribes and Pharisees, because you traverse sea and land to make one convert; and when he has become one, you make him twofold more a son of hell than yourselves.'[1] In both cases let us remain firm to the sound teaching of God the Master, namely, that the Christian life be consonant with holy baptism and that to none may eternal life be promised, if he will have lacked either one or the other. He who said: 'unless a man be born again of water and the Spirit, he cannot enter into the kingdom of God,'[2] also said: 'unless your justice exceeds that of the Scribes and the Pharisees, you shall not enter the kingdom of heaven.'[3] In truth, He says of them: 'The Scribes and the Pharisees have sat on the chair of Moses. All things, therefore, that they command you, observe and do. But do not act according to their works;

1 Cf. Matt. 23.15.
2 John 3.5.
3 Matt. 5.20.

for they talk but do nothing.'[4] Their justice is 'to talk and
do nothing.' That is why He willed that our justice 'to talk
and do' abound over theirs; if it will not have abounded,
there will be no entrance for us into the kingdom of heaven.
Not that anyone ought to be so exalted that he would dare,
I shall not say boast before others, but even believe himself
that he is without sin in this life. He ought to remember that,
unless there were certain sins so serious that they must be
punished with excommunication, the Apostle would not say:
'you and my spirit gathered together with the power of our
Lord Jesus to deliver such a one over to Satan for the
destruction of the flesh, that his spirit may be saved in the
day of our Lord Jesus Christ';[5] and also: lest 'I should mourn
over many who sinned before and have not repented of the
uncleanness and immorality that they practised.'[6] Moreover,
if there were not certain sins which must be healed, not by
that humility of penance such as is given within the Church
to the penitents properly so called, but by definite remedies
of discipline, the Lord Himself would not say: 'go and show
him his fault, between thee and him alone. If he listen to
thee, thou hast won thy brother.'[7] Finally, if there were not
certain things without which this life could not go on, He
would not put into prayer the daily healing remedy for
which He teaches us to pray: 'And forgive us our debts, as
we also forgive our debtors.'[8]

---

4 Matt. 23.2,3.
5 1 Cor. 5.4,5.
6 Cf. 2 Cor. 12.21.
7 Matt. 18.15.
8 Matt. 6.12.

Chapter 27

(49) It seems to me that I have adequately presented my position in regard to that whole controversy, which revolves about three issues.

The first is the mixture of good and wicked in the Church, similar to the mixture of wheat and cockle. Here we must be cautious against giving the impression that these likenesses—either the wheat and the cockle, or the unclean animals in the ark,[1] or any other pertinent figure of Scripture—have been pointed out to imply that the discipline of the Church, which is spoken of in the likeness of the valiant woman: 'Austere are the ways of her house,'[2] has grown lax. On the contrary, they have been emphasized to prevent the indiscretion of folly, rather than the severity of diligence, from advancing to the point of presuming to separate the good from the bad, as it were, by impious schism. Nor is there any intention by means of these parables and predictions to counsel slothfulness to the good whereby they might become careless where they ought to exercise precaution, but, rather, to counsel patience with which to endure in the firm doctrine of truth what they are not able to amend. Because unclean animals entered the ark with Noe, that is no reason why bishops ought to grant baptism to impure dancers who ask for it; yet they are certainly less offensive than adulterers. By this allegory it is prophesied that in the Church there will be the impure by reason of tolerance, not because of corruption of doctrine or dissolution of discipline. Furthermore, the unclean animals did not break their way into the ark through any part of the structure, but, because the ark was an

---
1 Cf. Gen. 7.3.
2 Cf. Prov. 31.27. St. Augustine seems to be translating from the Septuagint.

integral whole, they entered by the one and only entrance which the architect had made.

The second question seems to indicate that the candidates must be taught faith alone prior to baptism, and, after baptism, instructed in Christian morality. Unless I am mistaken, I have amply demonstrated that it is the duty of the guardian, at the time when all the faithful who ask for the sacrament are listening intently and anxiously to all that is being taught, not to be silent in regard to the punishment with which the Lord threatens those living evil lives, lest in baptism itself, to which the guilty one comes for the remission of all sins, there is matter for very serious sin.

The third question is the most dangerous of all. And since it has received too little consideration and treatment not in accordance with divine eloquence, that whole idea seems to me to have sprung up which promises to the most vicious and disgraceful sinners—even if they persist in their sinful living but believe in Christ and receive His sacrament—that they will attain salvation and everlasting life, contrary to the most evident judgment of the Lord, who answered the young man yearning for eternal life: 'if thou wilt enter into life, keep the commandments,'[3] and enumerated 'which commandments,' clearly indicating the sins to be avoided which obviously bar one from eternal salvation, because faith without works is useless.[4]

In answer to the three questions of the controversy I have, in my opinion, adequately demonstrated and made sufficiently evident that the wicked must be tolerated in the Church in such a way that ecclesiastical discipline will not suffer; that candidates for baptism must be instructed not only to hear and accept what they must believe, but also to live as befits that belief; that life without end must be promised to the faithful with such precision that no one will harbor the

---
3 Matt. 19.17.
4 Cf. James 2.20.

illusion that he can attain it with a dead faith useless for salvation because it is without works, but only by means of the faith of grace 'which works through charity.'[5] Nor has it been my purpose to find fault with the faithful dispensers of God for negligence or slothfulness, but, rather, to reprove the obstinacy of certain individuals who refuse to accept the Lord's talents, and compel the Lord's servants to use their adulterous money instead. At the same time, not for anything would they want to be classed with the evil servants such as St. Cyprian mentions,[6] who renounce this world in words alone, not in deeds; although not even in words do they renounce the works of the devil, since they publicly announce without any embarrassment that they intend to remain in their state of adultery. In conclusion, if my adversaries are apt to say anything which by chance my discussion has failed to touch upon, I am sure that it would be of such nature that an answer would be totally unnecessary, either because their comment would be irrelevant to the problem under debate, or because it would be so trivial that it could easily be refuted by anyone at all.

---

5 Cf. Gal. 5.6.
6 Cyprian, *De lapsis* 6.470,471.

THE CREED

(De symbolo ad catechumenos)

Translated by
SISTER MARIE LIGUORI, I.H.M., Ph.D.

INTRODUCTION

VERY LITTLE is definitely known about the *De symbolo ad catechumenos*. Possidius, in his *Indiculum*, merely notes three sermons on the Creed.[1] In *PL* 38 there are four sermons attributed to St. Augustine in which the Creed is expounded to catechumens. Sermons 212, 213, and 214 were delivered on the occasion of the *traditio symboli*, that is, the imparting of the Creed,[2] and Sermon 215 on the *redditio symboli* or the rectitation of the Creed.[3]

Of the four sermons *De symbolo ad catechumenos* in *PL* 40 that are there associated with the name of St. Augustine, the Benedictines of St. Maur considered only the first as genuine. The other three fall far short of the genius of Hippo. Their want of polish in diction and style, their lack of gravity, erudition, and intellectual acumen are noticeably at variance with all his other writings.[4] The Creed, too, as it is formulated in them, differs from the one used by St. Augustine.[5]

---

1 Cf. A. Wilmart, 'Operum S. Augustini Elenchus,' *Miscellanea Agostiniana* II (Rome 1931) 205: '175 De symbolo tractatus tres.'
2 All three sermons were delivered about fourteen days before Easter; Sermon 212 between 410 and 412; Sermon 213 before 410; Sermon 214 in 391 or possibly 423. Cf. A. Kunzelmann, 'Die Chronologie der Sermones des Hl. Augustinus,' *Miscellanea Agostiniana* II (Rome 1931) 417-520.
3 No specific date known. Cf. Kunzelmann, *op. cit.*
4 'Admonitio,' *PL* 40.625-626.
5 Cf. E. Portalié 'Saint Augustin,' *DTC* I 2 (Paris 1909) 2310.

The first and approved *De symbolo,* moreover, bears striking resemblance in content to the exposition of the Apostle's Creed in *De fide et symbolo*[6] which St. Augustine presented to an impressive audience, when, as a simple priest, he took part by request in the Council held at Hippo in October, 393.[7] Naturally, however, there is this difference between them: the lecture—long, philosophical, dogmatic, carefully planned and prepared—was delivered to the general Synod of African Bishops, men of knowledge and experience; the sermon was preached as an instruction to catechumens, who, for the most part, had little or no knowledge of religious matters. Dogma was, in fact, kept from them by the discipline of the secret until they were actually members of the Church.

One of the chief duties of bishop in the Christian Church was preaching. In the first Christian centuries, the Sacrifice of the Mass was unthinkable without a homily from the bishop. St. Augustine, however, had been commanded to fulfill this office when still only a priest. Then, after Valerius, Bishop of Hippo, died and Augustine succeeded him—four or five years after his ordination to the priesthood—preaching continued to play a dominant role in his life. To it he gave all the ardor and zeal of his temperament, the brilliance of his native endowment, and the refinement of his long years of rhetorical training.[8]

It goes without saying that the African Father was an eloquent and stirring preacher, enthusiastically received. He is pre-eminent for his deep psychological insight and great power of adapting his thought and expression to the comprehension level of his audience or auditor. He had the gift of eliciting the right responses and reactions from his

---
6 Cf. above, *Faith and Works* 1.1; 1.4; 4.8; 5.11; 7.14. 7.18; 9.16-21.
7 V. J. Bourke, *Augustine's Quest of Wisdom* (Milwaukee 1945), 132; cf. G. Bardy, *Saint Augustin, l'homme et l'oeuvre* (Paris 1946) 164-169; also, *Retractationes* 1.17 (*PL* 32).
8 Cf. Kunzelmann, *op. cit.* 417-419.

hearers who, although sometimes noisy, listened to him, nevertheless, with avidity and devotion.⁹

De symbolo ad catechumenos is an excellent example of the fine sympathy and understanding of one sensitively aware of the individual need of those before him. It may well represent the effort of the priest who, as bishop, was to become the consummate master of the theory and art of catechising, as *De catechizandis rudibus* so clearly indicates. The bishop, too, was a perfect example of that personal love for mankind and God which he strongly demanded of the catechist. His was ever a tender regard for the catechumens whom, on every occasion, he never ceased to encourage and exhort to ask for the sacrament of baptism.

Pertinent to an appreciation of the preacher's art of teaching is a comparison of the *De symbolo ad catechumenos* with the *Tractatus de symbolo*,¹⁰ the first of the thirty-three sermons found in the Wolfenbüttel collection and edited by Dom Morin for the Augustinian fifteenth centenary. The two sermons necessarily cover the same material, but differ in emphasis because of the experience, learning, preparation, and previous instructions of those addressed. *De symbolo*, for example, in treating of the Trinity, develops in great detail the equality and relation of Father and Son; the *Tractatus de symbolo* stresses the procession of the Holy Spirit. The virgin maternity of Mother Church is likened to the virginal maternity of the Mother of God in the latter; the former dwells on the Incarnation of the Son as contrasted with His eternal nativity. Strangely enough, there is no

---
9 Cf. Bardy, *op. cit.* 213-263; cf. also, H. Pope, O.P. *Saint Augustine of Hippo* (Westminster, Md. 1949) 139-194.
10 This sermon is practically identical with Sermon 213, *PL* 38 (1841) 1060-1065. It is longer by two additional sections, the first and last. Morin believes *Tractatus de symbolo* to be the genuine sermon because of its wording of the Creed, and distinctly Augustinian clausulae. Cf. 'Sermones Moriniani I—Ex Collectione Guelferbytana I, *Miscellanea Agostiniana* I (Rome 1930), 441-450.

overlapping of Scripture in the two sermons; St. Augustine does not repeat himself here. There are, however, at least seven parallels in which not only the thought but also the manner of expression is reproduced with some identity in diction. A few examples will illustrate the great preacher's manner of self-repetition, a natural habit which does not in the least detract from his evident awareness of the limitations and resources of his audience.

A part of the instruction on the omnipotence of God is almost word perfect in the two sermons, as (1.2): *'Deus omnipotens est: et cum sit omnipotens, mori non potest, falli not potest, mentiri non potest . . . Quam multa non potest, et omnipotens est, et ideo omnipotens est, quia ista non potest'* just escapes complete identity with (2.21-26): *'Nam ego dico quanta non possit: non potest mori, non potest peccare, non potest mentiri, non potest falli; tanta non potest, quae si posset, non est omnipotens.'*

In the following parallels, St. Augustine has caught the difficulties of those whom he is preparing for the sacrament of baptism which they will probably receive the following week on Easter Sunday (7.15): *'Nemo dicat: Illud feci, forte non mihi dimittitur. Quid fecisti? quantum fecisti? Dic immane aliquid quod commisisti, grave horrendum . . .'* echoes in the *Tractatus* (2.10-14): *'Nemo dicat: Non mihi potest dimittere peccata. Quomodo non potest omnipotens? Sed dicis: Ego multum peccavi. Et ego dico: Sed ille omnipotens est. Et tu: Ego talia peccata commisi, unde liberari et mundari non possum.'*

The present translation of *De symbolo ad catechumenos* follows the Benedictine text as reproduced in *PL* 40 (1887) 627-636.

THE CREED

Chapter 1

RECEIVE, MY SONS, the rule of faith which is called the Creed. When you have received it, write it on your hearts; recite it daily to yourselves. Before you go to sleep, before you go forth, fortify yourselves with your Creed. No one writes the Creed so that it can be read; let your memory be your codex that you may be able to review it if it should happen that forgetfulness effaces what diligence has given you. You will believe what you hear yourself saying, and your lips will repeat what you believe. The Apostle says truly: 'For with the heart a man believes unto justice, and with the mouth profession of faith is made unto salvation';[1] this is the Creed that you will be going over in your thoughts and repeating from memory. These words that you have heard are scattered throughout the divine Scriptures. They have been assembled and unified to facilitate the memory of dull mankind in order that everyone will be able to say the Creed and adhere to what he believes. Can it be that up to this point you have heard merely that God

---
1 Rom. 10.10.

is all-powerful? You are beginning to hold Him as a Father when you will be born of Mother Church.

(2) You have already received, you have meditated, and you have clung to the fruits of your meditation, so that you may say: 'I believe in God, the Father Almighty.' God is all-powerful, and, since He is all-powerful, He cannot die, He cannot be deceived, He cannot lie, and, as the Apostle says, 'he cannot disown himself.'[2] Very much He cannot do, yet He is all-powerful; because He cannot do these things, for that very reason is He all-powerful. If He could die, He would not be all-powerful; if He could lie, if He could be deceived, if He could deceive, if it were possible for Him to do an injustice, He would not be omnipotent; because, if it were in Him to do any of this, such acts would not be worthy of the Almighty. Absolutely omnipotent, our Father cannot sin. He does whatsoever He wills: that in itself is omnipotence. He does whatever He wishes well, He does whatever He wishes justly, but, whatever is evil, that He does not will. No one has the power to resist the Omnipotent and not do what God wills. He made heaven and earth, the sea, and all the creatures that are in them, visible and invisible; invisible, as in heaven the Thrones, Dominions, Principalities, Powers, Archangels, Angels, all of whom will be our fellow citizens if we shall have lived rightly. He made the visible creatures of heaven the sun, moon, stars. He adorned earth with His terrestrial animals; He filled the sky with winged creatures, land with moving and creeping things, the sea with fish; He filled all regions with their proper creatures. He made the mind of man to His own image and likeness; that is where the image of God is—in the mind. That is why the soul cannot be comprehended even by itself, where the image of God is. For this purpose have we been made, to be lord and master over all other creatures, but through the

---

2 2 Tim. 2.13.

sin of the first man we have fallen and have all come into the inheritance of death. We have become lowly mortals, filled with fears and errors. This is the wage of sin. Every man is born with this penalty and guilt.[3] That is the reason, just as you have seen today, just as you know, even little children are breathed upon and exorcized, so that the hostile power of the devil who deceived mankind in order to gain possession of men may be driven out of them. It is not, then, a creature of God that is breathed upon and exorcized in infants, but him under whose sway all are who are born with sin, for he is the prince of sinners. Now, on behalf of one who fell and thereby sent all to death there was sent into the world One without sin, who would lead back to life all who believed in Him, by liberating them from the power of sin.

Chapter 2

(3) We believe, therefore, in His Son, also, that is, the only Son of the Almighty Father, our Lord. When you hear the words, 'the only Son of God,' acknowledge that He is God. It cannot be that the only Son of God is not God, for God begot what He is, although He is not the Person whom He begot. Furthermore, if the Son is the true Son, He is what the Father is; if He is not what the Father is, He is not the true Son. Consider mortal creatures of earth: Whatever a thing is, that is what it generates. Man does not beget an ox, a sheep does not beget a dog, nor a dog a sheep. Whatever begets, begets according to its kind. Remember, therefore, and with fortitude, firmness, and fidelity, that God the Father has begotten this, that He Himself is omnipotent. These mortal creatures beget through corruption. Is this how God begets? A mortal being begets according to

---

3 Cf. Gen. 1-3.

its kind, an immortal according to its kind; corruptible begets corruptible; incorruptible, incorruptible; the corruptible begets by corruption, the incorruptible by incorruption; precisely what itself is, that it begets, so that one begets one and only one. You know when I went over the Creed with you I put it this way, and you ought to believe it this way: We believe in God the Father Almighty and in Jesus Christ, His only Son. When you believe that He is the only Son, believe, too, that He is Almighty, for it is not that God the Father does what He wills and God the Son does not do what He wills. There is only one will of the Father and Son because there is only one nature. The will of the Son cannot, in any degree whatsoever, be separated from the will of the Father. God and God, both one God; Almighty and Almighty, both one Almighty.

(4) We are not introducing two gods in the way that some teach two gods and say: God the Father and God the Son, but greater God the Father and lesser God the Son. Both are what? Two gods? You blush to say it; blush, then, to believe it. You say the Lord God the Father and the Lord God the Son; the Son Himself says: 'No man can serve two masters.'[1] Are we going to be in His family in a position similar to a large household where there is a *paterfamilias* who has a son, so that we, too, shall say the greater Master, the lesser Master? Shun such a thought. If you think such thoughts in your heart you are setting up an idol in your soul. Reject it, by all means. First believe, afterwards understand. On the other hand, when God grants almost instant understanding to one who believes, remember that it is a gift of God, not human frailty. Nevertheless, even if you do not yet understand, believe: one God the Father; God Christ, the Son of God. Both are what? One God. How are both said to be one God? In what way? Do you wonder?

---
1 Matt. 6.24.

In the Acts of the Apostles it says: 'Now the multitude of the believers were of one heart and one soul.'[2] There were many souls; faith had made them one. There were many thousands of souls; they loved one another, and the many are one; they loved God in the fire of charity and from a multitude they arrived at the oneness of beauty. If love made so many souls one soul, what is that charity in God where there is no diversity, only integral equality? If on earth and among men there can be such great love that many souls became one soul, then where the Father is ever inseparable from the Son, the Son inseparable from the Father, are both able to be other than one God? But those souls could have been called both several souls and one soul. God, moreover, in whom there is an ineffable and supreme union, can only be called one God, not two gods.

(5) The Father does what he wills; the Son does what He wills. Do not think the Father is almighty and the Son is not almighty. It is an error; blot it right out of you. Let it not abide in your memory; let it not be imbibed in your faith, and if by chance some one of you should imbibe it, let him spit it out. The Father is omnipotent; the Son is omnipotent. If the Omnipotent has not begotten the omnipotent, He has not begotten a true Son. What are we saying, brethren, if the greater Father has begotten a lesser Son? What have I said, He has begotten? Man, a greater person, begets a son, a lesser person, that is true, but that is because the father grows old and the son grows up, and by growing attains the form of his father. The Son of God, if He does not grow, since God cannot grow old, was begotten perfect; indeed, begotten perfect. If He does not grow, yet does not remain less, He is equal. That you may know the Omnipotent is begotten from the Omnipotent, hear Him who is Truth itself. What Truth says about Himself, that is true. What

---
2 Acts 4.32.

does Truth say? What does the Son who is Truth say? 'Whatever the Father does, this the Son also does in like manner.'³ The Son is omnipotent in that He does everything that He has willed to do. Now, if the Father does anything which the Son does not do, the Son spoke falsely when He said: 'Whatever the Father does, this the Son also does in like manner.' But, since the Son spoke truth, believe: 'Whatever the Father does, this the Son also does in like manner' and you have believed in the Omnipotent Son. Even if you have not pronounced that word in the Creed, that is what you have expressed when you have believed in only one God. Does the Father have anything which the Son does not have? That is what the blaspheming, heretical Arians say, not I. But I, what do I say? If the Father has anything which the Son does not have, the Son lies who says: 'All things that the Father has are mine.'⁴ Many and innumerable are the testimonies which prove that the Son is the true Son of God the Father, and God the Father begot the true Son God, and Father and Son are one God.

Chapter 3

(6) This only Son of God the Father Almighty, let us see what He did for us, what He suffered on account of us. He was born of the Holy Spirit and the Virgin Mary. He, so great a God, equal to the Father, was born humbly of the Holy Spirit and the Virgin Mary that he might heal the proud. Man exalted himself and fell; God humbled Himself and arose. What is the humility of Christ? God stretched forth His hand to fallen man. We have fallen; He has come down from heaven. We were lying prostrate; He stooped

---
3 John 5.19.
4 John 16.15.

down to us. Let us take His hand and let us rise again that we may not fall into punishment. This, then, is His bending down to us: 'He was born of the Holy Spirit and the Virgin Mary.' This very nativity as man is both lowly and lofty. Whence lowly? Because as man He was born of men. Whence lofty? Because He was born of a virgin. A virgin conceived, a virgin brought forth, and after bringing forth remained a virgin.

(7) Then what happened? 'Suffered under Pontius Pilate.' Pontius Pilate was performing the office of governor and was himself judge when Christ suffered His Passion. The time when Christ suffered is linked to the name of the judge Pontius Pilate: the time when He suffered, was crucified, died, and was buried. Who? What? For whom? Who? The only Son of God, our Lord. What? Crucified, died, and was buried. For whom? For the sacrilegious and for sinners. Great condescension! Great grace! 'What shall I render to the Lord, for all the things that He hath rendered to me?'[1]

(8) He was begotten before all time, before all ages. Begotten before. Before what, since there is no before with Him? Absolutely do not think of any time before that nativity of Christ whereby He was begotten of the Father. I am speaking of the nativity by which He is the Son of God Almighty, His only Son our Lord. This is the nativity of which I am speaking first. Do not suppose that in this nativity there was a beginning of time; do not imagine any interval or period of eternity when the Father was and the Son was not. From when the Father was, from then the Son likewise. And what is this 'from when' where there is no beginning in time? The Father has always been without beginning, the Son, always without beginning. And how can it be, you ask, that He was begotten if He has no beginning? Co-eternal from eternity. The Father has never been when

---
1 Ps. 115.12.

there was not the Son, yet the Son was begotten by the Father. Where can I find any analogy at all? We are among the things of earth; we are among visible creatures. Let earth give me a comparison; it offers none. Let the element of the waters give me some likeness; it has none to give. Let any animal offer an analogy; it cannot. An animal, to be sure, generates; it is both that which generates and that which is generated, but first the father is and afterwards the son is born. Let us find coevality and let us believe in co-eternity. If we should be able to find a father coeval with his son and a son coeval with his father, we would believe God the Father coeval with His Son, and God the Son co-eternal with His Father. On earth we can find something coeval, but we are unable to find any co-eternal. Let us extend coevality and let us believe co-eternity. Some one perhaps may interrupt you and say: When can a father be found coeval with his son, or a son coeval with his father? That the father may beget, he precedes in age; that the son may be born, he follows in age; but this father coeval with his son, or the son with the father, how can this be? Think of the father as fire and the son as its brilliance; see, we have found coevals. The very instant fire begins, immediately it brings forth brilliance; the fire is not before the brillance, nor the brilliance after the fire. And if we should ask which begets which, the fire the brilliance or the brilliance the fire, straightway common sense, an inborn wisdom, makes you all cry out: Fire the brilliance, not brilliance the fire. Behold the father beginning, behold the son at the same time, neither coming before nor following after. Behold, therefore, the father beginning; behold the son beginning simultaneously. If I have shown you a father beginning, and a son at the same time beginning, believe in the Father not beginning, and with Him the Son Himself not beginning; the Father eternal, the Son co-eternal. If you are making progress, you understand; make an effort now to go on. You are being born, but you ought also to grow, because no one begins from a state of perfection. It was permitted for the Son of God to be born perfect, because He was born without time, co-eternal with the Father, preceding all things; not in time, but in eternity. Hence, He was begotten co-eternal with the Father, and of that generation the Prophet said: 'Who shall declare his generation?'[2] Begotten of the Father without time, He was born of the Virgin in the fullness of time. Time had started before this nativity from a virgin. At the opportune moment, when He willed, when He knew, then He was born; for He was not born without willing to be born. No one of us is born because he wills it, and no one of us will die when he wills it. God was born when He willed it, and when He willed it He died. He was born as He willed to be born, of a virgin; He died as He willed to die, on the Cross. Whatever He willed, that He did: He was man in such manner as to hide the Godhead; God the assumer, man the assumed, one Christ, God and man.

(9) What shall I say about His Cross? What shall I tell you? He chose the most extreme form of death in order that His martyrs would fear no kind of death. He made known His doctrine in the man; in the Cross He gave them an example of patience. There was His task, that He was crucified: the execution of the task, the Cross; the reward of the task, the Resurrection. In the Cross He showed us what to endure, in the Resurrection what we ought to hope for. Truly, as the supreme Gladiator, He said: Do, and endure; do the work and receive the reward; strive in the contest and you will be crowned. What is the work? Obedience. What is the reward? Resurrection without death. Why have I added: without death? Because Lazarus rose and died;

2 Isa. 53.8.

Christ rose and 'dies no more; death shall no longer have dominion over him.'³

(10) Scripture says: 'You have heard of the patience of Job, and you have seen the purpose of the Lord.'⁴ How much Job endured when he was stripped and was shunned, when he feared with a great fear, when he trembled all over! And what did he receive? Double what he had lost. Let no one, however, be willing to suffer patiently for the sake of a temporal reward and say to himself: I shall bear this loss; God will give me back twice as many sons; Job received everything back twofold, and begot as many sons as he had buried. Were they not, therefore, twice as many? Certainly they were twice as many, since the others were still living.

Let no one say: Let evils come; I will put up with them and God will repay me in the same measure as He repaid Job. That is no longer patience; that is greed. If that holy man had not had patience, he would not have so courageously held up under all the misfortunes that befell him. What proof do we have that God restored all to him? 'Hast thou considered,' said the Lord, 'my servant Job, that there is none like him in the earth, a man without a complaint, a true worshiper of God?'⁵ What a testimony, brethren, did that holy man merit from God! Yet his wife wanted to deceive him with her evil persuasion, even to having the appearance of that serpent which had deceived the first man⁶ made by God in the Garden of Paradise, and now thought that he could also deceive this man, who was pleasing to God, by suggesting blasphemy. How much Job suffered, brethren! Who could suffer so much in his possessions, in his household, in his children, in his own flesh, in his very own wife, the temptress who remained for him? But even her who had

---
3 Rom. 6.9.
4 James 5.11.
5 Cf. Job 1.8; 2.3.

been spared the serpent would have taken away long before if she had not abetted him, since it was through Eve that he had vanquished the first man. He had preserved Eve!

How much Job suffered! He lost everything he had. His house fell into ruins. Would that that were all! It crushed his children to death. But because patience had retained such a great hold on that man, what did he answer? Listen: 'the Lord gave, and the Lord hath taken away: as it hath pleased the Lord so is it done: blessed be the name of the Lord.'[7] He took away what He gave; would He be lost, too, He who gave? He took away what He gave. As if Job were to say: 'He has taken everything; let Him take all; let Him dismiss me naked, but let me keep Him. For, what is lacking to me, if I have God? What do other things profit me, if I have not God?' His flesh was afflicted; he was struck with an ulcerous scab from his head to the soles of his feet. Corrupt matter was flowing from his sores and he was swarming with vermin. Yet he proved himself resolute and constant to his God. The woman—the handmaid of the Devil, not the comforter of her husband—meant to induce him to blaspheme God: 'How long,' she said, 'are you going to endure all this? Speak some word against the Lord and die.'[8] Because he had been humiliated, therefore, he was exalted. And the Lord did this that He might make his example known to men; on the other hand, He kept greater things in heaven for his servant. Job humbled, He exalted; the devil elated, He humbled: since 'One he putteth down, and another he lifteth up,'[9] However, dearly beloved brethren, let no one look for a reward in this life when he suffers any tribulations of this kind; for example, if one should endure any loss, let him beware of perhaps saying to himself: 'the Lord gave,

---
6 Cf. Gen. 3.1-6.
7 Job 1.21.
8 Cf. Job 2.9.
9 Ps. 74.8.

and the Lord hath taken away: as it hath pleased the Lord so is it done: blessed be the name of the Lord'[10] in order to receive back twofold what he had lost. Patience, not avarice, gives glory to God. If you seek to receive back double the things you have lost and for that reason praise God, you are praising Him from greediness, not from love. Do not let it so much as occur to you that such is the example of that saintly man, for you are deceiving yourself. When Job was bearing all things, he was not looking for a twofold return. Both his first confession when he suffered the loss of all his possessions and carried the bodies of his children to the grave, and his second confession when he endured patiently the flowing infections of his flesh, testify to what I am saying. These are the words of his first confession: 'the Lord gave, and the Lord hath taken away; as it hath pleased the Lord so is it done: blessed be the name of the Lord.' He could have said: 'The Lord gave, the Lord has taken away; He who has taken can give again, can restore more than He has taken.' He did not say that, but, 'as it hath pleased the Lord so is it done': because it pleases Him, let it please me; let not what has pleased the good Lord displease His obedient servant; let not what has pleased the Physician displease the sick man. Hear, now, his other confession: 'Thou hast spoken,' he said to his wife, 'like one of the foolish women: if we have received good things at the hand of God, why should we not receive evil?'[11] He did not add, what would be true, if he had said it: 'The Lord is powerful, He can restore my body to its former health, and what He has taken from us He is able to multiply in return.' He did not say this, lest it seem that he suffered his torments with such hope before him. He did not say such things; he did not look for such things. It was for our instruction that God

---
10 Job. 1.21.
11 Job 2.10.

gave to him who was expecting nothing; it was for us to learn that He was with Job, because, if He had not restored everything to him as He did, we could by no means have been able to see his hidden crown. What, then, does divine Scripture say in exhorting us to patience and the hope of future rewards, not present ones? 'You have heard of the patience of Job, and you have seen the purpose of the Lord.'[12] Why the 'patience of Job,' and not: 'You have seen the purpose of Job himself?' You would open your jaws for twice as much; you would say: 'Thanks be to God, let me bear up under this and I shall receive twice as much, just like Job.' 'The patience of Job, the purpose of the Lord.'[13]

The patience of Job we know, and the purpose of the Lord we know. What purpose of the Lord? 'O God, my God, why hast thou forsaken me?'[14] These are the words of our Lord hanging on the cross. God abandoned Him, as it were, for present happiness, but did not abandon Him for eternal immortality. There is the purpose of the Lord. The Jews held Him, the Jews insulted Him, the Jews bound Him, they crowned Him with thorns, they dishonored Him by spitting upon Him, they scourged Him, they heaped abuses upon Him, they hung Him upon a tree, they pierced Him with a lance, finally they buried Him; He was, as it were, abandoned. By whom? By those insulting Him. Have patience, therefore, that you may rise from the dead and not die, that is, never die as Christ never dies; for so we read: 'Christ, rising from the dead, dies now no more.'[15]

---

12 James 5.11.
13 Cf. James 5.11.
14 Ps. 21.2.
15 Rom. 6.9.

Chapter 4

(11) Believe: 'He ascended into heaven.' Believe: He 'sitteth at the right hand of the Father.' Understand that to sit here means to dwell in the same sense that we say of anyone: he has lived in that country for three years. Scripture employs the same expression, as: 'a certain man dwelt in the city many days.'[1] Now, does this mean he sat and never rose? In this connection: the abodes of men are called seats. Where their seats are is there always sitting, no rising, or walking, or lying down? Yet these are called seats. Believe, then, in this way: Christ dwells on the right hand of God the Father; He is there. Do not let your heart say: 'What is He doing?' Do not seek what is not given you to find. He is there; that is enough for you. He is happy with a happiness that is called the right hand of the Father; the name, the right hand of the Father is of happiness itself. If we accept in its physical sense that He sits at the right hand of the Father, the Father will be at His left. Is it proper for us to arrange them in this order: the Son to the right, the Father to the left? There, all is on the right because there is no misery in heaven.

(12) 'From thence He shall come to judge the living and the dead': the living, those who are still alive; the dead, those who have gone before. It can be interpreted in this way, too: The living are the just; the dead the unjust. He judges both, giving each his due. To the just He will say in judgment: 'Come, blessed of my Father, take possession of the kingdom prepared for you from the foundation of the world.'[2] Prepare yourselves for this, hope for these blessings; for this live, and so live with this before you, for this

---
1 Cf. 3 Kings 2.38.
2 Matt. 25.34.

believe, for this be baptized, that to you may be said: 'Come, blessed of my Father, take possession of the kingdom prepared for you from the foundation of the world.' What does He say to those on His left? 'Go into everlasting fire which was prepared for the devil and his angels.'[3] Thus will the living and the dead be judged by Christ. We have spoken of the first nativity of Christ, without time; we have spoken of the other nativity, in the fullness of time, the nativity of Christ from a virgin; we have spoken of the Passion of Christ; and we have spoken of the judgment of Christ. Everything has been said which had to be said about Christ, the only Son of God, our Lord; but not yet is the Trinity completed.

Chapter 5

(13) The Creed continues: 'And in the Holy Spirit.' This Trinity is one God, one nature, one substance, one power, supreme equality, no division, no diversity, perpetual charity. Do you want to know that the Holy Spirit is God? Be baptized and you will be His temple. The Apostle says: 'Or do you not know that your members are the temple of the Holy Spirit, who is in you, whom you have from God?'[1] God has a temple, Solomon, king and prophet, was, for example, commanded to build a temple to God. If he had built a temple to the sun or the moon, or star, or an angel, would not God have condemned it? Because he built a temple to God, he showed that he worshiped God. And of what did he build it? Of wood and stone, since God deigned to make a home for Himself on earth through His servant, where He might be petitioned, where He might be re-

---
3 Cf. Matt. 25.41.

1 1 Cor. 6.19.

membered. That is why blessed Stephen says: 'Solomon built him a house. Yet not in houses made by hands does the Most High dwell.'[2] If, then, our bodies are the temple of the Holy Spirit, what manner of God is He who built a temple to the Holy Spirit? God of course, for, if our bodies are the temple of the Holy Spirit, He who made our bodies also built the temple for the Holy Spirit. Listen to the Apostle who, when he was speaking of the different members to stress the absence of dissension in the body, says: 'God has so tempered the body together in due portion as to give more abundant honor where it was lacking.'[3] God created our body; God created the grass. Who created our body? Where do we find proof that God creates the grass? He who clothes is the very One who creates. Read the Gospel: 'But if God so clothes the grass of the field, which today is alive and tomorrow is thrown into the oven.'[4] Therefore, He who clothes creates. And the Apostle: 'Senseless man, what thou thyself sowest is not brought to life, unless it dies. And when thou sowest, thou dost not sow the body that shall be, but a bare grain, perhaps of wheat or something else. But God gives it a body even as He has willed, and to each of the seeds a body of its own.'[5] If, therefore, God builds our bodies and our bodies are the temple of the Holy Spirit, have no doubt that the Holy Spirit is God. And do not add the Holy Spirit as if you were naming a third god, because the Father, Son, and Holy Spirit are one God. And so believe.

---

2 Acts 7.47,48.
3 1 Cor. 12.24.
4 Matt. 6.30.
5 1 Cor. 15.36-38.

Chapter 6

(14) After the praise of the Trinity comes 'the holy Church.' God and His temple have been pointed out. 'For holy is the temple of God,' says the Apostle, 'and this temple you are.'[1] This is holy Church, the one Church, the true Church, the Catholic Church, fighting against all heresies; she can fight, but she cannot be conquered. All heresies are expelled from her as if they were dead branches pruned from the vine; she herself, however, remains fixed in her root, in her vine, in her charity. The gates of hell shall not prevail against her.[2]

Chapter 7

(15) 'The forgiveness of sins.' You have the Creed in its perfection in you when you receive baptism. Let no one say: 'I have committed that sin; perhaps it is not forgiven me.' What have you done? How great a sin have you committed? Tell me anything terrible that you have done, something serious, horrible, something that makes you shudder just to think about it; whatever you might have done, did you kill Christ? There is nothing worse than that crime, because there is nothing better than Christ. What a diabolical thing it is to kill Christ! Nevertheless, the Jews killed Him, and afterwards many believed in Him, and drank His Blood. The sin which they had committed was forgiven them. When you have been baptized, hold to the good life in the commandments of God that you may preserve your baptism up to the very end. I do not say to you that you will live here without sin, but they are venial sins which we cannot avoid in this life. Baptism was devised for all sins; for slight sins without

---
1 1 Cor. 3.17.
2 Cf. Matt. 16.18.

which it is impossible to live, prayer was found. How does the prayer go? 'And forgive us our debts, as we also forgive our debtors.'[1] We are cleansed but once by baptism; daily we are cleansed by prayer. But do not commit those sins that compel your separation from the Body of Christ; God forbid that you should! They whom you see doing penance have committed crimes, either adultery, or some other outrage; that is the reason why they are doing penance. If their sins were slight, daily prayer would be enough to destroy them.

Chapter 8

(16) Within the Church, sins are forgiven in three ways: by baptism, by prayer, and by the greater humility of penance; yet God does not forgive sins except to the baptized. Those sins which He forgives in the first way He forgives only to the baptized. When? When they are being baptized. Sins which are forgiven afterwards to those who pray and repent are forgiven them because they have been baptized. For, how can those who are not yet born say 'our Father'? As long as they are catechumens, all their sins are still upon them. If this is true of catechumens, how much more so is it of pagans, of heretics? But we do not remove baptism from heretics. Why? Because they possess baptism in the same way that a deserter from the army possesses a mark. So, too, do the heretics have baptism. They have it, but unto damnation, not unto the crown. But, if a deserter should resume service after he has reformed, does one dare to remove his mark?

---

1 Matt. 6.12

Chapter 9

(17) We believe also in 'the resurrection of the body' which has gone before us in Christ, and the body which has gone before us in the Head awaits resurrection. Christ is the Head of the Church, the Church is the Body of Christ.[1] Our Head has arisen from the dead, has ascended into heaven; where the Head is, there, too, are the members. How, then, do we accept the resurrection of the body? Let no one by any chance think it the same as the resurrection of Lazarus. That you may know that it is not the same, the words 'unto life everlasting' are added. May God regenerate; may God preserve and watch over you; may God bring you unto Himself who is Life Everlasting. Amen.

---

1 Cf. Eph. 5.23.

FAITH AND THE CREED

(De fide et symbolo)

Translated by
ROBERT P. RUSSELL, O.S.A., Ph.D.
Villanova University

INTRODUCTION

HE SHORT WORK entitled *Faith and the Creed* was occasioned by the Plenary Council of Hippo celebrated in October, 393.¹ The task of addressing the Council on the subject of the Creed was entrusted to Augustine, who had been ordained priest scarcely two years before by the aging Valerius, Bishop of Hippo. The choice of Augustine as spokesman for the Council is all the more significant when it is recalled that local custom in Africa reserved to bishops the right of preaching to the faithful. This action of the African bishops in making Augustine their spokesman shows clearly the esteem and authority already enjoyed by the future Doctor of the Church.

In his *Retractations* (1.7) Augustine acknowledges that it was at the insistence of close friends that he was prevailed upon to publish the discourse delivered before the African episcopate. If due allowance is made for possible expansion and literary revision, it may be assumed that the treatise *Faith and the Creed* reproduces, in substance, Augustine's historic address to the Council of Hippo in 393.

The present work of Augustine is but the first of several devoted to the general theme of faith and the articles of the

---
1 Cf. Hefele, *History of the Councils of the Church* (Edinburgh 1896) 2 394-395.

Creed. There follows next in order *The Christian Combat,*[2] composed in 397, which is closer to the first treatise not only in time but also in content and form. Important stylistic differences, however, separate these works widely. *The Christian Combat* was written purposely 'for the brethren who were not proficient in the Latin language.'[3] The present work, a written account of Augustine's discourse to the African bishops, conforms in literary quality to the high standards of composition set by the ecclesiastical documents of the time and place. From a literary point of view, *Faith and the Creed* has been judged one of Augustine's finest compositions.[4]

A third work, bearing the title *On Faith in Things Unseen*[5] and written about 399, shows first the reasonableness of faith and its necessity even in human affairs and then demonstrates the credibility of faith which is divine and supernatural. In *Faith and Good Works,* Augustine insists that adult candidates for baptism resolve firmly upon a good life before being admitted to the sacrament and stresses the important teaching that faith alone, without good works, is insufficient for eternal salvation.

Augustine's most complete and systematic handling of the subject of faith and the Creed is to be found in his *Enchiridion,* or *Handbook, On Faith, Hope, and Charity.*[6] The treatise is mostly given over to the subject of faith. Hope is limited to an explanation of the Lord's Prayer and the closing chapters extol briefly the dignity and primacy of charity in the Christian life.

---

2 Translated by R. P. Russell, O.S.A., in Volume 2 of this series (rev. ed., New York 1950).
3 *Retractationes* 2.3.
4 Cf. F. Di Capua, 'Il ritmo prosaico in S. Agostino,' in *Miscellanea Agostiniana* (Roma 1931) 2.665.
5 Translated by Roy J. Deferrari and Sister Mary Francis McDonald, O.P., in Volume 4 of this series (New York 1947).
6 Translated by Bernard M. Peebles in Volume 2 of this series.

A span of nearly thirty years separates Augustine's initial effort from his definitive work known as the *Enchiridion*. These three decades bear witness to the development of Augustine's theological thought and remind us of his admonition that readers of his works observe the proper chronological sequence if they would properly understand the history of his intellectual and religious evolution.[7] The *Enchiridion*, which has been aptly described as the saint's 'only systematic treatment of the Church's doctrine as a whole,' is a work of theological maturity and one wherein the reader may find those typically Augustinian positions on the nature and necessity of grace as well as the related problems of original sin and predestination.

The earlier and more compendious work, *Faith and the Creed*, is distinguished for its simplicity and brevity in the formulation of the main articles of belief. Here Augustine sets the pattern, followed later in *The Christian Combat*, of setting forth the doctrines of faith together with appropriate references to the specific heresies in question. *Faith and the Creed* is not without historical significance, for it stands as an important landmark in the life of the great African Doctor, whose influence was soon to spread from provincial Africa and mold the theological learning of the Western Church for centuries to come.

Finally, *Faith and the Creed* furnishes further evidence for the conclusion of scholarly research on the origin of the Creed, that the early Church, far from being indifferent to religious dogma, was vitally preoccupied with its proper understanding and correct formulation.[8]

The present English translation has been made from the critical edition of J. Zycha, in *Corpus Scriptorum Ecclesiasticorum Latinorum* 41 (Vienna 1900).

---

[7] *Retractationes* prol. 3: 'Whoever reads my works in the order in which they are written will see, perhaps, how I have made progress by writing.'

[8] Cf. J. de Ghellinck. *Patristique et moyen âge* I (Bruxelles-Paris 1946) 224.

SELECT BIBLIOGRAPHY

Texts:

Sancti Augustini Hipponensis episcopi opera VI (Paris 1695), (Maurist edition), reproduced in *PL* 40.181-196.
J. Zycha, ed., *Corpus Scriptorum Ecclesiasticorum Latinorum* (Vienna 1900) 41.3-32.
H. Smith, ed., *De fide et symbolo* (London 1926).

Translations:

'Of Faith and of the Creed,' in *Library of the Fathers* (Oxford 1847) 15-36.
'Treatise on Faith and the Creed,' *Works of Aurelius Augustine*, ed. Marcus Dods (Edinburgh 1883) 9.339-370.
M. H. Barreau: *Oeuvres Complètes de Saint Augustin* (Paris 1869) 21.223-241, trans. M. H. Barreau, with Latin text.
J. Rivière: *Oeuvres de Saint Augustin*, Bibliothèque Augustinienne (Paris 1947) 9.13-25, trans. J. Rivière, with Latin text.

Supplementary Works:

P. Alfaric, *L'évolution intellectuelle de saint Augustin* (Paris 1918); *Les écritures manichéennes* (Paris 1918).
G. Bardy, 'Manichéisme,' in *DTC* 9, cols. 1841-1895.
F. C. Burkitt, *The Religion of the Manichees* (Cambridge 1925).
J. de Ghellinck, S.J., *Patristique et moyen âge* I (Bruxelles-Paris 1946).
F. Di Capua, 'Il ritmo prosaico in S. Agostino,' *Miscellanea Agostiniana* II (Rome 1931) 665ff.
J. Finaert, *L'évolution littéraire de saint Augustin* (Paris 1939).
E. Gilson, *L'introduction à l'étude de S. Augustin* (3rd ed., Paris 1949).
C. Hefele, *A History of the Councils of the Church*, trans. H. N. Oxenham (Edinburgh 1896).
H. Leclercq, 'Images,' in *DACL* 1.1 (Paris 1926) cols. 214ff.
J. Tixeront, *Histoire des dogmes* (Paris 1922-1924).
G. Verbeke, *L'évolution de la doctrine du pneuma du stoicisme à S. Augustin* (Paris-Louvain 1945).

FAITH AND THE CREED

Chapter 1

THE FACT THAT 'the just man lives by faith'[1] is a matter of Scripture as well as a truth corroborated by the very weighty authority of apostolic tradition. And since this faith requires of us the service of both heart and tongue, we must be mindful both of justice and salvation, for the Apostle says: 'With the heart a man believes unto justice, and with the mouth profession of faith is made unto salvation.'[2] Since we who expect to reign in everlasting justice can, in fact, only be saved from this wicked world, if, while ourselves for our neighbor's salvation, we profess with our lips the faith we bear about in our heart, we must exercise a pious and careful vigilance to see that this faith in us is not sullied in any point of belief by the deceitful snares of heretics.

As expressed in the Creed, the Catholic faith is familiar to believers who have learned it by heart in as few words as the subject permits. In this way the truths to be believed are framed in few words for the benefit of those who have been

---
1 Hab. 2.4; Gal. 3.2.
2 Rom. 10.10.

born again in Christ, for beginners and young ones whose faith has not yet been made strong by a careful training in the spiritual meaning of the divine Scriptures. This faith is to be expounded to them at greater length as they advance and rise to the heights of divine knowledge along the sure path of humility and charity.

It is, therefore, underneath these few words which comprise the Creed that most heretics have attempted to conceal their poisonous wares. God in His mercy has withstood them and does so now through the agency of men possessed of spiritual insight. These have been found worthy not only to embrace and believe the Catholic faith as set forth in the words of the Creed, but also to possess a knowledge and understanding of it, being further aided by enlightenment from the Lord. For it is written: 'Unless you believe, you shall not understand.'[3]

A detailed treatment of the faith is a help in defending the Creed. This does not mean it should take the place of the Creed as something to be learned by heart and recited by those seeking to receive the grace of God. But it does help to safeguard the truths found in the Creed from the snares of heretics by an appeal to Catholic authority and by the erection of a stronger defense position.

Chapter 2

(2) Some heretics have tried to make people believe that God the Father is not almighty.[1] They have not been rash

---

3 Isa. 7.9 (Septuagint).

1 Augustine's preoccupation at this time with the Manichaean heresy is evidenced here as well as in other passages of the present work. The sect arose in Persia about the middle of the third century and spread

enough to say this, yet, on the basis of their teaching, they are open to the charge of entertaining such an opinion and belief. They affirm the existence of a nature which Almighty God did not create from which He fashioned this world, which, they admit, is harmoniously designed. Thus they carry their denial of God's omnipotence to the extent of believing that He was unable to make the world unless in its production He made use of another pre-existing nature which He Himself had not produced. This comes about, of course, from a habit of sense perception which observes carpenters, builders, and artisans of every kind who cannot bring their skill to full realization without the aid of ready-made material.

This much they do understand: that the Maker of the world is not almighty if He could not make the world unless some nature, unproduced by Him, were available to aid Him in the way of material. But, if they grant that an Almighty God is the Maker of the world, they are constrained to acknowledge that He produced the things He made out of nothing. Since He is almighty, there could be nothing in existence of which He would not be the Creator.

Even if God did make one thing from another, as man from slime, He surely did not make it out of something He had not produced Himself, because He made out of nothing the earth from which the slime comes. And if He made the heaven itself and the earth, that is to say, the world and all things in it, out of some kind of matter, (as it is written:

---

so rapidly that it soon gained a stronghold throughout the Roman Empire. Dualistic in its metaphysical basis, Manichaeanism taught the co-existence of two eternal and antagonistic principles or 'roots', Light and Darkness. The present world was produced to bring about the restoration of particles of Light lost through conflict with the hostile elements of Darkness. In carrying out his cosmic plan, the King of Light had to avail himself of the elements of Darkness, thus contracting a dependency hardly consistent with the nature of an omnipotent and inviolable Deity. For a more detailed exposition cf. titles by G. Bardy, P. Alfaric, and F. C. Burkitt in Select Bibliography.

'Thou hast made the world out of invisible matter,'[2] and also from 'unformed' matter, as some copies have it), we are not to suppose for a moment that this same matter, though unformed and invisible or however it existed, could have existence of itself, as if it were co-eternal and coeval with God. But whatever mode of being matter did have, enabling it somehow to exist and assume the form of differentiated reality, this it had only from Almighty God, to whose bounty any reality, formed as well as unformed, owes its existence. But there is this difference between what is 'formed' and 'unformed': the 'formed' being has its form already, while the 'unformed' is capable of having it.[3] But He who confers upon things their form is the same One who also endows them with the capacity for form. It is from Him and in Him that there is had the fairest and the changeless pattern of all things. Hence, it is He alone who bestows upon a being not only the perfection of beauty but also its capacity for becoming beautiful.

Accordingly, we are perfectly right in believing that God made the world from nothing, because even if the world was made from some kind of matter, that matter has itself been made from nothing. Thus there first was produced the capacity for forms and then form was given to such things as were formed, in keeping with God's well-ordered bounty. We have made this assertion so no one will think that the utterances of sacred Scripture are at variance with one another, for it is written both that God made the world from

---

2 Wisd. 11.18.
3 The distinction drawn here between the complete reality (*formatum*) and the incomplete and underlying principle (*formabile*) suggests the analogous pre-Christian doctrine of Hylomorphism. Augustine is careful, however, to stress the fact that the production of the primordial matter or world-stuff is to be ascribed to the direct creative act of God. In *De Genesi ad litteram* (1.15.29) he expressly denies any kind of temporal priority to this primordial matter, declaring that the creative act terminates simultaneously in the production of both aspects of being.

nothing and that the world has been made from unformed matter.

(3) Therefore, as believers in God the Father Almighty, we are constrained to hold that there is no creature in existence that has not been created by the Almighty. And since He has created all things through the Word, this Word is also called the Truth[4] and the Power and the Wisdom of God.[5] He who is proposed for our belief as the Lord Jesus Christ is made known to us by many other names, such as 'our Liberator and Ruler'[6] and 'Son of God.' For, He who made all things through Him was alone able to beget that Word through whom all things were fashioned.

Chapter 3

We also believe in Jesus Christ, the Son of God, the Only-begotten of the Father, that is, the one God, our Lord. Yet, we must not think of this Word as we do our own words, words which, once uttered by the voice and tongue, pass away with the movement of the air and last no longer than their sound. That Word abides in a changeless state, for the words referring to Wisdom have been spoken about the Word Itself, that, 'Remaining in herself, she renews all things.'[1] He is also called the Word of the Father because it is through

---

4 Cf. John 14.6.
5 Cf. 1 Cor. 1.24.
6 In earlier works Augustine avoids the term *salvator* because of its unclassical standing and prefers the expression *liberator* to represent Christ the Redeemer. The term *salvator* is later used approvingly, a fact which evidences Augustine's gradual assimilation and mastery of the Christian terminology. Cf. *De Trinitate* 13.10.14. For a study of Augustine's literary development, cf. J. Finaert, *L'évolution littéraire de saint Augustin* (Paris 1939).

---

1 Wisd. 7.27.

Him that the Father is made known. In giving utterance to the truth we aim to disclose our thoughts to the hearer by words and to bring to the knowledge of another through such signs what we hold hidden away in our heart. Similarly, that Wisdom which God the Father begot is most fittingly styled His Word since it is through Him that the innermost nature of the Father is revealed to worthy souls.

(4) But, there is a great difference between our mind and the words by which we endeavor to express that same mind. We do not, of course, beget the vocal sounds, but we form them, and it is the body that supplies the basic material in their formation. There is a vast difference between mind and body. In begetting the Word, God begot the same nature as Himself. Neither did He produce the Word from nothing or from some kind of matter already found and fashioned in creation, but begot from Himself the same nature as Himself.

If we examine carefully our motive for speaking, we shall see that this is also our aim—provided we are not lying but telling the truth. For, what other objective do we have but to introduce, if such a thing were possible, this very mind of ours into the mind of the hearer so it can be known and fully grasped while we really remain within ourselves, not withdrawing from ourselves? Yet we bring into existence a sign by which our knowledge is engendered in another. As a result, another mind is, so to speak, brought forth by the mind through which this self-revelation is made. We endeavor to do this by means of words, by facial expressions, and by gestures of the body, being eager to disclose by so many devices, as it were, the thought content which is present within. We are unable to give perfect expression to a reality of this kind and, consequently, the speaker's mind can not be

FAITH AND THE CREED   321

fully disclosed; whence it also follows that there is room left for telling lies.

But God the Father, who has been both willing and able to reveal Himself perfectly to souls destined to know Him, has, for the sake of revealing Himself, begotten that self-same Reality which is one with Him who has begotten It. The Son is called also His Power and Wisdom because He has made and ordered all things through Him. Accordingly, it is said of the Son: 'He reacheth from end to end mightily and ordereth all things sweetly.'[2]

Chapter 4

(5) Consequently, God's Only-begotten Son was not made by the Father, since, in the words of the Evangelist, 'all things were made through him';[1] neither was He begotten in time, seeing that the eternally wise God enjoys the eternal possession of His Wisdom; neither is He unequal, that is, inferior in some respect, to the Father, for the Apostle also says: 'Who being set up in the form of God did not think it robbery to be equal to God.'[2]

Hence; they must also be excluded from the Catholic faith who hold that the Son is the same Person as the Father,[3] for this Word being present with God could only be present with God the Father, and whoever exists alone is equal to no one. Also excluded are all who say the Son is a creature,

---

2 Wisd. 8.1.

1 John 1.3.
2 Phil. 2.6.
3 Reference is here made in a general way to those heresies which denied the real distinction between the Father and the Son and taught that the Persons of the Trinity are merely different aspects of one and the same divine Person. Cf. J. Tixeront, *Histoire des dogmes* (Paris 1924) I 353ff.

though not the same as other creatures.⁴ For, no matter how excellent they say a creature is, if it is a creature it has been produced and made. 'Produce' is the same as 'create,' although, in keeping with Latin usage, the term 'create' is sometimes employed in place of the word 'beget.' But the Greek language makes a distinction: what they call *ktísma* or *ktísis* we designate as 'creature,' and when we wish to avoid ambiguity in speaking we do not say 'create,' but 'produce.' Therefore, if the Son is a creature, He has been made, no matter how excellent He is. But we believe in Him as the One through whom *all* things were made, and not as the One through whom everything else [except Himself] was made. In no other way can we understand the expression 'all things' except as meaning all things that have been made.

(6) Inasmuch as 'the Word was made flesh and dwelt among us,'⁵ this same Wisdom begotten of God has deigned also to become a creature among men. This is the import of the passage which reads: 'The Lord created me in the beginning of his ways.'⁶ By 'the beginning of his ways' is meant the Head of the Church, namely, Christ, in His assumed human nature. Through Him a pattern of life has been given us, that is to say, a sure path by which we may come to God. For we who have fallen through pride could only return [to God] through humility. Thus was it said to the first creature of our race: 'Taste, and you shall be as God.'⁷

---

4 Augustine has in mind the error of subordinationism, which, in one form or another, denied the absolute equality and consubstantiality of the Son with the Father. It was only after the Gothic invasion of North Africa that Augustine came to grips directly with Arianism. About 428 he took part in a public dispute at Hippo with the Arian bishop, Maximinus. Cf. *Collatio cum Maximino Arianorum episcopo* (PL 42.709-743).
5 John 1.14.
6 Prov. 8.22. The Vulgate reading has 'possessed' (*possedit*) for 'created' (*creavit*).
7 A free paraphrase of Gen. 3.5.

As I was saying, our Saviour has Himself deigned to exemplify in His own Person that humility which is the path over which we have to travel on our return [to God]; for 'he did not think it robbery to be equal to God, but emptied himself, taking the form of a slave.'[8] Hence, the Word through whom all things were made was 'in the beginning of his ways' created man.

In so far, therefore, as He is the Only-begotten, He is without brothers, but in so far as He is the 'first-born' He has deigned to call all those His brothers who, subsequent to and in virtue of His being first, are born again unto God's grace through filial adoption,[9] in accordance with the teaching of the Apostle.[10]

Only one *natural* Son, then, has been begotten of the very substance of the Father and having the same nature as the father: God of God, Light of Light. We, on the contrary, are not light by our nature, but are illumined by that Light which enables us to shine forth with wisdom. 'For it was the true light,' as it is written, 'that enlightens every man who comes into the world.'[11]

Now, in addition to our belief in the eternal truths, we also include the temporal mission of our Lord, which He deigned for our sake to take upon Himself and to discharge for our salvation. To the extent that He is the Only-begotten Son of God, the expressions 'has been' and 'will be' cannot be employed, but only the term 'is'; because what 'has been' no longer exists and what 'will be' does not yet exist. Therefore, He is unchangeable, without the character and variation of time. And it is my opinion that the special kind of name which He intimated to His servant Moses as His own has no other basis for its origin. For, when Moses was asking how

---
8 Phil. 2.6,7.
9 Luke 8.21.
10 Heb. 2.11.
11 John 1.9.

he should reply as to who sent him, in the event the people to whom he was sent should make little of him, he received this answer from the One speaking: 'I AM WHO AM.' And to this He added the further statement: 'This shalt thou say to the children of Israel: HE WHO IS hath sent me to you.'[12]

(7) I trust, then, that it is evident to spiritually minded souls that no nature can be opposed to God. For, if He *is,* and of Him alone properly speaking this term can be said, then God has nothing for an opposite. Whatever has true existence remains unchangeable. Whatever undergoes change was something which it is no longer and will be something which it is not as yet. If anyone were to ask us what the opposite of 'white' is we would answer 'black'; if asked the opposite of 'hot' we would answer 'cold'; if asked the opposite of 'fast' we would answer 'slow'; and so on in similar case. But, when asked the opposite of that which 'is', we answer rightly that it is 'nothing'.

(8) But, in accordance with His temporal plan, as I have mentioned, our changing nature was assumed by the unchangeable Wisdom of God for our salvation and regeneration through the working out of God's liberality. Consequently, we include in the scope of our faith the deeds accomplished in the order of time for our salvation, professing our belief in Him as the Son of God who was born of the Virgin Mary through the work of the Holy Spirit. It is by this Gift of God, namely, the Holy Spirit, that the exceeding humility of so great a God has been bestowed upon us. He has thus deigned to take upon Himself a complete human nature within the Virgin's womb, dwelling within His mother's inviolate body and leaving it inviolate at His departure.[13]

---

12 Exod. 3.14.
13 A striking statement testifying to the Church's ancient and abiding belief in the perpetual virginity of the Mother of God. The somewhat traditional formula used to express the threefold aspect of Mary's virginity, *ante partum, in partu, post partum,* is equivalently found in Augustine: *Illa enim virgo concepit, virgo peperit, virgo permansit* (*Sermo* 51.11.18).

The heretics level insidious attacks against this temporal plan in a number of ways. But, if a person holds fast to the Catholic faith and believes that a complete human nature, namely, body, soul, and spirit,[14] was assumed by the Word of God, he is protected well enough against the heretics. Since this assumption was actually accomplished for the sake of our salvation, we should be on our guard against the notion that any particular component of our nature had no share in the assumed nature and is unrelated to our salvation. Except for the shape of his bodily members, diversely assigned to the different species of animals, man differs from the beast only by reason of his rational soul, which is also called the mind. How can that faith be sound which teaches that the Wisdom of God assumed that part of our nature which we possess in common with the beast but not the part which is illumined by the light of Wisdom and proper to man?[15]

(9) We must likewise repudiate those who deny that the Lord Jesus Christ had Mary for His mother on earth, since

---

14 Although the terms 'soul' and 'spirit,' employed to represent the incorporeal part of man's nature, do not always have a fixed meaning for Augustine, a fair degree of consistency is observable in their use. 'Soul' (*anima*) has the broader connotation and signifies the quickening principle of all living things, rational and irrational; it is not to be confused with the masculine form *animus*, which Augustine would appear to identify with the highest power of the human soul. 'Spirit' (*spiritus*) has a twofold meaning for Augustine: scriptural and philosophical. Taken in the former sense, 'spirit' represents the highest faculty of the human soul which raises man above the lower animals; the philosophical meaning of 'spirit,' borrowed from the Stoics, stands for the imaginative power or sense-memory, common to both man and beast. G. Verbeke has traced the development of the doctrine of the 'spirit,' or *pneuma*, from its Stoic origins to Augustine. *L'évolution de la doctrine du pneuma du stoicisme à S. Augustin* (Paris-Louvain 1944). For a more detailed account of Augustine's vocabulary dealing with the soul, cf. E. Gilson, *L'introduction à l'étude de S. Augustin* (3rd ed., Paris 1949) 56-57.

15 Apollinaris, a Syrian bishop of the fourth century, denied that Christ had a rational soul in his attempt to defend the perfect unity of the two natures in Christ. Cf. Tixeront, *op. cit.* 2.94ff. A similar error had been taught earlier by Lucian of Antioch. Cf. Tixeront, *op. cit.* 2.27.

His temporal plan ennobled each sex, both male and female.[16] By possessing a male nature and being born of a woman He further showed by this plan that God has concern not only for the sex He represented but also for the one through which He took upon Himself our nature.

Nor should this remark of Christ compel us to deny His mother: 'Woman, what is it to me and to thee? My hour is not yet come.'[17] He is rather giving us to understand that, as God, He had no mother, for by changing water into wine He was making ready to reveal the personal character of His majesty. It was as man, however, that He was crucified. That was 'the hour that had not yet come' when He said: 'What is it to me and to thee? My hour is not yet come'; that is to say, 'the hour when I will acknowledge thee.' Then it was, as a man on the cross, that He acknowledged His human mother and commended her in a most human fashion to the Apostle He loved most.[18]

Nor should we be disturbed by the fact that when His mother's and brothers' arrival was announced to Him, He replied: 'Who is my mother and who are my brethren?'[19] This episode should rather be a lesson that relations are not to be considered whenever they stand in the way of our ministry of preaching the word of God to the brethren. If anyone supposes that He had no mother on earth just because He said: 'Who is my mother?' he will be forced to deny as well that the Apostles had fathers on earth, since He imposed on them this command, saying: 'Call no one on earth your father, for one is your Father, who is in heaven.'[20]

---

16 The heresy of Docetism denied the physical reality of Christ's human nature and thus deprived Mary of her prerogative of divine maternity. The Manichaeans held an analogous position. Cf. Tixeront, *op. cit.* 3.22-79.
17 John 2.4.
18 John 19.26,27.
19 Matt. 12.48.
20 Matt. 33.9.

(10) Nor should the thought of the inner body of a woman weaken our belief [in His human birth], as if this kind of generation on the part of our Lord would appear objectionable just because the unclean take an unclean view of it.[21] The Apostle is perfectly right in declaring that 'the foolishness of God is wiser than men'[22] and that 'for the clean all things are clean.'[23]

People who hold this view ought, then, to observe how the rays of this sun of ours (which in fact they do not extol as God's creature but adore as God)[24] are everywhere spread over stenches from sewers and over every kind of foulness. The sun here is operating according to its nature, yet it is not thereby made sordid by contamination of any kind, even though visible light is by its nature in somewhat close contact with sordid visible objects. Was it not, then, a much easier matter for the Word of God, being neither corporeal nor visible, to escape contamination from a woman's body wherein He assumed human flesh together with a soul and spirit? Through the medium of these, the majesty of the Word takes up a more hidden abode, removed from the frailty of a human body.

So it is evident that the Word of God could not in any way be defiled by a human body, since even the human soul itself does not suffer defilement on this account. It is not when the soul rules over, and gives life to, the body that it is defiled by the body, but when it craves for the fleeting pleasures of the body. Now, if these [heretics] want to avoid stains on the soul, they ought rather to have a dread of all such untruths and sacrileges.

---

21 In Sermon 12 Augustine enlarges in a more popular vein on the anti-Manichaean theme that the Incarnation of the Word in no way compromised the sanctity of the divine Nature.
22 1 Cor. 1.25.
23 Titus 1.15.
24 Sun worship found a logical place in the Manichaean cosmogony where the sun is represented as a divine emanation. Cf. *Contra Secundinum Manichaeum* 20.

Chapter 5

(11) But the humility of our Lord in undergoing human birth was too little for Him to do for us; in addition, He deigned to die for mortal man. 'He humbled himself, becoming obedient unto death, even to the death of the cross,'[1] so none of us would recoil from a form of death which men look upon as utterly disgraceful, even though we might be able to face death itself fearlessly. Accordingly, we believe in Him who was crucified under Pontius Pilate and was buried; the name of the judge had to be added for a proper understanding of the time.

In professing belief in His burial, however, we are reminded of the new tomb which was to bear witness of Him at the time of His resurrection unto the newness of life, just as the Virgin's womb had done at the approach of His birth. For, as no other dead person was buried in that tomb,[2] either before or after, so no mortal being was conceived in that womb, either before or after.

(12) We also believe that He rose from the dead on the third day, the First-born among the brethren who are to follow. These He has called unto the adoption of the sons of God[3] and has deigned to make them His fellow sharers and co-heirs.

Chapter 6

(13 We believe He has ascended into heaven, unto that realm of bliss which He has promised us, also, saying: 'They will be as the angels in heaven,'[1] in that city which is the

---

1 Phil. 2.8.
2 Cf. John 19.41.
3 Cf. Eph. 1.5.

---

1 Matt. 22.30.

mother of us all, the everlasting Jerusalem in heaven.[2] Our belief in the assumption of an earthly body into heaven is wont to give offense to certain godless people, pagans and heretics alike.[3] Pagans, for the most part, are eager to draw us into discussion with arguments taken from the philosophers purporting to prove that nothing made of earth can exist in heaven. They are unfamiliar with our Scripture and fail to grasp the proper meaning of the words: 'There is sown a natural body, there arises a spiritual body.'[4]

This statement was not meant to imply that the body is changed into, and becomes, a spirit, for even now our body has not been turned into and made a soul, though it is said to be quickened by the soul. By a 'spiritual body' we mean one so docile to the spirit that it is fit for a heavenly abode, seeing that its every weakness and all its earthly blemishes have been changed and transformed into a steadfastness and purity of a heavenly kind. This is the kind of change the Apostle is also referring to when he says: 'We shall all rise, but we shall not all be changed.'[5] And where the same Apostle declares that 'we shall all be changed,' he is teaching us that this is not a change for the worse, but for the better.

But it is sheer curiosity and a waste of time to inquire as to the 'where' and 'how' of the Lord's body in heaven; we have only to believe that it is present in heaven. It is not for our feeble powers to search into the hidden things of heaven; but it *is* the part of faith to entertain lofty and worthy notions about the excellence of the Lord's body.

---

2 Gal. 4.26.
3 Among the pagans, belief in the resurrection of the body was assailed with particular vehemence by Porphyry, a neo-Platonic philosopher of the third century. Cf. *De civitate Dei* 13.19. The religious error of the Jewish sect of the Sadducees concerning the same doctrine was continued almost from earliest Christian times by both Gnostics and Manichaeans. Cf. Tixeront, *op. cit.* I 175; 471 n.1.
4 1 Cor. 15.44.
5 1 Cor. 15.51.

Chapter 7

(14) We believe, too, that He sits at the right hand of the Father. Nevertheless, we are not to imagine that God the Father is therefore bounded by a kind of human configuration so that the notion of a right or left side should arise in mind when one thinks about Him. Nor should the mention of the Father's being 'seated' lead us to suppose He is doing so with knees bent; otherwise we shall fall into that sacrilegious belief which the Apostle abominates in those men who have changed the glory of the incorruptible God into the image of a corruptible man.[1]

It is a wicked thing for a Christian to erect in his temple such a likeness of God;[2] it is more wicked still to erect it in the heart wherein is found the true temple of God—provided that heart be cleansed from worldliness and misbelief. The expression 'at the right hand' must therefore be understood in this sense: to exist in a state of perfect blessedness, where there is justice and peace and joy. Similarly, the 'goats' are placed on the left side;[3] that is to say, they live in a condition of utter wretchedness because of the weight and torments of their sins.

The reference, therefore, to God's being seated does not signify a position of the limbs but the power to judge, a power ever present to His majesty whereby He is always

---

1 Rom. 1.23.
2 It is doubtful that Augustine has in mind any specific ecclesiastical legislation prohibiting images of the Deity in churches. Viewed in its context, the passage would appear to be a simple reiteration of the prohibititions already contained in Scripture. Almost a century earlier the Spanish Council of Elvira enacted its famous canon forbidding pictures in churches, probably with a view to safeguarding recent Christians from the danger of relapsing into idolatry. In any case, the canon would appear to be disciplinary rather than dogmatic. Cf. H. Leclercq, *Dictionnaire d'archéologie chrétienne et de liturgie* 1.1, cols. 214-215.
3 Cf. Matt. 25.23.

dealing with men according to their merits. At the Last Judgment, however, the glory to come of the Only-begotten Son of God, Judge of the living and the dead, will manifest itself with a brilliance, striking and unmistakable.

Chapter 8

(15) We also believe that at the appropriate time He will come from heaven and judge the living and the dead. We may understand by these words the just and sinners; or we may give them this meaning: that the 'living' are those whom He will find alive on earth, while the 'dead' are those who are to rise at His coming. His plan for time, unlike His divine generation, is not a matter of the present only, but embraces also the past and future. For, our Lord 'was' on earth; now He 'is' in heaven; and He 'will be' the Judge of the living and the dead when He appears in His glory. He will come just the way He ascended, according to the authoritative teaching found in the Acts of the Apostles. It is in view of this temporal plan that He is speaking in the Apocalypse where it is written: 'These things he spoke, who is and who was and who is coming.'[1]

Chapter 9

(16) Once our Lord's divine generation and human dispensation have been set forth and proposed for belief, there is added thereto belief in the Holy Spirit, in order to round out our faith concerning God. The Holy Spirit is not

---
1 The corresponding passage in the Vulgate reads: 'I am the Alpha and the Omega, the beginning and the end, says the Lord God, who is and who was and who is coming, the Almighty.'

inferior in nature to the Father and the Son, but is, so to speak, consubstantial and co-eternal; for this Trinity is one God. This does not mean that the Father is the same Person as the Son and the Holy Spirit. It means, rather, that the Father is the Father, the Son is the Son, and the Holy Spirit is the Holy Spirit, and that this Trinity is one God, as it is written: 'Hear, O Israel, the Lord thy God is one God.'[1]

But, if we are asked about the Persons in particular and someone says to us: 'Is the Father God?' we will reply that He is God. If asked whether the Son is God, we will answer that He is. And if a like question is raised about the Holy Spirit, we shall have to reply that He is none other than God. We must be very careful not to understand the term 'God' in the sense in which it has been said of men: 'You are gods.'[2] For they are not God by nature who have been made and fashioned by the Father, through the Son, and by the liberality of the Holy Spirit. It is to the Trinity Itself that reference is made where the Apostle says: 'For from him and in him and through him are all things.'[3] Hence, while replying that the individual Person is God in answer to the question about the Persons in particular—whether the Father, the Son, or the Holy Spirit—no one should suppose that we are worshiping three Gods.

(17) It is not surprising that words like this are spoken about the unspeakable Nature. Something akin happens in the case of those objects that we behold with bodily eyes and discern by sense perception. When we are asked about the source of a stream, we may not say it is the river itself; if asked about the river, we may not call it the source; again, we may not refer to the drinking water coming from the source or the river as the source or the river. Yet, if we are asked separately about the members in this trinity called

---
1 Deut. 6.4.
2 Ps. 81.6.
3 Rom. 11.36.

water, we answer in each instance that it is water. If I inquire whether that is water in the source, water is given in reply; if we inquire whether that is water in the river, the answer is no different; and no other reply will be possible in the case of the drinking water. Nevertheless, we do not say there are 'three waters,' but 'one water.'

We must, of course, take care that no one will represent the unspeakable nature of the divine Majesty as if he were thinking about that visible and material source of the stream, or about the river or the drinking water. In these instances, the water now at the source flows out into the river and has no fixed resting place; when it flows from the river, or source, it becomes drinking water; it does not remain in the same place from which it is drawn. In this way it is possible for the water to be denominated now as 'source,' again as 'river,' and at an other time as 'drinking water.'

But we have stated that in the Trinity it is impossible for the Father to be at any time the Son, or for the Son to be at any time the Father; for, as in the case of a tree, the root alone is the root, the trunk is nothing else but the trunk, and only the branches may be called branches. The reality called 'root' may not be styled 'trunk' or 'branches'; nor is it possible for the wood of the root to shift about somehow so as to be found now in the root, then in the trunk, and at another time in the branches. It is able, rather, to exist only in the root, though the rule about the use of the term holds good: the root is 'wood'; the trunk is 'wood'; the branches are 'wood.' Nevertheless, we do not speak of 'three woods,' but of 'one wood.'

If these examples show a degree of dissimilarity because there is a variation in thickness of the wood to justify our speaking of 'three woods,' then the following will at least be granted by all: If three cups are filled from the one source, we may speak of three cups; we may not speak of 'three waters,' however, but only of 'one water.' Yet, if asked about the cups in particular, you may reply that water is found in any one of them, even though in this example there is no such shifting of the water from the source to the river as we mentioned.

These material illustrations have been given, not because of a sameness with that divine nature, but because of a 'oneness' that is discernible even in sense objects. In this way we are able to see how any three objects, no matter what they are, can bear one particular name, not only as separate units but also when taken together. Nor should anyone think it strange or absurd that we call the Father 'God,' the Son 'God,' and the Holy Spirit 'God,' yet say that there are three Gods in this Trinity but one Substance.

(18) Learned and religious men have indeed dealt with the subject of the Father and the Son in numerous works. As far as humanly possible, they have endeavored to show in these writings how the Father and the Son are not one Person, but One in nature; and to intimate what is proper to the Father and what is proper to the Son: how the former is the Begetter, that latter, the Begotten; the former does not have His origin from the Son, the latter has His origin in the Father; the former is the Principle of the Son, for which reason He is also called the 'head of Christ';[4] but Christ, too, is called the Principle[5] [Beginning], but not of the Father; the latter [the Son] is called the Image of the former[6] though He differs in no respect and enjoys absolute equality. These matters are treated at greater length by those who do not aim at presenting so brief an exposition of the whole Christian faith as we do.

Therefore, in so far as He is the Son, He receives existence

---
4 Cf. 1 Cor. 11.3.
5 Cf. John 8.25.

from the Father, though the latter does not receive it from Him. Many statements are found in the Scriptures concerning the Son in so far as He has, in His unspeakable mercy and in keeping with His temporal plan, taken upon Himself a human nature, a created nature, that is, and one destined for a more glorious transformation. These statements have been put in such a way as to occasion error in the ungodly minds of heretics who want to teach before they understand.

Such expressions as the following lead them to believe that the Son is not equal to the Father or consubstantial with Him: 'For the Father is greater than I';[7] and the head of the woman is the man, and the head of the man is Christ; but the head of Christ is God';[8] and 'then He Himself [the Son] will also be made subject to him who subjected all things to him';[9] and 'I go to my Father and your Father, to my God and your God.'[10] There are other similar statements, but no one of them has been made to indicate an inequality of nature and substance. Otherwise these statements would not be true: 'I and the Father are one';[11] and 'He who sees me sees also the Father';[12] again, 'the Word was God,' for He was not made since all things have been made through Him;[13] also, 'He thought it not robbery to be equal with God';[14] and so with other similar places.

The former declarations were made partly with a view to one mode of operation of the human nature He assumed, in view of which it is said that 'He emptied himself'.[15] This does not mean that Divine Wisdom, being absolutely un-

---
6 Cf. Col. 1.5.
7 John 14.28.
8 1 Cor. 11.3.
9 1 Cor. 15.28.
10 John 10.17.
11 John 10.30.
12 John 14.9.
13 John 1.1,3.
14 Phil. 2.6.
15 *Ibid.*

changeable, has undergone change, but that He chose to reveal Himself to men in so lowly a manner. These declarations, therefore, which the heretics falsely interpret, were so made partly with a view to this mode of operation [of His human nature] and partly to show that the Son owes His existence to the Father; in fact, He also owes it to the Father that He is equal and like the Father Himself. The Father on the contrary, owes nothing of His existence to another.

(19) But, as yet, the subject of the Holy Spirit has not been so extensively and thoroughly covered by the learned and outstanding commentators of the sacred Scriptures as to enable us to see readily what is also proper to Him whereby we call Him neither the Father nor the Son, but the Holy Spirit.[16] They simply proclaim Him to be the Gift of God, so we may believe that God does not communicate a Gift less perfect than Himself. They refrain, however, from saying that the Holy Spirit is begotten of the Father, for Christ is the Only-begotten; or from saying that He is begotten of the Son, as if He were the grandson of the Father Most High. They nevertheless do not assert that the Holy Spirit owes His existence to no one, but rather that He owes it to the Father from whom all things have their being. Otherwise, we would be setting up *two* Principles without an origin—a wholly false and absurd position and one that does not pertain to the Catholic faith, but to the error of a certain class of heretics.[17]

There are, however, some who have ventured to hold that the Holy Spirit is the common bond between the Father

---

16 Augustine acknowledges that in the West literature dealing with the Holy Spirit was scant. In giving definite form to the doctrine of the Holy Spirit, he probably consulted polemical works on the subject from the pens of Greek writers, some of whose works were made accessible to the West by such contemporaries as St. Jerome. Cf. Tixeront, *op. cit.* 2.269-273.

17 A further allusion is made here to the metaphysical dualism of the Manichaeans mentioned in Chapter 2.

and the Son, the Godhead, so to speak, which the Greeks call *theótēta*. Accordingly, as the Father is God and the Son is God, the Godhead Itself by which They are mutually united—the One by the generation of the Son and the Other by cleaving to the Father—is made equal with Him by whom He was begotten. As I was saying, these commentators assert that this Godhead is the Holy Spirit, which they would also have us understand as the mutual Love and Charity of both [Father and Son].

They uphold this view of theirs by a number of testimonies from Scripture, as by the statement: 'Because the charity of God is poured forth in our hearts by the Holy Spirit who has been given to us,'[18] or by various other such testimonies. They also rest their view on the very fact that we are reconciled to God by the Holy Spirit. Hence in our referring to Him also as 'God's Gift,' they would see a sufficient indication that the Holy Spirit is the Charity of God. For, we are reconciled to Him only by love, by reason of which we are called the 'sons of God.'[19] We live no longer as slaves under fear, for perfect love casts out fear.[20] We have also received the spirit of liberty 'whereby we cry, "Abba! Father!"'[21] Moreover, since we have been reconciled and restored to His friendship through charity, we shall be enabled to understand all the hidden things of God. Thus it is said of the Holy Spirit: 'He will lead you to all truth.'[22] It is for this reason that the courage which filled His Apostles, at His coming, to preach the truth is also rightly ascribed to charity,[23] since want of courage is attributed to fear, which is excluded by the perfect possession of charity.

---

18 Rom. 5.5.
19 Cf. 1 John 3.1.
20 John 4.18.
21 Rom. 8.15.
22 The Vulgate reads: 'He will teach you all truth.'
23 Cf. Acts 2.4.

The Holy Spirit is likewise called the 'Gift of God'[24] for the reason that no one finds enjoyment in the object he is perceiving unless he also loves it. Now, the act of enjoying God's Wisdom is nothing else than to cleave to Him by the bond of love. Nor can anyone take a permanent hold on the object of his perception except through love. And He is called the Holy Spirit (*spiritus sanctus*) for the reason that whatever is 'sanctioned' [*sanciuntur*] is sanctioned for the sake of permanence, there being no doubt that the term 'sanctity' [*sanctitatem*] is derived from 'sanction' [*a sanciendo*].

The partisans of this opinion (that the Holy Spirit is the common bond of the Godhead) invoke above all the testimony of the passage which reads: 'That which is born of flesh, is flesh; and that which is born of the Spirit is spirit.'[25] 'For God is Spirit.'[26] Reference is here made to our rebirth, not of the flesh according to Adam, but of the Holy Spirit according to Christ. Hence, when mention of the Holy Spirit is made in this passage which reads: 'For God is Spirit,' they say we are to observe that it did not state: 'For the spirit is God,' but did read: 'For God is spirit.' In this passage, then (they say), the Godhead Itself, common to the Father and the Son, has been called God, that is to say, the Holy Spirit. Further testimony is furnished by this statement of John the Apostle: 'For God is love.'[27] Here, again, he does not say 'Love is God,' but 'God is love,' signifying thereby that the Godhead Itself is love.

As for the fact that no mention is made of the Holy Spirit in the sequence of connected expressions wherein we read: 'For all things are yours, and you are Christ's, and

---
24 Cf. Eph. 3.7.
25 John 3.6.
26 John 4.24.
27 1 John 4.16.

Christ is God's,'[28] and 'The head of the woman is the man, and the head of the man is Christ, and the head of Christ is God,'[29] this, they say, is a working out of the principle that the connecting bond itself is not usually enumerated among the mutually connected parts. Hence it is that readers of finer discernment seem to recognize another reference to the Trinity Itself in that passage where it says: 'For from him and through him and in him are all things'[30]—*from him,* as from one who owes His existence to no one'; *through him,* as through the Mediator; *in him,* as in one who imparts stability, that is to say, one who brings about a bond of union.

(20) This opinion is opposed by those who think this common bond which we call 'Godhead,' 'Love,' or 'Charity' is not something substantial; they want the Holy Spirit represented in terms of a substantial reality. Yet they do not realize that the statement 'God is Love' could be made only if Love were a substance. These opponents are led astray, of course, because of habitual contact with corporeal objects; thus, when two bodies are so united that they are placed in juxtaposition, the union itself is not a body, since, as a matter of fact, the union is not to be found once those bodies become separated which had been united. Yet we do not think that this union has taken leave, so to speak, and gone elsewhere, the way the bodies do. People like this should rather do their utmost to obtain purity of heart so they can see that in the case of God's substance nothing like this can have place, namely, that the substance of God be one thing and the modification of the substance something different and apart from substance. On the contrary, whatever is knowable about God is something substantial.

Actually, it is an easy matter to have these truths stated

---

28 1 Cor. 3.22,23.
29 1 Cor. 11.3.
30 Rom. 11.36.

and assented to by belief, but their inner meaning can only be fully perceived by the pure of heart. Therefore, whether this is the true opinion, or something else, we must cling steadfastly to the faith wherein we call the Father God, the Son God, and the Holy Spirit God. Neither do we say there are three Gods, but one God, the Trinity; or that they differ in nature, but, rather, that they are of the same substance; or that the Father is at one time the Son, at another time the Holy Spirit, but rather that the Father is always the Father, the Son is always the Son, and the Holy Spirit always the Holy Spirit.

Let us make no rash pronouncement about things unseen, as if we understood them, but conduct ourselves as becomes believers; for these things cannot be seen except by the heart made clean. Furthermore, a person beholding these truths in the present life 'in part,' as it is said, and 'in an obscure manner'[31] cannot make his hearer also see them if such a one is hindered by defilement of heart. But, 'blessed are the clean of heart, for they shall see God.'[32]

Such is the faith we profess concerning God our Creator and Saviour.

(21) But, the precept of charity has been imposed upon us not only in reference to God—in the statement: 'Thou shalt love the Lord thy God with thy whole heart, and with thy whole soul, and with thy whole mind'—but also in reference to our neighbor, for it adds: 'Thou shalt love thy neighbor as thyself.'[33] Now, if this faith does not embrace the multitude and society of men wherein fraternal charity is operative, it bears less fruit.

---

31 Cf. 1 Cor. 13.12.
32 Matt. 5.8.
33 Luke 10.27.

Chapter 10

Accordingly, we believe in the holy Church; in the Catholic Church, that is, for heretics and schismatics both call their assemblies 'churches.' Heretics sully the purity of the faith itself by entertaining false notions about God, while schismatics withdraw themselves from fraternal charity by unlawful separation, though they believe the same things we do. Consequently, neither heretics nor schismatics belong to the Catholic Church: not heretics, for the Church loves God; not schismatics, because she has love for the neighbor. The Church readily pardons the neighbor's sins for the reason that she prays in her own behalf to be forgiven by Him who has reconciled us unto Himself,[1] blotting out all past offenses and beckoning us onward toward a new life. Until we enter upon this perfect life, we are unable to live sinless lives. But it makes a difference what kind of sins they are.

(22) There is no need to treat of the distinction of sins. But we must be sure to believe that our sins are not forgiven us at all if we have been unrelenting in forgiving offenses. Therefore, we also believe in the forgiveness of sins.

(23) There are three elements which make up man: spirit, soul, and the body. Again, they are spoken of as two, since the term 'soul' is also frequently included in the term 'spirit'; for the rational part of the soul, not found in the beast, is called the spirit.

The spirit is the foremost component of our being; the principle of life, called the soul, comes next, by which we are united to the body; last of all there is the body, which, because of its sense character, comprises the lowest element of our being.

This whole creation groans and travails in pain until now.[2]

---
1 Cf. 2 Cor. 5.18,19.
2 Rom. 8.22.

Nevertheless, the spirit has yielded its first fruits, for it has believed in God and is already possessed of a good will. This spirit is likewise called the 'mind,' with reference to which the Apostle says: 'With my mind I serve the law of God.'[3] Speaking in the same vein, he says in another place: 'God is my witness, whom I serve in my spirit.'[4]

But, while the soul is still hankering for carnal pleasures, it is called 'flesh' and resists the spirit. This resistance does not spring from the soul's nature but from a habit of sin. This is why it is said: 'With my mind I serve the law of God, but with my flesh the law of sin.' This habit of sin has been engrafted on our nature through human generation as a result of the first man's sin. Hence it is written: 'And we were once by nature children of wrath,'[5] that is to say, children of vengeance. It has come about in this way that we serve the law of sin.

The soul is made perfect in its nature when it obeys the spirit and follows it in its pursuit of God. Hence, 'the sensual man does not perceive the things that are of the spirit of God.'[6] But the soul does not become subject to the spirit in doing good as quickly as the spirit is brought into submission to God in regard to true faith and a good will. On the contrary, the tendency of the soul to waste itself upon the carnal and transitory is not always brought under speedy restraint. But, as the soul is itself purified by recovering the equilibrium of its nature under the mastery of the spirit, which is its head—and Christ is the Head of this head—we ought not give up hope that the body will also be restored to its true nature.

This, of course, will not take place so speedily as does the soul's restoration, just as the soul's restoration is not so

---
3 Rom. 7.25.
4 Rom. 1.9.
5 Eph. 2.3.
6 1 Cor. 2.14.

speedy as is that of the spirit. But it will happen at the right time, at the sounding of the last trumpet, when the dead shall rise incorruptible and we shall be changed.[7]

Accordingly, we also believe in the resurrection of the flesh, not merely because of a renewal of the soul, which is now called 'flesh' because of its propensity to the things of the flesh. On the contrary, this visible flesh, too, which is flesh by nature—the term being given to the soul not from its nature but from its carnal inclination—this visible flesh, I say, which is properly called flesh, will rise again, as doubtless we must believe. For the Apostle Paul seems, as it were, to be pointing to the flesh with his finger when he says: 'This corruptible must put on incorruption.'[8] At the mention of the word 'this' he is pointing his finger, as it were, at the flesh. Now, it is at things visible that we are able to point a finger, for even the soul could be called 'corruptible,' seeing that it is corrupted by immoral living. And when we read the sentence: 'and this mortal must put on immortality,'[9] reference is being made to the same visible flesh, since the finger is, so to speak, pointed at it again. Just as the soul can be called 'corruptible' through its immoral living, so, too, can it be styled 'mortal.' As a matter of fact, it is death for the soul to fall away from God.[10] This first sin of the soul in paradise is found in the sacred writings.

(24) The body, then, will rise again according to the tenets of the Christian faith—a faith that cannot lead us astray. If this belief seems incredible to anyone, that is because he is thinking of the flesh as it is now and not as it will be in the future, for at the moment of its spiritual transformation it will no longer be flesh and blood but only a body. Speaking with reference to the flesh, the Apostle

---

7 Cf. 1 Cor. 15.52.
8 1 Cor. 15.53.
9 *Ibid.*
10 Cf. Eccli. 10.14.

states: 'There is one flesh of beasts, another of birds, another of fish, another of snakes; and there are heavenly bodies and earthly bodies.'[11] He does not speak of 'heavenly flesh,' but does mention 'bodies,' both heavenly and earthly.

Whatever is flesh is also a body, but not every body is at the same time flesh. To begin with the things of earth: wood is a body, yet it is not flesh, while body and flesh both belong to man and beast. But in the heavenly realm there is no flesh, only pure and radiant bodies which the Apostle calls 'spiritual';[12] there are some who call them 'ethereal.' Consequently, the Apostle's assertion that 'flesh and blood shall not possess the kingdom of God'[13] does not go counter to the resurrection of the flesh, but proclaims what that reality which is now flesh and blood will be like in the future.

A person who does not believe that flesh can be transformed into this kind of nature has to be led to the belief step by step. If you ask him whether earth can be changed into water, this does not appear incredible to him in view of their natural affinity. If you ask him, again, whether water can be changed into air, he replies that this, too, is not impossible, since they are akin to one another. And if the question is proposed whether air can be changed into an ethereal, that is to say, into a heavenly body, the same natural affinity is a convincing argument in its favor.

Why, then, does the unbeliever not grant that what is possible through these successive stages—the transformation

---

11 1 Cor. 15.39,40. The Vulgate text omits the expression 'flesh of snakes' but includes 'flesh of men.'
12 Cf. 1 Cor. 15.44.
13 1 Cor. 15.50. In his *Retractationes* Augustine is careful to remove all possible ambiguity from his treatment of the glorified body. Its substantial idenity is especially stressed, while the evidence of Christ's risen body is invoked as a prototype of all glorified bodies at the resurrection. In conclusion, Augustine directs his readers to a more extensive treatment of the subject in *De civitate Dei* (1-17), where this 'difficult question is examined for the purpose of convincing non-believers.'

of earth into an ethereal body—can happen instantaneously and, in the words of the Apostle, 'in the twinkling of an eye',[14] by the intervention of that same will of God which made it possible for a human body to walk upon the waves?[15] In a similar way we observe with what amazing rapidity smoke can change into a flame.

Our flesh is, to be sure, made of earth, and philosophers admit that it is possible for any kind of body at all to be transformed and changed into every other kind of body. Yet, not infrequently, they oppose the resurrection of the body with arguments purporting to show that it is impossible for an earthly body to exist in heaven.

When the resurrection of the body will have become a reality and we are freed from the exigencies of a temporal existence, we shall experience the full enjoyment of life eternal with a love unspeakable and a constancy that shall never fail. Then will be fulfilled the words that are written: 'Death is swallowed up in victory. Where, O death, is thy sting? where, O death, is thy strife?'[16]

This is the faith imparted to Christian neophytes. They are to make profession of it in the few words contained in the Creed; to believers, these few words are well known. By believing them they are made subject to God, by being subject to God they live a good life, by a good life they obtain purity of heart, and with a pure heart they understand the things they believe.

---
14 Cf. 1 Cor. 15.52.
15 Cf. Matt. 14.25.
16 1 Cor. 15.39,40,50-54.

THE CARE TO BE TAKEN FOR THE DEAD

(De cura pro mortuis gerenda)

Translated by
JOHN A. LACY, M.A.
The Catholic University of America

INTRODUCTION

T. AUGUSTINE, Bishop of Hippo in North Africa, wrote *The Care to be Taken for the Dead* probably in 421, as he seems to indicate in his *Retractations*. The work is addressed to Paulinus, Bishop of Nola.

At Nola there was a church dedicated to St. Felix the Confessor, who had brought a great blessing to the people of Nola by his appearance during an attack on the town. This church had become a popular shrine for many of the devout of southern Italy. In the neighborhood lived a very devout lady, Flora, of noble birth. She had requested permission of the bishop to have her son Cynegius buried near the tomb of St. Felix. This permission was granted, but then she wanted to know whether it was of any advantage to his soul that his body was buried in the place dedicated to this saint. Paulinus told her that would work to his advantage. Then, as he thought more deeply on the matter, he began to be puzzled and without delay wrote a letter to his friend, the Bishop of Hippo, requesting that he set forth his views on the subject. After some delay, due to pressing engagements, St. Augustine wrote the present treatise to 'Your holiness, venerable fellow bishop Paulinus.'

The discussion is treated in a most learned and loving manner. It will be of great interest to all who are concerned over the neglect of the mortal remains of some loved one who has fallen in battle far from home. Many will find great consolation in their inability to render such visible service to their dead as they would wish to perform.

The text used is that of J. Zycha in *CSEL* 41.

THE CARE TO BE TAKEN FOR THE DEAD

Chapter 1

FOR A LONG TIME I have felt obliged to answer the request of your holiness, venerable fellow bishop, Paulinus, ever since you wrote to me through some of your servants concerning our most devout daughter Flora, asking me whether it is to the advantage of anyone after death to have his body buried near a memorial of some saint. For the above-mentioned widow had made a similar request of you concerning her son who had died in your region, and in your letter of consolation you related that the very thing which with motherly and pious devotion she had requested concerning the faithful youth Cynegius, that his body be buried in the Church of the most blessed Felix the Confessor, had been fulfilled.

And on this occasion it happened that you wrote to me through the same bearers of your letters, posing a question of this very nature and insisting that I reply what I thought of the matter, nor did you refrain from stating what you yourself thought. You write that these things do not seem to you to be the idle impulses of the devout faithful caring for their dead. You also add that it is of great significance that it is the practice of the universal Church to pray for their dead, and that, accordingly, it can be inferred that it is of advantage to a man after death if by the faith of his relatives such a place is provided for burying his body in which is visible the very aid of the saints which is sought by such method.

(2) Since these things are so, you indicate that you do not understand how the statement of the Apostle is not contrary to this belief, when he says: 'For we all shall stand before the tribunal of Christ in order that each one may receive according to the things which he has done in the body, whether good or evil.'[1] As a matter of fact, this judgment of the Apostle urges that what can be of profit after death be done before death, not then when what each man has earned before death must be accepted.

Yet, this question is thus solved, since by a certain kind of life there is acquired while one lives in the body that these works may bring some aid to the dead, and by reason of this: according to what they have done through the body they are aided by what has been done religiously in their behalf after the body. There are those whom these works aid in no way, whether they are performed in behalf of those whose merits are so evil that they are not worthy to be aided by such deeds or in behalf of those whose merits are so good that they have no need of them. Therefore, by the kind of life which each one has lived through the body it is brought about that whatever is done piously in behalf of a person is of advantage or is not of advantage when he has left the body. For, if there has been accomplished in this life no merit through which these things may be of advantage, in vain is any sought after this life. And so it happens that the Church, through the care relatives take for their dead,

---

1 Cf. 2 Cor. 5.10.

does not render in vain what religious service it can, yet each one receives according to what he has done through the body, whether good or evil, the Lord bestowing on each one according to his work. That what is provided can be of benefit to him after he has left the body has been acquired in the life lived in the body.

(3) This short reply of mine could have been a sufficient answer to your request, but I call your attention briefly to some other things involved which I think are worthy of discussion here. We read in the books of the Maccabees that sacrifice is offered for the dead.[2] Yet, even if it were read nowhere in the Old Testament, the authority of the universal Church which clearly favors this practice is of great weight, where in the prayers of the priest which are poured forth to the Lord God at His altar the commemoration of the dead has its place.

Chapter 2

Whether the location of his body is of any advantage to the soul of the dead requires more careful study. And we should especially inquire, not according to common belief, but according to the sacred writings of our religion, if it has any effect on the souls of men for enduring or for increasing their misery after this life, whether their bodies have not been buried. And we must not believe, as we read in Vergil, that the unburied are prohibited from sailing and crossing the river Styx because 'One may not cross the gloomy banks and foaming crest until his bones find peaceful rest.'[1] Who would open his Christian heart to these fabulous poetic imaginings, when the Lord Jesus asserts that

---
2 Cf. 2 Mac. 12.43.

---
1 *Aeneid* 6.327,328.

not a hair of the head of a Christian will perish? Even though they are in the hands of enemies who have power over them, they shall die secure. Indeed, He urged them not to fear them who, when they have killed the body, have no more that they can do. Concerning this point, I think I have said enough in the first book of the *City of God* to blunt the teeth of those who by attributing the destruction of the barbarians, which Rome has recently suffered, to Christian causes even hurl this abuse, that Christ did not come to the aid of His followers. And when it has been pointed out to them that He has received the souls of the faithful in view of the merits of their faith, they make insulting remarks about unburied bodies. This whole topic on burial I have explained[2] with words such as the following.

(4) But, I say, in so great a mass of dead bodies all could not have been buried. Yet a pious faith does not dread even this too much, since it holds to the belief that not even ferocious wild beasts would hinder those bodies at the time of resurrection. 'For not a hair of their heads shall perish.'[3] In no wise would Truth say: 'And do not be afraid of those who kill the body but cannot kill the soul,'[4] if it made any difference to the future life what evil men might wish to do with the bodies of the slain. Unless anyone is so absurd as to maintain that those who kill the body ought not to be feared before death lest they kill the body, but ought to be feared after death, lest they not permit the slain body to be buried! Is, then, the statement false which says: 'who kill the body and after that have nothing more that they can do,'[5] if they are able to do so great harm to the dead bodies? No, for Truth has not spoken falsely. It has

---
2 cf. *De civ. Dei* 1.12,13.
3 Luke 21.18.
4 Matt. 10.28.
5 Luke 12.4.

been said that they do some harm when they are slaying the body, for it has feeling while being slain, but later they have nothing which they can do, for there is no feeling in the slain body.

It is true that the earth has not covered many of the bodies of the Christians, but nothing has kept any one of them away from heaven and earth. All creation is filled with the presence of Him who knows how to resuscitate what He created. As the Psalmist says: 'They have given the bodies of thy servants as food for the fowls of the air, the flesh of thy saints to the beasts of the earth. They have shed their blood like water round about Jerusalem, and there was none to bury them.'[6] But he says this more to magnify the cruelty of those who do such things than the plight of those who have suffered them. For, although these things seem hard and bitter in the sight of men, 'precious in the sight of the Lord is the death of his saints.'[7] So, all these things—the care of the funeral arrangements, the establishment of the place of burial, the pomp of the ceremonies—are more of a solace for the living than an aid for the dead.

If an expensive funeral is of any advantage to an evil man, a cheap one, or none at all, is of no disadvantage to a devout soul. A large gathering of the household put on a great show in the sight of men for that rich man clothed in purple, but of much greater significance in the sight of the Lord was the service which the angels offered for the poor beggar covered with sores. The angels did not take the beggar into a marble tomb, but carried him to Abraham's bosom.[8] We have undertaken to defend the City of God against those who ridicule these things. Yet it is true that their own philosophers despised the care of burial. And, often,

---
6 Ps. 78.2,3.
7 Ps. 115.6.
8 cf. Luke 16.19-31.

entire armies, while they were dying for their earthly fatherland, did not care where they might lie afterwards, or for what beasts they might become food. Thus, the poets might write about this and be commended for the statement: 'He is covered by the sky, who has no grave.'⁹ How much less ought they to rail at Christians about unburied bodies? For the reformation of the body itself and of all its members is promised to Christians. They are brought together not only from the earth, but also from other elements from a most secret region where the dissolved bodies have gone. But they shall be restored and returned in an instant of time.¹⁰

Chapter 3

(5) Yet, the bodies of the dead, especially of the just and faithful, are not to be despised or cast aside. The soul has used them as organs and vessels for all good work in a holy manner. If a paternal garment or a ring or anything else of this kind is as dear to children as is their love for their parents, in no way are their very bodies to be spurned, since they are much more familiar and intimate than any garment we put on. Bodies are not for ornament or for aid, as something which is applied externally, but pertain to the very nature of the man. Hence, the funerals of the just men of old were cared for with dutiful devotion, the processions solemnized, and a fitting burial provided. Oftentimes, they themselves, while they were yet alive, gave directions to their sons concerning everything pertaining to their burial.¹ And Tobias by burying the dead is commended by the witness of an angel as having gained favor with God.² Also, our

---
9 Lucan, *Pharsalia* 7.819.
10 Cf. 1 Cor. 15.52.

1 Cf. Gen. 23; 25.9,10; 47.30.
2 Cf. Tob. 2.9; 12.12.

Lord Himself, knowing that He would rise on the third day, praised the good work of a devout woman and said that her work was worthy of mention, because she had poured precious ointment upon His body and had done it for His burial.³ And they are highly commended in the Gospel who took His body down from the cross and prepared it with reverent care for burial.⁴

Indeed, these examples are not intended to say that there is any feeling in dead bodies; rather, they are representative of God's care, for such works of piety are pleasing to Him. Also, such care for the bodies of our dead indicates a strong belief in the resurrection. From this we learn with profit how great can be the reward for the almsdeeds which we perform for the living who have feeling, if this which we do for the lifeless members of men as a part of our dutiful care receives so much praise from God. Indeed, there are other facts which the holy patriarchs wished to be understood concerning the burial or the removal of their bodies as having been spoken by the Spirit through the Prophets.⁵ But this is not the proper place for elaborating on these matters, since what I have stated is sufficient.

If these things which are necessary for sustaining the living—such as food and clothing, although these may be lacking with severe inconvenience, do not overcome the virtue of endurance and suffering in valiant men, and do not erase piety from their minds, but, rather, make it more fruitful by exercising it—how much less does the lack of those things which are usually associated with the funeral arrangements and the burial of dead bodies bring misery to those who are at rest in the hidden abodes of devout souls! And because of this fact, when these things were lacking

---
3 Cf. Matt. 26.7-13
4 Cf. John 19.38.
5 Cf. Gen. 47.30; 50.24.

for the dead bodies of Christians in that devastation of the great city, or even of other towns, it was neither the fault of the living, who were not able to provide them, nor was it a hardship for the dead, for they were not aware of the lack.

Such, then, is my opinion on the subject of burial. In fact, I have transferred it from another book of mine to this one for you, because it could be explained more easily in this way than by stating the same thing in another manner.

Chapter 4

(6) And if this is true, a place provided for burying bodies among the memorials of the saints is surely a matter of good human affection in attending to the funeral of one's own relatives. Indeed, if there is some religious requirement that they be buried, there can be some when the question is considered as to where they shall be buried. But, when such comforts are sought for the living by which their pious intentions toward their own loved ones are evident, I do not see what aids there are for the dead except for this purpose, that, while the living are worshiping in the place where the bodies of those whom they love are buried, they may commend to the same saints, as if to patrons, those whom they have undertaken before the Lord to aid by prayer. Actually, they could do this even if they had not been able to bury them in such places. For no other reason are those things which plainly become sepulchres of the dead said to be memorials or monuments, unless it is because of this: Memorials admonish us to think of and to recall to our memory those who have been taken away by death from the eyes of the living, lest by forgetfulness they be removed from our hearts also. The name *memoriae* shows clearly that this is the meaning, and *monumentum* is also thus called because it should admonish the mind, that is, it

calls something to the attention of the mind. For this reason, the Greeks use the word *mnēmeion* for what we call a memorial or a monument, because in their language memory itself, by which we remember, is called *mnēmē*. When, therefore, the mind recalls where the body of a very dear one has been buried, and the place happens to be in the name of a venerable martyr, to the same martyr he commends the beloved soul in a spirit of prayerful recollection and affliction. And when such a disposition is shown for the dead by very dear Christian friends, there is no doubt that they are benefited by these devotions, if when they were living in the body they merited such things to be to their advantage after this life. Indeed, if some necessity permits bodies to be buried, or does not give any opportunity for them to be buried in special places, those supplications in behalf of the dead are not to be passed over. Such prayers are to be made for all the dead in a Christian and Catholic society, even though there be a silent mention of their names which the Church undertakes in the general commemoration. In this way commemoration is made by one devoted mother for those who lack such prayers, whether parents, or sons, or any relations whatsoever, or friends. If, however, these supplications which are made with true faith and devotion for the dead should be lacking, there would be no advantage to their souls, I think, however holy the places be in which their lifeless bodies are buried.

Chapter 5

(7) When, therefore, a faithful mother desired the body of her faithful son who had died to be placed in the church of a martyr, if she truly believed that his soul was being aided by the merits of the martyr, this, because she so

believed, was a kind of prayer, and as such was of advantage, if anything was of advantage. And the fact that she frequently returns in spirit to the same sepulchre and there commends her son by prayers more and more aids the soul of her dead son. It is not the location of the dead body, but the living devotion of the mother out of memory of the place which affords this aid. At the same time, the love for the one who is commended, as well as for the saint to whom the loved one is commended, has a beneficial effect on the devout soul of the one who is praying. Those who pray by using the members of the body, as when they bend the knees, when they extend the hands, or even prostrate themselves upon the ground, or whatever else they do in a visible manner, they do that which indicates that they are suppliants although their invisible will and the intention of their heart is known to God, for He has no need of such outward signs to indicate that the human mind is in a state of supplication to Him. By doing this a man excites himself more to a proper state for praying and lamenting more humbly and fervently, and, somehow or other, since these movements of the body cannot be made except by a previous movement of the mind, by these same actions of the visible man, the invisible soul which prompted them is strengthened. Then, by reason of this the devotion of one's heart is strengthened, because he has resolved that these prayers be made and has made them. Yet, if anyone is held back or restrained from this method so that he is unable to make these outward signs, the soul of the man certainly prays in his most secret chamber before the eyes of God, where in spirit he is urged on, and even prostrates himself. Indeed, then, it is a matter of very great importance where one buries the body of his dead relative. And when one supplicates God in behalf of some dear soul after his devotion has chosen a holy place and there has buried the body, the recollection of the holy place renews and increases the devotion of him who selected the place. Yet, even if a devout person is not able to bury in the place of his choice one whom he loves, he by no means ought to cease from the needed prayers in making his commendation. In whatever place, then, the flesh of the dead body lies, or does not lie, repose must be sought for the soul. For, when the soul departed, it retained its sensation by which it is possible to distinguish in what manner each one exists, whether his life is good or evil. For not from the flesh does the soul expect its life to be helped; the soul itself furnished life for the flesh, and, withdrawing, took this life away, but when it returns it shall give it back. The flesh does not provide the merit of the resurrection for the spirit; rather, the spirit for the flesh, whether it shall restore the life for punishment or for glory.

Chapter 6

(8) We read in the *Church History* which Eusebius wrote in Greek, and which was translated into Latin by Rufinus, that the bodies of the martyrs in Gaul were exposed to dogs and that the remains of the dogs and the bones of the martyrs were cremated as thoroughly as possible and that all these ashes were scattered on the Rhone River, that nothing at all might remain to be remembered. We should believe that this was divinely permitted for no other reason than that Christians through their trust in Christ might learn how to despise this life. What was done to the bodies of the martyrs with an intense ferocity, if anything could have harmed them so that their most valiant souls would not find blessed repose, otherwise would not have been permitted. In very fact, it has been stated that the Lord said: 'Do not be afraid of those who kill the body, and after

that have nothing more that they can do,'[1] not because He would not permit them to do anything with the bodies of their dead, but because, whatever they would have been permitted to do, nothing would happen to lessen the Christian joy of the dead, nothing as a result would affect the feeling of the living after death, nothing would work to the harm even of their very bodies to prevent their rising intact.

Chapter 7

(9) Yet from that love of the human heart, because of which 'no one ever hated his own flesh,'[1] if men believe that anything would be lacking to their bodies after death which in their own people or country the solemnity of burial demands, they become sad like men, and before death they fear for their bodies that which has no effect on them after death. Thus we read in the Book of Kings that God through a Prophet threatens another Prophet who transgressed His word, that his body should not be returned to the sepulchre of his fathers. Scripture records it in these words: 'Thus saith the Lord: Because thou hast not been obedient to the Lord, and hast not kept the commandment which the Lord thy God commanded thee, and hast returned and eaten bread, and drunk water in the place wherein he commanded thee that thou shouldst not eat bread, nor drink water, thy dead body shall not be brought into the sepulchre of thy fathers.'[2]

If we consider the extent of this punishment according to the Evangelist where we learn that, after the body has been

---
1 Luke 12.4.

---
1 Cf. Eph. 5.29.
2 3 Kings 13.21,22.

slain, there is no occasion to fear that the lifeless members will suffer, it should not be called punishment. But, if we consider it in relation to the love of a man for his own flesh, then he might have been frightened and saddened while living at what he was not to feel when dead. This, then, was the nature of the punishment: The soul grieved that something would happen to its body, although, when it did happen, the soul did not grieve. Only to this extent did the Lord wish to punish His servant, for it was not from his own obstinacy that he refused to carry out the command, but, because of the deceit of another person who was deceiving him, he thought that he obeyed when he did not obey.

It is not to be imagined that one has been so annihilated by the teeth of a beast that his soul has then been snatched away to infernal punishment, since the same lion who slew his very body guarded it. Even the beast of burden on which the man had been riding was unhurt and with great courage stood in the presence of the wild beast at the destruction of his master. By this miraculous sign it is made clear that the man of God was corrected temporarily even at the point of death rather than that he was punished after death. On this subject the Apostle Paul, when he had made mention of certain unpleasant infirmities and death experienced by many, said: 'But if we judged ourselves, we should not thus be judged by the Lord. But when we are judged, we are being chastised by the Lord, that we may not be condemned with the world.'[3]

Well did the man who had deceived the man of God bury him with honor in his own tomb and give orders that he himself should be buried next to his bones, hoping thus to spare his own bones. He knew that the time would come according to the prophecy of that man of God when Josias, king of the Jews, would dig up in the land the bones of

---
3 1 Cor. 11.31,32.

many dead and with them defile the sacrilegious altars which had been set up for graven images. He spared that tomb where the Prophet lay who more than 300 years before had predicted these things. And because of him the burying place of the man who deceived him was not violated.[4] By that love because of which no one ever hated his own flesh he provided for his own corpse, while he had slain his soul by deceit. From this fact, then, because each one naturally loves his own flesh, it was punishment for him to learn that he would not be in the tomb of his fathers. So he took care that his bones be spared by burying them next to him whose tomb no one would violate.

Chapter 8

(10) The martyrs of Christ in their strivings for truth have conquered this love of one's flesh. And it is not strange that they despised what they would not have felt after they had met death, since they could not be conquered by those tortures which they felt while living. Just as God was able to restrain the lion from doing further harm to the body of the Prophet who had been slain, and changed the killer into a guardian, so, I say, He was able to keep the bodies of His own who had been slain from the dogs to whom they had been cast. In like manner He could have frightened in countless ways the savagery even of men who dared to burn the dead bodies or to scatter the ashes. But this proof ought not have been lacking to the manifold variety of temptations, otherwise the fortitude of a confession of the faith which did not yield to the savagery of the persecutions for the saftey of the body might fear for an honorable burial; finally, in order that faith in the resurrection of the body might not

---
4 Cf. 3 Kings 13.24-32; 4 Kings 23.16-18.

become fearful over the destruction of the body. Therefore, this ought also to have been allowed, so that, even after these experiences of such great horror, the martyrs remaining fervent in the confession of Christ might also become witnesses of this truth, in which they had learned that those who had slain their bodies had nothing which they might do afterwards, since whatever they might do to the bodies of the dead was as if they did nothing. For, in all flesh that lacks life, he who has left the body can be aware of no injury to the lifeless body, nor can He who created it lose anything. But in the midst of what was being done to the bodies of the dead, although the martyrs were enduring them fearlessly with great fortitude, among the brethren there was great grief, because no opportunity was given to them to pay just dues at the burial of the saints, and the vigilance of the cruel guards did not permit them to take away secretly any relics, as history likewise bears witness.[1] And thus, although no misery came upon those who had been slain, in the dismemberment of their bodies, in the burning of their bones, in the scattering of the ashes, a great sorrow did torture those who were unable to bury anything of theirs, because they themselves in a certain manner felt for those who had no feeling in any manner, and where now there was no passion on the part of the one, there was a wretched compassion on the part of the other.

Chapter 9

(11) Those men were praised and called blessed by King David who had bestowed the merciful kindness of burial on the dry bones of Saul and Jonathan, in keeping with

---
1 Cf. Eusebius, *Hist. Eccl.* 5.1.

that wretched compassion which I have mentioned.[1] But, pray tell, what compassion is bestowed on those who have no feeling? Or should one remember that the unburied were not able to cross the infernal river?[2] May this be far from the Christian belief! Otherwise, it worked out very badly for so great a multitude of martyrs whose bodies could not be buried, and for them Truth emptily said: 'Do not be afraid of those who kill the body and after that have nothing more that they can do,'[3] if they were able to do them such great wrongs as to prevent their crossing over to the desired places. But, without any doubt, this is exceedingly false, for it is no hindrance to the faithful to be denied burial of the bodies. Also, it is of no advantage if burial be granted the godless. Why, then, are those men said to have done an act of mercy in burying Saul and his son, and blessed by good King David for this, unless it be that the hearts of the compassionate are favorably affected when they are concerned over the well-being of other bodies of the dead? Or is it because of that love which keeps one from ever hating his own flesh that they do not wish such things to happen after their own death to their own bodies, so that what they wish to be done for them when they shall have no feeling they care to do for others who now have no feeling, while they themselves still have feeling?

Chapter 10

(12) Certain visions are reported which seem to bring into this discussion a question that should not be neglected. In fact, some dead persons are reported to have appeared either in a dream or in some such fashion to the living,

---
1 Cf. 2 Kings 2.5.
2 Cf. Vergil, *Aeneid* 6.327.
3 Luke 12.4.

who were ignorant as to where their bodies were lying unburied. After pointing out these places to them, they admonished them to provide for them the burial which had been lacking. Now, if we state that these things are false, we shall seem indifferently to go against the writings of certain of the faithful and against the senses of those who affirm that such things have happened to them. One must reply that it is not to be assumed that the dead have knowledge of these things merely because they seem to say them or to point them out or to seek them in dreams. The living often appear to the living while they are asleep, although they are entirely unaware of making any such appearance, and hear from them, as they speak, the things which they have dreamed, namely, that they saw them in their dreams doing or saying something. It is possible for someone to see me in his dreams indicating to him something that has happened, or predicting to him something that is to happen, when I am entirely ignorant of this and do not care what he may dream, or whether he is awake while I am sleeping, or he is asleep while I am awake, or whether we both are awake or asleep at one and the same time when he experiences the dream in which he sees me. Why, then, is it so strange if the dead, without their knowledge and not perceiving these things, are seen by the living in sleep and say something which, upon awaking, they realize to be true?

I might believe that this is done by the workings of angels. It may be permitted from above, or it may be ordered, that they may seem in their sleep to say something about the burying of their own bodies, when truly they whose the bodies are know nothing of this. Even this sometimes happens advantageously for some kind of solace for the living who are related to those dead whose images appear to them while dreaming, or that by these friendly admonitions to mankind the humanity of burial is commended. For, although burial may not help the dead, if one neglects it he may be considered irreligious. However, at times when false visions have been seen, men are led into great errors, which they ought to resist. Suppose someone should see in his dream what Aeneas by a false report of the poet is said to have seen among the dead, and then the image of someone not buried should appear to him and should say such things as Palinurus is said to have spoken to Aeneas.[1] Then, on awaking, he should find the body in the very place where he heard that it was lying when he was dreaming. If then, on being admonished and requested to bury the body he had found and because he finds this to be true, he should believe that the dead are buried so that their souls may pass over to those places from which he dreamed that the souls of the unburied are prohibited by a wicked law, would he not by holding such a belief depart far from the path of Truth?

Chapter 11

(13) However, human weakness seems to be such that when anyone sees in his sleep one who is dead he thinks he sees the soul of the dead person. But, when he has dreamed of a living person, he feels confident that it is the likeness of the person and not his soul or body which has appeared to him. This amounts to the belief that the souls but not the likeness of the dead in the same manner without their knowledge may appear to those sleeping. Indeed, when we were at Milan, we heard of the following incident: Payment of a debt was demanded of a certain son, whose father, without the knowledge of the son, had made full settlement before his death, but had not received back the original note which was now produced. The son became very sad and

---

1 Cf. Vergil, *Aeneid* 6.337-383.

was wondering why his father as he was dying had not told him what he owed, since he had made a will. Then the same father appeared to his son, who was now quite anxious. While the son was sleeping his father told him where he might find the receipt which would acknowledge full payment of his original note. And when the son found this and presented it, not only did he throw off the slander of the false claim, but also recovered his father's signature, which the father had not recovered when he repaid the loan. Here, indeed, the mind of a man is thought to have exercised a care for his son and to have come to him sleeping, that he might inform his ignorance and so set him free from a great annoyance.

But, at almost the very same time at which we heard the above report, another story came to us at Milan from Eulogius, a rhetorician at Carthage. He was a disciple of mine in this art, and he himself told me the same story after we had returned to Africa. The story is as follows. When Eulogius was teaching the rhetorical works of Cicero to his pupils, as he was reviewing the lecture which he had intended to deliver the following day, he came upon an obscure passage, and, not being able to determine the exact meaning, could scarcely sleep. On that very night I expounded to him in his dream the passage which he did not understand. Indeed, not I, but my image, and without my knowledge, and so far across the sea, either doing or dreaming something else, and caring not at all for his worries! In what way such things happen I do not know, but in whatsoever way they do happen, why do we not believe that they happen in the same way, namely, as one in his sleep sees a dead person, so he sees a living person? In both instances it happens to those who neither know nor care who dreams of their images, or where, or when.

Chapter 12

(14) Quite similar indeed to dreams are some of the visions of people who are awake. They have disturbed feelings, such as those who are mad or raving in some manner. They even talk with themselves, as if they actually were speaking with someone present. They even converse with those who are absent more than with those who are present, whose images they think of, whether they be of persons living or dead. However, the ones who are living do not know that they are seen by them and that they are conversing with them. They are not really present nor are they actually conversing. Yet, because of their disturbed feelings men suffer such imaginary visions. In this manner, also, these who depart from this life seem to men, who are so affected, as if they were really present, although they are absent and altogether ignorant of whether anyone sees them in his imagination.

(15) A situation quite similar to this is the following. Some persons are at times drawn from the senses of the body and are taken with such visions more deeply than when they are asleep. To these the images of the living and of the dead appear. But, when they were brought back to their senses, they said that they had seen certain dead persons. Indeed, they are believed to have been with them. But those who also hear that images of the living, although they are absent and unaware of it, have been seen in like fashion pay no attention to these reports.

A certain man, Curma by name, of the township of Tullium, which is next to Hippo, was a poor member of the Senate, scarcely qualified to be a magistrate of the town, merely a simple country fellow. When he was taken ill, he was out of his mind and lay almost dead for some days. There was the faintest breath in his nostrils, barely felt on one's hand when held near, and this was the only sign of life that kept him from being buried as dead. He moved no limb, he took no nourishment, he gave no indication with his eyes or by any other sense of the body that he was aware of any imposed annoyance. Yet he saw many things, just as in a dream. Finally, after many days, upon awaking, he reported all that he had seen. As soon as he opened his eyes he said: Let someone go to the house of Curma the smith and see what is going on there. And on arriving there it was discovered that Curma the smith had died at the very moment when Curma the magistrate had come out of his coma, almost returning from death. Then, to those who were intently curious, he indicated that Curma the smith had been ordered brought in when he himself was dismissed. The fact was, he said, that he, Curma the magistrate, had been ordered brought to those regions of the dead, when the order was intended for Curma the smith.

Therefore, in those visions, just as in his own dreams, among those of the dead whom he saw being treated each according to his own merits he recognized some even whom he knew to be alive. Indeed, I might have believed him had he not seen during those so-called dreams some who are even living to this day, some clerics of his own district. And he was told by their priest that he should be baptized by me at Hippo, something which he said had already been done. Thus he had seen in that vision a priest, clerics, me myself among the living, and in the same vision he later saw dead persons. Now, why should not one believe that he saw the dead in the same way in which he saw the living, namely, both dead and living being absent and ignorant of any such incident, and that he did not see real persons and places, but only the likenesses of both persons and places? For he saw the place where the priest was with the clerics, and Hippo where he thought he was baptized by me. But he certainly was not in these places at the time when he seemed to himself to be there, for he did not know what was going on there at the time, and without doubt he would have known if he had really been there. These things, then, are seen which are not actually present, but sketched, as it were, in shadowy imaginings.

Finally, after relating these many things that he had seen, he added that he had been led into Paradise and that he was told when he was dismissed to return to his family: 'Go, be baptized, if you wish to be in this place of the blessed.' Then, on being admonished that he be baptized by me, he replied that this had already been done. Again, the same one advised him as before: 'Go, receive true baptism, for you saw in a vision that baptism of which you spoke.'

After he recovered, he came to Hippo. And, as Easter was drawing near, he gave his name among the other catechumens who were seeking baptism, although like many others he was unknown to us. For he took care not to make known that vision to me or to anyone of our group. He was baptized, and after having fulfilled the duties of the Easter season, he returned home. After two years or more had passed, I discovered all these things, at first through a certain friend of mine and of his who was a guest at my table, when we were speaking of such things. Then I insisted and brought it about that he relate these things in person to me with some of his own trustworthy citizens as witnesses of his marvelous sickness, that he lay almost dead for many days, and also who knew of that other Curma the smith, as I have related above. And with respect to all these incidents, when he was relating them to me, they recalled that they had heard them at that time from him, thus confirming his account. And because of this, just as he saw his baptism and me myself and Hippo and the church and the baptistry, not in reality, but in mental representations, so also did he see certain other living persons, although the same living persons were ignorant of any such thing.

Chapter 13

Why, then, do we not agree that in like manner those dead persons were present only in the mind of the dreamer, and without the knowledge of the same dead?

(16) Why do we not believe that these are the workings of angels through a dispensation of the providence of God, who puts to good use both good and evil according to the incomprehensible depth of His judgment?[1] Are the minds of mortal men thus strengthened or weakened, or consoled or frightened, by a realization of the fact that to each individual mercy is shown or punishment imposed by Him to whom the Church, not in vain, ascribes mercy and judgment?[2] As each one shall wish, let him receive what I shall say.

If the souls of the dead were taking part in the affairs of the living, and they themselves were speaking to us when we see them in our dreams (that I may be silent about others), my devout mother would be with me every night, for she followed me on land and sea that she might be with me. Far be it that she should have become for the sake of a happier life cruel to this extent, that, when anything grieves my heart, she would not console her grieving son whom she loved so fondly! She never wished to see me sorrowful. Truthfully, then, does the inspired Psalmist write: 'When my father and my mother forsook me, the Lord received me.'[3]

---
1 Cf. Rom. 11.33.
2 Cf. Ps. 100.1.
3 Cf. Ps. 26.10.

If, then, our parents have forsaken us, how do they take part in our cares and affairs? However, if our parents are not interested, who are the others among the dead who know what we are doing or what we are suffering? Isaias the Prophet says: 'For Thou art our Father, because Abraham hath not known us, and Israel hath been ignorant of us.'[4] God promised to the patriarchs who believed in Him a multitude of descendants. And the Prophet Isaias says that the patriarchs do not know their living descendants. If so great patriarchs did not know what was going on as concerns their own offspring, how do the dead associate themselves with the affairs of the living to learn of and to assist them in their deeds?

How do we say that they have been advised who have died before the coming of the evils which followed their death, if after death they perceive whatever misfortunes befall the human life? Or is it that we are mistaken when we imagine that they are at rest when the restless life of the living concerns them? What is this, then, which God promised to the most devout king, Josias, for a great reward, telling him that he would soon die in order that he might not see the evils which He was threatening to send upon that place and that people? The words of God are these: 'Thus saith the Lord the God of Israel: My words which you have heard and which you feared from my mouth when you heard what I said about this place and those who dwell in it, that it be forsaken and become a curse, and you rent your garments and wept in my sight, shall not come to pass, saith the Lord of hosts. Behold I shall bring thee to thy fathers, and thou shalt be brought with peace, and your eyes shall not see all the evils which I bring upon this place and those who dwell in it.'[5] And Josias, alarmed at the dire

---
4 Isa. 63.16.
5 Cf. 4 Kings 22.18-20.

threats of God, wept and tore his garments and then was made secure by an early death from all future ills, because he would so rest in peace that he would not see those evils.

The souls of the dead, then, are in a place where they do not see the things which go on and transpire in this mortal life. How, then, do they see their own graves or their own bodies, whether they are buried or lie exposed? How do they take part in the misery of the living, when either they are suffering their own evil deserts, if such they have merited, or they rest in peace, such as was promised to this Josias? For there they undergo no evils either by enduring them themselves or by compassionate suffering for others, but are liberated from all evils which when they lived here they endured for themselves and out of compassion for others.

Chapter 14

(17) Someone might say: If the dead have no care for the living, how did that rich man who was being tormented in hell ask father Abraham to send Lazarus to his five brothers who were not yet dead and to deal with them lest they come to the same place of torments? When that rich man said this, did he know anything of what his brothers were doing, or what they were suffering at that time? Thus, being evil he suffered more because he had a care for the living, for he did not know what they were doing, just as we have a care for the dead, although we do not know what they are doing. For, if we had no care for the dead, we would not be in the habit of praying for them. In short, Abraham did not send Lazarus, but replied that the five brothers had Moses and the Prophets with them and that they should hear them so as not to come to such torments.

Someone raises another objection: How did father

Abraham himself not know what was going on here when he knew that Moses and the Prophets were here, that is to say, their books which men might read and obey, thus avoiding the torments of hell; when, finally, he knew that the rich man had lived in luxury, while Lazarus in toils and pains had spent his days in poverty? He says this to him: 'Son, remember that thou in thy lifetime hast received good things, and Lazarus in like manner evil things.'[1] Then he knew the things which had been done among the living, not among the dead. Truly he did not know of them when they were happening among the living, but he could have learned of them from Lazarus after the rich man and Lazarus were dead. I say this, for the Prophet Isaias cannot be false in saying: 'Abraham hath not known us.'[2]

Chapter 15

(18) Then it must be admitted that the dead do not know what is going on here, but, when something is happening here, the dead actually hear about it later from those who at their death go from here to them. Truly, they do not report everything. They are allowed to remember and to report only the things which are proper for those dead to hear. Also, from angels who are aware of the things which go on here the dead are able to hear whatever He who governs all determines is proper for each one to hear. For, unless there were angels who can be present in the abodes of the living and the dead, the Lord Jesus would not have said: 'And it came to pass that the poor man died and was

---
1 Luke 16.25.
2 Isa. 63.16.

borne away by the angels into Abraham's bosom.'[1] Thus, the angels who carried from this place to that the one whom God wished are able at one time to be with the living, at another time to be with the dead. For, the souls of the dead are able to know some things which go on here which they ought to know. Further, those who ought to know such things know not only the present or the past, but also by divine revelation the things which are to come—just as the Prophets, but not everybody, while they were living here received revelation. However, not even the Prophets knew everything, but only such things as the providence of God decided ought to be revealed to them.

Also, some can be sent to the living from the dead, just as in the opposite direction divine Scripture testifies that Paul was snatched from the living into Paradise.[2] Samuel the Prophet, although dead, predicted future events to King Saul, who was alive, although some think that it was not Samuel himself who was able to be called forth by some magic,[3] but that some spirit so allied with evil works had feigned a likeness to him—yet the Book of Ecclesiasticus, which Jesus the son of Sirach is said to have written, but because of some similarity of style is thought to be the work of Solomon, contains in praise of the fathers the fact that Samuel prophesied even though dead.[4] If there is objection to this book on the ground that it is not in the canon of ancient Hebrew Scripture, what are we going to say of Moses, who in Deuteronomy is certainly recorded as dead and again in the Gospel of St. Matthew is reported to have appeared to the living along with Elias who did not die.[5]

---

1 Luke 16.22.
2 Cf. 2 Cor. 12.2.
3 Cf. 1 Kings 28.7.
4 Cf. Eccli. 46.16-23.
5 Cf. Deut. 34.5; Matt. 17.3.

Chapter 16

(19) The following offers another solution of this question: How do the martyrs by their very benefactions, which are given to those who seek, indicate that they are interested in human affairs, if the dead do not know what the living are doing? For, not alone by the operations of his benefactions, but even to the very eyes of men, did Felix the Confessor appear, when Nola was being besieged by the barbarians. You take pious delight in this appearance of his. We heard of this not by uncertain rumors, but from trustworthy witnesses. In truth, things are divinely shown which are different from the usual order nature has given to the separate kinds of created things. Just because our Lord, when He wished, suddenly turned water into wine[1] is no excuse for us not to understand the proper value of water as water. This is a rare, in fact, an isolated instance of such divine operation. Again, the fact that Lazarus rose from the dead[2] does not mean that every dead person rises when he wishes, or that a lifeless person is called back by a living one just as a sleeping person is aroused by one who is awake. Some events are characteristic of human action; others manifest the signs of divine power. Some things happen naturally; others are done in a miraculous manner, although God is present in the natural process, and nature accompanies the miraculous. One must not think, then, that any of the dead can intervene in the affairs of the living merely because the martyrs are present for the healing or the aiding of certain ones. Rather, one should think this: The martyrs through divine power take part in the affairs of the living, but the dead of themselves have no power to intervene in the affairs of the living.

---
1 Cf. John 2.9.
2 Cf. John 11.44.

(20) This question as to how the martyrs aid those who certainly are aided by them surpasses the powers of my intelligence. Are they themselves by their own power present at one moment in places so diverse and separated by such great space between them, or are they wherever their memorials are, or even beyond their memorials wherever they are thought to be? Or are they in a place suited to their own merits, removed from every association with mortals, yet continuing to pray for the needs of their suppliants? This would resemble our prayers for mortals with whom, indeed, we are not present and do not know where they are or what they are doing. And does Almighty God, who is everywhere present, neither fixed to us nor remote from us, when He hears the prayers of the martyrs, bring about through the ministry of angels, which is everywhere, those solaces for men to whom He judges that in the misery of this life such solaces should be given? Further, does He by a marvelous and unbelievable goodness and power bestow the merits of His martyrs where and when and how He wishes, but especially through their memorials, since He knows that this is expedient for us for building up our faith in Christ? For the martyrs have suffered because of their confession of Christ. This question is so deep that I cannot comprehend it, and so complex as to defy all my efforts to scrutinize it successfully. But, in which of these two ways are we aided by the martyrs? Or is it possibly by both ways, so that at one time these aids are secured through the very presence of the martyrs and at another time through angels who assume the appearance of the martyrs? I do not wish to say. I should prefer, rather, to seek out these things from those who know.

For there is somebody who knows them, but not the one who seems to himself to know while he does not know. The gifts are of God, who bestows freely some on these persons, others on those, according to the Apostle Paul, who says: 'Now the manifestation of the Spirit is given to everyone for profit. To one through the Spirit is given the utterance of wisdom; and to another the utterance of knowledge, according to the same Spirit; to another faith, in the same Spirit; to another the gift of healing, in the one Spirit; to another the working of miracles; to another prophecy; to another the distinguishing of spirits; to another various kinds of tongues; to another interpretation of tongues. But all these things are the work of one and the same Spirit, who allots to everyone according as He will.'[3] Of all these spiritual gifts which the Apostle has mentioned, the discernment of spirits is the gift which enables one to know things just as they should be known.

Chapter 17

(21) One must believe that the famous monk, John,[1] was such a person. He is the one whom the elder Theodosius, the emperor, consulted as to the outcome of the civil war. He truly had the gift of prophecy. Such gifts are not distributed one to one man, another to another, but I do not doubt that one person can have more than one gift.

A certain very religious woman was quite impatient to see this famous monk, and was urgently insisting through her husband that her request be granted. But the monk was unwilling to see her, for he never granted an audience to women. However, he said to the husband: 'Go, tell your wife that she will see me tonight, but in her dreams.' And this did happen. And he gave her such advice as ought to be

---

3 1 Cor. 12.7-11.

1 John of Lycopolis. Cf. '*Joannes* (487),' William Smith-Henry Wace, *Dictionary of Christian Biography* 3.403; also *De civitate Dei* 5.26.

given to a faithful wife. When she awoke she told her husband that she had seen such a man of God, and mentioned what she had heard from him. Thereupon he knew that she had seen John, the monk. And when he discovered this from the facts, he retold it to me. He was a serious and noble man and most worthy to be believed. But, if I had seen that holy monk myself, because, as the report goes, he was being questioned most patiently and was answering most wisely, I would have asked him this very question: Did you in person come to that woman in her dreams, that is, was it your spirit in the likeness of your body, just as we dream of ourselves in the likeness of our own body? Or were you doing something else, or, if asleep, were you dreaming something else, or did such a vision appear to the woman in her sleep through an angel, or even in some other fashion? And did he by a revelation of the spirit of prophecy find out beforehand that this would occur so that he himself might promise it? For, if he conversed with her while she was dreaming, this could have been so by a miraculous gift, not by a natural gift; by the grace of God, not by a natural faculty. If, however, he himself was doing something else, either sleeping or occupied in other visions when the woman saw him in her sleep, clearly something else took place such as that incident which we read of in the Acts of the Apostles.[2] Here the Lord Jesus is speaking to Ananias about Saul, and telling him that Saul saw him coming to him. But Ananias himself knew nothing of it. Regardless of what answer that man of God might make to me on this point, I would continue to ask him, concerning the martyrs, whether they are present in person during dreams or in whatever other manner they might wish to appear to those who see them, and especially when demons in men confess that they are tortured by the martyrs and

---

2 Cf. Acts 9.10-19.

ask them to obey them, or, whether these things are done at the will of God through the workings of angels for the honor and commendation of men, while the martyrs are in a place of peaceful quiet, separated far from us for beholding much better visions, and there praying for us.

For, at Milan, near the tomb of the martyr-saints Gervase and Protase, the demons, while making mention of the martyrs, also acknowledged in like manner Ambrose the bishop, who was still living, calling him by name and imploring him to spare them. Now St. Ambrose, the bishop, was doing something else at the time and was altogether unaware when this was done. Is the answer really this: At one time these things are done through the very presence of the martyrs, at another time through the presence of angels? Can we learn these two things and, if so, by what signs? Or does anyone have the power to be aware of these things and to draw a distinction, except one who has that gift through the Spirit of God, who distributes suitable gifts to each as He wishes? John the monk would, I think, explain all these things to me as I might wish, that I might learn from his instruction, and that the things which I might hear I might discover whether they are really true, or that I might believe in the things that I do not know when he tells me what he knows. He might even reply using holy Scripture, and say: 'Seek not the things that are too high for thee, and search not into things above thy ability; but the things that God hath commanded thee, think on them always.'[3] This I would gratefully accept, for it is a great gain if it should become clear that we should not even try to understand some obscure and uncertain facts which we were not able to understand, and if we should learn that it is of no disadvantage if we do not understand the things we wish to know, thinking that such knowledge is a gain when it is not.

---
3 Eccli. 3.22.

Chapter 18

(22) Since this is so, we should not think that any aid comes to the dead for whom we are providing care, except what we solemnly pray for in their behalf at the altars, either by sacrifices of prayers or of alms. Even this does not benefit all for whom it is done, but only those who while they lived made preparation that they might so be aided. But, even though we do not know who these are, we ought none the less to do such works for all Christians, so that no one of them may be neglected for whom these aids can and ought to come. It is better that there be a superabundance of aids for those to whom these works are neither a hindrance nor a help, than that there be a lack for those who are thus aided. Yet, each one does this more diligently for his own friends and relatives, in order that a like service may be performed in his behalf by his friends and relatives. Regardless of what is spent for burying the body, it is not an aid to salvation, but a duty of our humanity according to that love by which 'no one ever hated his own flesh.'[1] Then, it is fitting that one exercise what care he can for the body of his relative, when the one who used to exercise the care has already died. And if they do this who have no faith in the resurrection of the body, how much more ought we who have faith that a duty of this kind is due to a dead body which shall rise again and live forever? And this is in some way a testimony of one's faith. Truly, the fact that one is buried in a memorial of a martyr seems to me to benefit the dead only in this respect, namely, that in commending the dead to the patronage of the martyr the desire for supplicating in his behalf is increased.

(23) Thus you have such a response of mine as I have been able to render to those questions which you thought I

---
1 Cf. Eph. 5.29.

should seek out. If it is longer than necessary, please forgive me, for it was undertaken because of my love for conversing with you. In what manner your esteemed pleasure shall receive this book please let me know by a return letter from you. And our brother in Christ and our fellow priest, Candidianus, the bearer of this letter to you, will without doubt make it more pleasing. When I became acquainted with him through your letter, I received him with my whole heart. I now regret to send him back, for His presence has brought much consolation to us in the love of Christ. I must confess that I have obeyed you because of his insistence. For so many problems demand my attention that my reply would have failed your request unless, indeed, he by his constant reminding had not allowed me to forget.

IN ANSWER TO
THE JEWS

(Adversus Judaeos)

Translated by
SISTER MARIE LIGUORI, I.H.M., PH.D.

INTRODUCTION

ST. AUGUSTINE does not mention the *Tractatus adversus Judaeos* in his *Retractations*. This omission raises two obstacles to any agreement upon a probable date of composition. If the treatise were written as a book, then its probable date would be after the *Retractations*, that is, 428-429. This theory Blumenkranz sees as the only basis for the traditional date 428 or 429.[1] On the other hand, if the *Tractatus* is a sermon, it would have no place in the *Retractations*, which was restricted to books, as St. Augustine had reserved the review of his epistles and sermons for later consideration.[2] Portalié,[3] Schanz,[4] Bardenhewer,[5] classify the *Adversus Judaeos* as a sermon among St. Augustine's apologetic or polemical writings. Following a

---

1 B. Blumenkranz, *Ein Beitrag zur Geschichte der jüdisch-christlichen Beziehungen in den ersten Jahrhunderten* (Basel 1946) 208. Blumenkranz rejects M. Zarb's chronology (cf. 'Chronologia operum sancti Augustini,' *Angelicum* 11 [1934] 87).
2 Cf. *Retractationes*, prol. I.
3 E. Portalié, 'Saint Augustin,' *DTC* I 2 (Paris 1909) 2291-2292.
4 M. Schanz, *Geschichte der römischen Litteratur* IV 2 (Munich 1920) 417.
5 O. Bardenhewer, *Geschichte der altkirchlichen Literatur* IV (Freiburg 1924) 460.

suggestion in Schanz,[6] moreover, Blumenkranz demonstrates conclusively that the *Tractatus* bears all the characteristics of the sermon in form, style, and diction.[7]

The fifty-sixth *quaestio* of the *De diversis Quaestionibus*,[8] Epistle 196 to Asellicus,[9] and probably Sermon 91,[10] St. Augustine likewise directs against the Jews. His commentaries on them throughout his writings—on their blindness, their rejection of Christ and consequent reprobation, the loss of their heritage to the Christians—is in accordance with the traditional attitude of earlier Christian writers. St. Augustine's original contribution to Jewish-Christian relations, however, is his interpretation of the Jewish dispersion as the Church's witness among all nations, of the Messianic mission of Christ. Since this same idea of bearing witness occurs in the *De civitate Dei* (18.46) where St. Augustine gives it exhaustive treatment, and since the *Tractatus* presumes the understanding of this whole chain of ideas and at the same time exhibits the habit of the preacher to use the same idea repeatedly, Blumenkranz sets the *terminus post quem* of *Adversus Judaeos* at 425—if this be the accepted date for *De civitate Dei*.[11]

---

6 *Op. cit.* 419.
7 Blumenkranz, *op. cit.* 200-202.
8 Cf. Possidius, *Librorum, tractatum, et epistolarum Sancti Augustini indiculus* 2 (*PL* 46). A. Wilmart, in 'Operum S. Augustini Elenchus,' *Miscellanea Agostiniana* II (Rome 1931) 149-233, presents some strong conjectures that Possidius based his *Indiculum* on St. Augustine's catalogue of his own writings.
9 Possidius, *loc. cit.: Epistola ad Asellicum episcopum*—'de cavendo Judaismo.' Cf. *CSEL* 57 (1911), ed. Goldbacher.
10 Cf. *PL* 38.565-571: 'De verbis Evangelii Matthaei ubi Dominus interrogavit Judaeos, cujus filium dicerent esse Christum.' Cf., also, Possidius, *loc. cit.*: 'adversos quos supra dictos contra Judaeos tractatus duo.' Schanz (*op. cit.* 419) thinks that Sermon 91 may be the other of the two sermons noted by Possidius.
11 Blumenkranz, *op. cit.* 207-209,211. Pope gives 426 as the date for the completion of *De civ. Dei.* Cf. H. Pope, O.P., *Saint Augustine of Hippo* (Westminster, Maryland 1949) 377.

It was natural for St. Augustine to refer to the Jews in his writings and sermons wherever and whenever occasion demanded. He could scarcely avoid reference to them in his Scriptural commentaries and reflections any more than he could overlook their presence in society. It was natural, moreover, to be alert to the not insignificant problem they created in his province. The Jews formed no small part of the population of Hippo and Carthage and, though many were true to their religious beliefs and customs, others, with their careless morals and contentious ways, presented a serious difficulty to the zealous bishop in his solicitude for the members of his Christian flock who were only too ready to revert to the practices and customs of their pagan and Jewish ancestry.[12]

The persuasive firmness and kindness of the bishop, so evident in this sermon, might almost be construed as an invitation to the Jews to come into the Church.[13] Still, the *Adversus Judaeos* apparently contributed more to the struggle against Jewish influence on the Church and served as a warning to his own Catholics and catechumens to shun the society of a people so baneful in its influence upon their morals and faith.[14] It is with this fact in mind that the translation of the title *In Answer to the Jews* emphasizes that argumentative aspect of *adversus* which would equip the Christians with ready answers to the taunts, criticisms, and even enticements of their unbelieving fellow townsmen.

The following translation of *Adversus Judaeos* is based on the Benedictine text of St. Maur in *PL* 42 (Paris 1886) 51-64.

---
12 Blumenkranz, *op. cit.* 68; cf. also Pope, *op. cit.* 6-8.
13 Cf. below, 10.15.
14 Blumenkranz, *op. cit.* 203-204, 211.

IN ANSWER TO THE JEWS

Chapter 1

THE BLESSED APOSTLE Paul, the teacher of the Gentiles in faith and truth, admonishes us with precepts when he exhorts us to remain firmly fixed in the same faith of which he was made the fitting minister; he instils fear in us by example when he says: 'See then, the goodness and the severity of God: his severity towards those who have fallen, but the goodness of God towards thee if thou abidest in his goodness.'[1] Assuredly he said this about the Jews who, as branches of that olive tree which was fruitful in its root of the holy patriarchs, have been broken off on account of their unbelief, so that, because of the faith of the Gentiles, the wild olive was grafted on and shared in the richness of the true olive tree after the natural branches had been cut off. He warns, however: 'do not boast against the branches. But if thou dost boast, still it is not thou that supportest the stem, but the stem thee.'[2] And since some of the Jews are saved, he immediately adds:

1 Rom. 11.22
2 Rom. 11.17,18.

'otherwise thou also wilt be cut off. And they also, if they do not continue in unbelief, will be grafted in; for God is able to graft them back.'[3] They, however, who persist in their unbelief are judged by the Lord, who says: 'but the children of the kingdom will go into the darkness outside: there will be the weeping and the gnashing of teeth.'[4] Of the Gentiles, on the contrary, who persevere in goodness, He says in addition: 'many will come from the east and from the west, and will feast with Abraham and Isaac and Jacob in the kingdom of heaven.'[5] By the just severity of God, therefore, the unbelieving pride of the native branches is broken away from the living patriarchal root, and, by the grace of divine goodness, the faithful humility of the wild olive is ingrafted.

(2) When these Scriptural words are quoted to the Jews, they scorn the Gospel and the Apostle; they do not listen to what we say because they do not understand what they read. Certainly, if they understood what the Prophet, whom they read, is foretelling: 'I have given thee to be the light of the Gentiles, that thou mayest be my salvation even to the farthest part of the earth'[6] they would not be so blind and so sick as not to recognize in Jesus Christ both light and salvation. Likewise, if they understood to whom the prophecy refers which they sing so fruitlessly and without meaning: 'Their sound hath gone forth into all the earth: and their words unto the ends of the world,'[7] they would awaken to the voice of the Apostles, and would sense that their words are divine. Consequently, testimonies are to be selected from sacred Scripture, which has great authority

---

3 Rom. 11.22,23.
4 Cf. Matt. 8.12.
5 Matt. 8.11.
6 Isa. 49.6.
7 Ps. 18.5.

among the Jews, and if they do not want to be cured by means of this advantage offered them, they can at least be convicted by its evident truth.

Chapter 2

(3) First of all, however, this error of theirs must be refuted, that the Books of the Old Testament do not concern us at all, because we observe the new sacraments and no longer preserve the old. For they say to us: 'What is the reading of the Law and the Prophets doing among you who do not want to follow the precepts contained in them?' They base their complaint on the fact that we do not circumcise the foreskin of the male, and we eat the flesh of animals which the Law declares unclean, and we do not observe the Sabbath, new moons and their festival days in a purely human way, nor do we offer sacrifice to God with victims of cattle, nor do we celebrate the Pasch as they do with sheep and unleavened bread, nor do we revere the other ancient sacraments which the Apostle classifies under the general expression of shadows of things to come,[1] since at their time they signified events to be revealed which we have accepted and recognized as already revealed, so that with the shadows removed we are enjoying their uncovered light. It would take too long, however, to dispute these charges one by one; how we are circumcised by putting off the old man and not in despoiling our natural body; how their abstinence from certain foods of animals corresponds to our mortification in habits and morals; how we present our bodies a living sacrifice, holy and pleasing to God before whom we intelligently pour forth our souls in holy desires, instead of in blood; how we are cleansed from all

---
1 Cf. Col. 2.17.

iniquity by the Blood of Christ as the Immaculate Lamb. Christ is even prefigured in the old sacrifices by the goat because He took the likeness of our flesh of sin; nor does one who recognizes Christ as the greatest victim refuse to see Him, in the horns of the cross, prefigured in the bull. When we find rest in Him we truly observe the Sabbath, and the observance of the new moon is the sanctification of our new life. Christ is our Pasch; our unleavened bread is sincerity of truth without the leaven of decay. If there are any other events over which there is no need for delay at this time, events which have been represented by those ancient signs, they have come to an end in Him whose kingdom will be without end. It was necessary, indeed, that all things be fulfilled in Him, who came to fulfill, not to destroy, the Law or the Prophets.[2]

Chapter 3

(4) Christ, then, did not change the ancient signs of events to come by censuring them; He changed them by their fulfillment. As there were signs which announced that Christ had already come, so there were signs foretelling that He would come. What else is intended to be meant when certain psalms, which the Jews themselves read and esteem with the authority of sacred writings, are so designated that they have written in their titles 'For those things that shall be changed.'[1] The text of these same psalms actually foretells Christ. They were so designated because they foretold the change that Christ would make—just as we know that through Christ the change has been fulfilled, so that the people of God, now the Christians, no longer have to keep

---
2 Cf. Matt. 5.17.

---
1 Cf. Ps. 44.1.

the observances of the days of the Prophets; not because the observances have been condemned, but because they have been changed; not that the realities, that were themselves signified, might be lost, but that the signs of the events might befit their times.

Chapter 4

(5) Accordingly, in Psalm 44 (for that is the first of the psalms bearing the title, 'For those things that shall be changed'—where one also reads: 'A canticle for the Beloved'), Christ is quite evidently manifested: 'Thou art beautiful above the sons of men';[1] 'Who though he was by nature God, did not consider being equal to God a thing to be clung to.'[2] In this psalm it is said to Him: 'Gird thy sword upon thy thigh,'[3] because He was about to speak to men in His human flesh. By the figure 'sword,' speech, of course, is signified; by thigh, the body, for He 'emptied himself, taking the nature of a slave,'[4] that He who through His divinity was 'beautiful above the sons of men' through infirmity might become what another Prophet said of Him: 'and we have seen him, and there is no beauty in him, nor comeliness; but His countenance is downcast, and He is acquainted with the infirmity.'[5] The same Psalm 44 shows very plainly that Christ is not only man but also God, for it continues: 'Thy throne, O God, is for ever and ever: the sceptre of thy kingdom is a sceptre of uprightness. Thou hast loved justice, and hated iniquity: therefore God, thy God, hath anointed thee with the oil of gladness above thy fellows.'[6] Christ is named, in fact, from the word 'anointing,'

---
1 Ps. 44.3.
2 Phil. 2.6.
3 Ps. 44.4.
4 Phil. 2.7.
5 Cf. Isa. 53.2,3.
6 Ps. 44.7-8.

which in Greek is *chrisma*. He Himself is God anointed by God, who changed this corporeal into a spiritual anointing, along with the rest of the sacraments. This psalm speaks to Him also of the Church: 'The queen stood on thy right hand, in gilded clothing; surrounded with variety.'[7] Here is signified the variety of languages of all the people within the Church, in whom, nevertheless, there is one simple faith, for 'All the beauty of the king's daughter is within.' The psalm then addresses the Church: 'Hearken, O daughter and see'; hear the promise, see it fulfilled; and 'forget thy people and thy father's house.' Thus the new is fulfilled; thus the old is changed. 'And the king shall greatly desire thy beauty.' The beauty, which He Himself made through Himself, He did not find in you. How could you be beautiful in His eyes when you were disfigured with your sins? So that you will not think, however, that your hope must be placed in men, the Prophet goes on to say: 'for he is the Lord thy God.'[8] That you might not despise the nature of a slave, that you might not scorn the infirmity of the Mighty One and the lowliness of the Lofty One, he says: 'He is thy God.' In what appears small, the Mighty One hides; in the shadow of death hides the Sun of Justice; in the reproach of the Cross, the Lord of Glory. No matter that persecutors put Him to death, or unbelievers deny Him, 'He is the Lord thy God.' Through His Body are changed the things that before were prefigured through shadows.

---

7 Ps. 44.10,14,15.
8 Cf. Ps. 44.14,11,12.

Chapter 5

(6) Psalm 68 also includes in its title the words: 'For the things that shall be entirely changed.'[1] This psalm sings of the Passion of our Lord Jesus Christ, assuming to Himself even certain words of His members, that is, of His faithful. For He Himself did not have any sin, but carried our sins; whence the psalm says: 'and my offenses are not hidden from thee.'[2] Here is written and foretold what we read in the Gospel as having happened: 'And they gave me gall for my food, and in my thirst they gave me vinegar to drink.'[3] In Him, therefore, the old events have been changed which the title of the psalm predicted were to be changed. The Jews, reading the psalm and not understanding it, think that they are saying something when they ask us how we accept the authority of the Law and the Prophets since we do not observe the rites which there are prescribed. We do not observe them because they have been changed; those rites have been changed, moreover, which were foretold would be changed. We believe in Him by whose revelation they have been changed; hence, we do not observe the rites prescribed there because we understand what is being prophesied, but we hold fast to the promises made there. Moreover, they who make these charges against us have inherited the bitterness of their parents, who gave the Lord gall for His food; are still emulating the ancients who offered Him vinegar to drink. That is the reason why they do not understand that in the gall and vinegar the following anathema is fulfilled, 'Let their table become as a snare before them, and a recompense, and a stumblingblock.' They themselves have become full of gall and bitterness in serving food of gall and

---
1 Cf. Ps. 68.1.
2 Ps. 68.6.
3 Cf. Matt. 27.34,48; Mark 15.23; John 19.29.

vinegar to the Living Bread. How else do they look upon these prophecies in the psalm: 'Let their eyes be darkened that they see not,' and how are they to be upright in order to lift up their heart, they about whom it has been foretold, 'and their back bend thou down always'?[4] These prophecies have not been made, however, about all the Jews; only about those to whom the predictions apply. These indictments do not concern those who believed in Christ at that time because of these very prophecies, nor those who have believed in Christ up to the present or who, henceforth, up to the end of the world, will believe in Christ, that is, the true Israel who will see the Lord face to face. 'For they are not all Israelites who are sprung from Israel; nor because they are the descendants of Abraham, are they all his children; but: Through Isaac shall thy posterity bear thy name. This is to say, they are not the sons of God who are the children of the flesh, but it is the children of promise who are reckoned as a posterity.'[5] They belong to the spiritual Sion and the cities of Juda, that is, to the churches about whom the Apostle says, 'And I was unknown by sight to the Churches of Juda, which were in Christ,'[6] since a little later in the same psalm appears, 'For God will save Sion, and the cities of Juda shall be built up. And they shall dwell there, and acquire it by inheritance. And the seed of his servants shall possess it; and they that love his name shall dwell therein.'[7] When the Jews hear these words they take them in their natural meaning and imagine an earthly Jerusalem which is in slavery with her children, not our eternal mother who is in heaven.[8]

---

4 Cf. Ps. 68.22-24.
5 Rom. 9.6-8.
6 Gal. 1.22.
7 Ps. 68.36,37.
8 Cf. Gal. 4.25,26

Chapter 6

(7) Psalm 79 is likewise entitled: 'For the things that shall be changed.'[1] In this psalm among other things is written: 'look down from heaven, and see, and visit this vineyard: And perfect what thy right hand hath planted: and upon the son of man whom thou hast confirmed for thyself.'[2] This is the vineyard of which is said: 'Thou hast brought a vineyard out of Egypt.'[3] Christ did not plant another; by His coming He changed that one into a better vineyard. Accordingly, we find in the Gospel: 'He will utterly destroy those evil men, and will let out the vineyard to other vine-dressers.'[4] The Gospel does not say: 'He will uproot, and will plant another,' but, 'this same vineyard He will let out to other vine-dressers.' The City of God and congregation of the children of promise must be filled with the same community of saints by the death and succession of mortal men, and at the end of the world will receive its due immortality in all men. This same thought is expressed differently by means of the fruitful olive tree in another psalm, which says: 'But I, as a fruitful olive tree in the house of God, have hoped in the mercy of God for ever, yea, for ever and ever.'[5] It was not because the unbelievers and the proud had been broken away and the branches were on that account unfruitful and the wild olive of the Gentiles was ingrafted that the root of the patriarchs and Prophets died. 'For if thy people, O Israel,' says Isaias, 'shall be as the sand of the sea, a remnant of them shall be saved,'[6] but through Him about whom the psalm says: 'and upon the son of man whom thou hast confirmed for thyself,' and

---

1 Cf. Ps. 79.1.
2 Ps. 79.15,16.
3 Ps. 79.9.
4 Matt. 21.41.
5 Ps. 51.10.
6 Cf. Isa. 10.22.

about whom is reiterated, 'Let thy hand be upon the man of thy right hand: and upon the son of man whom thou hast confirmed for thyself. And we depart from thee.'[7] Through this Son of Man, Christ Jesus, and from His remnant, that is, the Apostles and the many others who from among the Israelites have believed in Christ as God, and with the increasing plenitude of the Gentiles, the holy vineyard is being completed. Thus, in the passing of the old rites and in the institution of the new, the title of the psalm, 'For the things that shall be changed,' is fulfilled.

(8) Consequently, it is necessary to review with the Jews the more evident testimonies. Whether they consent to them or dissent, they cannot escape being sensible to them: 'Behold the days shall come, saith the Lord, and I will make a new covenant with the house of Jacob: not according to the covenant which I made with their fathers, in the day that I took them by the hand to bring them out of the land of Egypt.'[8] This change, certainly having been foretold, is not indicated through the titles of psalms for the understanding few; it is expressed in the unmistaken proclamation of the Prophet. Clearly, a new covenant is promised, not according to that covenant which was made with the people when they were led out of Egypt. Since, then, there are in the Old Testament precepts which we who belong to the New Testament are not compelled to observe, why do not the Jews realize that they have remained stationary in useless antiquity rather than hurl charges against us who hold fast to the new promises, because we do not observe the old? Just as it is written in the Canticle of Canticles: 'The day has broken, let the shadows retire,'[9] the spiritual meaning has already dawned, the natural action has already ceased. 'The

---
7 Ps. 79.16,18,19.
8 Jer. 31.31,32
9 Cf. Cant. 2.17.

God of gods, the Lord hath spoken: and he hath called the earth from the rising of the sun to the going down thereof';[10] certainly the whole world is called to the new covenant which another psalm also makes known: 'Sing ye to the Lord a new canticle: sing to the Lord, all the earth.'[11] Not, then, as the God of gods formerly spoke from Mount Sinai to one people, whom He called from Egypt, but He has spoken in this manner in order to summon the earth from the rising of the sun to its setting. If the Jew were willing to understand the speech he would hear this call, and would be among those whom the same psalm addresses: 'Hear, O my people, and I will speak to thee: O Israel, and I will testify to thee: I am God, thy God. I will not reprove thee for thy sacrifices: and thy burnt offerings are always in my sight. I will not take calves out of thy house: nor the goats out of thy flocks. For all the beasts of the woods are mine: the cattle on the hills, and the oxen. I know all the fowls of the air: and with me is the beauty of the field. If I should be hungry, I would not tell thee: for the world is mine and the fulness thereof. Shall I eat the flesh of bullocks? or shall I drink the blood of goats? Offer to God the sacrifice of praise: and pay thy vows to the most High. And call upon me in the day of trouble: I will deliver thee, and thou shalt glorify me.'[12] Assuredly, here, too, the change of the ancient sacrifices is manifest. God foretold that the time would come when He would no longer accept the old sacrifices; He revealed to His worshipers a sacrifice of praise. He did not make this revelation because He was seeking after praise from us as if He needed it, but that in our praise He was looking to our salvation. The closing of the psalm makes His purpose quite evident: 'The sacrifice of

---
10 Ps. 49.1.
11 Ps. 95.1.
12 Ps. 49.7-15.

praise shall glorify me: and there is the way by which I will show him the salvation of God.'[13] What in truth is the salvation of God, if not the Son of God, the Saviour of the world; the Son as day from the Father as day, that is, Light from Light, whose arrival the New Testament has revealed? So, too, where it is said: 'Sing ye to the Lord a new canticle: sing to the Lord, all the earth. Sing ye to the Lord and bless His name,'[14] He Himself is at once shown to be worthy to be proclaimed, and it is added: 'shew forth his salvation from day to day.'[15] He Himself as priest and victim has fulfilled the sacrifice of praise, granting pardon for evil works and lavishly bestowing the grace to perform good works. The sacrifice of praise is offered to the Lord by His worshipers for this end: 'Let him who takes pride, take pride in the Lord.'[16]

Chapter 7

(9) When the Jews hear the following words from the psalm, they answer with their heads held high: 'We are they; the psalm is about us; it is said to us. We are Israel, the people of God; we recognize ourselves in the words of the speaker: "Hear, O my people, and I will speak to thee: O Israel, and I will testify to thee." '[1] What shall we say to these things? We know, of course, the spiritual Israel about which the Apostle says: 'And whoever follow this rule, peace and mercy upon them, even upon the Israel of God.'[2] The Israel, however, about which the Apostle says:

---

13 Ps. 49.23.
14 Ps. 95.1,2.
15 Ps. 95.2.
16 1 Cor. 1.31.

---

1 Cf. Ps. 49.7.
2 Gal. 6.16.

'Behold Israel according to the flesh,'[3] we know to be the natural Israel; but the Jews do not grasp this meaning and as a result they prove themselves indisputably natural. It may be well to address them for just a little while as if they were present: And so you belong to that people whom 'the God of gods hath called from the rising of the sun to the going down thereof'?[4] Were you not brought from Egypt to the land of Canaan? Not thither were you called from the rising of the sun to its setting, but from there you were dispersed to the rising of the sun and to its setting. Do you not rather belong to His enemies referred to in the psalm; 'My God shall let me see over my enemies: slay them not, lest at any time they forget thy law. Scatter them by the power'?[5] That is the reason why, not unmindful of the Law of God, but bearing that same Law about for a covenant to the Gentiles and a reproach to yourselves, you unknowingly are ministering the Law to a people that has been called from the rising to the setting of the sun. Or will you really deny it? Then, too, those events foretold with such great authority, fulfilled with such manifestation— do you either with great blindness fail to consider them, or with remarkable impudence refuse to acknowledge them? What reply, then, are you going to make to what the Prophet Isaias proclaims: 'And in the last days the mountain of the house of the Lord shall be prepared on the top of mountains, and it shall be exalted above the hills, and all the nations shall come to it, and shall say: Come and let us go up to the mountain of the Lord, and to the house of the God Jacob, and he will teach us the way of salvation, and we will walk in it: for the law shall come forth from Sion, and the word of the Lord from Jerusalem.'[6] Or here,

---
3 1 Cor. 10.18.
4 Cf. Ps. 49.1.
5 Cf. Ps. 58.12.
6 Cf. Isa. 2.2,3.

too, are you going to say: 'We are they,' since you heard the house of Jacob and Sion and Jerusalem? As if we were denying that Christ the Lord according to the flesh is from the seed of Jacob, Christ who is represented by the mountain lifted high above the tops of the mountains because by His height He transcends all heights; or are we to deny that the Apostles and those Churches of Judaea, which after the Resurrection of Christ continued to believe in Him, belong to the house of Jacob; or is another people to be understood as the spiritual Jacob other than the Christian people themselves, who, although younger than the people of Judaea, have surpassed them in increases and have replaced them, that the Scripture might be fulfilled in the figure of the two brothers, 'and the elder shall serve the younger'?[7] Sion, however, and Jerusalem, although spiritually understood as the Church, are nevertheless a fitting witness against the Jews, because from that place where they crucified Christ the Law and the Word of God has proceeded to the Gentiles. The Law, in fact, which was given them through Moses, on account of which they are quite proudly exalted and by virtue of which they are far better convicted, is understood to have come forth from Mount Sinai, not from Sion and Jerusalem. After forty years, to be sure, they arrived with the Law itself at the land of promise where Sion is, which is called Jerusalem. They did not, however, receive it there or from there. The Gospel of Christ and the Law of faith certainly did proceed from there, just as the Lord Himself said after His Resurrection when speaking to His disciples and showing them that the prophecies of the divine Scriptures had been fulfilled in Himself: 'Thus it is written; and thus the Christ should suffer, and should rise again from the dead on the third day; and that repentance and remission of sins should be preached in his name to all the

---
7 Gen. 25.23.

nations, beginning from Jerusalem.'[8] See what Isaias prophesied: 'for the law shall come forth from Sion, and the word of the Lord from Jerusalem.'[9] There according to the promise of the Lord, the Holy Spirit came down and filled those who were assembled in the one house and prompted them to speak in the native languages of all 'the people' gathered together.[10] From there they went out and preached the Gospel to the understanding of all nations. Just as the Law which proceeded from Mount Sinai had been written by the Finger of God, signifying the Holy Spirit, fifty days after the celebration of the Pasch, in the same way, this Law which proceeded from Sion and Jerusalem is written on the tablets of the heart of the holy Evangelists by the Holy Spirit—not on tablets of stone—on the fiftieth day after the true Pasch of the Passion and Resurrection of the Lord Christ, on the day on which the Holy Spirit who had been promised before had been sent.

(10) Go now, O Israelites by nature, not by spirit; go now and even contradict this very apparent truth. When you hear: 'Come and let us go up to the mountain of the Lord, and to the house of the God of Jacob'[11] say: 'We are of the house of Jacob,' so that like blind men you may dash against the mountain, and with your face badly bruised you smash your head the worse. If you sincerely want to say: 'We are they' [the house of Jacob], say it when you hear: 'for the wickedness of my people was he led to death.'[12] This is said about Christ whom you, in your parents, led to death; just like a sheep was led to sacrifice, that the Pasch which unknowingly you celebrate, unknowingly you fulfill in your madness. If you truly want to say: 'We are the

---
8 Luke 24.46,47.
9 Isa. 2.3.
10 Cf. Acts 2.1-6.
11 Isa. 2.3.
12 Isa. 53.8.

house of Jacob,' then say it when you hear: 'Blind the heart of this people, and make their ears heavy, and shut their eyes.'[13] Then say: 'We are they,' when you hear: 'I have spread forth my hands all the day to an unbelieving and contradicting people.'[14] Say: 'We are they,' when you hear: 'Let their eyes be darkened that they see not; and their back bend thou down always.'[15] In these and other prophetic words of this kind say: 'We are they.' Without any doubt you are, but you are so blind that you say you are what you are not, and do not recognize yourselves for what you really are.

Chapter 8

(11) Listen carefully for just a minute to what I am going to say in reference to these even more obvious testimonies. Most certainly, when you hear: 'in good Israel,' you say: 'We are Israel,' and when you hear: 'in good Jacob,' you say: 'We are Jacob.' And when you are asked why, you reply: 'Because Jacob himself is also Israel, and we are descendants of the patriarch; hence, we are distinguished by the merited name of our father.' We are not, therefore, rousing you from a deep and heavy sleep to spiritual matters which you do not grasp. Nor are we now attempting to show you, blind and deaf as you are in your spiritual senses, how these words are to be accepted spiritually. Surely, just as you admitted and as a perusal of the Book of Genesis manifestly affirms, Jacob and Israel are one and the same;[1] that is the reason why you boast that the house of Jacob is

---
13 Isa. 6.10.
14 Isa. 65.2.
15 Ps. 68.24.

---
1 Cf. Gen. 32.28.

the house of Israel. What did the Prophet Isaias mean, however, when he announced that a mountain would be prepared on the summits of the mountains, to which all peoples were going to come? The Law and the Word of God was going to proceed from Sion and Jerusalem to all nations, not from Mount Sinai to one nation. This we see most evidently fulfilled in Christ and the Christians. A little later, the Prophet says: 'O house of Jacob, come ye, and let us walk in the light of the Lord.'[2] Here, surely, you will speak your usual piece: 'We are the house of Jacob'; but listen a moment to what follows, and when you have said what you want to say, hear what you do not want to hear. The Prophet continues: 'For he has cast off his people, the house of Israel.'[3] Here say: 'We are the house of Israel'; here acknowledge yourselves and forgive us for reminding you of these facts. If you hear them willingly, they are said for your encouragement; if, however, you hear them indignantly, then they are said for a reproach. Yet, they must be said, whether you are willing or unwilling. Behold, not I, but the Prophet whom you read—through whom you cannot deny God has spoken, to whom you cannot deny the authority of the sacred Scriptures—at the Lord's command vehemently cries out and lifts up his voice like a trumpet[4] and, rebuking you, says: 'O house of Jacob, come ye, and let us walk in the light of the Lord.' You, in the person of your parents, have killed Christ. For a long time you have not believed in Him and you have opposed Him, but you are not yet lost, because you are still alive; you have time now for repentance; only come now. You should have come long ago, of course, but come now; your days are not yet ended; the last day is still to come. Or, if you

---

2 Isa. 2.5.
3 Cf. Isa. 2.6.
4 Cf. Isa. 58.1.

believe that as the house of Jacob you have followed the Prophet, that now you are walking in the light of the Lord, declare yourselves the house of Israel which He has cast off. We have shown both, those whom with His divine call He has separated from that house, and those whom He cast off because they did not heed the call. Not only did He call the Apostles from that house, but even after the Resurrection He called a great many peoples. That is why, as we mentioned earlier, He cast off those whom you imitate by your unbelief, and by imitating them you are lingering in the same danger of destruction. If, on the contrary, you are they whom He called from there, where are those whom He cast off? For yo‧ annot say that He cast off any other nation, when the Prophet cries out: 'For he has cast off his people, the house of Israel.' See what you are, not what you boast to be. Moreover, He also cast off that vineyard from which He expected a yield of grapes and received thorns instead, and as a result commanded His clouds not to rain down upon it. Furthermore, He called them away from there to whom He says: 'Judge between me and my vineyard;'[5] about whom the Lord also says: 'And if I cast out devils by Beelzebub, by whom do your children cast them out? Therefore they shall be your judges';[6] to whom He makes this promise: 'you shall also sit on twelve thrones, judging the twelve tribes of Israel.'[7] That is where the house of Jacob, which has been called and has walked in the light of the Lord, will sit to judge the house of Israel, that is, the people of that house whom He has cast off. How is it that, according to the same Prophet: 'The stone which the builders rejected: the same is become the head of the corner,'[8] unless because circumcised and

---

5 Isa. 5.3.
6 Matt. 12.27.
7 Matt. 19.28.
8 Ps. 117.22; cf. Isa. 28.16.

uncircumcised meet and unite in the keystone, like the union of two adjacent walls, as it were, in the kiss of peace. That is the reason that the Apostle says: 'For he himself is our peace, he it is who has made both one.'[9] They who have followed His call—whether from the house of Jacob or from the house of Israel—are cleaving to the corner-stone and walking in the light of the Lord; they, however, whom He cast off from the house of Jacob or Israel are themselves builders of destruction and rejecters of the corner-stone.

Chapter 9

(12) Lastly, O Jews, if you try to distort these prophetic words into another meaning according to the dictates of your heart, you resist the Son of God against your own salvation. If you, I say, choose to understand by these testimonies that the house of Jacob or Israel is the same people, both called and cast off—not called in respect to some and cast off in respect to others, but the entire house called to walk in the light of the Lord, inasmuch as the reason why the house had been cast off was because its people were not walking in the light of the Lord; or some of the house certainly were called and others cast off in such a way that without any separation having been of the Lord's table as regards the sacrifice of Christ; both called and cast off were under the same old sacraments, to be sure, both those who walked in the light of the Lord and observed His precepts and those who rejected justice and deserved to be abandoned by it—if you choose to interpret these testimonies in this manner, what are you going to say and how will you interpret another Prophet who cuts this reply away entirely, shouting with unmistakable manifestation: 'I have no pleasure in you saith

---
9 Eph. 2.14.

the Lord Almighty: and I will not receive a gift of your hand. For from the rising of the sun even to the going down, my name is great among the Gentiles, and in every place sacrifice is offered to my name, a clean oblation: for my name is great among the Gentiles, saith the Lord Almighty.'[1] Finally, with what words do you cry out against such evidence? Why do you continue to exalt yourselves so impudently beyond measure that you perish all the more miserably and with graver destruction? 'I have no pleasure in you,' He says; not anyone, but 'the Lord Almighty.' Why do you glory so much in the seed of Abraham, you who, whenever you hear Jacob or Israel, or the house of Jacob or the house of Israel, whenever any praise is uttered, assert so energetically that such praise can refer only to you? The Lord Almighty says: 'I have no pleasure in you, and I will not receive a gift of your hand.' Certainly, you cannot deny that here the Lord not only refuses to receive a gift from your hands, but you do not offer Him a gift with your hands. Only one place has been established by the Law of the Lord where He commanded you to offer a gift with your hands; He absolutely forbade any other place. Since, therefore, you have lost this place through your own fault, you dare not offer in any other place the sacrifice which He permitted you to offer there. Behold fulfilled to the letter what the Prophet says: 'And I will not receive a gift of your hand.' If in the earthly Jerusalem you still had a temple and altar, you could say that the prophecy has been fulfilled in the pagans among you whose sacrifices the Lord does not receive; of others from among you and in you, however, who keep the commandments of God He does accept gifts. It can be said, therefore, that according to the Law that has come from Mount Sinai there is not one of you who is able to offer sacrifice with his hands. Nor was the prophecy and its

---

[1] Mal. 1.10,11.

fulfillment such that the prophetic judgment permits you to answer: 'We do not offer flesh with our hands, but with our hearts and lips we offer praise as the psalm: "Offer to God the sacrifice of praise."'[2] Even here He opposes you who says: 'I have no pleasure in you.'

(13) In the next place, do not suppose that because you do not offer sacrifice and God does not accept it from your hands, a sacrifice is not being offered to God, which He certainly does not need who needs the goods of no one of us. Nevertheless, since He is not without sacrifice which is for our benefit, not His, He adds: 'For from the rising of the sun even to the going down, my name is great among the Gentiles, and in every place sacrifice is offered to my name, a clean oblation: for my name is great among the Gentiles, saith the Lord Almighty.' What do you say to that? Open your eyes at last, at any time, and see, from the rising of the sun even to its setting—not in one place as established with you, but everywhere—the sacrifice of the Christians is being offered; not to any god at all, but to Him who foretold these events, to the God of Israel. For this reason, in another place, He says to His Church: 'And he who delivered you, the very God of Israel shall be called the God of all the earth.'[3] Search the Scriptures through which you believe that you have eternal life.[4] Actually, you would have it, if you recognized Christ in the Scripture and cleaved to Him. Search the sacred writings carefully; the same writings bear witness to the world about this sacrifice which is being offered to the God of Israel, not by your nation alone from whose hands He foretold He would not take the gift; it is being offered by all nations who say, 'Come and let us go up to the mountain of the Lord';[5] not in one place, in the earthly Jerusalem, as

---
2 Ps. 49.14.
3 Cf. Isa. 54.5.
4 Cf. John 5.39.
5 Isa. 2.3.

you were bidden; everywhere, even in Jerusalem itself, according to the order of Melchisedech, not according to the order of Aaron. It was said to Christ and about Christ long before it was prophesied: 'The Lord hath sworn, and he will not repent: Thou art a priest forever according to the order of Melchisedech.'[6] What does 'The Lord hath sworn' mean except that He confirmed with unshaken truth what He said? What is the meaning of 'he will not repent' if not that absolutely for no reason whatsoever will He change this priesthood? God does not repent as man does. We speak of repentance in God despite the idea of anything changing which was instituted by God and thought to be lasting. In the same sense He says: 'The Lord hath sworn, and he will not repent; thou art a priest forever according to the order of Melchisedech.' He shows clearly enough that He had repented, that is, He had willed to change the priesthood which He had established according to the order of Aaron. We see the fulfillment of both: of Aaron, there is no longer any priesthood in any temple; of Christ, the priesthood continues everlastingly in heaven.

(14) To this light of the Lord the Prophet calls you when he says: 'O house of Jacob, come ye and let us walk in the light of the Lord.'[7] You 'house of Jacob' whom He has called and elected, not 'you' whom He has cast off, 'For he has cast off his people, the house of Israel.'[8] Whoever of you from the house of Jacob choose to come, you will belong to that house which He has called; you will be free from that house which He has cast off. The light of the Lord in which the Gentiles walk, that is the light about which the same Prophet speaks: 'I have given thee to be the light of the Gentiles, that thou mayest be my salvation

---

6 Ps. 109.4.
7 Isa. 2.5.
8 Isa. 2.6.

even to the farthest part of the earth.'⁹ To whom, if not to
Christ, is this said? In whom is it fulfilled if not in Christ?
This light is not in you of whom it has been said over and
over again: 'God has given them a spirit of stupor; eyes
that they may not see, and ears that they may not hear,
until this present day.'¹⁰ Not in you, I say, is this light, for
with plenty of blindness you rejected the stone which was
made the corner-stone. 'Come ye to him and be enlightened.'¹¹
What is 'Come' if not believe? Where may you go in order
to come to Him, since He is the stone of which Daniel the
Prophet speaks, that stone which grew into such a mighty
mountain that it filled the whole earth?¹² The Gentiles who
also say: 'Come and let us go up to the mountain of the
Lord' do not seek to go and reach a fixed place anywhere in
the world. Wherever they are, that is where they ascend,
because sacrifice is offered in every place according to the
order of Melchisedech. Similarly, another Prophet says:
'God shall consume all the gods of the Gentiles of the earth:
and they shall adore him every man from his own place.'¹⁴
Therefore, when you hear: 'Come to him,' you do not hear:
Prepare ships or pack animals, and load yourselves with your
victims, and go a great distance to the place where God will
receive your sacrifice of devotion, but: Come to Him who is
being preached in your ears, come to Him who is being
glorified before your eyes. You will not be worn out with
walking, for you come to Him there where you believe in Him.

---

9 Isa. 49.6.
10 Cf. Rom. 11.8.
11 Ps. 33. 6.
12 Cf. Dan. 2.35.
13 Isa. 2.3.
14 Soph. 2.11.

Chapter 10

(15) Dearly beloved, whether the Jews receive these divine testimonies with joy or with indignation, nevertheless, when we can, let us proclaim them with great love for the Jews. Let us not proudly glory against the broken branches; let us rather reflect by whose grace it is, and by much mercy, and on what root, we have been ingrafted. Then, not savoring of pride, but with a deep sense of humility, not insulting with presumption, but rejoicing with trembling,[1] let us say: 'Come ye and let us walk in the light of the Lord,'[2] because His 'name is great among the Gentiles.' If they hear Him and obey Him, they will be among them to whom Scripture says: 'Come ye to him and be enlightened: and your faces shall not be confounded.'[3] If, however, they hear and do not obey, if they see and are jealous,[4] they are among them of whom the psalm says: 'The wicked shall see, and shall be angry, he shall gnash with his teeth and pine away.'[5] 'But I,' the Church says to Christ, 'as a fruitful olive tree in the house of God, have hoped in the mercy of God forever, yea forever and ever.'[6]

---
1 Cf. Ps. 2.11.
2 Isa. 2.5.
3 Ps. 33.6.
4 Cf. Rom. 11.11.
5 Ps. 111.10.
6 Ps. 51.10.

THE DIVINATION OF DEMONS

(De divinatione daemonum)

Translated by
RUTH WENTWORTH BROWN, Ph.D.
University of Southern California

INTRODUCTION

MENTION IS MADE of the *The Divination of Demons* in the second book of the *Retractations* among the works written after Augustine was elevated to the episcopacy: 'About the same time I was constrained, in consequence of a discussion, to write a brief work, which, as is indicated by its title, deals with the divination of demons. In a certain passage of this book I wrote: "Sometimes, too, the demons with all ease discern the intentions of men, not only as they are expressed by the voice, but also as they are conceived in reflection, when certain phases of thought are one by one manifested physically." Here I made a statement upon a very abstruse subject with a bolder pronouncement than was proper. That these matters do come to the knowledge of demons has been disclosed even by some evidence of experience. Yet whether, when men deliberate, certain physical indications are afforded, discernible to demons, but hidden from us, or whether demons recognize these matters by another power, and that a power of the spirit, is a question very difficult, or entirely impossible, for men to discover.'[1]

---

1 *Retractationes* 2.30.

The phrase 'about the same time' associates the work chronologically with the publication of the treatises against the Donatists during the years 406-411. No evidence for a more precise dating has appeared.

The setting of a dialogue is presented in the first lines, where we find a group of lay brothers assembled in the presence of the bishop at an early morning hour in the week after Easter. A conversation arises concerning the opposition of pagan arrogance and its worldly wisdom to Christian teachings. St. Augustine's participation in the discussion is clearly indicated by the use of the first person. The other disputants remain anonymous and impersonal. At the end of the second chapter, the conversation closes with the departure of the bishop to appear before a congregation of the people. He promises, before leaving, to resume the discussion at a later time. This pledge is fulfilled in Augustine's discourse that occupies the eight remaining chapters.

The *De divinatione daemonum* is rarely mentioned in works dealing with St. Augustine as thinker and writer. The existence of evil in a world governed by an omnipotent and a just God is discussed in the two opening chapters. Readers will, however, turn to other writings of Augustine for more profound and satisfying expositions of his views upon this universal problem. The short treatise was composed to meet a contemporary situation, and thus is not without its significance.

The temple of Serapis[2] in Alexandria had been demolished some years before by the patriarch Theophilus, who doubtless acted upon an edict of Theodosius. This structure was the greatest of the Isis-Serapis temples, frequented by Greeks as well as by Egyptians. Through the patronage of the

---
2 Cf. E. A. W. Budge, *The Gods of the Egyptians* (London 1904) 2.195-201.

Macedonian Ptolemies, Serapis worship had flourished, and, after the Roman conquest, it spread into the provinces and even established its shrines in Rome. The image[3] of Serapis, destroyed with the temple, was of pure Greek type; Bryaxis, one of the four sculptors of the Mausoleum of Halicarnassus, was said to have been its creator. The Egyptian conception of a beast-headed divinity had given place to an anthropomorphic statue, which identified the Egyptian god of the afterlife with the Greek Hades.

The loss of the Serapeum meant the almost complete obliteration of the cult. Certain of the rites, doubtless the most objectionable ones, were still practiced clandestinely. A report was spread that the downfall had been known in advance and foretold by the priests of Serapis.

The purpose of the discussion, as we learn in the first chapter, is to provide the Christian lay brothers with answers to pagan arguments. This end is not accomplished through the denial of the possibility of divination in pagan cults; Augustine seeks, rather, to inspire and confirm the group in their faith in the one God and to strengthen their convictions in the truth and righteousness of scriptural prophecy.

The subject of prescience among demoniac powers receives elaborate treatment in the *City of God*,[4] where we are made quite aware of the extensive learning of Augustine in the ancient lore of divination. Abundant citations occur from Plato, Plotinus and other Neo-Platonists, from Varro, Cicero, and especially from the man of Madaura, Apuleius, whose *De deo Socratico* is frequently mentioned. *The Divination of Demons*, in contrast, entirely omits learned references. The lay brothers to whom the arguments are addressed would,

---

[3] See Plutarch, *Moralia*, 'Isis and Osiris' 361.28. Here it is related that Ptolemy Soter, prompted by a dream, had the statue conveyed from Sinopê to Alexandria.
[4] Notably in Books 8-9.

in all probability, have been but meagerly equipped in erudition to match their wits with the Greek followers of the Egyptian god. Their power must be derived from another source. Thus, Scriptural quotations are abundant.

This slight work, then, is interesting as a record of the time when the mockers were still 'vaunting their learning,' though these mockers were 'fewer this year than they were the year before.' We may also read it as an example of St. Augustine's ability and readiness to respond to the needs of the day.

The present translation has been based upon the Vienna text of J. Zycha (1900).

SELECT BIBLIOGRAPHY

Texts:

J. P. Migne, *Patrologia Latina* 40 (Paris 1887) 581-592.
J. Zycha, *Corpus Scriptorum Ecclesiasticorum Latinorum* 41 (Vienna 1900) 597-618.
St. Augustin, *Oeuvres complètes* (Paris 1870) 22.130-142. Benedictine text with a French translation by M. H. Barreau *et al.*

Secondary Works:

V. J. Bourke, *Augustine's Quest of Wisdom* (Milwaukee 1947).
H. Lindau, 'Augustin und das Dämonische,' *Zeitschrift für Kirchengeschichte* 36 (1916) 99-108.
H. I. Marrou, *Saint Augustin et la fin de la culture antique* (Paris 1938).
J. E. C. Welldon, *S. Aurelii Augustini De civitate Dei*, 2 vols. (London 1924).

THE DIVINATION OF DEMONS

Chapter 1

N A CERTAIN DAY within the holy octave of Easter, when in the early morning many Christian lay brothers were present with me and we had taken our seats in the familiar place, a conversation arose concerning the Christian religion as opposed to the arrogance and, as it were, the notable and great knowledge of the pagans. I thought that this conversation, recorded and completed, should be set down in writing, without indicating the identity of the disputants.[1] They were, however, Christians and in their contrary arguments appeared chiefly to be searching for replies which they should make to the pagans. Thereupon, when a question was asked concerning the divination of demons[2] and a declaration was made that some one had foretold the downfall of the Temple of Serapis,[3] which had

---
1 The dialogue form is employed in 1-2, although no names are assigned to participants.
2 Augustine, following Plato, derives *daemon* from a Greek word meaning knowledge. Cf. Plato *Cratylus* 398; also *De civitate Dei* 9.20.
3 The downfall occurred in 391. The temple's splendor is described by Ammianus Marcellinus 22.16.

taken place in Alexandria, I replied that one should not marvel that demons could know and predict that downfall was impending their own temples and images, and other events, also, in so far as it is allowed them to know and to foretell.[4]

(2) Then the following response was presented to me: 'Well, then, divinations of this kind are not evil nor do they displease God. Otherwise, the Omnipotent and Just would not permit them to be made, if they were evil and unjust.' I replied that these occurrences were not bound to appear just, on the ground that the most omnipotent and just God permits them to take place.[5] Surely, there are acts which manifestly are unjustly committed, like murders, adulteries, thefts, pillage and other crimes of like nature. Although these acts undoubtedly displease a just God, for the very reason that they are unjust, this same Omnipotent One, by the fixed order of His judgment, permits them to occur, by no means with impunity, but to the condemnation of those by whom the acts that displease a just God are committed.

(3) A counter-argument was advanced that, while, to be sure, one could not doubt that God is omnipotent and just, nevertheless He is not concerned with these human sins which are committed against the society of mankind, while they are being committed, and therefore they may occur. Surely, they could not have been committed at all, if the Omnipotent had not permitted them. Yet, under no consideration, certainly, could one believe that He disregarded those former occurrences such as have to do with the actual practice of religion, and for that reason they could not have taken place, unless they had been pleasing to Him. Thus, they should not be regarded evil. To this argument, too, I made reply. Now, however, those acts are displeasing to Him, in that

---
[4] Cf. *De civitate Dei* 9.21-22 upon God's permission to the demons to prophesy and the limitations placed upon their knowledge.
[5] Cf. *De ordine* 2.4f. for exposition of the place of evil in the divine order.

the temples and images are being overthrown and those sacrificial rites of the heathen, if ever they are performed, are punished. So, then, just as it was maintained that these acts could not have been performed unless they had pleased God, and on that ground they must be regarded as good since they please the Just, so it may be said that they could not have been prohibited, overthrown, and punished unless they displeased God. If at that time they were performed righteously, inasmuch as they were disclosed as pleasing God through the fact that He permitted them, so now they are performed unrighteously, because they are disclosed as displeasing to God, inasmuch as He bids or allows their overthrow.

Chapter 2

(4) In answer to my argument someone brought forth these counter-statements: 'Such acts as those are surely unlawful now, but they are not evil. They are unlawful for the reason that they take place contrary to the laws by which they are forbidden. They are, however, not evil, because, if they were evil, they assuredly would never have pleased God. Furthermore, if they had never pleased Him, they would have taken place without the permission of Him who can do all things and who would not disregard such matters, since they are so important that they are performed in opposition to the very religion by which God is worshiped, if they are performed wickedly.' Hereupon I interposed: 'If,' I said, 'they are not evil, inasmuch as they are proved to be pleasing to God by the fact that the Omnipotent allows them to occur, how will it be a good thing that their performance is forbidden and that they are overthrown? If, however, it is not good that those things that are pleasing to God are overthrown, the Omnipotent would not allow

their overthrow to take place, for this also is an occurrence opposed to the religion by which God is worshiped, if things which please God are overthrown by men. Yet, if God permits this downfall, although it is an evil occurrence, one must not account those former acts good solely because the Omnipotent allowed them to take place.'

(5) Someone said in reply that it must be granted that those practices do not rightly occur now, nay more, that they no longer occur at all, because they are now displeasing to the Omnipotent. They were pleasing to Him, nevertheless, when they occurred. We, certainly, do not know wherein they were pleasing then, nor, on the other hand, wherein they are displeasing now. For all that, it is certain that they could not have taken place then if they had not been pleasing to the Omnipotent, nor could they have ceased now unless they had displeased the Omnipotent. Thereupon I spoke. 'Why, then,' I said, 'are there even now performed in secret such acts as are either continually concealed or, if they are detected, are punished, if the Omnipotent permits none of these things to occur except such as please Him, the Just One, since to Him as just nothing unjust could be pleasing?' An answer was made to this query that worship of that nature does not actually take place at present, for those former rites, declared the disputant, which were recorded in the pontifical books[1] are not performed. Certainly, in former times their performance was a righteous act. It is demonstrated that they were then pleasing to God by the very fact that the Omnipotent and Just suffered them to occur. Now, however, whatsoever forbidden sacrifices are carried on secretly and lawlessly should not be compared with the former priestly type of worship. They should be regarded in the same class with ritual which is performed in the season of night. All unlawful rites like these are assuredly

---

1 Of the cult.

forbidden and condemned even in their pontifical books. Hereupon I replied: 'Why, then, does God actually permit such acts to take place, if He overlooks none of the sins which are committed against religion? That He does have regard for such sins must be admitted above all by those who venerate the pontifical books, since they maintain that those deeds which are forbidden in the books are assuredly divinely forbidden. How, pray, are they divinely forbidden, except that they are displeasing to God? By forbidding them He certainly discloses not only that the deeds are displeasing to Him, but that He is concerned with respect to them and that He does not in any way overlook them. Thence we conclude that a just God may disapprove an act, yet, omnipotent as He is, may permit it.'

(6) After this discussion, it was granted that an act need not be regarded as being performed justly and righteously on the ground that God, although He took care to have it forbidden, allowed it to occur. It must be admitted that even those evil deeds which are committed in opposition to the religion by which God is worshiped both displease a just God and are permitted in the order of His judgment by an omnipotent God. But it was decided that we must now discuss another subject, namely, whence arise the divinations of demons, or of those, whatsoever they may be, whom the pagans call gods.[2] We must certainly take care that we do not perchance deem these acts good because the Omnipotent permits them to take place, but for the reason that they are so great that it seems that they can only be attributed to the power of God. To these questions I promised that I would make reply later, since the hour was now at hand when I must appear before the assembly of the people.[3]

---
2 Cf. *De civitate Dei* 9.23.
3 The convention of the dialogue is abandoned here. St. Augustine's discourse begins with the following chapter.

I have not delayed, now that leisure for writing is afforded, to revise the early discussion and to supplement it with the following discourse.[4]

Chapter 3

(7) The nature of demons is such that, through the sense perception belonging to the aerial body,[1] they readily surpass the perception possessed by earthly bodies, and in speed, too, because of the superior mobility of the aerial body, they incomparably excel not only the movements of men and of beasts but even the flight of birds. Endowed with these two faculties, in so far as they are the properties of the aerial body, namely, with keenness of perception and speed of movement, they foretell and declare many things that they have recognized far in advance. At this, because of the sluggishness of earthly perception, men wonder. The demons, too, through the long period into which their life is extended, have gained a far greater experience[2] in events than accrues to men because of the brief span of their lives. Through these faculties which the nature of the aerial body has allotted, demons not only foretell many things that will occur but also perform many miraculous acts.[3] Since man can neither tell nor perform these things, certain individuals think it proper to serve the demons and to render them divine

---

4 '*et illa retexere et ista subtexere*': the paronomasia of the Latin can not be reproduced in English.

---

1 Cf. *De civitate Dei* 8.14-18 where is presented the Neo-Platonic view of a threefold division of living beings with rational souls, the gods occupying heaven, men the earth, and demons the air. The *De deo Socratico* of Apuleius is the chief source, but Augustine refutes the argument that demons are superior to men and that they are worthy of worship. Mention of the aerial bodies of demons is frequent in the *De divinatione* and in *De civitate Dei*. Cf. *De civitate Dei* 18.15 *et passim*; *De agone Christiano* 3; *Contra Academicos* 1.7; *et al.*
2 Cf. *De civitate Dei* 9.22.
3 Cf. *Ibid.* 21.6 for demons as workers of miracles.

honors. To this service they are prompted especially by the vice of curiosity, because of their desire for a false happiness and for an earthly and temporal success. Those, however, who cleanse themselves from these desires and do not allow themselves to be lifted up and carried away by them, but who search out and love something which is forever of the same nature, by partaking of which they may be blessed, first of all conclude that they should not regard demons so far superior to themselves, because the demons have an advantage in their keener bodily perception, the aerial, to be sure, that is, one that is derived from a more subtle element. As a matter of fact, in the case even of earthly bodies, men do not think that beasts, whose sense perceptions are in many respects more keen than their own, should be preferred to themselves.[4] For example, because the keen-scented dog uncovers the hiding quarry with a sense of smell so very keen that he affords to man a certain guidance for capturing his prey, they do not for that reason regard him as possessed of wiser intellect, but of keener bodily sense. Nor do they so highly esteem the vulture, because, when a corpse is exposed, he flies to it from an unforseen distance; nor the eagle, because it is said that, while she is flying aloft, from that great distance she discerns the fish swimming under the waves and, as the waters beat mightily upon her, she thrusts forth her feet and her talons and seizes her prey. Nor do they so regard many other kinds of living creatures who, while pasturing, stray among herbs hurtful to their well-being and do not touch any of those by which they may be harmed. Man, on the other hand, has scarcely learned by trial to avoid the poisonous herbs and fears many harmless varieties because they have not been tested.[5] From these

---
4 Cf. *Ibid.* 8.15 for a comparison of the physical powers of men and animals.
5 Cf. Cicero, *De natura deorum* 2.47.122

circumstances it is easy to conjecture how much keener may be the sense in aerial bodies. Nevertheless, no wise man would conclude that demons who are endowed with such perception should be preferred to good men. This statement I would also make concerning swiftness of body. In this excellence, too, men are also so surpassed, not only by birds but by many quadrupeds as well, that in comparison with those creatures men may be regarded as heavy as lead. For all that, human beings do not think the tribes of animals superior to themselves. By capturing them, taming them, and subjecting them to such use and convenience as their own will imposes, men govern beasts not by physical force, but by the power of reason.[6]

Chapter 4

Now, that third faculty of demons, namely, that by long experience in events they have learned to prognosticate many happenings and to announce them in advance, is lightly esteemed by those who take diligent pains to discern these circumstances according to the validity of the most true light. Even so, it comes about that honorable young men do not think that evil old men excel them through having undergone many experiences and being on this account, so to speak, wiser. Likewise, men do not account as superior to themselves doctors, sailors, and farmers, whose wills are perverted and whose characters depraved, on the ground that they respectively make such pronouncements in advance concerning diseases, storms, and the phases of orchards and fruits that they seem to one inexperienced in matters of the kind to prophesy.

(8) As to the fact that demons not only predict some

---
6 Cf. *De diversis quaestionibus LXXXIII* 13.

future events, but even perform certain miracles, assuredly through that actual superiority of the body, why do not wise men make light of it? It is true that many sinful and abandoned men so train their bodies that, by diverse arts, they can perform such remarkable feats that those who do not know about them and have never seen them scarcely believe, even when they are told. How much have rope-dancers and other theatrical performers[1] done that caused wonderment! How much have artisans and especially mechanics! Are they for that reason better than men who are good and endowed with holy piety? I have mentioned these matters in order that he who regards them without stubbornness and without the vain arrogance of controversy may consider this likewise: If, while each one uses the somewhat gross material that is at hand, either that of his own body, or of earth and water, namely stones and wood, and various metals, certain men can produce such great works that those who are unable to equal them frequently, in their amazement, call the producers in comparison with themselves divine, while actually some of the producers are superior in the arts, but some of the admirers superior in character, how much greater and more marvelous deeds in proportion to the faculty and facility of their most subtle body, that is, the aerial, can demons perform! For all that, because of the depravity of their will, and especially because of the haughtiness of their arrogance, and the malice of their envy, they are unclean and perverted spirits! Moreover, how effective is the element of air, in which their bodies surpass, to produce invisibly many visible results, to move, to change, and to overthrow is too long a story to set forth now. I think that it will occur readily to one who deliberates even moderately.

---

[1] Cf. *De civitate Dei* 2.4-11 upon the immoralities of the stage.

Chapter 5

(9) Wherefore, one must know in the first place, since the divination of demons is the subject of discussion, that they very often foretell acts which they themselves intend to perform.[1] They often receive the power to induce diseases, to render the very air unwholesome by vitiating it, and to counsel evil deeds to men who are perverted and greedy for earthly gains. They are aware from the character of these men that they would agree with them if they should counsel such acts. They persuade them, however, in marvelous and unseen ways, entering by means of that subtlety of their own bodies into the bodies of men who are unaware,[2] and through certain imaginary visions mingling themselves with men's thoughts, whether they are awake or asleep. Yet sometimes they foretell, not the deeds which they themselves perform, but future events which they recognize in advance through natural signs which cannot reach the senses of men. Surely, because the physician foresees outcomes that one ignorant of his art does not foresee, one need not for that reason esteem him divine. Moreover, what is remarkable if, even as the physician, when the temperature of the human body is either disturbed or changed, foresees that the health will be either good or bad, so a demon in the state and condition of the atmosphere, known to him and unknown to us, foresees storms that will arise? Finally, too, with all ease they discern the intentions of men, not only as they are expressed by the voice, but also as they are conceived in reflection, when certain individual phases of the mind are expressed in the body. These disclosures are truly miraculous to those who do not know the acts intended; for, to be sure,

---
1 Cf. *De civitate Dei* 9.22.
2 Cf. *De diversis quaestionibus LXXXIII* 12, for a vivid description of an evil spirit permeating the senses of man.

just as an especially violent emotion is reflected in the countenance so that inward meditations are to some extent recognized outwardly by men, so it should not be incredible if even milder thoughts afford some indications through the medium of the body. These cannot be recognized by the dull sense of men, but can be through the keen perception of demons.[3]

Chapter 6

(10) By this faculty and faculties of this kind, demons foretell many events that will come to pass. Yet, far above them is the loftiness of that prophecy which God brings to pass through the holy angels and prophets. For, whatsoever these holy ones prophesy of that which God has ordained, they hear from Him, that they may prophesy. When they declare that which they hear from Him, they do not deceive nor are they deceived. Absolutely true are the pronouncements of the angels and the Prophets. Still, it is regarded as an offense that demons should hear and predict some matters of like nature, as if it were something of an offense that not only the good but the wicked as well should not keep silent concerning utterances that were spoken with the intent that they should be known to men.[1] Yet, even among men, we see that precepts of a good life are celebrated alike by the righteous and the depraved. It does not at all hinder, in fact it furthers the wider knowledge and reputation of truth, when even those who contradict it by their evil characters speak what they know concerning it. In their other predictions, nevertheless, demons are usually deceived and deceive. They are indeed mistaken, since, when they announce

---
[3] Cf. *Retractationes* 2.30, where this passage is cited.

[1] Cf. *De civitate Dei* 9.21; *De Trinitate* 4.17.

their own intentions, a command suddenly is issued from on high which shatters all their plans. The case would be similar if any men whatsoever, who were subject to certain potentates, should think that their superiors would not prevent them from performing an act and should promise that they would perform it. Yet, those in whom the superior authority rested might, on the basis of another better plan, suddenly prevent the entire deed that had been intended and arranged. They make some mistakes, too, in regard to natural phenomena. Like doctors, sailors, and farmers, they prognosticate, but demons do this far more keenly and far more excellently through the more alert and active perception of their aerial bodies. The demons make mistakes, I say, because even these phenomena of nature are unexpectedly and suddenly changed by the angels, devotedly serving God on high, in harmony with another plan unknown to the demons. Even so, some mishap from without may befall a sick man to cause his death, although the doctor had promised that he would survive, since all previous symptoms assured recovery. For example, some of the sailors, viewing the state of the atmosphere, had predicted that the wind would blow for a long time. Our Lord Christ, sailing with his disciples, commanded the wind to be still 'and there was a great calm.'[2] Likewise, the husbandman might promise that a vineyard would that year bear much fruit, understanding, as he did, the nature of the soil and the number of the plants. Yet, in that year, an unforeseen storm might break it down, the command of some despot might uproot it. Thus, many circumstances contributing to the foreknowledge and prediction of demons, such as are discerned in advance in the minor and more ordinary cases, these are obstructed and changed in more important and mysterious conditions. Then, too, they also deceive with a

---

2 Matt. 8.26.

desire to deceive and with malicious intent, that they may rejoice in the error of men. But, that they may not lose the weight of their authority among their own worshipers, they take pains that their failure be attributed to their seers and to the interpreters of their signs, claiming that they were mistaken or that they prevaricated.

(11) How, then, is it remarkable if, when downfall was already impending for temples and idols—a downfall which the prophets of the most high God foretold so long in advance—Serapis, a demon,[3] betrayed this event, close at hand, to some one of his own worshipers, so that he, though yielding and fleeing, might in a sense commend his own divinity?

Chapter 7

They are actually put to flight, or, rather, they are fettered and dragged off by higher orders, and they are estranged from their own places, that in respect to the very powers by which they held sway and for which they were worshiped, the will of God may be accomplished, who so long before foretold among all people that this would come to pass and commanded that the deed should be accomplished through His own faithful servants. Why, then, should the demon [Serapis] not be permitted to foretell this event, since he knew even beforehand that it was impending for him, inasmuch as this prediction was attested also by the Prophets? These matters were recorded by them and it was granted to the wise to understand how watchfully they must shun the guile of demons and banish their worship. For a long time before, the demons kept silent in their own temples concerning the things that would come to pass, although, because

---

3 On the pagan gods as demons, cf. *De civitate Dei* 9.23, *et passim*; Lactantius, *Divinae institutiones* 4.27.

of the utterances of the Prophets, they could not have been unaware of them. When, later, the events began to draw near, they wished, as it were, to foretell them, so that they might not be deemed ignorant and vanquished. Nevertheless, not to mention other instances for the present, long ago there had been foretold and recorded that which the Prophet Sophonias says: 'The Lord shall prevail against them, and shall cast out all the gods of the Gentiles of the earth: and they shall adore Him every man from his own place, all the islands of the Gentiles.'[1] Possibly those gods who were worshiped in the temples of the Gentiles did not believe that those events would occur to them, and consequently did not wish them to be noised abroad through their own seers and diviners. Even so, their own poet represents Juno as not wholly believing that which Jupiter had spoken with regard to the death of Turnus. Now, Juno is proclaimed by them a power of the air. She, according to Vergil, speaks thus:

Now dread doom is awaiting the guiltless, else in vain error
Truthless I stray. Mocking my fears, O thou art able,
Repent thee, and change to a kindlier way thy providence
    o'er him.[2]

So, then, either the demons, that is, the powers of the air, doubted that those very disasters which they had known as foretold by the Prophets could happen to themselves, and for that reason did not wish the predictions of the Prophets to become known—and thereby one may understand the character of the demons—or, though they knew that these things would most surely come to pass, they kept silent through their temples, that they might not even then begin to be abandoned and despised by understanding men, because

---
1 Cf. Soph. 2.11.
2 Vergil, *Aeneid* 10.630-632.

witness was given concerning the coming downfall of their temples and idols to those Prophets who forbade that they be worshiped. But now, certainly, after the time has arrived in which should be fulfilled the pronouncements of the Prophets of the one God, who calls those gods of theirs false and most sternly commands that they be not worshiped, why should not even the demons be permitted to declare that which has been accomplished? Therefore, it should the more clearly appear that either they did not in the least believe these prophecies in advance, or that they feared to announce them to their worshipers. Finally, it is evident that, having nothing further to accomplish, they determined to display their power of divination even in the very instance in which they are now detected as having pretended their divinity.[3]

Chapter 8

(12) As to the statement that the remaining worshipers of pagan gods make, that these events were foreknown and even included in certain books belonging to them, although one should regard the inclusions as compiled from events after their occurrence, the rejoinder is that, if they were authentic prophecies, they should have become known in their temples to their peoples long before their occurrence. Thus, our prophecies are repeated, not only in our churches, but also—a circumstance which is valid as a powerful testimony against our enemies—in the synagogues of the Jews.[1] Nevertheless, those actual prophecies, which they with difficulty pronounce rarely and secretly, should not disturb us, if some demon is constrained to betray to his worshipers

---
3 Antithesis and paronomasia: *ostendere divinationem — simulasse divinitatem*.

1 Cf. *De fide rerum quae non videntur* 6; *De symbolo* 4.

a matter which he had learned from the declarations of the Prophets or from the oracles of the angels. Why should this not take place, since it is not an assault upon the truth, but a testimonial for it. Certainly, this argument, the only one which should be required of them, they have never previously presented, nor will they ever hereafter try to present, unless fictitiously, namely, that their gods through their seers have ever dared to predict or speak anything against the God of Israel, a God concerning whom their most learned authors, who could read and know all these matters, have questioned as to what god He was rather than been able to deny Him as God. Furthermore, that God, whom no one of them ventured to deny as the true God, who, if one denied, would not only have subjected him to the punishment due, but would have convinced him by the sure consequences, that God whom, as I have said, no one of them dared deny as the true God, through His own seers, that is, through the Prophets, declared with manifest proclamation, commanded with manifest power, and accomplished with manifest truth both that the false gods should be entirely abandoned and that their temples and idols should be overthrown. Knowing this, who is so foolish that he would not prefer to worship the God whose worship even the gods that he has been worshiping do not gainsay? Doubtless, when one begins to worship Him, he will not be at all inclined to worship those whose worship He whom he worships forbids.[2]

Chapter 9

(13) I mentioned a little earlier and now repeat that it was foretold by His Prophets that the Gentiles, casting out their false gods whom they formerly worshiped, would

---
2 Note antithesis and word-play.

worship Him. It is said: 'The Lord shall prevail against them, and shall cast out all the gods of the Gentiles of the earth: and they shall adore Him every man from his own place, all the islands of the Gentiles.'[1] Nor shall it be the islands alone, but even so all Gentiles, even as also all islands of the Gentiles, since in another passage he does not name 'islands,' but the whole earth. He says: 'All the ends of the earth shall remember and shall be converted to the Lord: And all the kindreds of the Gentiles shall adore in his sight. For the kingdom is the Lord's; and he shall have dominion over the nations.'[2] That these words were to be fulfilled through Christ appears clearly both in many other testimonies and from the very psalm from which I have quoted the previous passage. For, when a little earlier the Lord Himself was telling through His Prophet that His Passion would come to pass, He said: 'They have dug my hands and feet. They have numbered all my bones. And they have looked and stared upon me. They have parted my garments among them; and upon my vesture they cast lots.'[3] Shortly after, the Psalmist introduces that passage which I have set down, in which it was said: 'All the ends of the earth shall remember and shall be converted to the Lord,' and so on. Yet, in record to that testimony which I have presented formerly, in which it was said: 'The Lord shall prevail against them, and shall cast out all the gods of the Gentiles of the earth,' it is clearly disclosed, from the fact that 'shall prevail' is introduced, that it is likewise prophesied that the heathen will first contend against the Church and, in so far as they are able, persecute the Christian name, with the intent that, if it could be accomplished, it should be blotted out entirely from the earth. Because He was to

---

1 Cf. Soph. 2.11.
2 Ps. 21.28,29.
3 Ps. 21.17-19.

overcome them through the suffering of the martyrs, the magnitude of the miracles, and the subsequent faith of the peoples, it was spoken thus: 'The Lord will prevail against them.' For, it would not have been said: 'He will prevail against them,' unless they had resisted Him, as they fought against Him. Wherefore, in the psalm, also, it is thus prophesied: 'Why have the Gentiles raged, and the peoples devised vain things? The kings of the earth stood up, and the princes met together, against the Lord, and against his Christ.'[4] Shortly after, he says: 'The Lord hath said to me: Thou art my son, this day have I begotten thee. Ask of me, and I will give thee the Gentiles for thy inheritance, and the utmost parts of the earth for thy possession.'[5] That is why in another psalm are spoken the words that I have quoted above: 'All the ends of the earth shall remember and shall be converted to the Lord.' By these and similar examples from the Prophets, that prophecy is disclosed which we see fulfilled through Christ, namely, that it was to come to pass that the God of Israel, whom we know as the one true God, would be worshiped, not among His own people alone, which was called Israel, but among all the Gentiles, and that He would drive out the false gods of the Gentiles both from their temples and from the hearts of their worshipers.

Chapter 10

(14) Now let those supporters go[1] on and even now dare to defend ancient vanities against the Christian religion

---
4 Ps. 2.1,2.
5 Ps. 2.7,8.

---
1 *Eant nunc*: a formula of contemptuous dismissal frequent in Augustan writers. Cf. Vergil, *Aeneid* 7.425.

and against the true worship of God, that they may perish in noise. This also is foretold concerning them in the psalms, when the Prophet says: 'Thou hast sat on the throne, who judgest justice. Thou hast rebuked the Gentiles, and the wicked one hath perished: thou hast blotted out their name for ever and ever. The swords of the enemy have failed unto the end: and their cities thou hast destroyed. Their memory has perished with a noise: but the Lord remaineth forever.'[2] It is needful, therefore, that all these sayings be fulfilled: nor, seeing that those very few who have remained dare to vaunt their vainglorious doctrines and to mock at the Christians as wholly unlearned, should we be moved, so long as we see that in them those prophecies are accomplished. In truth, the Christians' very foolishness of ignorance, which to the humble and the holy and to those diligently devoted to it appears the lofty and the only true wisdom—this foolishness, at it were, of the Christians—has, I say, brought their enemy to their present scanty numbers, even as the Apostle says: 'God has made foolish the wisdom of this world.' Thereafter he adds a saying, wondrous if one understands it, and continues thus: 'For seeing that in the wisdom of God the world, by wisdom, knew not God, it pleased God, by the foolishness of our preaching, to save them that believe. For both the Jews require signs, and the Greeks seek after wisdom: But we preach Christ crucified, unto the Jews indeed a stumbling block, and unto the Gentiles foolishness: But unto them that are called, both Jews and Greeks, Christ the power of God and the wisdom of God. For the foolishness of God is wiser than men; and the weakness of God is stronger than men.'[3] Then let them mock with all their might at our ignorance and foolishness, as they call it, and let them vaunt their own learning and wisdom. So much

---

2 Ps. 9.5-8.
3 1 Cor. 1.20-25.

I know, that these mockers of us are fewer this year than they were the year before. Ever since 'the Gentiles have raged, and the people devised vain things'[4] against the Lord and against His Christ, when they shed the blood of the saints and laid waste the Church, even to this time and henceforth they are each day diminished. We, however, are emboldened against their reproaches and insolent mockeries by the prophecies of our God. In this very matter we see them fulfilled and we rejoice. Thus, indeed, He speaks to us through the Prophets. 'Hearken to me, you that know what is just, my people, who have my law in your heart; fear ye not the reproach of men, and be not overcome by their slander, nor consider it of great moment that now they scorn you. For as a garment they shall in time be wasted, and the moth shall consume them as wool, but my justice shall remain forever.'[5] Let them, nevertheless, read this writing of ours, if they deem it meet. When their refutal reaches us, we shall reply, as God shall grant us aid.

---
4 Ps. 2.1.
5 Cf. Isa. 51.7,8.

INDEX

INDEX

Aaron, 412
Abraham, 6, 28, 37-39, 42-44, 46, 51, 355, 374-376, 392, 398, 410
abstinence, 229, 393
actors, 263
Adam, 4, 58, 149
Adam, Karl, 7
adoption, 190
adulterer, 14, 15, 18, 32, 65, 70, 71, 72, 74, 77, 93, 94, 104, 106, 108, 111, 113, 114, 115, 118, 119, 122, 124, 128, 153, 180, 223, 229, 250, 251, 259, 261, 262, 263, 266, 267, 280
adulteress, 15, 18, 63, 64, 74, 93, 94, 103-115, 122, 124, 126, 128, 250, 266
adultery, 4, 13, 16-20, 31, 32, 46, 56, 59, 63, 69-77, 93-95, 98, 102-119, 122-126, 128, 129, 131, 163, 164, 177, 222, 229, 231, 232, 234, 236, 239, 241, 242, 245, 256, 259, 264, 266-268, 276, 277, 282, 422

advocate, 271
Aeneas, 368
Alexandria, 18, 419 n., 422
Alfaric, P., 314, 317 n.
allegory, 280
allurements, 275
Alpha and Omega, 331 n.
altars, 364
Ambrose, St., 3, 136, 138, 146 n., 382
Ananias, 381
anathema, 397
ancients, 36, 37
Angels, 290, 355, 376, 379, 431, 436
Anna, 21, 51
Antoninus, Emperor, 109
Anulinus, 199 n.
Apostle, 11, 16, 18, 20, 23-30, 33, 42, 48, 50, 61-66, 68, 70, 71, 77-98, 100, 102-106, 115-117, 121, 143, 145, 155, 156, 159-167, 174, 181, 183, 190, 194, 196, 202, 204, 223-225, 230,

232-235, 238, 241, 243, 244, 246-248, 253-256, 259, 264, 267, 268, 271, 273, 274, 279, 286, 289, 304, 305, 315, 321, 323, 326, 327, 329, 330, 332, 337, 342-345, 392, 393, 398, 400, 402, 404, 408, 409, 439
Apollinaris, 325 n.
Apuleius, 419, 426 n.
Arians, 294, 322 n.
Ascension, 236
Asellicus, 388
Augustine, St., Works cited: *City of God*, 10, 23, 30, 35, 36, 329, 344, 354, 380, 388, 399, 419-421; *Confessions*, 98, 200; *Enchiridion*, 146, 312, 313; *Letters*, 150, 184, 215, 218; *Retractations*, 37, 46, 56, 135, 137, 138, 215, 219, 286, 311-313, 344, 387, 417, 431; *Sermons*, 143, 146, 149, 150, 200, 285, 287, 324, 327; others, 56, 59, 135, 136, 144-146, 149, 150, 184, 199, 318, 319, 422, 426, 430, 431, 435
avarice, 300

baptism, 35, 98, 100, 107, 123, 139, 150 n., 204, 215-217, 221, 222, 229-232, 234, 237, 239, 240, 242-245, 250-252, 254, 258, 261-268, 277-281, 287, 288, 305, 306, 312, 372
baptistry, 373
barbarians, 354

Bardenhewer, Otto, 7, 387-389
Bardy, Gustave, 7, 8, 286 n., 287 n., 289 n., 314, 317 n.
Bareille, G., 150 n.
Barnabas, 79
Barreau, M. H., 314, 420 n.
Batiffol, P., 7
beasts, 355
Beelzebub, 408
Bellarmine, Robert, 7
Benedictines, 285
bishop, 36, 262, 280, 286, 287, 311, 349, 382, 389
blasphemy, 277, 298
Blood, of Christ, 81, 107, 305, 394
Blumenkranz, B., 387-389 nn.
Body, of Christ, 259, 306, 357
Bourke, V. J., 220 n., 286 n.
Bread, of the Lord, 231, 398
brilliance, 296, 331
Bryaxis, 419
Budge, E. A. W., 418 n.
bull, 394
Burkitt, F. C., 7, 314 n., 317 n.

Cabrol, F., 200 n.
Caecilian, 227
Canaan, 403
Canaanite, 180, 258, 259
Candidianus, 384
Cappello, Felix, 7
Carthage, 369, 389
catechists, 215, 230, 236, 245, 287
catechumens, 35, 98, 100, 122,

204, 215, 217, 231, 233, 234, 242, 286, 287, 306, 372, 389
Catholics, 85, 135, 216, 315, 389
Cato, 36, 232
cattle, 393, 401
Cavallera, F., 7
Cayré, F., 7
Ceillier, Dom Remy, 7
celibacy, 42, 155, 171, 173
centurion, 180, 186
Cephas, 79
chalice, 231
charity, 20, 23, 79, 80, 83, 87, 101, 129, 139, 148, 149, 151, 179, 189, 191, 193, 202, 210, 224, 247, 248, 250, 251, 253-255, 257-259, 268, 269, 272, 273, 276, 282, 293, 304, 305, 316, 337-341
chastity, 14, 21, 26, 37, 44, 46, 48, 50, 109, 110, 119, 128, 130, 131, 151, 153, 155, 162, 166, 178, 184, 192, 197, 201, 202, 204; *see also* continence
chrisma, 396
Christ, 5, 6, 10, 21, 31, 36, 37, 41, 42, 48, 50, 51, 78, 79, 89, 91, 93, 95, 97, 100, 107, 109-114, 122, 123, 129, 131, 139, 141, 143-145, 149-152, 154, 159, 163, 167, 168, 170, 174, 179, 180, 182, 183, 186, 189, 192, 194, 202, 205, 215, 221-224, 227, 234-239, 241, 243, 244, 249-261, 265, 268-271, 273-281, 292, 294, 295, 297, 298, 301-303, 305-307, 316, 319, 322, 325 n., 326 n., 334-336, 338, 339, 353, 361, 364, 365, 376, 379, 381, 384, 388, 392, 395, 398, 400, 404, 405, 407, 409, 414, 432, 437-440; as Head, 149, 150, 307, 322, 342; as Lord, 11, 12, 18, 21, 23, 26, 28, 29, 41, 42, 44, 47-49, 56, 61, 65, 68-70, 73, 75, 77-80, 83-93, 96, 97, 100, 102, 107, 108, 112, 113, 117, 120, 126, 131, 155-158, 160, 166, 167, 173, 177, 179, 180, 185, 190, 191, 197, 199, 201, 206, 207, 212, 221-226, 229, 231, 232, 235-237, 239, 241, 244-247, 249-255, 258, 260, 262, 265, 267-282, 295, 208-301, 319, 322, 323, 325, 327, 331, 332, 340, 353, 355, 356, 358, 361-363, 373, 374, 376, 378, 381, 397-414, 432, 434, 437, 438; as Priest, 206; as Saviour, 22, 62, 64, 79, 84, 99, 110, 149, 249, 275, 276, 278, 281, 323, 340, 402; as Son of God, 174, 185, 186, 226, 236, 237, 243, 249, 255, 266, 270, 271, 287, 291-297, 319, 321-324, 331-340, 402, 409; as Son of Man, 41, 42, 174, 186, 207, 400
Christians, 4, 41, 56, 57, 59, 68, 77, 84, 90, 93-95, 97, 102, 109, 118, 121, 143 n., 150-152, 169, 170, 182, 205, 215, 221, 230,

232, 233, 248, 257, 258, 264, 265, 274, 278, 330, 355-357, 361, 383, 388, 389, 394, 404, 407, 411, 421, 439
non-Christian, 87, 88, 151, 217
Christianity, 98, 120, 121
Chrysostom, St. John, 138
Church, The, 5, 30, 35, 59, 65, 78 n., 100, 135, 136, 139, 141, 143 n., 145, 150 n., 151, 154, 170, 187, 192, 199 n., 204, 216, 217, 223-229, 231, 232, 236, 261-263, 279-281, 286, 287, 305-307, 311, 313, 320, 341, 351-353, 373, 388, 389, 396, 398, 404, 414, 437, 440
Cicero, 369, 419, 427
clouds, 276, 277
cockle, 227, 228, 232, 260, 280
coevality, 296
co-heirs, 328
Combès, Gustave, 7, 56 n.
commandments, 269, 270, 273, 275, 276, 281
commemoration, 353
communion, 217
competentes, 217, 230, 231, 264
concubinage, 30, 266
concupiscence, 6, 13, 16, 24, 58, 169, 183, 247, 257
confession, 300
Confessor, 349, 351
confidence, 278
confirmation, 150 n.
conscience, 252
Consentius, 218

continence, 2, 17, 20, 22, 37, 39-45, 49, 50, 57, 62-65, 69, 86, 102, 113, 116-119, 127, 128, 130, 131, 137, 151, 153, 155, 162, 164, 166, 167, 169, 177, 182, 184, 196-198, 201, 202, 229
converts, 215, 261, 278
corner-stone, 409, 413
Cornish, C. L., 7
corruption, 292
Covenant, New, 58, 107, 400, 401
Creed, 217, 240, 266, 285, 286, 287, 289
Crispina, 199
Crispus, 238
cross, 297
crucifixion, 238
Cunningham, W., 7
Curma, 370, 371
Cynegius, 349
Cyprian, 97 n., 184 n., 200 n., 265 n., 282 n.

dancers, 280
David, King, 107, 365, 366
Dawson, Christopher, 7
deception, 250, 263
Deferrari, R. J., 312 n.
defilements, 275, 276
de Ghellinck, I., 4, 7, 313 n., 314 n.
Deliverer, 156
demons, 381, 382, 416, 417, 421, 425, 426, 428
denarius, 172, 173
Dermine, J., 7

destruction, 249, 253, 279, 354
Devil, 11, 41, 160, 179, 252, 259, 260, 282, 291, 299, 303; *see also,* Satan
Di Capua, F., 312 n., 314
Diocletian, 199 n.
diptychs, 200 n.
discipline, 228
disobedience, 45, 46
divination, 416, 417, 419, 421, 422, 425, 435
divorce, 19, 57, 59, 62, 110, 118, 124
docetism, 326 n.
Dods, Marcus, 314
dogs, 225, 227-229, 258, 277, 291, 361, 364
Donatists, 227, 418
dreams, 368, 371, 373, 380, 381
drunkards, 251, 263
dualism, 336 n.

Easter, 285 n., 288, 372, 418, 421
Egypt, 240, 241, 243, 399-401, 403, 418, 420
Elias, 377
Elvira, Spanish Council of, 330
envy, 178
episcopate, 311
error, 226, 393
Esmein, A., 7
Essenes, 147 n.
Eucharist, Holy, 150 n.
Eulogius, 369
eunuchs, 127, 168-171, 187, 202, 236, 237, 243

Euphasia, 109
Eusebius, 361, 365
Evagelists, 72, 73, 76, 201, 362
Eve, 4, 58, 299
excommuication, 223, 224, 264, 279
exorcism, 217, 229

faith, 248-250, 253, 254, 258, 261, 262, 268, 269, 272, 276-278, 281, 282, 311, 389, 396
feast, marriage, 260
fecundity, 36, 144, 145, 150-152, 154, 155
fidelity (*fides*), 1, 4, 13, 14, 16, 48, 57, 59
Felix, St., 349, 351, 378
filth, 252, 277
Finaert, J., 314, 319 n.
fire, 244, 249, 250, 252-254, 257, 272-274, 277, 293, 296, 303
flesh, 342-345, 362, 364, 383, 394, 395, 398, 401, 405, 411
flora, 349, 351
folly, 280
forgiveness, 305
fornication, 12, 17, 19, 20, 24, 25, 32, 35, 46, 57, 61, 65-69, 71, 83, 85, 97, 102-105, 114, 122, 124-126, 129, 153, 157, 168, 241, 244, 251, 256, 262
foundation, 250, 252, 254-256, 302, 303.
fowls, 355
Froget, J., 7
funeral, 355, 358

Gaius, 238
gall, 397
Gaul, 361
generation, 36, 37, 47, 48, 50, 58, 59, 116, 297, 327, 331, 337
Gentiles, 29, 84, 90, 391, 392, 400, 403, 404, 410-414, 434, 436-439
Gervase and Protase, Sts., 382
Gift, of God, 337, 338
Gilson, E., 314, 325 n.
gladiators, 264
Gnostics, 329 n.
goats, 330
God, 6, 9-11, 21, 22, 26, 27, 29, 32, 35-38, 40, 48-51, 66, 80, 82-89, 91, 96, 98, 105, 107, 108, 110, 111, 119, 120, 123-125, 129, 131, 137, 141, 144, 146, 147, 151, 152, 155-157, 160, 161, 168, 169, 172, 173, 178, 180, 181, 183, 190, 192, 194-199, 201, 202, 206, 207, 209, 210, 212, 223, 224, 226, 227, 232, 233, 235, 238, 239-244, 246-252, 255-273, 276-278, 282, 287, 290-307, 316-345, 353, 357, 360, 362, 363, 373, 374-399, 401-414, 418, 419, 422-425, 431-440; Almighty, 290-292, 294, 317-319, 331 n., 397, 410; Creator, 10, 22, 25, 151, 317, 340; Father, 181, 185, 195, 205, 206, 210, 226, 240, 266, 271, 287, 290-304, 306, 316, 319-323, 330, 332-340, 374, 402; the Omnipotent, 290, 293, 422-425
Godhead, 297, 337, 338
gold, 250, 255-257
Goliath, 45
Gospel, 12, 41, 55, 73, 75, 79, 84, 91, 112, 120, 126, 145, 182, 232, 238, 239, 243, 249, 259, 260, 271, 304, 357, 377, 392, 399, 404, 405
gossipers, 183
grace, 247, 249, 268, 273, 274, 282, 313
Greeks, 75, 359, 361, 396, 418, 439
Gregorian Code, 109-110
guardian, 281
guilt, 291

Hades, 419
hair, 354
Halicarnassus, 419
hand, right, 330
harlots, 187, 221, 244, 250, 251, 259, 261, 263, 264, 268
hay, 251, 255-257
Hefele, 311 n., 314
heresy, 135, 136, 305, 316 n., 321 n., 326 n.
heretics, 306, 315, 316, 325, 329, 336, 341
Herod, 265
Hippo, 285, 311, 322 n., 349, 370-372, 389
Holy of Holies, 188

horns, of the cross, 394
humility, 180-182, 184, 185, 188, 198, 202, 203, 205, 206, 208, 210-212, 279, 316, 322, 323, 414
hylomorphism, 318

idolatry, 224, 242, 243, 244, 251, 256, 264, 330 n.
idols, 32, 242, 243, 433
images, 330 n., 364
immorality, 61-64, 66, 70-77, 93, 94, 102, 113, 114, 127, 429 n.
immortality, 11, 17, 20, 155, 279, 301, 343, 399
impurity, 264
Incarnation, 236, 287, 327 n.
incest, 20
incontinence, 15, 17, 24, 43, 49, 50, 112-117, 122, 130
incorruption, 155, 292
incredulity, 268
infidelity, 57, 268
infidels, 271
iniquity, 253, 268, 395
injustice, 290
insufflation, 217
intercourse, sexual, 9, 11, 12, 15-17, 20-24, 29-32, 40, 41, 46-50, 108, 116, 117, 147, 171, 231
Isaac, 47, 51, 392, 398
Israel, 42, 180, 240, 324, 332, 374, 398, 401-403, 406-412, 436, 438
Israelites, 11, 19, 58, 59, 84, 241, 268, 398, 400, 405

Jacob, 51, 392, 400, 403-410
Jerome, St., 3, 135-139, 184 n., 200 n., 336 n.
Jerusalem, 33, 175, 267, 329, 355, 398, 403-405, 410-412
Jews, 4, 147, 241, 242, 274, 278, 301, 305, 363, 387-404, 409, 414, 435, 439
John the Baptist, St., 6, 41, 42, 244, 245, 266, 268
John of Lycopolis, 380-382
Jonathan, 365
Joseph, 4
Josias, 363, 374, 375
Jovinian, 3, 135, 136, 138
Joyce, G. H., 5, 8
Juda, 117, 398
Judaism, 143 n.
judgment, 271, 281; last, 331
Julian Law, 109
Juno, 434
Jupiter, 434
Just One, the, 422-424
justice, 289, 395

Kavanagh, D. J., 56 n.
kidnapers, 258
Kunzelmann, A., 285 n., 286 n.

Labriolle, P. de, 8
Lactantius, 433 n.
Ladomérsky, N., 5, 8, 58
Lamb, the, 47, 173-177, 188, 189, 194, 204, 207, 208, 394
Latin, 361
Law, the, 19, 38, 39, 42, 79, 80,

83, 84, 87, 93, 105, 107, 112, 114, 121, 190, 239-248, 263, 269-273, 393, 394, 397, 403-405, 407, 410
Lazarus, 297, 307, 375-378
leaven, 394
Leclercq, H., 150 n., 314, 330 n.
Lent, 217
liberty, 275
licentiousness, 41, 251
life, 271, 272
light, and darkness, 317 n.
Lindau, H., 420 n.
Lord's Prayer, 217
Lot, wife of, 277
Low Sunday, 217
Lucan, 356
Lucian, of Antioch, 325 n.
lust, 29, 32, 239, 273

Madaura, 419
malice, 274, 275
Manichaeism, 3, 42, 49, 55, 135, 137, 317, 326 n., 329 n., 336 n.
Marcellinus, Ammianus, 421 n.
Mariology, 139
Marrou, H. I., 8, 420 n.
Martha, 21
martyrs, 40, 42, 199 n., 200, 202, 359, 361, 364-366, 378, 379, 381-383, 438
Mary, Virgin, 4, 21, 51, 138, 139, 141, 145-148, 150, 154, 163, 174, 210, 287, 294, 295, 324, 325, 326 n., 398
Mary, 21

Mass, 286
Master, 92, 185, 206, 207, 225, 278, 292
maternity, 326 n.
matricides, 258
matrimony, 5 154, 265
Maur, St., 285, 389
Maurist text, 218
Mausbach, J., 5, 8
Maximinus, 322 n.
McDonald, Sister M. Francis, 312 n.
Melchisedech, 412, 413
mercy, 45, 257, 277, 278, 316, 335, 399, 414
Migne, J. P., 7, 218, 420 n.
Milan, 136, 138, 368, 369, 382
Milne, C. H., 8
miracles, 380, 429, 438
mire, 275
misery, 302
Mitterer, 218 n.
monastery, 135
money, 261
monk, 380-382
monogamy, 58
Montgomery, W., 8
monuments, 358, 359
moon, new, 393, 394
Morin, Dom, 287 n.
mortality, 11, 19
mortification, 393
Moses, 19, 59, 112, 223, 278, 323, 375-377, 404
mother, a faithful, 359, 360
mysteries, 240

nativity, 287, 303
negligence, 282
neighbor, 253, 256
Neo-Platonists, 419, 426 n.
Nero, 199 n.
nets, 262
Noe, 280
Nola, 349, 378
Noldin, H., 8
nuns, 200, 211

obedience, 45, 46, 49, 196
obstinacy, 282
offspring, 4, 10, 29, 32, 34, 37, 48, 58, 116, 150, 154
ointment, 357
olive, 392, 399
omnipotence, 288, 317
Onan, 117
oracles, 228, 436
Orders, Holy, 5
ordination, 35, 36, 48
oxen, 291, 401
Oxenham, H. N., 314

pagans, 4, 19, 35, 42, 57, 84, 85, 216, 274, 329, 410
pain, 341
paradise, 298, 377
parricides, 258
Pasch, the, 393, 405
Passion, 225, 239, 295, 303, 405
paterfamilias, 292
patience, 42, 223, 228, 229, 280, 297-301
Patriarchs, 6, 29, 37, 39, 42, 46, 47, 49-51, 58, 143 n., 144 n., 357, 374, 391, 399, 406, 418
Paul, St., 4, 41, 56, 57, 85, 89, 90, 143 n., 163, 190, 191, 199 n., 216, 218, 234, 238, 247-250, 253, 254, 257, 277, 343, 363, 377, 379, 391
Pauline privilege, 78 n.
Paulinus, 349, 351
Peebles, B. M., 312 n.
penance, 107, 122-124, 222, 279, 306
Pereira, B., 4, 8
perfection, 246, 297
perjurers, 258
Perrone, E. Vincent, 8
persecution, 265, 277
Peter, St., 27, 28, 42, 174-176, 209, 234-236, 239, 241, 248, 249, 251-253, 267, 274-277
Peters, J., 8
Pharisees, 180, 181, 187, 193, 198, 278
Philip, 236, 237, 243
Phinees, 223
piety, 357, 429
Pilate, Pontius, 295, 328
Pius XI, Pope, 3
Plato, 419, 421 n.
Plotinus, 419
Plutarch, 232 n., 419
polyandry, 58
polygamy, 6, 58, 144 n.
Pollentius, 55-57, 61, 101
Pope, Hugh, 8, 218 n., 287 n., 388 n.

Portalié, E., 3, 8, 218 n., 285 n., 387 n.
Possidius, 56, 285, 388 n.
Pourrat, P., 5, 8
Prat, F., 143 n.
prayer, 306
preacher, 90, 91
predestination, 271, 313
pride, 178, 179, 182, 183, 192, 193, 198, 207, 208, 211, 212, 247, 322, 414
priesthood, 412
procreation, 4, 12, 16, 18, 24, 25, 28, 29, 31, 37, 49, 117
progeny, 10, 22, 32, 36, 50, 145, 150, 169
propagation, 58, 188
prophecy, 140, 336, 380, 398, 410, 419, 431, 435, 439, 440
prophets, 33, 42, 84, 168, 169, 239, 268, 270, 297, 357, 362, 364, 374-377, 392-400, 403, 407-413, 431, 433-440
Porphyry, 329 n.
propitiation, 271
proselytes, 278
prostitution, 20, 25, 97, 251, 257, 265
proverb, 275
Providence, 373
Ptolemies, 419
publicans, 180, 181, 186-188, 198, 208, 225, 245, 268
purification, 39, 277
purity, 276, 341

rebirth, 338
Red Sea, 240-243
regeneration, 100, 105, 106, 241, 324
relics, 365
repentance, 241, 245, 252, 254, 264, 266, 404
resurrection, 236, 237, 271, 272, 297, 307, 328, 329 n., 343-345, 354, 357, 361, 364, 404, 405, 408
Reuter, A., 8
Rhone River, 361
Rivière, J., 314
Roman Law, 121
Rome, 135, 136, 354, 419
rope-dancers, 429
Rufinus, 361
Russell, R. P., 312 n.

Sabbath, 393, 394
sacrament (*sacramentum*), 4, 5, 18, 35, 36, 48, 59, 105, 106, 154, 222, 223, 230, 232, 242-244, 257, 258, 263, 281, 288, 393, 396
sacrifice, 401, 402, 410, 411, 413; of the altar, 200, 286
Sadducees, 329 n.
Saint-Martin, J., 7
salvation, 253, 254, 256, 262, 273, 274, 289, 315, 324, 325, 383, 392, 401, 402, 409, 412
Samaritan, 80
Samuel, 377

sanctity, 26, 35, 36, 48, 176, 211, 212, 338
Sara, 6, 28, 44
Satan, 17, 117, 159, 223, 224, 279
Saul, 107, 365, 366, 377, 381
scandals, 193
sceptre, 395
Schanz, M., 387 n., 388
schism, 227, 280
schismatics, 341
scribes, 187, 278
Scripture, Holy, 10, 12, 18, 45, 49, 56, 59, 73, 77, 121, 139, 160-166, 171, 178, 195, 198, 217, 218, 224, 226, 228, 232, 234, 237, 238, 241, 243, 244, 246, 249, 251, 253, 254, 269, 271, 273, 274, 277, 278, 280, 288, 289, 298, 301, 315, 316, 318, 329, 335, 336, 362, 377, 382, 392, 404, 407, 411, 414; *see also,* Testaments, two; quotations from, or references to, individual Books:
Acts of the Apostles, 35, 201, 234-237, 241, 268, 293, 304, 331, 337, 381, 405
Apocalypse, 47, 139, 145, 173, 204, 205, 331
Canticle of Canticles, 400
Colossians, 186, 231, 335, 393
1 Corinthians, 13, 18, 20, 23, 24, 26-28, 33, 35, 36, 40, 43, 44, 48, 49, 61, 63, 64, 77-81, 83-93, 96, 97, 100, 102, 103, 111, 115-117, 144, 152, 154, 155, 157, 158, 161, 163, 165-167, 172, 177, 179, 183, 189-195, 199, 200-202, 212, 221-224, 231, 237, 238, 244, 248, 250-254, 256, 257, 261, 263, 279, 303-305, 319, 327, 329, 334, 335, 339, 340, 342-345, 356, 363, 380, 402, 403, 439
1 Corinthians, 57
2 Corinthians, 44, 50, 145, 154, 170, 175, 204, 206, 223, 243, 279, 341, 352, 377
Daniel, 21, 163, 211, 212, 413
Deuteronomy, 11, 19, 84, 90, 168, 332, 377
Ecclesiastes, 28, 120
Ecclesiasticus, 51, 178, 182, 198, 206, 209, 343, 377, 382
Ephesians, 20, 109, 145, 194, 235, 255, 307, 328, 338, 342, 362, 383, 409
Esdras, 84, 116
Exodus, 177, 223, 240, 242, 324
Galatians, 43, 89, 148, 151, 193, 239, 248, 251, 254-257, 259, 263, 264, 268, 272, 275, 276, 282, 315, 329, 398, 402
Genesis, 9-11, 38, 47, 117, 144, 277, 280, 291, 299, 322, 356, 357, 404, 406
Habacuc, 315
Hebrews, 19, 46, 206, 241, 323
Isaias, 168, 170, 175, 178, 190, 192, 207, 297, 316, 374, 376, 392, 395, 399, 403, 405-408, 411-414, 440

James, 71, 181, 185, 195, 197, 199, 209, 248-252, 254, 255, 258, 262, 268, 277, 281, 298, 301
Jeremias, 400
Job, 40, 192, 197, 203, 298-301
John, 12, 100, 107, 108, 120, 173, 175, 182, 188, 206, 209, 210, 225, 234, 248, 267, 269-272, 278, 294, 319, 321-323, 326, 328, 334, 335, 337, 338, 357, 377, 378, 411
1 John, 190, 205, 207, 209, 240, 269-271, 337, 338
Jude, 248, 276, 277
1 Kings, 45, 377
2 Kings, 107, 366
3 Kings, 302, 362, 364
4 Kings, 364, 374
Luke, 21, 45, 56, 73-76, 93, 94, 111, 119, 120, 126, 129, 146, 147, 173, 175, 180, 181, 186-189, 191, 193, 195, 198, 201, 209, 222, 245, 249, 260, 268, 323, 340, 354, 355, 362, 366, 376, 377, 379, 405
2 Maccabees, 353
Malachias, 410
Mark, 56, 73-76, 93, 94, 111, 222, 227, 249, 397
Matthew, 12, 18, 19, 29, 41-43, 51, 62, 63, 70, 72-76, 79, 93, 94, 99, 111-113, 117, 121, 125-127, 144-146, 148, 149, 152, 155, 157, 168, 170, 172, 175-177, 180, 181, 185-188, 193, 197, 199-201, 203, 204, 206-208, 222, 225-228, 231, 239, 245, 246, 249, 252, 253, 255, 258-262, 265, 266, 269, 270, 277-279, 281, 292, 302-306, 326, 328, 330, 340, 345, 354, 357, 377, 392, 394, 397, 399, 408, 432
Micheas, 38
Numbers, 39, 223
1 Peter, 28, 174-176, 209, 239, 252, 274, 275
2 Peter, 248, 249, 253, 275, 276
Philippians, 31, 41, 147, 179, 181, 192, 203, 223, 321, 323, 328, 335, 395
Proverbs, 185, 188, 199, 203, 280, 322
Psalms, 10, 19, 83, 96, 140, 154, 173, 177, 180, 188-192, 194, 196, 197, 208, 210, 232, 247, 253, 270, 295, 299, 301, 332, 355, 373, 392, 394-403, 406, 408, 411-414, 437-440
Romans, 24, 80, 85, 93, 98, 103, 105, 121, 128, 143, 148, 172, 187, 189-192, 194, 195, 197, 203, 237, 238, 247, 248, 267, 269, 271, 273, 274, 289, 298, 301, 315, 330, 332, 337, 339, 341, 342, 373, 391, 392, 398, 413, 414
Sophonias, 413, 434, 437
1 Thessalonians, 11, 29
2 Thessalonians, 225
1 Timothy, 23, 27, 35, 40, 48,

96, 113, 117, 149, 170, 183, 184, 187, 224, 226, 227, 258, 259, 277
2 Timothy, 196, 290
Titus, 35, 327
Tobias, 356
Wisdom, 11, 196, 270, 318, 319, 321
seducers, 264
Seleucia, 199 n.
sensuality, 274, 275
sepulchres, 358, 360, 362
Serapeum, 419
Serapis, 418, 419, 421, 433
serpent, 298, 299
Serrier, G., 8
sheep, 291, 393, 405
Sheridan, E., 6, 8
Sinai, Mount, 401, 404, 405, 407, 410
Sinope, 419 n.
Sion, 398, 404, 405, 407
Siricius, Pope, 3, 135, 136, 138
sister, 148
slavery, 398
Sodom, 277
sodomites, 251, 258
Solomon, 270, 303, 377
souls, 325 n., 329, 341, 342, 355, 357, 361, 377, 393
spirit, 325 n., 329, 341, 342
Spirit, Holy, 26, 85, 86, 96, 163, 170, 192, 207, 226, 234-236, 244, 247, 259, 266, 269, 273, 277, 278, 287, 294, 295,

303, 304, 324, 331, 332, 334, 335, 337-340, 380, 405
springs, dry, 275-277
Stephen, 303
Stephanas, 238
sterility, 31, 144
Stoddard, J. L., 143 n.
Stoics, 325 n.
straw, 253
Styx, 353
subordinationism, 322 n.
sun, worship of, 327 n.
superiors, 262
Susanna, 21, 51, 163, 164
swine, 99
symbolism, 4, 5
Synod, of African Bishops, 286
Syria, 131

temperance, 32, 40
temple, 252, 330
Tempter, 94, 95
Testament, New, 29, 32, 90, 91, 97, 107, 265, 274, 400
Testament, Old, 33, 51, 90, 91, 143 n., 190, 192, 353, 393, 400
Thagara, 199 n.
Thebeste, 199 n.
Thecla, 199
Theodosius, 380, 418
Theophilus, 418
Thomas Aquinas, St., 3, 6
Tillemont, L. de, 8
Tixeront, J., 8, 314, 321 n., 325 n., 326 n., 329 n., 336 n.
tomb, 328, 349, 355, 364

transformation, 343, 344
transgression, 269, 273
Trinity, 85, 226, 287, 303, 305, 321 n., 332-334, 339
truth, 293, 294, 319, 354, 366, 368
Tullium, 370
Turnus, 434

unbelievers, 265, 272

Valerius, 286, 311
Varro, 419
Vazquez, G., 4, 8
veil, 184
Verbeke, G., 314, 325 n.
Vergil, 353, 366, 368, 434, 438
vermin, 299
vine, 305
vinegar, 397, 398
vineyard, 399, 400
vipers, 244
virgins, 6, 21, 23-25, 35, 45-47, 85-87, 97, 139, 143, 145-151, 153-175, 184 n., 187, 188, 193-195, 197-199, 201, 202, 204, 231, 236, 294, 295, 297, 303, 324, 328

virginity, 3, 20, 45, 46, 50, 135, 137-139, 141, 143, 145-148, 150-152, 159-179, 182, 188, 189, 193, 198, 199 n., 202, 203, 206, 209, 226, 227, 324 n.
visions, 382, 430
vomit, 275
vows, 146 n., 183, 203, 401

water, 278
Welldon, J. E. C., 420 n.
Wernz-Vidal, 8
wheat, 227, 228, 232, 260, 280
widowhood, 166
Wilmart, A., 285 n., 388 n.
wine, 40, 231
wisdom, 319-325, 335, 338
Word, divine, 165, 188, 319, 320-323, 325, 327, 404, 407
works, good, 248-254, 258, 261-263, 266-269, 281, 282, 312

Zaccaeus, 45, 186
Zarb, M., 387 n.
Zebadee, 181
Zycha, J., 7, 218, 219, 313, 314, 350, 420

www.ingramcontent.com/pod-product-compliance
Lightning Source LLC
Chambersburg PA
CBHW032022290426
44110CB00012B/631